JOAN OF NAVARRE

This book is the first full-length biography of Joan of Navarre, a fascinating royal woman who became duchess of Brittany and queen consort of England through her two marriages in 1386 and 1403 respectively.

Joan was enmeshed in the turbulent politics of the later Middle Ages as her extensive family and marital connections meant she was related to most of the royal houses of Western Europe—as well as the key protagonists of the Hundred Years War. The large foreign entourage that Joan brought with her to England, and her family ties across the Channel, made her unpopular with her subjects and her loyalties suspect, provoking several purges of her household and culminating in a charge of treason on which she was detained for several years. Yet Joan returned to court in her later years and fought vociferously to the end to retain queenly rights, revenues, and position. Ultimately, this book highlights Joan's political agency and tenacity, bringing her out of the historical shadows and into the foreground of high politics in fifteenth-century England and Europe.

Joan of Navarre is a useful resource for all students and scholars interested in queenship studies, women's history, and European politics during the later Middle Ages.

Elena Woodacre is a Reader in Renaissance History at the University of Winchester. She is an expert in queenship and royal studies, having published extensively in this area, and she was the lead editor of *The Routledge History of Monarchy* (2019). Elena is also Editor-in-Chief of the *Royal Studies Journal*, founder of the Royal Studies Network, and edits two book series, including *Lives of Royal Women* with Routledge.

Lives of Royal Women

Series Editors:-
Elena Woodacre, Ellie.Woodacre@winchester.ac.uk
Louise Wilkinson, LWilkinson@lincoln.ac.uk

This series features academic, yet accessible biographies of royal women - consorts, dowagers, royal mothers and female sovereigns - inclusive of all periods, cultures and geographic regions. These biographies include a deep engagement with the premise of queenship studies and the exercise of the queen's office (or equivalent), in addition to covering the lives of particular women. The series is divided into three sub-strands: Queens of England (blue), Queens and Empresses of Europe (purple), and Royal Women of the World (red).

Maria of Austria, Holy Roman Empress (1528-1603)
Dynastic Networker
Rubén González Cuerva

Anne of Bohemia
Kristen L. Geaman

Early English Queens, 650–850
Speculum Reginae
Stefany Wragg

Joan of Navarre
Infanta, Duchess, Queen, Witch?
Elena Woodacre

JOAN OF NAVARRE

Infanta, Duchess, Queen, Witch?

Elena Woodacre

Routledge
Taylor & Francis Group
LONDON AND NEW YORK

Cover image: Coronation of Joan of Navarre, *The Pageant of Richard Beauchamp*, British Library Cotton MS Julius E IV, folio 2v.

First published 2023
by Routledge
4 Park Square, Milton Park, Abingdon, Oxon OX14 4RN

and by Routledge
605 Third Avenue, New York, NY 10158

Routledge is an imprint of the Taylor & Francis Group, an informa business

British Library Cataloguing-in-Publication Data
A catalogue record for this book is available from the British Library

Library of Congress Cataloging-in-Publication Data
A catalog record has been requested for this book

ISBN: 978-0-367-20348-1 (hbk)
ISBN: 978-0-367-20347-4 (pbk)
ISBN: 978-0-429-26102-2 (ebk)

DOI: 10.4324/9780429261022

Typeset in Bembo
by MPS Limited, Dehradun

To Joan of Navarre, for being a gift that kept on giving and for being endlessly patient with me while I slowly put together the pieces of her rich and fascinating life to write this book. This book is dedicated to her and all the other women who have been relegated to the footnotes of history and whose life stories need to be told.

CONTENTS

FIGURES

MAPS

TABLES

ACKNOWLEDGEMENTS

My thanks to all of the colleagues who have offered their support and expert advice throughout the research and writing process, including those who offered feedback and ideas on conference papers and drafts of the book or helped with thorny queries on documental sources. Special thanks go to my colleague at Winchester, Dr James Ross, for his deep knowledge of palaeography and the collections at the National Archives, as well as being a sounding board for many theories and ideas about Joan's life; to Professor Chris Woolgar for his thoughts on Joan's household books and generously sharing archival finds; and to Drs Caroline Dunn, Rita (Marguerite) Keane, Núria Silleras Fernández, Erika Graham-Goering, Michele Seah, Zita Rohr, and Angela Clark for their thoughts on draft chapters of the book and to my co-editor Professor Louise Wilkinson for her comments on the final manuscript.

NOTES AND ABBREVIATIONS

Notes

All manuscript references are from The National Archives (TNA), London, unless otherwise noted. All translations in the text are also my own unless otherwise noted. Where there is considerable variation in the name used for a particular figure, I have decided to use the one which is most frequently used for them, rather than complete consistency with using the Spanish, French, or English version of their name. Some variation in usage has been deliberate to avoid confusion when several figures had the same first name, such as Blanca of Navarre, queen of France, who is referred to as Blanche to avoid confusion with her niece and grandniece with the same name.

Abbreviations

Titles are given in full in the bibliography.

ADLA	Archives départmentales de Loire-Atlantique
Actes JIV	*Recueil des actes de Jean IV, duc de Bretagne*
AGN	Archivo General de Navarra
BL	British Library
BnF	Bibliothèque National Français
CCR	*Calendar of Close Rolls* (accessed via British History Online unless otherwise noted)
CIM	*Calendar of Inquisitions Miscellaneous*
CFR	*Calendar of Fine Rolls*
CPR	*Calendar of Patent Rolls* (accessed via British History Online unless otherwise noted)
Catálogo	*Catálogo de la Seccion de Comptos, Documentos*
Foedera	*Rymer's Foedera* (accessed via British History Online unless otherwise noted)
GSR	*Gascon Rolls* (accessed via the Gascon Rolls Project website unless otherwise noted)
HoP	*History of Parliament Online*
King's Works	Brown, Colvin, and Taylor, eds., *History of the King's Works*, 2 vols.
Lobineau	*Histoire de Bretagne*
L&M JV	*Lettres et mandements de Jean V, duc de Bretagne*
Monstrelet	*La Chronique d'Enguerran de Monstrelet en deux livres avec pièces justificatives 1400–1444*
Morice	*Memoires pour servir de preuves a l'histoire ecclesiastique et civile de Bretagne*
ODNB	*Oxford Dictionary of National Biography*
Papal Registers	*Calendar of Papal Registers Relating to Great Britain and Ireland*
POPC	*Proceedings and Ordinances of the Privy Council of England*

PROME	*Parliament Rolls of Medieval England* (accessed via British History Online unless otherwise noted)
Saint-Denys	*Chronique du religieux de Saint-Denys*
Signet Letters	*Signet Letters of Henry IV and Henry V*
Walsingham	*The Chronica Maiora of Thomas Walsingham 1376–1422*
Usk	*The Chronicle of Adam Usk 1377–1421*

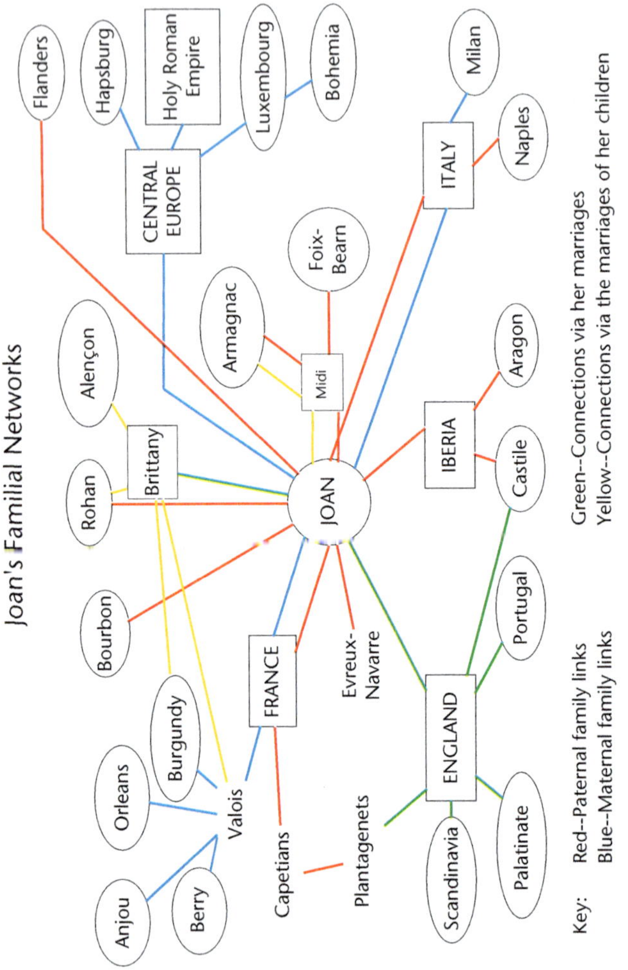

FIGURE 0.1 Joan's family network.

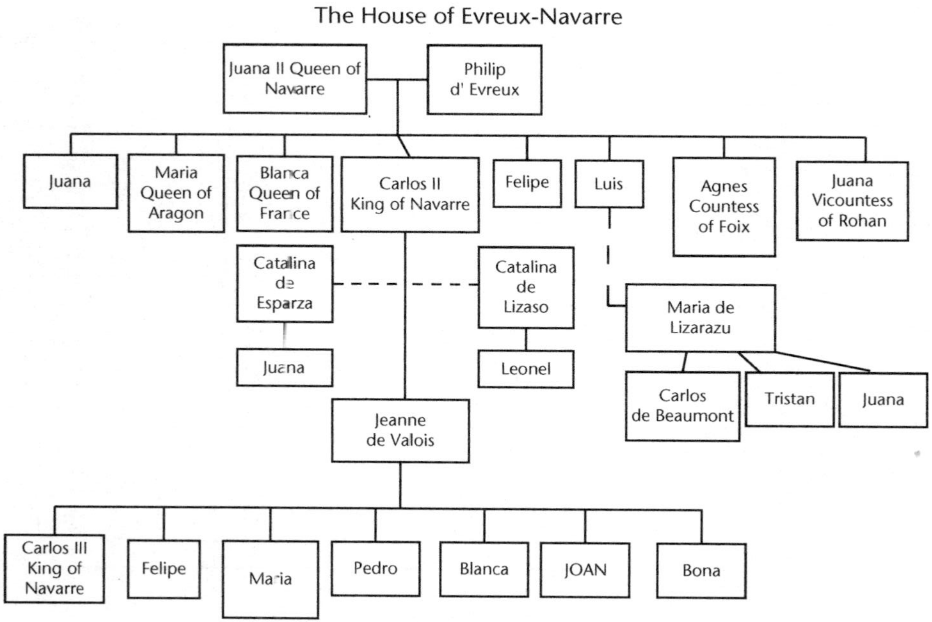

FIGURE 0.2 Descendants of Juana II of Navarre.

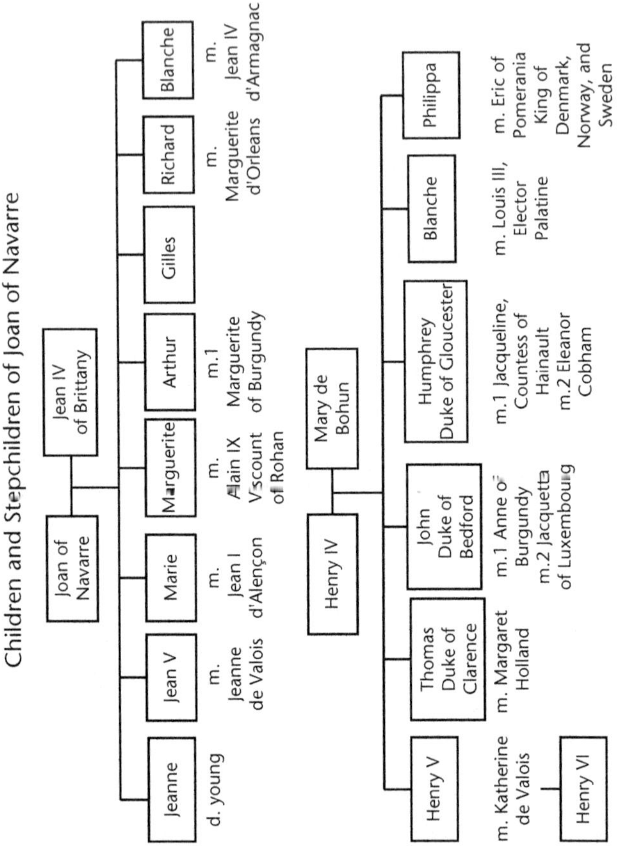

FIGURE 0.3 Joan's children and stepchildren.

INTRODUCTION

> *Joanna, or Jane of Navarre, the consort of Henry IV, is one of those queens of England whose records, as connected with the history of this country, are of a very obscure and mysterious character; yet the events of her life, when traced through foreign chronicles and unpublished sources of information, are replete with interest, forming an unprecedented chapter in the history of female royalty.*[1]

Queens have long been a source of fascination to writers of all types, chroniclers, historians, biographers, novelists, and journalists, from the ancient world to the modern day. The reigns (and love lives) of queens such as Elizabeth I, Cleopatra, and Catherine the Great have been perhaps over-examined, as have the lives of many queens whose reigns came to tragic and untimely ends such as Marie Antoinette, Mary Queen of Scots, Lady Jane Grey, and Anne Boleyn. Queens who lived in politically turbulent times, such as the women of the Wars of the Roses, and controversial consorts and regents such as Catherine de Medici, Hurrem Sultan, or Nur Jahan have also received considerable interest from scholars and popular culture. Yet other queens' lives pass "under the radar", failing to grasp either academic or popular attention. Joan of Navarre is one of

DOI: 10.4324/9780429261022-1

these queens who is not well known, even among specialists in queenship and medieval history—yet as Agnes Strickland noted in the quote above, her long life is "replete with interest". Joan lived in Iberia, France, and England; she was daughter of an intensely controversial father, a duchess in a divided Breton court, and later the wife of a usurper king who fought off attacks by rebels and Parliament to preserve his position. She was living at the epicentre of the Hundred Years War, with ties on all sides and divided loyalties at the famous battle of Agincourt, and was accused of witchcraft by her stepson—Joan hardly had a quiet or boring life, so why has there been little written about her?

This next section will aim to resolve this quandary by examining the treatment of Joan by various types of scholars and writers including English and Breton historians as well as queenly biographers or prosopographers. Various key themes resonate most strongly in the historiography of Joan: her marriages, motherhood, agency, and of course perhaps her most distinguishing feature, the accusation of treason or witchcraft. Intriguingly, Joan's agency and political activity throughout her long career is the area which has without doubt received the least attention. Joan is often portrayed as an onlooker to events with little connection to or influence on the chaos that often surrounded her. However, that impression stems from the chronicles, which rarely feature princesses, duchesses, queens, or dowagers apart from commenting on scandalous events or key moments in their life cycle, such as births, marriages, and deaths. This impression has been passed along by later writers and historians. This has also had an impact on Joan's minimal impression in popular culture—the seeming lack of material to work on has meant that she rarely appears in plays, films, and novels, unlike some of the more famous (or infamous) aforementioned queens. Shakespeare omitted her completely from his so-called "Hollow Crown" or history plays, even though she played a prominent role in the reigns of Henry IV and V, and aside from a recent novel by Anne O'Brien, there have been few attempts to tell Joan's story. After briefly charting how she has been portrayed in other works, we will then turn to the particular approach that this book—the first full-length study on Joan of Navarre—takes to document and discuss her life.

Tracing Joan's treatment in historiography

Unsurprisingly perhaps, Joan barely registers on the radar of Navarrese historians, as she left the realm in her late teens to marry, and there is little documentary evidence of her childhood; as a younger daughter of the king of Navarre, this is entirely logical. Where she does register is in terms of her marriages, particularly her first marriage to the duke of Brittany in 1386, which was significant as the last major alliance crafted by her father, Carlos II, before his death the following year. While the primary sources demonstrate that Joan continued to maintain close ties with her homeland and family after she left the Pyrenean realm, she is rarely mentioned in national histories and narratives of the reign of Joan's brother Carlos III, although the relationship between Navarre and Brittany is occasionally touched on. Effectively, in the eyes of Navarrese historians, Joan appears to be merely a pawn who made two marriages which enhanced their diplomatic connections. Joan's ongoing relationship with her family, including both her brother Pedro, who visited her frequently in Brittany, and her cousin Carlos de Beaumont, who joined her household in England and played a significant role at the English court, has not yet been deeply discussed.

It is perhaps Breton historians who have paid the most attention to Joan because she played a key role in the history of the Montfort dynasty, providing much needed heirs for her husband, Jean IV, after two childless marriages left him in danger of passing the duchy back to his bitter rivals, the Penthièvres. While there are no works specifically focused on her, Joan makes a frequent appearance in Breton historiography, from chronicles to general histories of the duchy, in biographies of her husband, Jean IV, and sons Jean V and Arthur de Richemont, and in several pieces focused specifically on duchesses.[2] After the death of Jean IV, Joan became regent for her young son Jean V—the analyses of her efforts to secure a smooth succession for her son through the effective use of ceremonial and her brief period of governance of the duchy is where Joan's agency shines most clearly in Breton historiography.[3]

There is a mood change in the treatment of Joan after 1400 as her controversial second marriage to Henry IV, which led to her giving up both the regency of the duchy and the custody of the majority of her children, provoked a great deal of comment in Breton historiography, which can be rather critical of her decision to remarry.[4] English historians, however, have taken a mixed view of the motivations behind Joan's decision to leave Brittany. Historians such as J.L. Kirby, Anne Crawford, and Ian Mortimer have often been sympathetic to Joan and towards her decision to leave Brittany for England, emphasising the notion of her sacrifice in order to marry Henry.[5] Yet, while Joan lived in England longer than anywhere else in her long life, for 34 years from 1403 until her death in 1437, generally English historiography has taken little notice of her. This is in part because the chronicles of the period have little time for her—Joan's arrival in England with a lavish wedding at Winchester and coronation at Westminster are certainly commented on by contemporary sources like the chronicles of Thomas Walsingham and Adam Usk, but then there are few mentions of her until she is accused of treason or possibly witchcraft.[6] Even then, considering how unusual and scandalous that accusation was, it is not given as much attention as one might expect—perhaps the chroniclers too recognised that the charge had little basis in reality, as we will discuss in Chapter 4.

More surprising, perhaps, is that Joan is barely mentioned in biographies of her husband Henry IV or analyses of his reign, although it is generally acknowledged that Joan and Henry had a strong relationship.[7] Brief mentions of her excessive dower and large foreign retinue give the impression that Joan was a lavish spender and nothing more than a drain on the Crown's purse, a reputation that we will explore more deeply in Chapter 5. Joan is often dismissed as an uninteresting queen or an expensive mistake on the part of Henry IV, who granted her a generous dower that he struggled to fund. Paul Strohm, in his chapter-long examination of her, describes her as "That Obscure Object of Desire" and even as a "problem".[8] As Joan was not a mother of a king she has been deemed to be of little significance and thus her political influence or agency has generally been glossed over by contemporary chroniclers and modern historians—yet as Strickland noted, there are considerable primary sources available which form the foundation of this current work, revealing a very different picture of her activity as both queen consort and dowager. Interestingly as well, Joan often appears to be a more engaged and significant player in French chronicles like the chronicle of Saint Denis and the Burgundian *Livre des Trahisons* than those which documented English events or even those of her native Navarre where she barely features, if at all.

Joan has also received little attention from queenly collective biographers; she generally only appears in collective biographies of queens which aim to include all of the English queen consorts of the Middle Ages, such as the collections by the Victorian biographers Hannah Lawrance, Francis Lancelott, Mary Howitt, and the famous compendium by the Strickland sisters, or more modern collections such as Lisa Hilton's compendium *Queens Consort.*[9] While all of the queenly biographers are theoretically focused on her role as queen of England, there is some coverage of her early years of Navarre and her tenure as duchess of Brittany, noting Joan's increasing influence and political agency over the course of her years in the duchy and her regency for her son Jean V. There are three key themes that are emphasised in the collective biographies: her role as a mother and her decision to leave her children behind in Brittany when she re-married, the accusation of treason or possibly witchcraft and detention under Henry V, and the repeated allegation that she was "avaricious".[10] The emphasis on the latter two elements has "coloured later characterizations" of Joan's life, even defining her to some extent as a "royal witch", as in the subtitle of Lisa Hilton's chapter on Joan in *Queens Consort* or Gemma Hollman's wider survey of royal women accused of witchcraft.[11] Indeed, another collective biographer, Petronelle Cook, notes that Joan's unique features were two "firsts" for English queens, being the first widow to marry a king of England (after the Norman Conquest) and the first to be accused of witchcraft.[12] However, Joan's later years, after she was released from detention on the spurious charge, are glossed over by the collective biographers; Cook summarises this entire period in one sentence by claiming that Joan "retreated into the obscurity she craved" to observe the great events and the lives of her sons from afar—yet as this book will demonstrate, Joan remained an engaged and active agent in administration and politics until her death.[13]

This brief historiography of Joan of Navarre not only gives an impression of her treatment in previous works but reveals wider issues with biographies and treatments of medieval queens in general. We return to this question of why Joan's life has received little attention despite being replete with scandal and interesting elements, including her controversial second marriage, the very unusual accusation of treason or witchcraft, and her political engagement in the Hundred Years War. Maternity is arguably a key factor here—in Brittany where she was the mother of multiple dukes and thus a critical dynastic linchpin, she has made an enduring impression in Breton historiography. However, in England, where she was the foreign wife of an unbeloved king and only a stepmother and step-grandmother in the reigns that followed, she appears extraneous to the master narrative of the period. Her brief treatment in the chronicles and national histories of England convinced later queenly biographers that there was little need to focus on her particularly unless they aimed to make a comprehensive survey of the queens of the period. Yet, those who did dig into her story, like Strickland, Howitt, Lawrance, and Lancelott, found much rewarding material for their collective biographies and acknowledged that Joan had been a woman of great significance in her own time. Indeed, as Hannah Lawrance commented, "scarcely even the name of the queen who gives the title to this chapter, is known to the majority of readers ... And yet this almost forgotten queen ... possessing commanding talents, was destined to act an important part, both in Bretagne and England".[14]

Overview of the work

This book aims to address the lack of a focused, comprehensive, full-length survey of Joan's long life, giving equal weight to the four key periods of Joan's life: her childhood as a Navarrese infanta or princess, her first marriage and time as duchess of Brittany, her second marriage to Henry IV which made her queen consort of England,

and her second long widowhood as a dowager queen. These periods will each form the basis of an individual chapter in the first section of the book and will trace her life in a chronological fashion. There will be a pronounced emphasis on the importance of family or personal relationships and politics—as a royal woman, these two elements were completely intertwined in Joan's life and formed its very foundation. Joan lived during particularly turbulent times—indeed the entirety of her life took place within the confines of the Hundred Years War and, as we will see, this conflict played a major role in her life as she was related to nearly all of the central figures in this conflict on both sides of the Channel. The context of this conflict and the political dynamics of the reigns of Joan's father, Carlos II, and brother, Carlos III of Navarre, and her two husbands, Jean IV of Brittany and Henry IV of England, will be woven into the chapters. However, a balance will be struck—it is not the intention to reprise the political history of the period as there are already excellent works which cover this in intensive detail, including Michael Jones's extensive scholarship on late medieval Brittany, Chris Given-Wilson's authoritative biography of Henry IV, Eloísa Ramírez Vaquero's work on Carlos III and the kingdom of Navarre, and Jonathan Sumption's multi-volume analysis of the Hundred Years War.[15] Yet what these works lack is Joan's connection with and position within the shifting politics of the period, which is what this book will try to supply—keeping her at the forefront of the narrative, rather than reducing her to a background character or a footnote as she has all too often been in previous works.

The second section of the book will take a radically different, thematic perspective on her life, examining her finances, her networks and affinity, and her patronage and possessions. The first of these chapters will take on the suggestion that Joan was "avaricious" by thoroughly examining her economic activity, particularly her administration of her Breton and English dower lands. Recent trends in queenship studies have begun to place greater focus on the financial activity of royal women, recognising their role as the controller of considerable monetary and landed resources and the key element this played in their exercise of both the queen's office and their own personal power and influence. This book is the first biography of Joan which moves beyond suggestions of greed and avarice to reveal that these epithets are actually reflections of her deep engagement with the management of her lands and revenues—from day-to-day administration with her vast network of officials from her office at Westminster Palace to the near constant battles she fought to retain and later regain her impressive collection of land holdings in both Brittany and England that she accrued as duchess and queen. The following chapter will trace Joan's networks of service, from the officials who assisted her in the administration of her dower lands to her household, noting the long-term loyalty of those who continued to serve her even as she transitioned between realms and was detained under suspicion of witchcraft. Finally, the last chapter brings together several elements: examining the places she inhabited, her personal and political piety, the possessions she surrounded herself with, and her acts of patronage which built on familial traditions and connections.

In summary, the first section will chart the key events of Joan's long life, from a young infanta, to becoming a wife and mother, a duchess and queen, and, finally, a matriarch of sorts—even if a controversial one—to an extended brood of children and stepchildren. The second section will move from understanding the events of her life to a deeper examination of her agency and activity, the people who surrounded her, and the places and objects that she possessed. Taken together, the intention is to build the richest possible picture of Joan's life and gain a deeper understanding of Joan as a woman in addition to being an infanta, duchess, and queen.

Notes

1 Agnes Strickland, *Lives of the Queens of England from the Norman Conquest; with Anecdotes of their Courts*, Vol. III (Philadelphia: Lea and Blanchard, 1848), 38.

2 Examples include Jean Kerhervé, "Arthur de Richemont, connetable et duc, Entre guerre et politique, dans la France du XVe siècle," in *2000 Ans d'Histoire de Vannes* (Vannes: Archives Municipales, 1993), 95–120; Jean-Pierre Leguay and Herve Martin, eds., *Fastes et malheurs de la Bretagne ducale 1213–1532* (Rennes: Ouest France, 1982); Michael Jones, *Ducal Brittany 1364–1399: Relations with England and France during the Reign of Duke John V* (Oxford: Oxford University Press, 1970).

Works on duchesses of Brittany range from *Petite Histoire des duchesses de Bretagne* aimed at children to Nicholas Kermabon's excellent PhD thesis on the dowers of the medieval duchesses: Nicolas Kermabon, "Le douaire des duchesses de Bretagne (13–15e)" (PhD thesis, Université de Rennes 1, 2007), 3 vols; Etienne Gasche, *Petite Histoire des duchesses de Bretagne* (Fouesnant: Yoran Embanner, 2011).

3 Arthur de la Borderie, "La jeunesse de Jean V, duc de Bretagne," *Revue de Bretagne de Vendee et d'Anjou* 23 (Mar 1900): 161–86; Michael Jones, "The rituals and significance of ducal civic entries in late medieval Brittany," *Journal of Medieval History* 29 (2003): 287–314; John Bell Henneman, *Olivier de Clisson and Political Society in France under Charles V and Charles VI* (Philadelphia: University of Pennsylvania Press, 1996).

4 For an extended discussion, see Elena Woodacre, "The Perils of Promotion: Maternal Ambition and Sacrifice in the Life of Joan of Navarre, Duchess of Brittany and Queen of England," in *Virtuous or Villainess? The Image of the Royal Mother from the Early Medieval to the Early Modern Era*, eds. Carey Fleiner and Elena Woodacre (New York: Palgrave Macmillan, 2016), 130–34.

5 J.L. Kirby, *Henry IV of England* (London: Constable, 1970), 135; Anne Crawford, "The King's Burden?—the Consequences of Royal Marriage in Fifteenth-century England," in *Patronage, the Crown and the Provinces in Later Medieval England*, ed. Ralph A. Griffiths (Gloucester: Alan Sutton, 1981), 35; Ian Mortimer, *The Fears of Henry IV; The Life of England's Self-Made King* (London: Vintage Books, 2008), 259.

6 For examples of chronicles which only mention her briefly at these key moments, see *The Chronica Maiora of Thomas Walsingham* 1376–1422, trans. David Preest (Woodbridge: Boydell, 2005); *The Chronicles of London*, ed. Charles L. Kingsford (Oxford: Clarendon Press, 1905); Chris Given-Wilson, ed. and trans., *The Chronicle of Adam Usk 1377–1421* (Oxford: Clarendon Press, 1997).

7 Indeed, a review of the newest biography of Henry IV by Chris Given-Wilson for Yale's important English Monarchs series remarks on the very few appearances that Joan makes in the book; see Alexander Brondarbit, "Review of Christopher Given-Wilson, Henry IV (New Haven, CT: Yale University Press, 2016)," *Royal Studies Journal* 4, no. 2 (2017): 247–49.

8 Paul Strohm, "Joanna of Navarre: That Obscure Object of Desire," in *England's Empty Throne: Usurpation and the Language of Legitimation, 1399–1422* (New Haven, CT: Yale University Press, 1998), 153–72.

9 Hannah Lawrance, *Historical Memoirs of the Queens of England, from the Commencement of the Twelfth Century*, Vol. 2 (London: Edward Moxon, 1840); Mary Howitt, *Biographical Sketches of the Queens of England …* (London: Henry Bohn, 1851); Francis Lancelott, *The Queens of England and their Times from Matilda, Queen of William the Conqueror to Adelaide, Queen of William the Fourth*, vol. 1 (New York: D. Appleton and

Company, 1859); Strickland, *Lives*; Lisa Hilton, *Queens Consort; England's Medieval Queens* (London: Phoenix, 2009).

10 See Strickland, *Lives*, 67; Lancelott, *Historical Memoirs*, 258; Howitt, *Biographical Sketches*, 166.

11 Quotation from Michael Jones, "Between France and England: Jeanne de Navarre, Duchess of Brittany and Queen of England (1386–1437)," in *Between France and England: Politics, Power and Society in Late Medieval Brittany* (Aldershot: Variorum, 2003), 12; Hilton, *Queens Consort*; Gemma Hollman, *Royal Witches: From Joan of Navarre to Elizabeth Woodville* (Cheltenham: The History Press, 2019). Elsie Prentys Thornton-Cook also dubbed Joan "The Witchcraft Queen" in her early 20th-century survey of England's queens: Elsie Prentys Thornton-Cook, *Her Majesty: The Romance of the Queens of England, 1066–1910* (London: Murray, 1926).

12 Petronelle Cook, *Queen Consorts of England: The Power behind the Throne* (New York: Margot Arnold, 1993), 90.

13 Cook, *Queen Consorts*, 92.

14 Lawrance, *Historical Memoirs*, 276.

15 Jones will be a touchstone throughout. His major works include Michael Jones, ed., *Recueil des actes de Jean IV, duc de Bretagne*, Vol. II, nos. 431–1196 (1383–1399) (Torquay: Devonshire Press, 1983); *Ducal Brittany*; and his brief but effective survey of Joan's life "Between France and England". Chris Given-Wilson, *Henry IV* (New Haven, CT: Yale University Press, 2016). Ramírez Vaquero is one of the most important scholars of Navarrese history, and while multiple pieces will be referred to in this work, her biography of Carlos III has been particularly helpful: Eloísa Ramírez Vaquero, *Carlos III, rey de Navarra, Principe de sangre Valois* (1387–1425) (Gijon: Ediciones Trea, 2007). Jonathan Sumption's impressive four-volume work on the Hundred Years War is very well known—the two volumes which have been most useful for Joan's life have been vols. 3 and 4; *Divided Houses: The Hundred Years War III* (London: Faber and Faber, 2009) and *Cursed Kings: The Hundred Years War IV* (London: Faber and Faber, 2016).

PART I

1

INFANTA: THE CONTEXT AND CONTENT OF JOAN'S EARLY YEARS

To begin Joan's story, we need to place her in the context of her family. While this means momentarily losing sight of Joan herself, running counter to our goal of keeping her in the picture at all times and narrating the events of the period from her perspective, this familial context is necessary to understand her own significance and how her blood and marital connections defined the whole of her life. Once her dynastic ties have been thoroughly explored in terms of both her immediate ancestors and contemporary family members, we will then explore her childhood years as an infanta in her native land among her Navarrese family—her siblings, aunts, cousins, and her father, the infamous Carlos II. We will then focus on Carlos and the challenging situation of Navarre during the early years of the Hundred Years War. This situation was made challenging by both the international political turbulence and the impact of Carlos II's own actions, earning him the sobriquet of "*el Malo*" or "the Bad". Again, this means taking our eye off Joan momentarily, but this political context provides a foundation for the final section of this chapter, the political alliance between Navarre and Brittany which created her first marriage, to Jean IV, in 1386. We will end the chapter as Joan made her transition from infanta to duchess, sailing up the Bay of Biscay to a new life in Brittany.

DOI: 10.4324/9780429261022-3

Family networks

In a later chapter we will focus on Joan's "networks of service", examining the men and women who served her in her household and administered the vast holdings of land that Joan accrued in both Brittany and England. Here we examine Joan's other networks—her familial ones through both blood and marriage. Both networks were vital to every aspect of her life. Joan's familial networks gave her position and status—she was born an infanta of Navarre, the daughter of a king and a descendant of an illustrious Franco-Iberian royal lineage. Her wide-ranging dynastic ties gave her further prestige, making her a desirable bride for Jean IV and Henry IV, which in turn made her a duchess and later a queen. Her connections to royal houses across Western Europe gave her potential influence—but also, as we will see, in later life made her loyalties suspect when her relations by blood and marriage were on the opposite sides of conflict. Indeed, given the context of the Hundred Years War, which dominated the political aspects of Joan's career and permeated the personal aspects of her life as well, various branches of her family were always on different sides of campaigns and factions, meaning that her loyalties were constantly strained and torn.

Joan of Navarre was blessed with a large, well-connected family as the chart of her family connections demonstrates (see Fig. 0.1). She was the daughter, granddaughter, niece, and cousin of kings and emperors. She carried Capetian blood in her veins through both sides of her family and was closely related to the Valois kings of France as well as the Holy Roman emperors of the House of Luxembourg, who were also the kings of Bohemia. She was also connected to the most powerful nobles of France, the dukes of Burgundy, Berry, and Orleans, as well as the counts of Foix and Armagnac in the Midi or southwest of France. Through the marriages of her family, as well as her English stepchildren, she could claim links to Castile, Aragon, Portugal, and the united kingdoms of Denmark, Norway, and Sweden, as well as the dukes of Milan and the kingdom of Naples.

Joan's extended family was her greatest asset, but while her lineage and connections elevated her into positions of power, her family ties often meant she had connections on both sides of serious conflicts. Later chapters will touch on the extended conflict in France, first between the partisans of the dukes of Orleans and Burgundy, and later between those of Burgundy and Armagnac—Joan was closely related to all parties by both blood and marriage. As we will see in this chapter, her father, Carlos II "the Bad", spent many years in opposition to Joan's maternal grandfather, the French king Jean II "the Good". The root of this conflict was another distinctive feature of Joan's ancestry—one which may in part account for her willingness to fight for her rights and position when under threat and her general political engagement—the legacy of regnant queenship. Joan's grandmother and great-great-grandmother were both regnant queens of Navarre, Juana I and II. Juana I married Philip IV of France and their marriage brought about the personal union of the two crowns which remained during the reign of their eldest son, Louis X of France and I of Navarre. When Louis died in 1316, his only living child at that point was his daughter Jeanne—while there is insufficient space to fully discuss the Capetian succession crisis that followed, we can quickly summarise it by noting that Jeanne was bypassed by both of her uncles in turn who became Philip V (and II of Navarre) and Charles IV (and I of Navarre).[1] In 1328, when both Philip and Charles had died leaving only female surviving issue, it was decided that the French throne would fall to the Valois, a subsidiary branch of the Capetian dynasty and that Jeanne would take the Navarrese throne as Juana II with her husband, Philip d'Evreux, starting the House of Evreux-Navarre of which Joan was a member. To prevent further squabbles between the Capetian princesses and their husbands and to block the accession of Edward III of England, whose mother Isabella was the daughter of Juana I and Philip IV, it was decided to block both female and female-line claimants to the French throne. Yet neither Juana II nor her son Carlos II forgot her claim to the French throne—these pretensions and sense of pride in his Capetian blood (which also came through his father's Evreux line) both motivated

Carlos's foreign policy and provided his daughter with a keen sense of her own royal position.

The royal couple: Joan's mother and father

Joan was named for these regnant queens of Navarre and also for her mother Jeanne de Valois, born in June 1343 to Jean II of France and Bonne of Luxembourg, daughter of the king of Bohemia and sister of the Holy Roman Emperor Charles IV. Jeanne was a very politically active queen who was deeply engaged as both a diplomat between her husband and her Valois family and as a regent or lieutenant in both Carlos's Iberian and French domains. While Jeanne died in 1373, when only 30 years of age and during Joan's infancy, she provided another example of active queenship for Joan to model herself on, alongside her ancestors the regnant queens and her influential aunts who we will discuss further shortly.

The marriage of Joan's parents was continually under threat and strain from the political situation and dynastic discord. Carlos II and Jeanne de Valois were married in an intimate, yet suitably resplendent, wedding in early 1352 at Vivier-en-Brie, when Jeanne was only eight years old.[2] Due to the bride's young age and the wider political situation, including a dispute between Jeanne's husband and father over her dowry, the couple were separated until 1360. While their reunion resulted in the birth in July 1361 of their son and heir, who would become Carlos III, and the birth of six further children including Joan herself, from Philippe Charon's comparison of their movements, it is clear that they were frequently separated during their nearly 20-year marriage. Indeed, Carlos was even accused of causing his wife's death by poison, necessitating an autopsy of the queen's body and the affidavit of his sister, Agnes countess of Foix, to verify that Jeanne had died of natural causes.[3] Yet Charon also argues that Carlos and Jeanne had a strong relationship, citing Carlos's trust in Jeanne as his regent, gifts sent from Carlos, and Jeanne's impassioned plea to free her husband during his imprisonment after the battle of Najera in 1367, as well as the seven children that they had together as evidence of a firm conjugal bond.[4]

Royal "bastards" in the House of Evreux-Navarre

Yet even if the marriage of Jeanne de Valois and Carlos II had been a good one, their conjugal bond did not prevent Carlos from taking mistresses and producing illegitimate children. Given their frequent separations, Jeanne's early death, and Carlos's decision not to remarry for the remaining 14 years of his life, his liaisons with other women are perhaps less surprising. However, both of Carlos's illegitimate children appear to have been born after his wife's death, indicating perhaps that his liaisons may have been a way of finding companionship as a widower rather than an indication of an unhappy marriage or a means to find companionship during their times apart. Carlos had two "natural" children, Juana, born c. 1374 to Catalina de Esparza, and Leonel, born c. 1378/9 to Catalina de Lizaso. Fernando Videgain Agos notes that both children were recognised, well cared for, and honoured by Carlos II.[5] His legitimate son and heir, Carlos III, treated both Leonel and Juana with respect and affection as members of his extended family. Leonel made an advantageous marriage and was named Vizconde de Murzabal, a position which came with substantial lands and revenues, and was also given the position of Mariscal del Reino. Leonel also left several illegitimate children—one of which, Felipe de Navarra, married the noblewoman Juana de Peralta and was also made Mariscal del Reino by Carlos III in 1424. Leonel's descendants continued to hold this position until the middle of the sixteenth century. Carlos II's illegitimate daughter Juana was consistently referred to in records from Carlos III's reign as the sister of the king and resided for an extensive period in the royal court, eventually marrying Juan de Béarn, baron de Beortegui, in 1397.

The illegitimate children of royal families have not been consistently or universally welcomed in dynastic history. Some kings have chosen not to acknowledge children born out of wedlock or have deliberately kept them in obscurity, to minimise the chances that they might prove any threat to the line of succession or legitimate siblings. Yet in Navarre, the preferment shown to illegitimate offspring demonstrates that they were valued for their royal blood as they were promoted through titles, service, and marriages which established them as important nobles in their own right, and they were allowed to use the royal coats of arms on their seals and devises. There appears to have been little stigma attached to their illegitimate ancestry, with the exception that they were not considered to be eligible for the succession to the throne. Yet while they were barred from the succession, in Navarre royal bastards were vitally important for dynastic service and building connections with the nobility as they formed strategic marriages with several houses, giving them a "preeminent role" in the realm.[6] Later, when Joan became queen of England, she came into contact with the Beauforts, the half-siblings of her husband Henry IV, who had been legitimised by his father John of Gaunt and also played a key role in the politics of the realm, and even, at the end of the fifteenth century, in the succession to the throne itself.

In the same generation as Joan and her half-siblings was another group of exalted royal bastards known as the Beaumonts, who were the children of Carlos II's brother Luis of Navarre, count of Beaumont-le-Roger. It is from this French title that the surname or sobriquet of de Beaumont for his illegitimate children derived, although the lands of the county and the title reverted to Carlos II on Luis's death in 1376 and was not granted to Luis's illegitimate offspring.[7] Luis of Navarre played an important part in Navarrese and European politics, as regent for Carlos II's French territories and later as the husband of Jeanne de Durazzo, a claimant for the throne of Naples. In addition to Luis's political acumen, he also gained a reputation as a womaniser—though he had no legitimate offspring with his Angevin wife, he left several illegitimate children. Videgain Agos commented that Luis never missed an opportunity for illicit relationships—apparently he had an eye for the ladies and a love of the hunt.[8]

Carlos was only one of Luis of Navarre's illegitimate children; his siblings Tristan and Juana were also born from Luis's relationship with Maria de Lizarazu, a Navarrese noblewoman who was accorded a level of respect as Luis's virtual wife, even referred to as *Condesa* or countess.[9] Carlos was likely born c. 1361 and it appears that he was the middle sibling, between his sister Juana who was born in 1359 and Tristan who may have been born c. 1363.[10] Carlos and his siblings were left in Navarre when their father departed for Italy and Albania to advance his position as duke of Durazzo, which he gained through marriage to the Neapolitan heiress; both Carlos and his sister Juana spent part of their early years in Estella—a key location for the education of royal offspring, including Joan herself as we will discuss shortly.[11]

There were no guarantees for Carlos de Beaumont and his siblings—as the illegitimate offspring of a royal prince, not the king himself, they were arguably more obscure and their father's death in 1376 left them without a clear protector, barring perhaps Juana who had been wed to Pées, Pedro, or Pey de Laxague in 1373.[12] Yet their uncle Carlos II treated them with both grace and favour and Beaumont was promoted in royal service to become alferez in 1379—the king noted that this appointment "certified to the good virtues, loyalty, mind [intelligence] and diligence of his beloved and loyal nephew".[13] He was also made castellan of St Jean Pied-de-Port in the same year, when he was likely only 18 years of age. In the same year, his younger brother Tristan was made a canon in the Cathedral of Pamplona—Carlos II had already generously funded his education after the death of the Infante Luis. In December 1381, Carlos II bestowed the palace and lordship of d'Asiain on his nephew and alferez Carlos de Beaumont—another sign of royal favour.[14]

The post of alferez was a key position with administrative, military, and diplomatic duties and Beaumont continued to serve Carlos III in this role after his accession in 1387. Although many of these diplomatic missions involved negotiations with Navarre's neighbours France, Aragon, and Castile, Beaumont's role also necessitated working with the English kings and their emissaries. Indeed Beaumont's earliest diplomatic missions involved England as part of an embassy to the English king Richard II in 1378 to negotiate the complicated situation regarding the possession of Cherbourg.[15] Beaumont appears to have made a favourable impression on Richard, as the king granted his request in December 1382 that Beaumont's brother-in-law, Pey/Pedro de Laxague, be allowed to build a sizable fortified house—this may be the building known as the "Maison Forte" of Gentein.[16] In the spring of 1385, Beaumont visited England on yet another diplomatic mission, which was probably tied to the situation in Cherbourg. Clearly he continued to be in Richard's good graces as in the same year the English king granted Beaumont the care and revenues of the castle of Mauléon and the vicomté de Soule and agreed to release the prisoner Tetbaut (Thibaut) de Poyloaut to the "mainprise" of Beaumont and his associates.[17] We will return to Beaumont's career in future chapters as he continued to play a major role in Anglo-Navarrese relations, as an international power broker and during Joan's tenure as queen of England.

Female family networks: Joan's formidable and formative aunts

Joan's aunts and great-aunts formed a vital part of Joan's family networks, both in terms of making important connections to dynasties across Western Europe and in directly influencing the course of Joan's life—particularly her childhood and years as duchess of Brittany. While Joan had several aunts, there are four who made the greatest impact as "models" and "moulders". The two who could be seen as "models" were her two aunts who were both dowager queens of France in Joan's lifetime, her great-aunt Jeanne d'Evreux, widow of Charles IV, and Blanca of Navarre (who will be referred to as Blanche so as not to confuse her with her niece and great niece), widow of Philip VI.[18] Both queens were widows who were not the mother of the heir, as Joan herself would be later in England. As Mariah Proctor-Tiffany has demonstrated in her evaluation of the precarious widowhood of Clémence of Hungary, the second wife of Louis X of France (and I of Navarre), this could have doomed these two women to a life of financial uncertainty and obscurity.[19] However, even though Jeanne and Blanche were not mothers of the heirs, they had given birth to princesses and continued to play a maternal role to stepchildren, nieces, and nephews. In this way, as Marguerite Keane notes, they were able to enact two key roles for dowager queens "which offered access to power"—that of mother and mediator.[20] Both women had very long periods as dowager queens, again like Joan herself in later years—Jeanne's widowhood lasted from 1328 to 1371 and Blanche's from 1350 to

1398. Yet, these two women retained significant political influence over the decades and were well known for their cultural patronage, becoming stabilising lynchpins in a court which was in considerable flux due to dynastic change and the political upheaval caused by the outbreak of the Hundred Years War with England and internal conflict between the great princes of the realm. Indeed, María Narbona Cárceles claims that in her later years Blanche functioned as "the memory of the court", called on for her knowledge of court ceremonial and protocol as a woman who had witnessed several coronations, including that of all the Valois queens—her own being the first of the new dynasty, making her the ideal person to organise the entry and coronation of Isabeau of Bavaria, bride of Charles VI.[21]

Jeanne and Blanche were close to one another and worked together to support the Navarrese cause in France—Carlos II owed a great deal to their diplomatic intervention during several periods of political crisis. Their first significant intervention came in mediating in the treaty of Mantes in 1354 and they were involved again in the treaty of Valognes in September of the following year—both treaties sought to heal the rift between Carlos II and Jean II and help to recover Carlos's patrimonial territory, which had been seized in northern France.[22] When Carlos II was imprisoned by Jean II from 1356 to 1357, the two queens were able to get a safeguard to take him to Paris. In August 1358 Navarrese forces took over Melun, which was a strategic town held by Blanche as part of her dower lands and a frequent residence of hers—Keane notes that it is not clear if Blanche was an "unwilling host" or if she actually invited the troops in to help her brother's side.[23] Blanche was involved in the ratification of the treaty of Pontoise in 1359 and in negotiating two further peace agreements in April 1364 and another, in concert with Jeanne d'Evreux, the following spring. Their last joint diplomatic venture was bargaining for Navarre's benefit at Vernon in March 1371, shortly before Jeanne d'Evreux's death. The combined blow of Jeanne's death and the death of Blanche's own daughter Jeanne, en route to her wedding to an Aragonese prince in the same year, heralded Blanche's semi-withdrawal from high politics.

However, Blanche continued to play an important role in serving the family, raising Carlos III in his younger years—he had been born at

Mantes in France, and when Jeanne de Valois returned to Navarre in January 1363, Carlos stayed with his aunt under her tutelage until 1366 and remained close to her for the rest of his life, visiting her during his trips to France.[24] The gifts Blanche left to Carlos III, and all of her surviving nieces and nephews, including Joan, in her will serve as testimony to her bond with and affection for her Navarrese family, which we will discuss further in the final chapter. In the same chapter, we will also discuss how Blanche also served as a model for Joan in terms of patronage, particularly in terms of the collection of books—Blanche, Jeanne d'Evreux, and Joan's grandmothers, Juana II and Bonne of Luxembourg, all set a template of queenly cultural patronage for Joan to follow. In sum, both Jeanne and Blanche were eminently respected for their political acumen, effective diplomacy, and influential cultural patronage—their example served as a model of dowager queenship that other royal women, particularly their niece Joan, sought to emulate.

Next, we turn from these "model" aunts to two other aunts who had important influence on Joan as "moulders", Agnes, countess of Foix, and Juana, viscountess of Rohan. The latter, the youngest of Joan's aunts, will be discussed further in the following chapter as a significant figure during Joan's tenure as duchess of Brittany. Juana, who was married to a prominent Breton noble, was a key proponent of a marriage between her niece and duke Jean IV, and once Joan was successfully installed in Brittany, her aunt's presence in the duchy arguably helped "mould" Joan from a Navarrese infanta into a Breton duchess.

Here, we will focus more on Agnes, who in many ways filled the role of mother to Joan during her childhood and thus played a crucial part in "moulding" Joan in her youth. Before discussing Joan's early years and Agnes's role in them, it is important to briefly explain the unusual circumstances which led to Agnes re-joining the Navarrese court. While some women chose to return to their native land if they were widowed, this was not the case for Agnes—rather she was repudiated by her husband, Gaston Fébus, count of Foix, in 1362. Agnes and Gaston had married in August 1349, but the death of Agnes's mother, the regnant queen Juana II, later that year from the Black Death left a problem which poisoned the marriage. Juana had been unable to pay all of Agnes's dowry before she died and

Carlos II's subsequent political challenges meant his money was needed for military campaigns rather than his sister's dowry payments. The couple lived in relative harmony for a dozen years but in 1362 a series of events brought their marriage to a shocking end. The first two events were ostensibly positive ones—the birth of a long-awaited heir, also named Gaston, in September, and an impressive victory in early December at Launac against Gaston Fébus' great regional rival, the count of Armagnac. Yet by Christmas he had sent his half-brother Arnaud-Guilhem to inform Agnes that she would be departing for Pamplona immediately, not to return unless she had the money to pay the remainder of her dower. Fébus' biographer Vernier argues that Agnes's surprising dismissal should be seen as motivated by personal reasons, as it was a very imprudent move politically which would gain the count nothing, noting it was likely that "a private estrangement between a husband and his wife, and a sudden impulse to end a situation that had become intolerable" was the real basis behind Fébus' vindictive actions.[25] According to Agnes's 1391 account of the situation, she was not only sent off in the dead of winter, but forced to abandon most of the personal items and jewellery that she had packed to take with her, and was only allowed to take her underclothes, one tapestry, and a dozen silver cups.

More importantly, perhaps, she also had to abandon her newborn son, the young Gaston. His story is also worth a brief digression here as it speaks both to the Navarrese political situation and the reputation of Joan's father, Carlos II. While Agnes was not allowed to return to her husband's court at Orthez, her son was permitted to visit her twice during his teens, in 1375 and 1378.[26] According to Froissart's famous chronicle, during this last visit Carlos II supplied young Gaston with a poison that he told his nephew was a love potion guaranteed to affect a reconciliation between his parents.[27] To truncate the story down to its bare bones, when he returned to Orthez the prince was found out before he was able to administer the poison and put in prison where his father Gaston Fébus accidentally killed him during an interrogation, even though he promised his lords that young Gaston would be spared. While Froissart's account is both over-dramatic, inconsistent in places, and may not be completely accurate, Fébus' biographer Richard Vernier notes that there are three fundamental facts which are also reflected in the chronicle: an attempt was made on Fébus' life, the lords were consulted about the situation, and Fébus either killed his son himself or had him killed.[28] However it took place, the repudiation of Agnes "had undoubtedly lit the slow fuse that would, seventeen years later, set off the deadly explosion", tragically culminating in the death of young Gaston.[29]

In terms of trying to understand this complicated situation, Pierre Tucoo-Chala has argued that Fébus was so empowered by the combination of the birth of an heir and victory over his rival that he felt able to sever ties with Navarre. Indeed, Tucoo-Chala has argued that Agnes's repudiation signalled "a complete political rupture between Orthez and Pamplona".[30] But while Richard Vernier agrees that Fébus may have felt liberated by his great victory over Armagnac in 1362, which may have partially inspired his actions, he notes that there was not an actual break between Navarre and Foix-Béarn after Agnes's return, mostly likely because Carlos II was not in position to add to his list of enemies nor in a position to make a military strike to avenge his sister. Yet even if Carlos could not strike at Gaston Fébus in a military or overt political sense, in Froissart's version of events, he still took revenge as a brutal poisoner who worked through his own nephew, putting him in harm's way as the unwitting agent of his assassination attempt. Froissart ends his tale of the death of the young Gaston by claiming "it was his father who accidentally killed him, but his real assassin was the King of Navarre".[31] Froissart had also claimed that Carlos had poisoned Charles V of France and this story lent considerable weight to Carlos's dark reputation as a poisoner or even a necromancer—a "black legend" which would later rebound on his daughter Joan.

Childhood and youth: Tracing Joan's early years

Happily, after all the trauma of her departure from Orthez, Agnes's arrival in Pamplona led to the development of a deep personal bond with her sister-in-law, Jeanne de Valois, and they became constant companions. Agnes even travelled with the Navarrese queen on her last trip to France in 1373. Signs of Jeanne's esteem and affection for

Agnes include the purchase of a new crown garnished with pearls and precious stones to replace the one Agnes left behind in Orthez. Jeanne also was willing to donate 3,000 livres towards the repayment of Agnes's dowry and worked with Fébus' mother, Alienor de Comminges, to try to work out a financial settlement which would enable a reunion of the count and countess, though Alienor's death scuppered their plans.[32]

Agnes's arrival at the Navarrese court in early 1363 enabled her to have a major impact on the upbringing of her nieces and nephews, including Joan, as she was *in situ* for all of their births, bar that of Carlos III, which had already occurred in 1361. Joan was the sixth child of Carlos II and Jeanne de Valois, after Carlos III, the short-lived Felipe, Maria, Pedro, and Blanca, who were all born between 1361 and 1368, although the exact dating and order is not completely concrete. Nor is the date of Joan's own birth—we know that she was born in Navarre, possibly at Estella, as Jeanne de Valois was based in the kingdom between 1366 and 1373. Jeanne spent much of this time ruling Navarre in her husband's stead, particularly during June 1369–September 1372 when Carlos II had gone back to France to negotiate over the return of his territories there. During this period—in Joan's infancy—Jeanne proved to be an effective regent during a very challenging political period. The queen defended the realm "with energy" against a possible Castilian invasion, signing an alliance with the king of Aragon, repairing defences and fortifications on the Castilian border, contracting mercenaries to supplement their forces, and putting down a revolt in the Ultrapuertos region in the north of the kingdom.[33] Jeanne ultimately prevented war with their Castilian neighbours by participating in peace negotiations brokered by the Pope and her brother Charles V. Jeanne's last political assignment was returning to France for further diplomatic negotiations with her Valois relatives in 1373.

Jeanne de Valois' last three children—daughters Blanca, Joan, and Bona were all born between 1366 and 1373. The exact dates can be hard to define as the births of princesses were not as heralded as those of potential heirs; for example, the contemporary Navarrese chronicle of Garcia d'Eugui comments on the birth of Joan's brothers Carlos and Pedro but does not mention any of their sisters.[34]

Blanca was likely born in 1367 or 1368 and Joan shortly after in 1368 or 1369. Bona, named for Jeanne de Valois' mother, Bonne of Luxembourg, was most likely born in 1373 considering that Carlos II was gone from June 1369 until September 1372. Indeed, the most likely scenario is that Jeanne died as a result of complications from giving birth to Bona—she was pregnant when she left Navarre in 1373 and according to the *Chronique des quatre premiers Valois* the queen died of "*mal d'enfanter*" or difficulties in childbirth.[35]

The first reference to Joan is also somewhat unclear—in 1369 there is a record of payment for the expenses of educating two girls at the Convent of Santa Clara at Estella, and one florin daily set aside for a teacher and a servant for them. One of these girls was Juana de Beaumont, natural daughter of Joan's uncle Luis of Navarre as noted previously, and the other was for one of Carlos II's own daughters. However, while the original document notes that this infanta was named Isabel, José Ramón Castro has listed this royal daughter as Joan instead in the calendared version of these records, known as the *Catálogo*.[36] There are two likely possibilities here: one is, as there is no clear indication in the records that this "Isabel" did exist, that the child referred to here was mostly likely Joan instead, or it is possible that Joan may have even been originally named Isabel and later called Joan after her mother's death. Whichever scenario was the case, it would make perfect sense that Joan was sent to the Clarissan convent at Estella during her childhood, as it was, as Nelly Ongay calls it, "*un espacio feminino por excelencia*", with a tradition of educating royal daughters.[37] While Joan may have had visits from her mother as an infant during Jeanne de Valois' period as regent, it is unlikely that Joan was able to create a lasting bond with her before the queen left the kingdom in the spring of 1373, never to return. Joan's aunt Agnes, who had accompanied Jeanne de Valois on her final journey to France and had been with her at her death, returned alone to Navarre in 1374 and became a mother figure to Joan and the other infantes. Agnes became the head of the household "of the Infantas", which included Joan's sisters Maria and Blanca and later also encompassed the two eldest daughters of Carlos III, Juana and Maria.[38]

The surviving records from this household are not complete during Joan's youth but do cover 1375–1377, when Joan was approximately six to nine years old and give almost complete coverage for Joan's last few years in the kingdom from the beginning of 1383 until her departure for her wedding on 27 July 1386, with the exception of 1385.[39] These records, along with their extensive analysis by Nelly Ongay, give an excellent idea of Joan's life and particularly her movements during her youth. In keeping with the itinerant nature of the Navarrese court itself, which was fairly typical of royal courts generally in the later Middle Ages, Joan and the infantas moved around the kingdom with some regularity. The household accounts note their daily location so we can track her movements—the place where the household was most frequently based in these accounts was Olite, where the household was in residence in July 1376, January 1377, late 1384, and early 1386. Olite was a principal residence of the Navarrese kings which Carlos II increasingly began to favour from 1372 and later it was developed by Carlos III into a spectacular Gothic palace, which has been restored in recent years as a key site associated with Navarre's medieval heritage.[40] In addition to Olite, we can see the household's peregrinations to other major royal palaces such as Estella, Tafalla, and Pamplona, as well as residences at Tiebas, Puente la Reina, Peralta, Caparroso, and Monreal.

The household accounts also reveal that while the infantas were based with their aunt Agnes, they also spent considerable time with their father, joining the king's household at several periods. During some of these periods, Agnes is not listed for one or two days at various points, suggesting that she may have taken some time away from the household, perhaps to visit sacred sites or have some respite from her duties as the infantas' virtual mother. While the infantas are often covered by the sweeping "*Madame de Foix et nos dames*", which groups the infantas together as "our ladies" in the daily summaries, changes to this phrasing can indicate some interesting possibilities. For example, there are periods when only Agnes and Joan are listed, such as a period in Monreal in late January and early February 1384, and on 25–26 January 1383, Agnes and Joan were briefly hosted by the king. Joan's departure for her wedding can be securely dated to 27 July 1386 by a change in this phrasing to indicate that only "Madame de Foix" and "Madame Maria" were present from 28 July.

Details from the household accounts can also give us an idea of what the infantas' life was like and the people who surrounded them, such as Agnes's confessor Father Guillaume (or Guilhem) who is noted in all the accounts. Ongay's detailed analysis of the account books breaks down the food consumed by the household of the infantas, noting that they ate a substantial amount of meat, fish, and poultry and that their rich diet underlined their privileged status as members of the royal family.[41] The detail of the expenses for the infantas reveals purchases of new shoes and clothes as they grew, medicines and the services of doctors and "barbers" when they were ill, purchases of paper and ink for their studies and letters, religious offerings made for feast days, and other more intimate details. For example, we know that Joan kept birds as pets as a child and later she kept them as an adult and gifted birds to others. Her father and brother kept a small royal menagerie at Pamplona which included at various points a mockingjay, a parrot, a pair of lions, a camel, a monkey, and an ostrich.[42] Joan and her sisters also had pet dogs—on 26 March 1386 there is the note of a purchase of "*un petit chien pour nos dames*" or "a little dog for our ladies", which may have added to the other small dogs who are noted elsewhere in the records.[43] Ongay's summary paints a colourful picture of the lives of Joan and her sisters: "The princesses lived, grew, prayed, visited sanctuaries, were entertained by performers, amused themselves with special birds and their food gave them an adequate diet for them to thrive".[44]

Altogether, through the limited but interesting evidence left to us, it appears that Joan had a good start in life—while her mother died before she was able to get to know her, she would have been raised with Jeanne de Valois' legacy as an active and able queen who had been deeply engaged in the administration and politics of the realm, ruling in tandem with Carlos II in a style similar to the co-operative "Team Players" mode of Carlos's parents, Juana II and Philip d'Evreux.[45] Joan also had the models of her aunts Jeanne d'Evreux and Blanche of Navarre—who also would have been held up to her as an example of effective queenship as consorts and dowagers. Closer to home, Joan was raised by her aunt Agnes, who might have lavished the love and care on her nieces the infantas that she was denied giving to her own son Gaston who remained in

Orthez. Joan would have met the young Gaston on his two fateful visits to Navarre and was raised with her sisters and cousins, both legitimate and illegitimate. She was educated both by the Poor Clares at Estella who began a lifelong connection with the Franciscan order and by her aunts as "models" and "moulders". Finally, she would have had the example of her father, the infamous Carlos "the Bad", in front of her as she grew and would have learned from both his successes and mistakes—in our next section, we will summarise the political situation of Navarre during Joan's childhood and consider the impact that it had on her first marriage and her long-term trajectory.

A tangled web: The politics of Carlos II

As alluded to throughout this chapter, the reign of Joan's father, Carlos II, was fraught with political challenges due in part to his own rivalries and ambitions and also from wider conflict between his allies and enemies in France, Iberia, and England. While it is not feasible to fully explore these here, we will briefly consider how these political affairs impacted both Joan's childhood and set in motion the events which led to her first marriage with Jean IV of Brittany, which will form the final section of this chapter.

Maria Raquel García Arancon summarises the political events of Carlos II's reign into three distinct phases.[46] The first phase of his reign, from his accession in 1349, began at peace with the king of France, Philip VI, who became his brother-in-law when he married Carlos's sister Blanche (who was originally betrothed to his son Jean) in 1350. Philip's death shortly thereafter brought Jean II to the throne—while Jean became Carlos's father-in-law when he married Jeanne de Valois in 1352, the tension between the French and Navarrese kings steadily rose, erupting in 1354 with the murder of Jean's favourite, Carlos de la Cerda (or Charles of Spain), in which Carlos II was deeply involved. As noted earlier, the French dowager queens Jeanne d'Evreux and his sister Blanche worked to try to heal the divisions between Jean II and Carlos II and tried to mitigate Carlos's imprisonment in 1356 for plotting against the French king with the English. Ironically, Jean II was taken prisoner himself in the same year and held by the English—although he was released in 1360 to collect bail, he later died in London in 1364 after returning to fulfil the terms of his captivity, as his hostage, Prince Louis, had escaped and his ransom had not yet been fully paid.

Joan was born in the middle of the second phase of Carlos II's reign which began with the death of Jean II and the accession of Charles V, his cousin and brother-in-law. This phase began with a difficult defeat for Carlos II and his English/Gascon allies at the hands of the French at Cocherel on 16 May 1364, which led to the loss of his territories in France.[47] This perhaps forced Carlos II to reorient himself towards Iberia, where in neighbouring Castile a war was being fought between Pedro "the Cruel" and his half-brother Enrique de Trastámara over the throne. Carlos II initially sought to remain neutral in the Castilian civil war and in the Papal Schism which opened up in 1378—Béatrice Leroy has noted that Carlos's shifts from neutrality to allegiance or shifts in allegiance have given him the reputation of being a wily, faithless politician immersed in *double jeux*, or double dealing. Instead, Leroy claims that both Carlos II and his son were not duplicitous but engaged in a skilful political strategy of "*politique de bascule*" or rocking from side to side based on their changing interests and the ever-shifting political landscape.[48]

A key period here was the 1370s, which coincides with the early years of Joan's childhood. As noted, in 1378 the Papal Schism opened when Gregory XI died, leading to the election of Urban VI under pressure from the Romans to elect an Italian pope after a string of popes who had been based at Avignon during the so-called "Babylonian Captivity". The French cardinals disavowed Urban and returned to Avignon where they elected Clement VIII instead. This had radical repercussions for European politics as divisions arose between those who supported the Roman pope or the Avignonese "anti-pope". While Carlos II initially chose a degree of neutrality, Carlos III became a strong adherent of Avignon, particularly during the reign of the Aragonese "Papa Luna", Benedict XIII. The French also chose to adhere to the Avignon anti-pope, but the English chose allegiance to the pope in Rome—Carlos II's initial reluctance to choose papal allegiance may have been part of his continual political oscillation between these cross-Channel rivals.

Carlos II's initial neutrality in the Castilian civil war had faded with a lean towards Pedro, who was supported by the English—Carlos sought to take advantage of the instability in Castile by seizing the cities of Logroño and Vitoria in 1368. As Enrique de Trastámara began to emerge as the stronger party and solidified his position against his Iberian neighbours, Carlos was forced to come to terms and sign the peace of Almazán in April 1375, losing Vitoria and Logroño but gaining a daughter-in-law, Leonor de Trastámara, who married his son, who later became Carlos III.[49] Around the time that the English crown passed from the elderly Edward III to his grandson in 1377, Carlos II began secret negotiations with the English on other potential royal marriages for one of his daughters with the young king Richard II, and another potential marriage between one of his daughters and a son of John of Gaunt—or alternatively between one of Gaunt's daughters and his son Pedro.[50] These negotiations are significant for multiple reasons—even though Joan is not specified here as the particular bride for either marriage, there is an irony here given that she eventually married John of Gaunt's son, Henry of Bolingbroke, and became queen of England as his wife. According to the deposition of Carlos's servant Jacques de Rue, the negotiations were well advanced and the English appeared to favour the idea of a Navarrese bride "because she was more noble and of higher lineage" than Joan's cousin, the imperial princess Anne of Bohemia, who who eventually became Richard II's wife.[51]

The other significant piece of these negotiations were their political repercussions—while they did not result in an Anglo-Navarrese marriage, when the French became aware of Carlos's overtures to the English, who were gearing up for another campaign against France, they responded with fury. In the path of this anger was Joan's brother, the heir Carlos, who had been dispatched to France in January 1378, along with Jacques de Rue and Pierre du Tertre, who had been involved in the negotiations with England. When Gaston Fébus alerted the king of France to the Navarrese machinations in the spring, Jacques de Rue was seized and revealed the entire plot, including the wider context of Carlos's surreptitious engagement with the English—Pierre du Tertre's eventual capture and trial provided more incriminating evidence.[52] Prince Carlos was summoned to meet his uncle Charles V at Senlis, where he was informed of the discovery of Carlos II's treachery with the English and effectively became a guest/hostage of the French—his Valois blood and the prince's accommodating cooperation with his uncle prevented him from being held as a true prisoner. Charles V then began to seize several key fortresses in the Evreux-Navarre territories in Northern France, starting with Breteuil in April, where another of Joan's brothers, Pedro, was taken when the fortress fell. Carlos, Pedro, and Bona, the youngest child of Carlos II and Jeanne de Valois, who as noted earlier was likely born and remained in France after her mother's death in 1373, were all held by Charles V as leverage while he moved against Carlos II and to prevent Pedro or Bona being married off to secure alliances with the English.[53] While Joan was safe at home in Navarre with her sister Maria, the two infantas may well have been missing not only their imprisoned siblings as well as their sister Blanca, who appears to have died in the same period.

The end of the 1370s proved to be a major political disaster for Carlos II, which signalled the start of the third and final phase of his political career. Carlos's attempt to craft new alliances was scuppered when his two neighbours in France and Castile worked together on a pincer move against him. In early 1378, Enrique of Castile moved in concert with his French allies, invading Navarre, as the French attacked the Navarrese holdings in Normandy. Castilian victories forced Carlos to concede to the treaty of Briones in March 1379 which compelled him to surrender to the infante of Castile 18 castles along with an elaborate system of hostages for each of the castles and for the cities of Pamplona, Sangüesa, Olite, and Laguardia.[54] In addition, the treaty stipulated that Carlos was forbidden from allying with or supporting England in any way, with a specific note that none of Carlos II's children could marry into the English royal house—not even to an illegitimate member of the dynasty.[55]

Yet the dire straits in which Carlos II found himself quickly began to ease slightly, giving him room to manoeuvre. Only two months after the Treaty of Briones, Enrique II of Castile died on 29 May, and Carlos's long-time rival and former brother-in-law Charles V of France followed soon after in September 1380. This brought two fairly young, untried monarchs to the thrones of France and

Castile—and in the following year his own son and heir was allowed to return to Navarre.[56] If Carlos could not forge a marriage alliance with his previous allies, the English, directly, his other option was to look for another prince who had similar political leanings for one of his daughters.

From infanta to duchess

Carlos's choice fell on Jean IV of Brittany, who had a similar scenario, being both a vassal of the king of France but also an autonomous ruler in his own right who was keen to keep his duchy outside direct French control. Carlos and Jean leant towards the English in their political sympathies, but both had been forbidden in treaties signed with the French to support the English.[57] While the Treaty of Guérande which Jean IV signed with France in 1381 required him to oppose any attempt of Carlos II to claim the French crown or provide support to Navarre against France, it was not clear that marriage between their respective houses was barred. A Breton-Navarrese marriage offered both Carlos and Jean several advantages, by allowing them to develop a deeper bond between two realms which shared a desire to support the English and prevent French control of their territories. The marriage also offered Carlos II a chance to "reactivate" himself politically by building up his allies in Northern France, while Jean IV appreciated that a Navarrese infanta could offer not only a connection to her father, the king of Navarre, but to her first cousin, the king of France, and her Valois uncles of Burgundy and Berry.[58] While an alliance with Navarre could appear to be potentially provocative to France, this marriage also offered an opportunity for a rapprochement with the French as Henneman noted: "a wife with Valois blood ... was surely more acceptable in Paris than his two previous English spouses".[59]

Jean had been married twice previously—first to Mary, daughter of Edward III of England, who died in 1361 shortly after they wed, and then to Joan Holland, daughter-in-law of the Black Prince, who had died in 1384—but no issue had been produced from either marriage. Jean wasted no time after the death of his second wife in looking for a third. Indeed, Michael Jones has noted that negotiations for a potential Navarrese marriage were so quickly in train that on the same day that the English court was holding a Mass for the death of Joan Holland on 27 November 1384, Joan's father, Carlos II of Navarre, was authorising his envoy to make terms with Jean IV for a matrimonial alliance.[60] Jean's need for an heir was particularly pressing not just due to his advancing years but because he had spent the better part of his life and reign fighting another branch of the ducal dynasty, the Penthièvres, over the right to the duchy. Should he die without issue, the Penthièvres would claim the ducal throne and all of his work to secure Brittany for the Montforts would be undone. Thus top of Jean IV's list of requirements for a Navarrese was a requirement that she be "*a laage de seze anz ou au desus et saine de toute maladie contagieuse*"—i.e that she was young ("sixteen years or younger"), healthy and thus presumably fertile, given that her mother, Jeanne de Valois, had produced three sons and four daughters.[61] At this stage, Carlos II had only two legitimate daughters left as both Blanca and Bona had passed away—indeed Bona had died in 1383, only a year before the Breton marital negotiations began. Out of the two surviving infantas, Joan seemed to fit the description of being "sixteen years or younger" best, as she would have been approximately 16 when the negotiations began in 1384, while Maria was roughly four years older.

A key figure who was important to orchestrating the match was the Breton noble the viscount de Rohan, married to Carlos II's youngest sister, Juana, who appears to have been influential in pushing the match forward.[62] Jean IV sent messengers with an initial approach to Carlos II in late 1384 which were cordially received, and a team of negotiators was dispatched to Brittany with instructions and the power to draft an agreement and Joan's explicit permission for negotiations to be contracted in her name.[63] On 12 April 1385 Jean IV wrote a polite and formal letter to thank Carlos II for sending Guillermo de Plantarosa, the master of the king's household, to Brittany to discuss terms and swore to receive Joan as his bride as long as the conditions established in the negotiations were met.[64] Plantarosa led an elite team which included two other royal counsellors, Francisco de Villapesa and Pierre Godeile, who was also the abbot of Monreal—to thank Plantarosa for his efforts, Joan gifted him cloth from Monstivillier.[65] In return, Jean IV sent his own team of Geoffroy de Poulglou, his chamberlain, and the lawyer Robert Brochereul, the seneschal of Nantes, to Navarre at the end of May 1386 to finalise the details just before the marriage and ensure that the contract was complied with.[66]

The Breton marriage was a significant political alliance for Joan's family and one that her father paid dearly for—knowing how vital the marriage was for Carlos II to gain a like-minded and supportive political friend in the French sphere, Jean IV had asked for a considerable dowry. Carlos had instructed his own negotiators not to promise more than 100,000 francs plus 12,000 francs-worth in jewels, but Jean IV ultimately asked for 200,000 gold francs—Joan's dowry was finally agreed at 120,000 gold francs plus another 6,000 francs allocated from the rents of the vicomté d'Avranches.[67] It was agreed that the dowry could be paid in instalments but nevertheless, for a kingdom which had been strapped by prolonged wars and economic difficulties, this was a nearly impossible sum to raise.[68] The substantial dowry plus the money needed for the lavish festivities as well as garments and jewels for the bride took a massive financial toll on not just the king but the kingdom itself, as Carlos II looked to the *buenas villas* or the major cities of the realm to assist with the hefty cost.[69] Ultimately, after extensive efforts to wring the money out of every crevice of the kingdom, Carlos could only send 46,986 francs by the time of the wedding—33,014 short of the first stipulated dowry instalment.[70] The wedding went ahead but the dowry was never paid in full; indeed, Joan's son Jean V ultimately brought a suit at the Tribunal de Paris against his uncle Carlos III for the unpaid sum in 1409.[71]

Not only did Carlos II have to raise money for the dowry from the realm, but he also had to fund the wedding celebrations, the bridal journey, and, most importantly, provide Joan with a trousseau fit for a princess. It appears that Carlos pressed various nobles and servitors for loans—even from Jehan le Roux, a key member of his son's entourage, to help him cover the costs of the wedding expenses.[72] The gold and silversmiths of the realm were given considerable work making a number of items for the infanta's trousseau, including silver tableware and particularly jewellery for the bride, including several crowns to help her transition to her new status as duchess and ensure she made a suitably royal impression in Brittany.[73] The bride had to be suitably clothed, as did her entourage, who were also representing Navarre, thus several payments were made just before Joan's departure in July 1386 for cloth "for the people who are accompanying the infanta Joan to Brittany".[74] While considerable sums were being spent on the bride, Joan also gave gifts to those she was leaving behind, including red and grey (presumably patterned) cloth which she gifted to the servitors of her sister Maria, who would have been part of the household of the infantas in which Joan had grown up, and gifted her aunt Agnes cloth of Monstivillier as well.[75] Finally, Joan's trousseau of household items such as a considerable quantity of sheets and bedclothes, foodstuffs, wine and spices, and her clothes had to be packed as well—in all there were nine pairs of coffers; four pairs for her clothes, one for her jewels, one for the items for her chapel, and the rest for household items.[76]

Joan's bridal trip in 1386 entailed an overland journey from Pamplona to Bayonne—as noted above, from the accounts of the infantas' household, we can ascertain that she departed the capital on 27 July. Joan moved northwards to the monastery of Roncevalles in the Pyrenees, an important stop on the pilgrim trail to Santiago de Compostela which has a long history of association with the rulers of Navarre, where she appears to have remained for a few weeks. Her father Carlos II visited her there on 30 July and again on 7 and 19 August—on the last occasion, Joan's brother Carlos joined them as well.[77] The royal party continued northwards to St Jean Pied de Port where there was a brief hiatus when Joan and her brother Carlos waited for a few days for their father who had made a detour to collect a little more cash for the dowry instalment. On 23 August they continued their journey to Irissarry, stopped at La Bastida de Clerenza the following day, and reached their destination of Bayonne on 25 August.[78]

The pieces were all coming together by the end of August—the dowry (or a portion of it) had been collected, the bride, royal entourage, and her trousseau had made it safely over the Pyrenees, and the papal dispensation for the match had come through.[79] After

Joan's arrival at Bayonne, there was a formal blessing of the match on 2 September in the Cathédrale Sainte-Marie conducted by Pierre Godeile, the abbot of Monreal, who had also been part of the negotiating team sent by Carlos II to Brittany. A group of emissaries from the Breton court had been sent to collect her and had arrived at San Sebastian in June in a flotilla of three boats captained by Pierre de Lesnerac. While Joan and her party travelled slowly overland, the flotilla had sailed from San Sebastian to Bayonne on the 10–12 July and had been waiting with decreasing patience for six weeks at the mouth of the Adour until the bride was ready to depart.[80] Finally, on 4 September, two days after the blessing at Bayonne, the flotilla departed with the bride, her household and goods in tow, and made a swift journey up the coast to Croisic—her wedding to Jean IV was celebrated nearby at Saillé near Guérande on 11 September and Joan's transition from infanta to duchess was complete.

Conclusion

In this chapter, we have not only been introduced to Joan, but we have placed her in the wider context of her wide-ranging and impressive family networks and the turbulent politics of her father's reign, which shaped her childhood and ultimately set her on the path to become duchess of Brittany. While we cannot say with certainty whether her childhood was a happy one, we have seen how her aunt Agnes played a key role in filling the gap left by Jeanne de Valois' death when Joan was only a toddler. Even though Joan's mother died in her early years, we can see the model of effective queenship that she and Joan's aunts, the French dowager queens Blanche of Navarre and Jeanne d'Evreux, created and the impact that this, along with the influence of her aunts Agnes and Juana, would have had in shaping Joan into the duchess and queen she would eventually become. Finally, this chapter has traced some of the key moments of the Hundred Years War in relation to Carlos II's controversial and troubled reign. This unfolding conflict, and political tension with her Valois cousins in France, continued to dominate Joan's life from her earliest days as infanta into her later roles as duchess of Brittany and queen of England, as we will see in the chapters to follow.

Notes

1 For more on both Juana I and II, see Elena Woodacre, *The Queens Regnant of Navarre: Succession, Politics and Partnership, 1274–1512* (New York: Palgrave Macmillan, 2013). On the succession crisis particularly, see pages 51–61, and Derek Whaley, "From *a* Salic Law to *the* Salic Law: The Creation and Re-creation of the Royal Succession System of Medieval France," in *The Routledge History of Monarchy*, eds. Elena Woodacre, Lucinda H.S. Dean, Chris Jones, Russell E. Martin, and Zita Eva Rohr (London: Routledge, 2019), 443–64.

2 Íñigo Arzoz Mendizábal, "Juana de Valois," in *Reinas de Navarre*, ed. Julia Pavon (Madrid: Silex, 2014), 620.

3 Nelly Ongay, "De Evreux a Olite: la condesa de Foix y su viaje de regreso de Francia," *Príncipe de Viana* 67, no. 239 (2006): 873.

4 Philippe Charon, "Jeanne de Valois, reine de Navarre et comtés d'Evreux (1343–1373)," *En la España Medieval* 32 (2009): 7–50.

5 Fernando Videgain Agos, *Los Bastardos de la casa real Navarra* (Pamplona: Ediciones y Libros S.A., 1979), 78.

6 María Narbona Cárceles, "Les bâtards royaux et la nouvelle noblesse de sang de Navarre (fin XIVe siècle – début XVe siècle)," *Revue du Nord* 31 (2015): 422. See also Maria Raquel Garcia Arancon, "Carlos II de Navarra: El circulo familiar," *Principe de Viana* 48 (1987): 608.

7 See Vicente Castañeda y Alcover, "El Condado de Beaumont-le-Roger," *Revista de Archivos, Bibliotecas y Museos* 88 (1926): 232–39.

8 Videgain Agos, *Los bastardos*, 96.

9 Jean de Jaurgain, "Les Beaumont-Navarre: Notes historiques et généalogiques," *Revista internacional de los estudios vascos (RIEV)*, 3, no. 1 (1909): 48.

10 Juana was baptised 2 Sept 1359, see Jaurgain, "Les Beaumont-Navarre", 47. There is less agreement on Tristan's birth date as other sources suggest he could have been born as late at 1370.

11 Videgain Agos, *Los bastardos*, 101. Narbona Cárceles, "Batards Royaux", 433 and Catálogo VII, no. 604, 9 April 1369.

12 Jaurgain, "Les Beaumont-Navarre," 49.

13 On Beaumont's appointment see D. José Yanguas y Miranda, *Diccionario de antigüedades del Reino de Navarra*, vol 1 (Pamplona: Javier Goyeneche, 1840), 116. Original text "*certificado de las buenas virtudes, lealdad, seso é diligencia de su amado é fiel sobrino*". See also Eloísa Ramírez Vaquero, "Carlos II. La Nobleza," *Principe de Viana* 48 (1987): 648.

14 On these marks of favour to the Beaumont siblings, see Videgain Agos, *Los bastardos*, 102; Jaurgain, "Les Beaumont-Navarre," 48–51.

15 Ramírez Vaquero, *Carlos III*, 67, n132. For more English context, see Jonathan Sumption, *Divided Houses: The Hundred Years War III* (London: Faber and Faber, 2016), 321–25 and 329–30.

16 GSR C 61/96, membrane 12, no. 66, 16 December 1382.

17 Edouard Perroy, ed., *The Diplomatic Correspondence of Richard II* (London: Royal Historical Society, 1931), 221–2, for the original grant and re-confirmation in GSR C 61/104, membrane 13, no. 20, 20 February 1394. Evidence of his diplomatic mission of 1385: 25 April 1385 Beaumont sent to "cierto lugar" to negotiate for the realm. Catálogo L, no. 786, 25 April 1385; Catálogo XV, no. 940, 29 May 1385, and no. 101, 9 July 1385. On the prisoner release see GSR C 61/104, membrane 2, no. 74, 11 May 1385.

18 For a good comparative biography of the two, see Jean-Marc Cazilhac, *Jeanne d'Evreux, Blanche de Navarre: Deux reines de France, deux douairieres Durante la Guerre de Cent ans* (Paris: L'Harmattan, 2010).

19 See Mariah Proctor-Tiffany, *Medieval Art in Motion: The Inventory and Gift-Giving of Queen Clémence de Hongrie* (University Park, PA: Penn State University Press, 2019).

20 Marguerite Keane, *Material Culture and Queenship in 14th-Century France: The Testament of Blanche of Navarre (1331–1398)* (Leiden: Brill, 2016), 8 and 74–75.

21 María Narbona Cárceles, "La 'Discreción hermosa': Blanca de Navarra, reina de Francia (1331?–1398). Una dama al servicio de su linaje," in *La dama en la corte bajomedieval*, ed. Martí Aurell (Pamplona: EUNSA, 2001), 106–7.

22 Narbona Cárceles, "Discreción hermosa," 105.

23 Keane, *Blanche of Navarre*, 53.

24 Narbona Cárceles, "Discreción hermosa," 86; Ramírez Vaquero, *Carlos III*, 11.

25 Richard Vernier, *Lord of the Pyrenees: Gaston Fébus, Count of Foix 1331–1391* (Woodbridge: Boydell, 2008), 147, see also 60 and 146.

26 Pierre Tucoo-Chala, "L'histoire tragique d'un couple au XIVe siècle: Agnès de Navarre et Gaston Fébus," *Principe de Viana Anejo: Homenaje José María Lacarra* 2 3 (1986): 749.

27 For Froissart's version of events, see Jean Froissart, *Chronicles*, trans. and ed. Geoffrey Brereton (London: Penguin Books, 1978), 263–74.

28 Vernier, *Pyrenees*, 154.

29 Vernier, *Pyrenees*, 156.

30 Tucoo-Chala, "L'histoire tragique," 747–79. Original quote is "*une rupture politique complète entre Orthez et Pamplune*".

31 Froissart, *Chronicles*, 274.

32 Tucoo-Chala, "L'histoire tragique," 748 and Vernier, *Pyrenees*, 149.

33 Arzoz Mendizábal, "Juana de Valois," 628–30.

34 Garcia d'Eugui, *Crónica d'Espayña de Garcia de Eugui*, ed. Aengus Ward (Pamplona: Gobierno de Navarra, 1999), 396. The chronicler notes "*Este rey caso con dona Johana, primogenita de Francia, & obo en ella dos fijos: a don Carlos & a don Pedro*".

35 Anon, *Chronique des quatre premiers Valois (1327–1393)*, ed. Siméon Luce (Paris: Jules Renouard, 1862), 244.

36 Catálogo VII, no. 604, 9 April 1369. The full document is reproduced in Maria Teresa Ruiz San Pedro, ed., *Fuentes documentales medievales del País Vasco. Archivo General de Navarra (1349–1387). V. Documentación Real de Carlos II (1368–1369)* (Donostia: Eusko Ikaskuntza, 2003), no. 2036, 9 April 1369.

37 Nelly Ongay Gambarte, "Notas Sobre la Vida Cotidiana de las Infantas Reales en los 'Hospitales' del Reino de Navarra (1365–1400): Alimentos, Vestidos, Religiosidad y Viajes," *Estudios de Historia de España* 17, no. 1 (2015): 62. See also Narbona Cárceles, "Batards Royaux," 433.

38 Ongay Gambarte, "Las infantas reales," 51–52.

39 The full list of surviving accounts are AGN "Registros de cuentas. Hostal." nos. 155 (August 1375, July–August 1376, January 1377), 175 (1383), 178 (1384), 187 (1386).

40 Angel J. Martin Duque, "Monarcas y Cortes Itinerantes en el Reino de Navarra," in *Viajeros, Peregrinos, Mercadores en el Occidente Medieval , XVIII Semana de Estudios Medievales* (Pamplona: Gobierno de Navarra, 1992), 264–65. See also Anthony Emery, *Seats of Power in Europe During the Hundred Years War: An Architectural Study from 1330–1480* (Oxford: Oxbow, 2016), 174–5.

41 Ongay Gambarte, "Las infantas reales," 53–61.

42 Nelly Ongay, "El Hostal de la Infanta Maria (1365–66)," *Principe de Viana* 64 (2003): 154.

43 AGN Registros 187, 26 March 1386, f.93v.

44 Ongay Gambarte, "Las infantas reales," 73–74. Original text: "*Las infantas viven, crecen, rezan, visitan santuarios, se diverten con la presencia de jugalares, se entretienen con pájaros especiales y son alimentadas a través de una dieta adecuada para lograr un crecimiento correcto*".

45 For more on the ruling partnership styles of Juana II and the other regnant queens and their consorts, see Woodacre, *Queens Regnant*, 166–68.

46 Maria Raquel Garcia Arancon, "El circulo familiar," 596–602.

47 Fabia Gray notes this defeat was "crucial for the possessions and the sphere of influence of the House of Evreux-Navarre in France": Fabia Anne Gray, "Formal and Informal Contacts between the House of Navarre and the English during the 14th Century Phase of the Hundred Years War" (PhD thesis, University of Nottingham, October 2005), 7.

48 Béatrice Leroy, "Neutralité ou double jeu? Le rôle du royaume de Navarre dans les relations internationales de la fin du XIVe siècle et du début de XVe siècle," in *Terres et Hommes du Sud*, ed. Christian Desplat (Biarritz: J&D Editions, 1992), 496. Original quote paraphrased above is "*Ces doubles jeux de Charles II et Charles III ne sont pas duplicité. Ils témoignent d'une très habile politique de bascule selon les intérêts du moment, ou de perspicacité pour savoir sur qui fonder l'avenir des relations*".

49 Jose Maria Lacarra, *Historia Politica del Reino de Navarra desde sus origenes hasta su incorporacion a Castilla*, vol. 3 (Pamplona: Editorial Aranzadi, 1973), 117–19; María Narbona Cárceles, "Leonor de Trastámara," in *Reinas de Navarra*, ed. Julia Pavón (Madrid: Silex, 2014), 653.

50 Lacarra, *Historia Politica*, 121; Sumption, *Divided Houses*, 313. For evidence of the Anglo-Navarrese negotiations, see Thomas Rymer ed., *Foedera, conventiones, literae, et cujuscunque generis acta publica...*, vol. 3, part 2 (London: Johannem Neulme, 1740), 53, 54, 57, 77, 79, 83.

51 Denis-François Secousse, *Recueil de pièces servant de preuves aux Mémoires sur les troubles excités en France par Charles II, dit le Mauvais* (Paris: Durand, 1755), 382. Original text is "*car c'estoit plus noblement & en plus hault lingnage*".

52 Sumption, *Divided Houses*, 317. The entire deposition of Jacques de Rue and the trial of Pierre du Tertre is in Secousse, *Preuves*, 373–437.

53 García Arancon, "El circulo familiar," 600. Nelly Ongay, "La boda de la infanta Juana con el duque Bretón Juan IV (1386). Las relaciones diplomáticas con Carlos II Evreux," *Estudios de Historia* 20 (2018): 144.

54 José Zunzunegui, "El Matrimonio de la Infanta Juana con el Duque de Bretaña: Navarra a fines de siglo XIV," *Principe de Viana* 4 (1943): 53; Lacarra, *Historia Politica*, 130–37.

55 Ongay, "La boda," 144; Lacarra, *Historia Politica*, 130–37.

56 Ramírez Vaquero, *Carlos III*, 42.

57 The Treaty of Guérande was signed 4 April 1381; Ongay, "La boda," 148; Zunzunegui, "El Matrimonio," 55.

58 Ramírez Vaquero, *Carlos III*, 49.

59 Henneman, *Olivier de Clisson*, 117.

60 Michael Jones, "Le voyage de Pierre de Lesnerac en Navarre, 1386," in *The Creation of Brittany: A Late Medieval State* (London: Hambledon, 1988), 177; see Catálogo XV, no. 599, 27 November 1384.

61 Zunzunegui, "El Matrimonio," 56. Quote from Letter 540B reprinted in full in Jones, "Lesnerac," 193–4.

62 Jones, "Between France and England," 3; Carlos II gave power to Jean de Rohan, his sister Juana, and Guillem Plantarosa to negotiate the marriage on 22 March 1385; Catálogo XV, no. 819.

63 Zunzunegui, "El Matrimonio," 56–57. For Joan's permission, see Catálogo XV, no. 599, 27 November 1384.

64 Letter 540A reprinted in full in Jones, "Lesnerac," 192–93. See also Catálogo XV, no. 857 and 861, 12 and 13 April 1385 respectively.

65 Zunzunegui, "El Matrimonio," 58. For the gift, see Catálogo XVI, no. 375, 6 September 1386.

66 Letter 589A reprinted in full in Jones, "Lesnerac," 195–96.

67 ADLA E7–9 and 10, dated 5 August 1386.

68 See Zunzunegui, "El Matrimonio," 57–59; Ongay, "La boda," 149–50; Letter 540B in Jones, "Lesnerac," 193–94.

69 See Juan Carrasco Perez, "Fiscalidad y circulación moneta en el Reino de Navarra: La dote de la infanta Juana, duquesa de Bretaña," *Anuario de Estudios Medievales* 22 (1992): 641–64 and "Le Royaume de Navarre et Le duché de Bretagne au cours du dernier tiers du XIVe siècle: politique matrimoniale et circulation monétaire" in *1491: La Bretagne, terre d'Europe*,

eds. Jean Kerhervé and Tanguy Daniel (Brest: Centre de recherche bretonne et celtique, 1992), 205–21.

70 There are many documents in the Catálogo which refer to the process of collecting the *ayuda* in 1385–6; for examples, see Catálogo XV, nos. 1009, 1137, 1272 and Catálogo XVI, nos. 71, 239, 273, 430, 432, 442, 727, 931–2, 1104.

71 Zunzunegui, "El Matrimonio," 67–68.

72 Catálogo XVI, nos. 301, 498 and 500, 18 July, 22 and 23 October 1386.

73 Catálogo XVI, nos. 183, 217, 242, 270, 277, 375, 18 April, 18 May, 8 June, 3 July, 6 July, and 6 September 1386.

74 Catálogo XVI, nos. 282–85, 8 July 1386.

75 Catálogo XVI, nos. 316 and 325, 26 and 27 July 1386.

76 Zunzunegui, "El Matrimonio," 66–7.

77 Catálogo LII, no. 933, summary 1386–87.

78 For the cost of the households of Joan and the infante Carlos on the journey, see Catálogo XVI, no. 365, 1 September 1386.

79 The papal dispensation from Clement VII is ADLA E37–2, 15 August 1386. See also Jones, "Lesnerac," 178, and for expenses related to procuring the papal dispensation, see Catálogo XV, no. 970, 11 June 1385, and Catálogo XVI, no. 1104, 26 June 1387.

80 Jones, "Lesnerac," 184.

2

DUCHESS: WIFE, MOTHER, REGENT

Joan arrived in Brittany in September 1386 as a young infanta, daughter of an infamous king whose politics had been controversial and divisive. She had two important assets which had convinced Jean IV to make her his new duchess: her august lineage and familial connections and her potential fertility. Joan arrived in the duchy at a time when Brittany was struggling to settle down after years of prolonged conflict over the succession between the Montfort and Penthièvre branches of the ducal dynasty. While Jean IV had been able to reassert his claim to the duchy and re-establish his rule after a period of exile in England, there was still considerable internal tension between Joan's new husband and the great lords of the duchy, particularly the powerful Olivier de Clisson, which still threatened to undermine Jean's rule. Joan had to negotiate this potentially treacherous political landscape and fill the role of duchess, which had not been completely fulfilled by either of Jean IV's previous wives, who had both been largely absent from the duchy and had failed to produce a much-needed heir to ensure the continuation of Montfort rule.

In spite of this difficult situation that Joan was presented with, her years as duchess of Brittany were an unqualified success. By the end

DOI: 10.4324/9780429261022-4

of her tenure, she had built a positive personal and political partnership with Jean IV, secured the succession with the birth of numerous sons and daughters, and assisted in stabilising the realm both internally and externally. This chapter will trace this period of Joan's life chronologically, investigating the challenges that Joan faced and how she responded to them, and mapping the transition she made not just from infanta to duchess, but from wife to mother and eventually to become regent of Brittany after the death of Jean IV in 1399.

The new duchess: 1386–89

As noted in the previous chapter, Brittany and Navarre were in very similar political situations. Both were small autonomous states, strategically located between two larger, rival powers. Both Joan's new husband, Jean IV, and her father, Carlos II of Navarre, had clashed repeatedly with the French king and struggled with the inherent tension of being both a vassal of the king of France and a peer as a territorial ruler. Arguably, Carlos II's situation was far more clear-cut in terms of being an independent ruler and his stature somewhat higher as a crowned king. However, Jean IV was keen to assert his independence and his quasi-royal standing in his own duchy. Michael Jones has argued that "without exaggeration it can be said that in the last ten years of this reign Jean IV acted as though he were an independent prince whose state was contiguous with and not within, the bounds of Valois France".[1] Beginning with Jean IV and continuing with his (and Joan's) heirs, the Montfort dukes adopted an increasingly royal stature in their representation, from iconography and visual depictions and in modes of address.[2]

Jean's marriage to Joan of Navarre could be seen as a means of strengthening his royal standing and stature. While his first wife had been an English princess, his second wife was, though a stepdaughter of a Prince of Wales, in effect the daughter of an English noble. Joan, on the other hand, was the daughter of a king and, as discussed thoroughly in the previous chapter, closely related to not only the kings of France, but many of the greatest lords of the realm and royal houses across Western and Central Europe. Not only could Joan boast an illustrious pedigree but indeed Jean's very selection of her as his bride could be seen as a signal of his changing political allegiances. Jean's English wives had been a product of his close political ties with England, who had given him support during the Breton war of succession. Jean's first wife was Mary of Waltham, a daughter of Edward III—their marriage was part of the English king's strategy to keep Brittany closely bound to England, but she died only months after their wedding in June 1361. Edward III required Jean IV to obtain his express permission to remarry, and when he eventually married again in 1366, it was to Joan Holland, the Black Prince's stepdaughter, thus renewing the Anglo-Breton bond.[3] However, Joan Holland's death in October 1384 removed this human tie to England and gave Jean IV a political opportunity to make alliances elsewhere. Henneman has argued that a clear change could be seen in Jean's relationship with England immediately after, demonstrating a "more independent stance in dealing with England in 1385 and 1386" which reflected both how the political landscape had changed and Jean IV's adaptability in steering a course between France and England as tension continued between the two powers.[4]

Thus Jean made a different choice with his third bride, choosing a young woman who had both blood ties to the Valois as well as a father who shared Jean's political sympathies with the English. Yet, looking beyond the political context of his three marriages, Joan was left with two considerable gaps which Jean's two English brides had not been able to fill. The first was establishing a strong presence for the duke's wife in Brittany—Jean's first duchess, Mary of Waltham, had never left England during her short tenure, which according to one contemporary source was only "thirty weeks" or approximately seven months, although the marriage may have been even shorter than this brief span.[5] Jean's second wife, Joan Holland, spent the bulk of her 18 years as duchess in her native England—indeed, while she was sharing Jean IV's exile from the duchy for some of this period (1373–79), she refused to return an additional four years after Jean was restored to power in Brittany. While Joan Holland did exercise the role of countess of Richmond in Jean's absence and look after her husband's interests in England, she did not establish a firm role for the duke's wife at the Breton court.

More importantly, perhaps, was the gap left by the two previous duchesses with regard to the succession. Joan had been brought in, effectively, as a brood mare, for after two marriages without issue, Jean IV was desperate for an heir. The first treaty of Guérande in 1365 clearly stipulated that if Jean IV failed to produce male heirs, the line would revert to his enemies, the house of Penthièvre.[6] In effect, this would mean that the entirety of Jean's struggles for the Breton succession and his reign would be pointless—the house of Montfort would disappear and his rivals would regain the ducal crown.

Joan soon proved her worth in terms of providing dynastic continuity, becoming pregnant only months after the wedding—as will be discussed further in Chapter 5, Joan was granted an extensive dower on 24 February 1387 when she was at the stage where her pregnancy would have been established.[7] Moreover, roughly ten days earlier on 15 February, the ducal couple had made a covenant of mutual donation of their possessions—the timing of these two documents suggests that Jean IV was keen to confirm his new wife's position now that she had effectively held up her end of the bargain by demonstrating her fertility.[8] This pregnancy and her more established position at the Breton court would have also reaffirmed the Navarrese alliance, which had been altered somewhat by the death of Joan's father, Carlos II, who had died on 1 January 1387—various accounts of his death, supposedly burned alive, were perhaps emphasised by those who wished to portray him as Carlos "the Bad" and make accounts of a horrific death compensatory for his supposed crimes in life.[9] Whatever the mode of his death, it brought Joan's brother, Carlos III, to the throne of Navarre, and Jean IV would have needed to consider the repercussions of this change to the Breton-Navarrese alliance which Joan personified.

Yet instead of solving Jean's succession issues, his remarriage and Joan's swift pregnancy may have only encouraged his enemies, the Penthièvres and Olivier de Clisson, to move against him. At the same time as Jean IV was negotiating with Carlos II to obtain a Navarrese bride, Clisson was negotiating a matrimonial alliance to marry his daughter Marguerite to Jean (or John of Blois), the Penthièvre heir. To achieve the marriage, Clisson had to seek a papal dispensation for the match, which was granted in 1386, around the time of Joan and Jean IV's wedding, and negotiate for the release of Jean de Penthièvre who was being held by the English. Jean IV engaged in strenuous diplomatic efforts with the English to block the release of his rival and aimed to secure strong allies in France to support him against his enemies with Joan's powerful uncles, the dukes of Berry and Burgundy.

The tense situation broke in the summer of 1387, when Jean IV moved against Clisson, inviting him to Vannes in late June, where he was arrested and forced to sign "a document which could only have been extorted from him by the direst threats" renouncing his matrimonial alliance with Penthièvre and turning over the Clisson and Penthièvre strongholds in return for his freedom.[10] Joan gave birth soon after, but the child was not the long-awaited son and heir that Jean IV had hoped for but a daughter, named Jeanne for her mother—and arguably her grandmother Jeanne de Valois and great-grandmother Juana II of Navarre.[11] Things became even worse for Jean IV as the backlash to his rash seizure of Clisson became apparent—Joan's cousin, Charles VI of France, was appalled at the arrest of Clisson, and the ransom agreements for Jean de Penthièvre suddenly bore fruit, resulting in his release on 19 November 1387 and his marriage to Marguerite de Clisson on 20 January 1388.[12] If Penthièvre and his new bride managed to produce a male heir, they would pose a serious threat to the Montfort line and the war for succession could reignite into open conflict. Moreover, this situation demonstrated a break within Joan's Valois family—previously her cousin Charles VI had been influenced by his uncles, the dukes of Berry and Burgundy, but here he had chosen to support Clisson, a man whom his uncles (and Joan's) and Jean IV were allied against, demonstrating that the so-called Marmouset faction now held greater sway over the king.[13]

Charles VI sent an ultimatum to Jean IV that he must restore the holdings of Clisson and Penthièvre, which Jean reluctantly agreed to do when he met with the French king in April 1388. But while Jean had been brought to heel by the French king, he had not given up on his attempts to block a Penthièvre heir from taking the duchy. In August 1388, he signed an agreement known as "the Articles" with England where he agreed that Richard II would be his heir, instead of the Penthièvres, if he died without issue—contravening the terms of the treaty of Guérande.[14] While this step seems somewhat premature given the youth of his bride and her rapid initial pregnancy after their marriage, Jean may have been recognising his own advancing age and the vagaries of infant mortality. Indeed, according to some sources, Joan may have borne a second daughter who died shortly after birth in 1388—others suggest that Joan's first pregnancy might have been twin girls.[15] It is possible that the Articles were drafted after Joan produced a second, short-lived daughter, prompting Jean to be less sanguine about the prospect of a male heir to follow him, or he may have simply sought to repair his relations with the English by throwing them the possibility of annexing Brittany even if he still had hope of a male heir. But by the end of the year, Jean had even more reason to be pessimistic about the succession as his first child, Jeanne, died on 7 December 1388.[16]

However, if Jean had been disappointed in her sex or had dismissed her as a potential heir in life, Jean-Yves Copy has argued convincingly that he treated her in death as his successor, using the symbology of the crown on her tomb to reinforce both his own quasi-royal status as duke and her place as a rightful heir, in spite of the provisions of the treaty of Guérande.[17] Yet all was not lost—Joan's next pregnancy followed swiftly after and resulted in the birth of a son, on Christmas eve 1389, at Vannes—the very place where Clisson had been arrested, turning the wheel of fortune back in Jean IV's direction and rallying the position of the Montforts through the advent of a male heir. The *Grandes Croniques de Bretaigne*, while truncating the time between her marriage and the birth of an heir, noted the joy generated by Joan's successfully bringing forth a male heir, underlining the importance of her fertility and maternity in the history of the duchy: "[on] Christmas Eve 1489, she gave birth to a son who was named Jean, which made the duke very happy, as his two previous wives had no children. And afterwards this lady had many other sons and daughters".[18] The birth of this long-awaited son, first named Pierre but then christened as Jean, resolved the long-standing crisis over the Montfort succession, which had come to a head in the early years of Joan's marriage to Jean IV and marked the end of the 1380s, leading to a new decade in which Joan would fully establish herself as an appreciated wife, a fertile mother, and an active duchess.

FIGURE 2.1 Illustration of Jean IV of Brittany, Joan of Navarre and their children, from Garrett MS. 40, "Missal, Carmelite use (French c. 1440–76)", folio 15v.

Source: Manuscripts Division, Department of Rare Books and Special Collections, Princeton University Library. Image supplied for use courtesy of Princeton University Library.

The 1390s: Maternity, family, and politics

While Joan's early years in the duchy had been marked by the crisis over the succession, the 1390s provided a more stable footing for Joan to mature into her marriage and new position. This decade in Joan's life was marked by three major elements which were themselves deeply intertwined: the births of six further sons and daughters (Arthur, Gilles, Richard, Marie, Marguerite, and Blanche), connections with and grafted by her Breton, Navarrese, and Valois family, and the continually turbulent politics of the period.

While Joan left the Navarrese court when she married, she was clearly not forgotten—documents from the Navarrese archives show a steady traffic between the two courts both to maintain familial ties and the Navarrese-Breton alliance which had been the reason for her marriage. Indeed the lengthy stay of Pierre Godeile, abbot of Monreal, secretary of the Navarrese king, in Brittany during 1387 on the king's business certainly indicates protracted discussions, likely triggered by the regime change in Navarre itself, as Joan's brother Carlos III had succeeded to the throne at the beginning of the year.[19] The exchange of frequent messengers bearing letters and gifts between the courts does seem to indicate a desire on the part of the young duchess to stay in close contact with her family: her messengers Bordat and Guiffre Alaoust and her squires Boloyte, Johan de Ochagavia, and Mahieu de St Germain made frequent trips to Navarre and back to the duchy—multiple payments were made to these men for trips between 1390 and 1400.[20]

Joan's interaction with her family was not only based on letters and gifts exchanged but on the physical presence of family members. One of these was her aunt, another Joan, Juana, or Jeanne of Navarre, the youngest sister of Carlos II, who had married the vicomte de Rohan, one of the most important nobles in Brittany, in 1377. Having her aunt at the Breton court must have been a source of reassurance to Joan and they appear to have formed a family bond as Joan granted a considerable pension to her aunt of 1,000 livres in 1402.[21] Joan was also geographically much closer to her aunt Blanche, dowager queen of France, as well as her Valois uncles and cousins at the French court.

An interesting incident during the early 1390s serves as a useful illustration of the intertwined nature of maternity, family, and politics, underlining the importance of Joan's family connections in the often tense relationship between France and Brittany. In late 1391 Joan's uncle, the duke of Berry, came to Nantes on behalf of Joan's cousin Charles VI of France, who was keen to see Jean IV reconciled with Olivier de Clisson and the Penthièvres. The *Saint-Denys* chronicle notes Joan's prominent presence in the party sent to welcome the duke, with her children and "a large cortege of illustrious ladies". Joan "graciously welcomed her beloved uncle and gave him the kiss of peace", asking after his health and exchanging news on the health of her family. Through her effusive welcome, which included entertainments and lavish gifts, the chronicler notes that she assured her uncle how delighted she was at his arrival.[22] This warm welcome could indicate both the strength of family feeling and a bond of alliance between Berry and Jean IV, as the chronicler notes that Berry was "the one that he loved best" out of all of Joan's uncles, the Princes of the Blood.

While this visit was clearly a success with regard to renewing family bonds between Joan and her uncle, the political element of Berry's visit nearly turned into a disaster. Berry aired the king of France's grievances against Joan's husband, Jean IV of Brittany, in front of an assembly of the Breton barons and demanded that the duke come to Tours to meet with Charles VI and reconcile with his enemies, Clisson and Penthièvre. Understandably, Jean was angered and was considering rebuffing the French embassy in his rage, a move which would have had serious repercussions and could have led to open war between the duchy and France. Again, family ties came to the rescue here—according to the chronicler of Saint Denis, Joan's brother Pedro was visiting the Breton court at the same time and sought Joan's help to intercede with her husband to prevent this political catastrophe. The chronicler notes that Joan promised to help as she wanted to keep peace between the duchy and France, noting that she was inclined towards the French "as the cousin of King Charles". This account emphasises how Joan deftly used both her wifely and maternal status in order to encourage Jean to work with her Valois relatives:

> She took her children in her arms, in spite of her encumbrance at the end of her term [of pregnancy] and went that night, unexpected, to the room of the Duke, followed only by a few of her ladies. I have learned from a reliable source that she went down on her knees before the Duke and in a voice broken by sobs she begged him to take pity on her and her children … she begged him to renounce his plans, so as not to

> alienate himself by an act of felony towards his king and the princes of the blood, who might after his [the Duke's] death protect his children.[23]

Michael Jones has noted that this episode highlights Joan's "talent for reconciliation which remained one of her most conspicuous traits", and we will continue to track her intercession and mediation as both duchess and queen.[24] This account was undoubtedly dramatised by the chronicler, however, with a deliberate emphasis on Joan's maternity and tearful emotion as a factor in her successful intercession. Intercession was an important element of a consort's role, and was not exclusively tied to maternity, as Joan's cousin and contemporary, Anne of Bohemia, who was queen of England at this time, was childless and yet praised for her extensive and successful intercession.[25] However, the added element of fertility and maternity could be seen as underpinning a consort's intercessory efforts, drawing on her role as mother of the heir as Joan did here by encouraging Jean to think of the impact on their children if Brittany and France went to war. A similar scenario can be seen with Philippa of Hainault's supposed intercession while heavily pregnant to help the burghers of Calais, made famous by Froissart—while this has been shown to be historically inaccurate, it reinforces the expectation of a consort's intercessory role along with the expectation of her fertility as the guarantor of dynastic continuity.[26]

While it is unlikely that this tale of intercession occurred exactly as the chronicler described, one element could well be accurate—Joan's pregnant state. While the birth dates and order of Joan's children is subject to some contradiction in various sources, it appears that Joan gave birth to Marie, her eldest surviving daughter, in February 1391, and another daughter, Marguerite, was likely born the following year in 1392. The duke of Berry visited in late 1391, when Joan could well have been pregnant with Marguerite, although most likely not "at the end of her term" as the chronicler suggests unless she fell pregnant again very shortly after Marie's birth.

Joan's growing family quickly became the focus of matrimonial alliances, in spite of their young age. The marriage of the heir, young Jean, was of primary importance, and articles were signed in April

1391 for a proposed marriage between the infant groom and a daughter of Jean III, the count of Armagnac, which was part of a wider "politico-military agreement" with the count and his brother, the count of Charolais.[27] However, this marital deployment of the heir was quickly reversed when the political situation changed—Jean III died in Italy in July of the same year without a male heir, which made his brother Bernard count of Armagnac. Then, as discussed previously, at the end of the year the duke of Berry had arrived to summon Jean IV to meet with the king of France at Tours—Joan's intercession and the proffered marriage between the Breton heir and one of Charles VI's own daughters assuaged Jean's anger at the summons and encouraged him to meet with the king. Jean IV went to Tours in January 1392 and eventually accepted the concessions that Charles VI wanted regarding Clisson and Penthièvre, and to reinforce their existing treaties with a matrimonial alliance between his young heir and Charles's year-old daughter Jeanne de Valois, although Jean penned a secret document that these concessions had been forced upon him.[28]

Yet matters with Clisson were hardly finished, as an assassination attempt was made on his life on 13 June 1392, only six months after Jean's meeting with the king of France. Charles VI was furious at the attack on his constable, which was blamed on the duke of Brittany who was believed to be hiding the assailant, Pierre de Craon, and encouraged by the Marmoset faction, the king prepared to attack Brittany to avenge the attempt on Clisson's life. Jean IV protested that he had nothing to do with the attack, and in Froissart's account reminded Charles of "the alliances that have been entered into between us" including "the marriage of our children"—while this appeared to satisfy Joan's uncles Berry and Burgundy, who were against the attack, Charles was keen to push on with the campaign.[29] Joan may have been distraught at the prospect of her cousin leading an army against her new marital home, but the campaign stopped abruptly on 5 August, when Charles VI had the first of his many attacks of madness—a tragedy for her cousin and indeed for France, but it saved Joan and her young family from potential ruin. The political pendulum swung the other way—Joan's uncle, the duke of Burgundy, seized control of the government while the king was incapacitated and dismantled the Marmoset faction, including Clisson, by accusing them of using their positions to line their own pockets. Burgundy made a deal with Jean IV to bring down Jean's enemy if the duke cut off contact with the English, and Clisson was forced to resign as constable of France in December 1392.[30]

Regardless of the whims of politics, Joan effectively spent the bulk of the 1390s in a state of pregnancy or postpartum, as after the birth of Marguerite in 1392 she then produced three more sons, which ensured that young Jean's life was not the only means of continuing the Montfort succession. On 24 August 1393, Joan gave birth at Suscinio, a favoured residence of the duke and duchess, which will be discussed further in Chapter 7, to her second son, Arthur, who would become a significant figure in the Hundred Years War and Breton history. He became known as Arthur de Richemont, in connection with the disputed honour of Richmond in England which had been held by the rulers of Brittany since the Conquest when William I bestowed it on his kinsman Alan Rufus of Brittany for his support for the invasion, and had been a continual bone of contention between the rulers of England and Brittany. Joan produced two more sons in the years which followed, Gilles in 1394 and Richard in 1395, and a final daughter, Blanche, born in 1396/7 and named for Joan's aunt, the dowager queen of France.

Marguerite and Blanche were later wed in a double wedding in 1407—while this was during the reign of their brother Jean V, they were furthering established patterns of alliance for both Jean IV and his Navarrese relatives. Marguerite married Alain, count of Porhoët, a scion of the powerful Breton house of Rohan—Joan's aunt, Juana of Navarre, was married to Alain's grandfather, Jean I of Rohan, and, as noted previously, the couple played a major role in furthering the arrangements for Joan's own marriage to Jean IV.[31] Blanche married Jean, the son of Bernard VII d'Armagnac, bringing about the alliance to which her father had initially pledged his young son and heir before changing course with a Valois bride.[32] When Blanche passed away c. 1416, Jean d'Armagnac then married Joan's niece, Isabel of Navarre, which offered Carlos III an alliance with the Armagnac faction during the Hundred Years War.

The marriage of Joan's first daughter, Marie, also demonstrates the shifting political tides of the 1390s between Brittany, England, and France and links to matrimonial alliances of her Navarrese family connected to the counts of Perche and Alençon. Richard II of England had become a widower when Anne of Bohemia died in 1394, and while he grieved for his wife, as they had no children it was imperative for Richard to remarry to beget an heir. An English embassy had been dispatched to Navarre and Aragon to negotiate a possible marriage for the king in February 1395, but while the embassy was travelling southwards, a French embassy, keen to prevent an Anglo-Aragonese marriage, arrived in England with a choice of three brides: Marie, the sister of the count of Harcourt and Aumale, Yolande, daughter of the duke of Bar, or Jeanne, daughter of the count of Alençon. J.J.N. Palmer noted that out of these candidates the Alençon marriage "would undoubtedly have brought Richard the greatest political advantage", as the family were important lords who held strategically located lands between Brittany and Normandy.[33] Yet none of these ladies were Iberian princesses, and when Richard did not immediately spring for any of these options, in May the French king wrote an emotional plea that he and Richard should put an end to decades of war with a peace sealed with the hand of his young daughter Isabella, which began protracted negotiations for an Anglo-French marriage.

In the midst of these negotiations, in November 1395, John of Gaunt was negotiating with Jean IV for a marriage between the houses of Lancaster and Brittany for his grandson Henry (later Henry V) with Joan's daughter Marie, which would cement a bilateral alliance between them that Jean IV hoped would get the support he needed to get back both the honour of Richmond and control of Brest.[34] While the matrimonial alliance suited both John of Gaunt and Jean IV, it did not suit Richard II, who reacted angrily to the news when John arrived back in England just after Christmas. Joan wrote two effusive letters to Richard II, in March 1396 and February 1397, to smooth over feathers ruffled by the proposed Lancastrian marriage.[35] In both letters she stressed that she was "desirous to hear of your good estate" and stressed her maternal role by noting the good health of her children. She also noted the good health of her husband in the 1396 letter, with a gentle plea regarding the "the deliverance of his lands", which appears to reference the ongoing dispute over the honour of Richmond or possibly the restoration of Brest. Joan signed off both letters with pledges that "if anything I can do over here will give you pleasure, I pray you to let me know it, and I will accomplish it with a very good heart, according to my power".

The blockage of the Lancastrian marriage and the Anglo-French negotiations opened up a new opportunity for Jean IV to redeploy Marie. Isabella de Valois had been betrothed to Jean, the count of Perche and Alençon heir, and now that she was being lined up to become the queen of England, Jean IV snapped up the young count of Perche for his own daughter, signing matrimonial agreements for Marie's marriage in June 1396, shortly after ratifying the marriage contract for his heir Jean with Isabella's sister, Jeanne de Valois.[36] A postscript to this marriage, which further underlines the importance of the Alençon family in the wider schemes of Breton and Navarrese matrimonial alliances, is the union of Joan's brother Pedro with Marie's sister-in-law, Catherine d'Alençon, in 1411.

Shortly after Marie's marriage was arranged with the count of Perche, Joan had the opportunity to attend the wedding of her cousin Isabella de Valois with Richard II, which had inadvertently made her daughter's own union with the Alençon family possible. While royal weddings are always an impressive occasion, this one was perhaps even more so as the English king came across the Channel to meet with his new father-in-law and bride in October 1396. Each king was accompanied by an impressive retinue of the most powerful lords of the realm and their ladies, in an event which Ian Mortimer describes as "one of the spectacles of the age, foreshadowing the later Cloth of Gold".[37] Contemporary chroniclers such as Froissart and the chronicler of Saint Denis commented on this important event; while Joan's specific presence is not mentioned in these accounts, her participation seems a given considering how important this event was to her Valois family and the fact that her husband was a noted attendee.[38] Moreover, as the great French and English lords, including Princes of the Blood, do appear to have brought their wives who played an active part in the proceedings, with the French ladies noted for hosting banquets and attending on the young Isabella de Valois, the new queen of England, it seems extremely likely that Joan herself would have been an active participant in her cousin's wedding festivities as well.

This spectacle had several outcomes beyond the royal marriage which were important for Joan and her family. On a personal level, it is very likely that she encountered Henry of Bolingbroke at this event, the man whom she would marry only a half a dozen years later. Neither Joan nor any of the other attendees at this event would ever have guessed that she would be her cousin Isabella's successor as queen of England or that Joan would be the first consort of an entirely new Lancastrian dynasty under Henry IV. This may not be the only time that she and Henry met, but it is one of the most likely possibilities, as it is less certain that Joan accompanied Jean IV to England when he became a member of the Order of the Garter in 1398.[39] Froissart and the *Grandes Croniques de Bretaigne* insist that Henry came to Brittany en route back to England to unseat his cousin Richard II in 1399—the *Grandes Croniques* note that Joan, "who was a very beautiful princess", received him with Jean IV when he arrived in the duchy.[40] Fernando de Ybarra repeats this scenario, noting a legend which claims that on his departure Joan gave him a bouquet of forget-me-nots, which later inspired his motto "*Soverayne*", most likely a shortening of "*Souveyne vous de moi*" or "Remember me".[41] However, Henry's biographers Chris Given-Wilson and Ian Mortimer are very clear that he departed from Boulogne, not Brittany, when he left France to unseat Richard II, though Mortimer notes Henry might have visited Brittany earlier in 1399.[42] While the significance of this meeting between Henry and Joan at the wedding festivities in 1396 was yet to bear fruit, a more tangible by-product of the meeting of Richard II and Charles VI was a confirmation that Brest and Cherbourg, which had been held by the English, would be returned to the duke of Brittany and the king of Navarre respectively, a major political benefit for Joan's marital and natal families.[43]

Joan had further opportunities to connect with her natal family in 1398, when Carlos III of Navarre also came to the Breton court for an extended visit. Carlos arrived on 27 June, not long after he had paid a visit to their aunt Blanche, the widowed queen of Philip VI of France. Carlos stayed in the duchy until the end of August, basing himself in Nantes for the first two weeks but later riding out to visit other regions of the duchy in the company of his brother-in-law, Jean IV. This visit clearly had political, rather than purely familial motives. Eloísa Ramírez Vaquero notes that the extended time that Carlos III had with his brother-in-law and other key Breton nobles, such as the powerful Olivier de Clisson, was a key opportunity to renew his alliance with Brittany and for them to consult with one another regarding their mutual stance vis-à-vis both England and France in an ever-shifting political landscape.[44] Indeed, Carlos signed pacts of alliance with both Richard II of England and Jean IV in August 1398, reflecting the same triangular dynamic between Navarre, Brittany, and England which had been a key factor in the creation of Joan's marriage. This visit was also an opportunity for Carlos to renew his relationship with his sister, whose marriage made her the physical bond between her natal family and Brittany, cementing their political alliance. Carlos also made connections at the Breton court; his expenses for this period include gifts not only to nobles but to the servants of the lords of Rohan and Clisson and to members of Joan's household, including 20 francs which was given to Joan's lady-in-waiting, Jehanne du Boiz, who had once been Carlos's wet nurse.[45]

The regent

Jean died in November 1399, leaving an heir and multiple spares, but his eldest son, who became Jean V, had not yet reached his majority, being only just shy of ten years old at the time, so a regency would clearly be needed. Jean IV entrusted this duty to Joan—she was now around 30 years old and had proven her worth as both duchess and mother. The regency was an excellent political opportunity for Joan, but also a serious challenge given the fractious politics of the duchy and the keen desire of her cousin, Charles VI of France, and her uncles, the French Princes of the Blood, to increase their control of the duchy, if not annex it altogether. Brittany had also been "piggy in the middle" between France and England over the course of the Hundred Years War. Moreover, as noted earlier, the Penthièvres, the ancient rivals of the Montfort dynasty, had unseated Jean IV during the early years of his reign and clearly still had ambitions for the ducal crown. As regent, Joan would have to protect her son's claim and steer a careful course through these turbulent political waters.

The first challenge she had to address was a confrontation between Jean IV and the major barons of the realm, Penthièvre, Rohan, and Clisson, which had reached a head in 1399, just before her husband's death. These three lords had taken an action against Jean IV at the Parlement of Paris in the spring of 1399, with wide-ranging grievances against the duke, particularly concerning taxes and complaints regarding ducal officers.[46] By September the Parlement had agreed to hear the appeal—the situation was unresolved by Jean IV's death in November. This was the most urgent item on her desk as Joan assumed the regency, as she knew that the support of these powerful barons was critical both for her regency and, more importantly, to solidify her son's position as the new duke. These three lords were all bound by ties of marriage and, together, the three lords were well positioned to prise the ducal coronet from her son's grasp. Indeed, Clisson's daughter Marguerite was married into the Penthièvre clan, who were rivals for the ducal throne—according to Lobineau's *Histoire de Bretagne*, Marguerite urged her father to kill the children of Jean IV so that her son could claim the duchy. Apparently, Clisson reacted to his daughter's suggestion so violently that he pushed her down the stairs and she retained a permanent limp, for which she was known thereafter as Marguerite *la Boiteuse* or "the lame".[47]

While Joan could not have known the contents of Clisson's conversation or his reaction to his daughter's murderous suggestion, Joan was well aware of the threat that the rebellious barons posed and how fragile her son's hold on the duchy was. Joan immediately dispatched her own lawyer to Paris to negotiate at the Parlement and moved to reach an accord with the three lords.[48] On 1 January 1400, exactly two months after her husband's death, Joan signed a treaty with Penthièvre, Rohan, and Clisson "to nourish peace, tranquility and accord" between them with the "*bon plasir*" of the king of France and the Parlement.[49]

As soon as she had the three barons on side and at peace, Joan became embroiled in a dispute with the Church, ironically with one of the bishops who had supported her in procuring peace with the barons. A local official, Jean de Malestroit, had seized a shipment of wine from merchants in Quimper as the necessary taxes had not been paid to the duke. The bishop of Quimper, outraged, seized the wine, proclaiming publicly in the main square of the town that the duke had no right to impose duty on it and summarily excommunicated Jean de Malestroit on 7 February 1400. Jean de Malestroit appealed to the duchess, who immediately dispatched two of her officers to remonstrate with the bishop and to appeal to the archbishop of Tours as metropolitan to revoke the excommunication and bring the bishop of Quimper back in line.[50] Yet while Morice's account suggests that the archbishop procured a speedy resolution to the crisis, which placated both the duchess and bishop, documentary evidence suggests that the dispute took over two years to resolve, possibly because the archbishop was distracted by another ecclesiastical rebellion in the duchy when he was shut out of the city of Dol on 25 May 1400, which resulted in the excommunication of the bishop and clergy there.[51]

Joan was able to secure a swifter resolution to another long-running dispute with the dame de Retz. Jean IV had effectively forced the dame de Retz to swap her lucrative lands for territory elsewhere in the duchy before his marriage to Joan in 1386—this land was later given to Joan as part of her dower lands.[52] The dame de Retz had appealed to the Parlement of Paris and even had support from Richard II of England for her plea for the return of her lands and castles. In 1393, the Parlement accepted her appeal and in 1399 Joan's uncle, the duke of Burgundy, acted as arbitrator to hammer out an accord. Joan signed off on this agreement on 1 September 1400, ending more than 15 years of dispute and getting another powerful family back into the ducal fold.

After resolving these disagreements between her husband and important nobles, Joan used ceremonial to her advantage to further secure her son's position, planning an elaborate coronation in

Rennes in March 1401. This was a key opportunity to publicly unite the nobles and prelates of the realm behind the young duke and his mother as regent. Joan both drew on and enhanced the traditional quasi-royal coronation rituals for the dukes of Brittany—indeed this ceremony was effectively set down as a template for later dukes to follow in the contemporary *Chronicon Brionese* or *Chronique de Saint-Brieuc.*[53] The duke, with a large entourage of nobles and his mother, the regent, presented himself at the Porte Mordelaise in Rennes on the afternoon of Tuesday 22 March 1401.[54] There he was made to swear upon sacred relics to defend the Church, the rights of the nobility to their lands, and to preserve the sovereignty, laws, and customs of the duchy before he was allowed entry to the city. The duke then kept vigil all night at the altar of St Peter in the cathedral. In the morning a great Mass was celebrated and the duke repeated his oaths before being invested with the ducal coronet and regalia. Clisson himself knighted the young duke and his brothers Arthur and Gilles. The procession filed out of the cathedral with the duke at the rear, and processed around the building before returning through the Great Door to make an offering. Then the procession, led by the duke and his brothers on horseback, continued through the streets of the city to the Market Hall where an impressive coronation banquet was held.[55]

Joan not only used the oaths of coronation to support her son's position, she also collected oaths of fidelity from knights and her servitors to secure their loyalty to her as regent. Shortly after her husband's death on 28 November 1399, she collected oaths from five knights as well as Geoffrey, lord of Quintin; Bertrand Gouyon, lord of Matignon; and Jean Raguenel, vicomte of Dinan, to herself and her young son Jean V. This was followed by oaths from other strategic personnel including Olivier de Maillechat, capitaine of Hédé; Jean de Painhouet, captain of the castle of Morlaix; and Jean de Langueouez, captain of the guard at Quimper.[56] She also moved to get the support of major cities of the duchy at the outset of her regency in 1400 by freeing the burghers of Vannes from the duty of the "*corvée de guet*" and confirming the privileges that Jean IV had bestowed on the city in 1397.[57]

From duchess to queen

While some of these oaths were made in the immediate aftermath of her husband's death, other oaths followed in late 1402 when Joan's proxy marriage to Henry IV had already been accomplished and her plans to leave the duchy and the regency were in train. As will be discussed further shortly, her matrimonial negotiations with Henry IV were concurrent with her efforts to crown her son in Rennes in March 1401, and thus it is unclear to what extent Joan's efforts to bring peace to the duchy were purely for the benefit of Brittany versus a means to free herself from the regency, by ensuring that her son's reign was stabilised before she left to pursue a new husband and a crown. Yet as she had demonstrated her political ability as regent, why give up her powerful position and leave Brittany at all?

The Breton historian Borderie praised Joan's regency claiming that she "seemed to have the secret of reconciling minds and unifying all of her subjects around her son" and bemoaned her abandonment of the regency. His logic for Joan's decision to leave Brittany for a marriage to Henry IV was that "the beautiful and still youthful duchess could not resist so flattering an offer".[58] Other historians, such as Knowlson, Jean V's biographer, and Fernando de Ybarra, have argued that Joan was driven by ambition and seized, or even created, the opportunity to upgrade her status from duchess to queen as soon as she was widowed in 1399.[59] However, some of Joan's collective biographers, such as the Victorian queenly prosopographers and even modern examples like Lisa Hilton, have framed Joan's decision in light of her widowhood—that Joan felt vulnerable as a young widowed mother and sought a powerful protector for herself and her large brood.[60] The issue of remarriage was a potentially thorny one for widows—James Brundage notes that medieval moralists were split on whether a widow should remarry or whether remarriage "signified shameless slavery to the voluptuous enticements of sexual passion".[61] Yet Barbara Hanawalt notes that a royal widow may not have had the same options as other women to become a vowess, remain single, or even choose their next husband, as that choice could be taken by her liege lord or natal family, who might want to use them to contract another matrimonial alliance.[62]

Michael Jones offers a more logical rationale for Joan's abandonment of the regency—that she knew that it would be short lived as her son would shortly reach the age of majority at 14 or 15 years old, thus she needed to carve out another role for herself beyond her widowhood and regency.[63] Clearly, remarriage to one of the most eligible men in Europe and the elevation to a royal crown was too good an opportunity to pass up—and, in her mind, may have been worth abandoning the regency and even her children for. It also offered her the possibility of deciding her own future in negotiating a marriage of her own choosing before her Valois cousins or her Navarrese family foisted a match on her that would be to their political benefit but not necessarily to her own liking.

Beyond Joan's issues of abandoning the regency and children, Henry's motivation for the match has long baffled historians—Paul Strohm went so far as to call Joan "that obscure object of desire".[64] Unlike Jean IV, Henry had no need to wed as he already had several heirs and he had other potential candidates, such as Lucia Visconti, cousin of the duke of Milan, who had formed an attachment to him when they met in 1393—a potential marriage with her was still under discussion in 1399.[65] Moreover, Joan brought no dowry and their marriage created a diplomatic storm that ultimately weakened relations with France and brought war, not peace, between England and Brittany. If Henry sought to control Brittany by marrying the regent, his strategy failed miserably. Given Joan's sacrifices and Henry's lack of immediate political or financial advantage, many have assumed that the pair were motivated by romance—that their previous meetings sparked a desire in Henry to wed Joan as soon as she was free. While we can never be certain of the potential emotional considerations of the pair, Henry might well have had a different set of motivations in mind. As an insecure king, whom many still saw as an illegitimate usurper, Joan's illustrious pedigree, her unquestionably royal status, and her extensive dynastic connections across Europe, as well as her regional connections in the Midi region close to English Gascony, may have been very attractive to Henry to bolster his own arguably shaky position. Indeed, it must be noted that concurrent with his own negotiations to marry Joan, Henry was arranging marriages for two of his daughters with European royal houses which resulted in his daughter Blanche marrying Louis III, elector Palatine, and Philippa wedding Eric of Pomerania. These three marriages for himself and his daughters were all part of a wider programme to build pan-European alliances and legitimise the new Lancastrian dynasty.[66]

In contrast to the extended and formal negotiations between Navarre and Brittany for Joan's first marriage, Henry and Joan conducted their negotiations with complete secrecy. Given the secretive nature of the discussions, it is difficult to say with complete certainty when they began; however, in the Close Rolls there is an entry on 7 February 1400, less than three months after the death of Jean IV, for the passage of Anthony Rys and Nicholas Alderwiche "who by command of the king are sailing to the duchy of Brittany with letters on his behalf addressed to the duchess".[67] Both men played a vital role in the negotiations—they returned to England for intense discussions in November 1401 and, as will be discussed in the last chapter, returned the following month laden with gifts for the duchess (and for themselves). Rys was particularly vital—he was clearly trusted by Joan as he was appointed as her procurator with full powers to negotiate on 15 March 1402 and stood in for her at the proxy ceremony at Eltham on 3 April.[68] On the king's side was another trusted individual, John Norbury, whose "long friendship with Henry IV particularly qualified him as a confidential agent in matters such as the arrangement of the King's marriage".[69] Only after the proxy ceremony did news of the match become more widely known, triggering a very negative reaction in the Breton and French court—precisely the reason why the pair had chosen to negotiate in a more personal and private fashion rather than formally and publicly as Jean IV and Carlos II had negotiated her first match.

Joan's Valois relatives—her cousin Charles VI and her uncles, the dukes of Burgundy and Berry—were very concerned about Brittany becoming subject to English influence through Joan's new husband. Burgundy was dispatched to the Breton court to take the regency from Joan and the custody of her four sons, Jean V, Arthur, Gilles, and Richard. Joan's two youngest daughters, Blanche and Marguerite, were initially allowed to go to England with her, but both returned home to Brittany only a few short years after

Joan's marriage to make marriages of their own.[70] The nobles of the Breton court reacted badly to the duchess's marriage as they were also keen to avoid English control and were not enthused about the choice of Burgundy for the regency—indeed antipathy to the match could be seen as a factor in increasing tension between Brittany and England, which broke out into open conflict only months after the wedding took place in 1403.[71]

While her Valois relatives were displeased by Joan's English marriage, her Navarrese relatives had quite a different reaction. Ramírez Vaquero argues that Carlos III may have seen this marriage as a way to solidify the alliance that he was attempting to build between England, Navarre, and Brittany.[72] She also hints that Carlos may have been involved in his sister's clandestine arrangements—as the cardinal of Pamplona appears to have been involved in Joan's efforts to obtain permission from Benedict XIII to marry, it is certainly possible that Carlos was involved in, or at least aware of, his sister's impending remarriage.[73] Joan's marriage also sat perfectly with the "*anglófilo*" alliances that Carlos was crafting at the same time with the marriages of his daughters Juana and Blanca with the heirs of Foix and Aragon, respectively, and offered the opportunity for a closer bond with the Castilian queen Catalina of Lancaster, Henry IV's half-sister, as well. However, this collection of English-leaning alliances for Navarre, and the fact that Carlos, now the brother-in-law of the king of England, had regained the strategic Channel port of Cherbourg, provided even more reasons for "all the alarms ringing in Paris" due to Joan's remarriage.[74]

Once the matrimonial agreement was finalised and the proxy marriage had taken place, the last piece of the puzzle was bringing the new queen to England to join her husband. One entry in the Close Rolls dated 25 March 1402 notes that a great fleet at sea was to be assembled in Southampton by 7 May to bring Joan safely across the Channel. Another entry a few months later, on 11 August, called for the port of Southampton to give passage to ships including one called *la Trinite* and another called *le Andreu* which were bringing the new queen to England.[75] Two weeks later, on 27 August, John Drax was commissioned to bring 20 ships from both Bristol and the mouth of the Thames and assemble them at Southampton, again to form a flotilla to ensure Joan's safe transit to her new realm.[76] There were even rumours in 1402 that Richard II would return and that Henry would then flee across the Channel to marry Joan.[77] Clearly, these preparations and even the rumours indicate that there was an expectation that Joan's arrival would follow on swiftly after the proxy wedding, but it took her longer to unwind her affairs as regent in Brittany. Joan's uncle, the duke of Burgundy, arrived in October 1402 to take on the regency and the custody of her sons and smoothed any tensions with his niece by showering her and her sons with gifts.[78] Joan and Jean V then on 18 November signed a treaty of alliance with Burgundy to be mutually allied against everyone except the kings of France and Navarre.[79] Once the transfer of power and guardianship from niece to uncle was achieved, Joan was free to depart for England—facing a rough winter's crossing in the New Year in order to make her transition from duchess to queen complete.

Conclusion

This chapter has outlined the key events in Joan's life during her 13-year marriage to Jean IV of Brittany. Joan arrived in the duchy as a teenager—young, inexperienced, and nubile—but matured over the course of her time as duchess to become a mother several times over, a wife who was appreciated and trusted by her older husband, and, through her engagement with the political crises and shifting alliances of her immediate and extended family, a woman who was prepared to take on the mantle of the regency and exercise it effectively to provide a strong foundation for her son Jean V's extended reign. Yet Joan was willing to let go of all she had built as duchess of Brittany, including giving up her position as regent and the custody of most of her children, to start a new life in England as Henry IV's queen. Whether motivated by love, ambition, or the desire to decide her own future, Joan took a major risk when she began secret negotiations with the English king. Her fateful decision to remarry entailed a move north across the Channel to England, even farther from her Navarrese homeland and separated from her children, cousins, and siblings in France as she transitioned from duchess to queen.

Notes

1 Michael Jones, *Ducal Brittany 1364–1399: Relations with England and France during the Reign of Duke John V* (Oxford: Oxford University Press, 1970), 114.
2 See Michael Jones, "'En son habit royal': Le Duc de Bretagne et son image vers la fin du Moyen Âge," in *Representation, Pouvoir et Royaulté*, ed. Joël Blanchard (Paris: Picard, 1995), 253–78.
3 James Bothwell, "An Emotional Pragmatism: Edward III and Death," in *Monarchy, State and Political Culture in Late Medieval England: Essays in Honour of W. Mark Ormrod*, eds. Craig Taylor and Gwilym Dodd (York: York Medieval Press, 2020), 60–1.
4 John Bell Henneman, *Olivier de Clisson and Political Society in France under Charles V and Charles VI* (Philadelphia: University of Pennsylvania Press, 1996), 114. Jones, *Ducal Brittany*, 204.
5 In "Le libvre du bon Jehan", Guillaume de Saint André comments "*Trente semaines furent ensemble/Sans plus ne moins come il me semble*" ("Thirty weeks they were together/Not more or less it seems to me"): Guillaume de Saint-André, *Chronique de l'État Breton*, eds. Jean-Michel Cauneau and Dominique Philippe (Rennes: Presses Universitaires de Rennes, 2005), 248.
6 Morice, I, cols. 1588–99; Erika Graham-Goering, *Princely Power in Late Medieval France: Jeanne de Penthièvre and the War for Brittany* (Cambridge: Cambridge University Press, 2020), 64–5.
7 ADLA E17-12, 24 February 1387.
8 ADLA E17-10, 15 February 1387. The ducal couple renewed their mutual donation on 2 February 1398; see ADLA E17-16.
9 See André Plaisse, *Charles, dit Le Mauvais, Comte d'Evreux, Roi de Navarre, Capitaine de Paris* (Evreux: Société Libre de L'Eure, 1972), 73–76, for four contemporary and early modern accounts of the death of Carlos II. For more on his funeral and will, see Nelly Ongay, "Testamento y exequias de Carlos II de Navarra," *Arquelogia, historia y viajes sobre el mundo medieval* 25 (2008): 72–82.
10 Michael Sumption, *Divided Houses: The Hundred Years War III* (London: Faber and Faber, 2009), 629–30.
11 There is some disagreement about date of birth, given alternately as June 1387 by Pere Anselme or August 1387 ("the Monday after the feast of the Assumption") from the *Chronicon aliud Brittanicum*, in Pere Anselme de Sainte Marie, *Histoire généalogique et chronologique de la maison royal de France*, vol. 1 (Paris: Compagnie des Libraries, 1712), 220; Lobineau, II, col. 365.
12 Jean-Yves Copy, "Du nouveau sure la couronne ducale bretonne: le temoignage des tombeaux," *Memoires de la Societe d'Histoire et d'Archeologie de Bretagne* 59 (1982): 175; Jean-Yves Copy, *Art, Société et Politique au temps des Ducs de Bretagne; Les gisants haut-Bretons* (Paris: Aux Amateurs de Livres, 1986), 107.

13 Eloísa Ramírez Vaquero, *Carlos III, rey de Navarra, Principe de sangre Valois (1387–1425)* (Gijon: Ediciones Trea, 2007), 60–1.
14 Jones, *Ducal Brittany*, 110; Copy "Coronne ducale," 176. The articles of 1388 are reprinted in *Ducal Brittany*, 212–14.
15 Lobineau claims that this second daughter was born in 1388 and died shortly thereafter "after having been baptized in the chapel of Sucinio by Guillaume de St. Andre". However, Pere Anselme has suggested that this second daughter was named Marie and was Jeanne's twin, instead of a second birth in 1388; see de Sainte Marie, *Histoire Généalogique*, 219–220; Lobineau, I, 471.
16 Lobineau, I, 471.
17 Copy, "Couronne ducale," *passim*.
18 Alain Bouchart, *Grandes Croniques de Bretaigne*, eds. Marie-Louise Auger, Gustave Jenneau, and Bernard Guenee, vol. II. 3 vols (Paris: Editions du Centre National de la recherche scientifique, 1986), 171. Original text is "*la vigille de Nouel quattre vingts et neuf, elle enfanta ung filz qui fut nomme Jehan, dont le duc fut moult joieulx, care de ses deux premieres femmes il n'avoit eu aucuns enfans. Et depuis eut celle dame plusieurs autres filz et filles*".
19 See Catálogo XVI, no. 881, 29 April 1387, and no. 884, 30 April 1387, for expenses paid to Godeile for his Breton trip.
20 For examples, see Catálogo XVII, no. 831, 9 June 1390; XIX, no. 830, 29 October 1392; XXI, no. 982, 20 August 1396; XXII, no. 69, 28 Jan 1396.
21 Foedera 8, 1 March 1403.
22 Saint-Denys, I, 723–25.
23 Saint-Denys, I, 727.
24 Michael Jones, "Between France and England: Jeanne de Navarre, Duchess of Brittany and Queen of England (1386–1437)," in *Between France and England: Politics, Power and Society in Late Medieval Brittany* (Aldershot: Variorum, 2003), 5.
25 On the intercession of Anne of Bohemia, see Kristen Geaman, *Anne of Bohemia* (London: Routledge, 2022), chapter 2, "She Settled Quarrels".
26 See John Carmi Parsons, "The Pregnant Queen as Counsellor and the Medieval Construction of Motherhood," in *Medieval Mothering*, eds. John Carmi Parsons and Bonnie Wheeler (New York: Garland Publishing, 1996), 39–63; Paul Strohm, *Hochon's Arrow: The Social Imagination of Fourteenth-Century Texts* (Princeton, NJ: Princeton University Press, 1992), 95–120; Anthony Musson, "Queenship, Lordship and Petitioning in Late Medieval England," in *Medieval Petitions: Grace and Grievance*, eds. W. Mark Ormrod, Gwilym Dodd, and Anthony Musson (Woodbridge: York Medieval Press, 2009), 156–72.
27 ADLA E8-1, 13 April 1381. Jones, *Ducal Brittany*, 123.
28 The documents for the matrimonial negotiations are ADLA E8-2, 3 and 4, dated 15, 24, and 26 January 1392 respectively. For more on the negotiations at Tours, see Morice, II, col. 577–90, and a copy of the matrimonial agreement for Jean and Jeanne is col. 590–93.

29 Jean Froissart, *Chronicles of England, France, Spain, and the adjoining countries, from the latter part of the reign of Edward II to the coronation of Henry IV*, ed. Thomas Johnes, vol. 2 (London: H.G. Bohn, 1852), 531.
30 See Jones, *Ducal Brittany*, 128–29; Sumption, *Divided Houses*, 796–801.
31 Alain Boulaire, *Les Rohan, "Roi ne puts, duc ne daigne, Rohan suis"* (Paris: Editions France-Empire, 2001), 30; Henneman, *Clisson*, 190; Morice, II, col 794–96; Lobineau, II, col. 794–96).
32 ADLA 9-3, 4, 5, and 8 dated 2 and 30 July 1406 and 20 June 1407, respectively. To note, while it is beyond the scope of this study, there was a later dispute over Blanche's unpaid dowry several decades after her death; see ADLA E9-8 and 14 for the original dowry agreement, both dated 15 April 1407 and ADLA E6, 7, 10, and 13 for the dispute, dated 20 January 1448, 19 November 1446, 6 July 1448, and 1 September 1448.
33 J.J.N. Palmer, "The Background to Richard II's Marriage to Isabel of France (1396)," *Bulletin of the Institute of Historical Research* 44, no. 109 (1971): 5 n3. See also Sumption, *Divided Houses*, 823–29.
34 ADLA E8-5, dated 25 November 1395, and E8-10, dated 1395. Jones, *Ducal Brittany*, 135–36. See also Chris Given-Wilson, *Henry IV* (New Haven, CT: Yale University Press, 2016), 91–2.
35 Both letters are printed in Anne Crawford, *Letters of the Queens of England* (Stroud: Sutton, 1997), 113–15. Crawford notes that these letters have repeatedly been misunderstood as letters to Henry IV during their matrimonial negotiations due to their affectionate nature.
36 ADLA E8-7 and 8 for the ratification of the French marriage, dated 26 April 1396 and E8-9 for Marie's marriage to Jean, count of Perche, dated 26 June 1396.
37 Ian Mortimer, *The Fears of Henry IV; The Life of England's Self-Made King* (London: Vintage Books, 2008), 133.
38 Jean Froissart, *Chronicles of England, France, Spain, and the adjoining countries, from the latter part of the reign of Edward II to the coronation of Henry IV, by Sir John Froissart*, ed. Thomas Johnes, vol. 2 (London: H.G. Bohn, 1852), 618–21; Saint-Denys, 450–73.
39 Jones, "Between France and England," 6–7.
40 Froissart, *Chronicles of England*, 685–7; Bouchart, *Grandes Croniques*, 223.
41 Fernando de Ybarra, *Matrimonios Reales Hispano-Británicos el el Medievo*, vol. I: *Póker de Reinas* (Salamanca: Universidad Pontificia de Salamanca: 1999), 302. For a discussion of Henry's motto and its meaning, see Mortimer, *Fears of Henry IV*, 384–87.
42 Mortimer, *Fears of Henry IV*, 170; Given-Wilson, *Henry IV*, 125–26. Jones also corrects Froissart's account in *Ducal Brittany*, 141.
43 Saint-Denys, 476–79.
44 Ramírez Vaquero, *Carlos III*, 117–20.
45 Catálogo XXII, no. 1080, dated 9 September 1398.
46 Henneman, *Clisson*, 191.
47 Lobineau, I, 498–9; Henneman, *Clisson*, 193; Michael Jones, "Marguerite de Clisson, comets de Penthievre et l'exercise du pouvoir," in *Femmes de*

pouvoir, femmes politiques durant les derniers siècles du Moyen Âge et au cours de la premiere Renaissance, eds. Éric Bousmar, Jonathan Dumont, Alain Marchandisse, and Bertrand Schnerb (Brussels: de Boeck, 2012), 349. Erika Graham Goering makes a note of caution of the veracity of this source and excellent point on the way in which the term "boîteuse" has been applying unfairly to several medieval women "as a conventional trope used (especially long after the fact) to slander elite women"; Graham-Goering, *Princely Power*, 36 n1.

48 Henneman, *Clisson*, 191.

49 Morice, II, col. 702 (treaty col. 701–3). Response Nantes Mediatheque ms 1695, no. 18, dated 22 January 1400.

50 Morice, II, col. 704–5 and ADLA E73-3 to 14, dated 18 Feb 1400–19 Apr 1402.

51 Morice, Pierre-Hyacinthe. *Histoire ecclesiastique et civile de Bretagne* (Paris: De l'imprimerie de Delaguette, 1750), 430; Lobineau, I, 499–500.

52 See Michael Jones, "Jean IV et le pays de Retz: l'exercise et les limites du pouvoir ducal a la fin du XIVe siècle," in *Echanges et pouvoirs au pays de Retz (Actes du colloque a Machecoul 14 Avril 2007)* (La Bernerie-en-Retz: Societe des Historiens du Pays de Retz, 2008), 31–41, and further discussion of the Retz lands in Joan's dower in Chapter 5.

53 Morice, I, cols. 81–2.

54 Jones, "Habit royal," 266.

55 See Michael Jones, "The Rituals and Significance of Ducal Civic Entries in Late Medieval Brittany," *Journal of Medieval History* 29 (2003): 289–90; Arthur de la Borderie, "La jeunesse de Jean V, duc de Bretagne," *Revue de Bretagne de Vendee et d'Anjou* 23 (Mar 1900): 163–64; Jones, "Habit royal," 263–68.

56 ADLA E143-29, 28 November 1399, E136-23, 28 October 1402, E138-7, 18 November 1402, E139-2, 25 September 1400.

57 Jean-Pierre Leguay, *Histoire de Vannes et de sa Region* (Toulouse: Privat, 1988), 67; *Inventaire Sommaire des Archives Communales antérieures à 1790*, Vol. 1: *Ville de Nantes* (Nantes: Imprimerie du Commerce, 1888), 4.

58 Borderie, "Jeunesse," 165.

59 George Akenhead Knowlson, *Jean V, duc de Bretagne et l'Angleterre 1399–1442* (Cambridge: W. Heffer & Sons Ltd, 1964), 25; de Ybarra, *Matrimonios Reales*, 304.

60 See Francis Lancelott, T*he Queens of England and their times from Matilda, Queen of William the Conqueror to Adelaide, Queen of William the Fourth*, vol. 1 (New York: D. Appleton and Company, 1859), 249–50; Hannah Lawrance, *Historical Memoirs of the Queens of England, from the Commencement of the Twelfth Century*, vol. 2 (London: Edward Moxon, 1840), 284–88; Agnes Strickland, *Lives of the Queens of England from the Norman Conquest; with Anecdotes of their Courts*, vol. III (Philadelphia, PA: Lea and Blanchard, 1848), 53–7; Lisa Hilton, *Queens Consort; England's Medieval Queens* (London: Phoenix, 2009), 359. For an extended discussion of Joan's remarriage and the perception of it, see Elena

Woodacre, "The Perils of Promotion: Maternal Ambition and Sacrifice in the Life of Joan of Navarre, Duchess of Brittany and Queen of England," in *Virtuous or Villainess? The Image of the Royal Mother from the Early Medieval to the Early Modern Era*, eds. Carey Fleiner and Elena Woodacre (New York: Palgrave Macmillan, 2016), 125–48.

61 James A. Brundage, "Widows and Remarriage: Moral Conflicts and their Resolution in Classical Canon Law," in *Wife and Widow in Medieval England*, ed. Sue Sheridan Walker (Ann Arbor: University of Michigan Press, 1993), 17.

62 Barbara A. Hanawalt, "Widows," in *The Cambridge Companion to Medieval Women's Writing*, eds. Carolyn Dinshaw and David Wallace (Cambridge: Cambridge University Press, 2003), 64–6.

63 Jones, "Between France and England," 9.

64 See Paul Strohm's consideration of the match, "Joanna of Navarre: That Obscure Object of Desire," in *England's Empty Throne: Usurpation and the Language of Legitimation, 1399–1422* (New Haven, CT: Yale University Press, 1998), 153–72.

65 Given-Wilson, *Henry IV*, 75, 101 n6, 120 n6.

66 See Anthony Tuck, "Henry IV and Europe: A Dynasty's Search for Recognition," in *The McFarlane Legacy: Studies in Late Medieval Politics and Society*, eds. R.H. Britnell and A.J. Pollard (Stroud: Alan Sutton, 1995), 116–22. See also Mortimer, *Fears of Henry IV*, 248.

67 CCR Henry IV, I, 7 February 1400.

68 Jones, "Between France and England," 10; Morice, I, 83–4.

69 C. Rawcliffe, "Norbury, John (d.1414), of Hoddesdon and Little Berkhampstead, Herts," in HoP.

70 Henneman, *Clisson*, 194; Bouchart, *Grandes Croniques*, 243–4.

71 Nicolas Travers, *Histoire civile, politique et religieuse de la ville et du comté de Nantes* (Nantes: Forest, 1836), 463.

72 Ramírez Vaquero, *Carlos III*, 132.

73 Jeanne-Marie Poupart, "Un mariage Anglo-Breton au XVe siècle," *Nouvelle Revue de Bretagne* 2 (March–April 1951): 85–6; Ramírez Vaquero, *Carlos III*, 130.

74 Ramírez Vaquero, *Carlos III*, 132.

75 CCR Henry IV, I, 25 March and 11 August 1402.

76 CPR Henry IV, II, 25 August 1402.

77 Given-Wilson, *Henry IV*, 209.

78 Borderie, "Jeunesse," 167.

79 L&M JV, IV, no. 1, 18 November 1402.

3

QUEEN: CHARTING TURBULENT WATERS AS HENRY IV'S CONSORT

The year 1402 was a pivotal transitional period for Joan. Her secretive matrimonial negotiations with Henry IV resulted in their proxy marriage in April. From that point she was effectively his bride and queen consort, yet their marriage needed to be formalised by her physical presence in the realm to undertake the ceremonies of a royal wedding and coronation which marked her installation into the queen's office as well as consummation of the marriage to make it fully valid. Yet she could not leave to start a new life as England's queen until her role as Brittany's duchess and regent was completed, which took her until the end of the year; the winter was not an ideal time to attempt a Channel crossing. Indeed a party headed by Henry's half-brothers Henry Beaufort, the bishop of Lincoln, and the earl of Somerset, as well as the earl of Worcester, had been sent to Brittany to collect Joan at the end of autumn 1402, but the bishop wrote from Plymouth on 9 December that they had to abandon the voyage and return to port as "*le vent soit si contrarie*" ("the wind was so contrary").[1] While Joan might have had a reasonable crossing similar to the smooth late-summer sailing up the Bay of Biscay for her first wedding if she had left in the summer of 1402 when Henry expected her, by the time she actually left in January 1403, she faced

DOI: 10.4324/9780429261022-5

stormy seas—perhaps an omen of the challenges she would face as Henry's consort.

Joan's journey began when she left Nantes on 26 December—she passed the new year in Vannes, a location where she had spent a considerable amount of time, one of Jean IV's primary residences and the birthplace of her eldest son, now Jean V. Joan and her party, including the courtiers who were accompanying her to England and her two youngest daughters, Marguerite and Blanche, then travelled on to the extreme northwestern point of the duchy, at Camaret, near Brest, where they took ship with the English fleet sent to bring the new queen to England on 13 January. Yet what should have been a brief journey ended up being an extended and challenging one—the party finally landed on 19 January at Falmouth, directly north across the Channel in the West Country, rather than Southampton, the centrally located port city just south of Winchester, where the wedding was set to take place. This necessitated Henry to rush westward to meet his bride at Exeter on 30/31 January and the entire royal party made a long and somewhat expensive journey overland via Bridport, Dorchester, and Salisbury to Winchester, where the wedding finally took place on 7 February.[2]

The new queen: Adjusting to the role

Henry IV's wedding to Joan at Winchester Cathedral was a deliberately impressive occasion. Winchester was strategically chosen for several reasons—on a practical level it was near the port of Southampton, the bride's intended landing site. Symbolically, it was a location with a very long history of royal events—from baptisms and burials to coronations and of course weddings as the former capital of Wessex and England. As Henry was a king who was not entirely stable on this throne—the first of a new dynasty, whom many believed was a usurper, connecting himself with centuries of royal history was a way to stress his legitimacy and continuity with the past. He was not the only king to use this strategy—Henry VII deliberately chose Winchester for the site of the birth and baptism of his heir Arthur in 1486 to reinforce the establishment of his own new dynasty. The first regnant queen Mary Tudor also chose

Winchester as the location for her own wedding in 1554 for similar reasons to Henry IV—proximity to the coast and connections to the past to strengthen her position, which had already been challenged by a usurping cousin and Wyatt's Rebellion. In Mary's case, she may have also chosen Winchester as it was far from the capital to avoid any potential backlash from Londoners against her new Spanish husband and his sizable foreign entourage on his arrival. While Henry IV may have been less concerned about a negative reaction to his Iberian-Breton bride, she too had a large number of foreigners accompanying her, so he may have felt it safer to bring her to London for her coronation once she had been firmly established as his new wife.

Henry was determined to welcome his bride to England with style—as will be discussed in detail in Chapter 7, he spent considerable sums on jewels and gifts for his bride as well as cloth of gold for her dresses. The event itself was also splendid, with expenditure for a runner of striped cloth to process down in the cathedral, which had been magnificently enhanced by the current bishop, William of Wykeham. The feast after the event, which likely took place in the bishop's palace next door, featured several courses of delicacies such as cream of almonds, pears in spiced syrup; a range of meats including cygnets, pheasants, and roasted venison; an equally splendid three-course fish menu for the clerics in attendance; and elaborate subtleties, effectively edible sculptures, in shapes such as a crowned eagle, a symbol repeatedly used by Henry which features on the couple's joint tomb at Canterbury.[3] The feast cost £522 12s—indeed Henry spent so much on the event that he needed loans of 500 marks from William Wykeham, the bishop of Winchester, and another 200 from Thomas Nevyle, the prior of the cathedral.[4] Yet the expenditure was all a necessary part of projecting majesty—through a lavish royal wedding and Joan's coronation at Westminster which followed later in the month, Henry was not only affirming her place as his bride and queen, but reaffirming his own standing as the rightful monarch of England.

The couple stayed for a few days in Winchester after the wedding and then headed towards the capital on 10 February, travelling slowly with their entourage and staying one night at Bishop Wykeham's impressive castle at Farnham with its recently renovated

Great Hall. Their immediate destination was not the city of London itself but Henry's favourite residence at Eltham to the east—Henry's development of the palace, including the additions he made for his new wife, will be discussed in detail in Chapter 7. While still at Winchester, summons had been sent out to the nobility to attend the new queen's coronation on 25 February at Westminster.[5] The couple travelled the short distance from Eltham to Westminster on the day before her coronation, where she appears to have made a formal entry according to a near contemporary source which notes:

> she [Joan] was brought to london And there the Maire and the Aldermen resceyved hyre in the moost worthy wyse that they coude and rood with hyre thurgh london to Westmynster And there she was crowned queen And there the king made a solempne feste in the worship of hire and of all the straungers that come with hyre.[6]

While this account comes from a sixteenth-century chronicle and thus was not an eyewitness account of the event, it does suggest that Joan was received in London and crowned with considerable pomp and ceremony. A comprehensive contemporary record of the coronation event itself is also lacking, but we can surmise a great deal from the *Liber Regalis*, a fourteenth-century manual for royal ceremonial which served as a foundation for the later medieval English monarchy.[7] If Joan was garbed according to the instructions of the *Liber Regalis*, she would have been wearing a purple tunic and robe "of one texture without any other working on it", with her hair loose and unbound, despite the fact that the twice-married queen was no longer a maiden. The key elements of the coronation are prayers said over the queen, the anointing with chrism or holy oil, and the conferral of the queen's regalia: the crown, ring, sceptre, and rod—although Joan is pictured holding an orb as well in the near contemporary illustration of her coronation in the *Beauchamp Pageant* manuscript.[8]

The *Beauchamp Pageant* manuscript also shows the festivities after the ceremonial, depicting a tournament in which Richard Beauchamp acted as the queen's champion, with Joan herself shown in the royal box watching the display of arms. Nor was Richard the only Beauchamp to be involved in Joan's coronation—his mother Margaret, countess of Warwick, appears to have served as chief pantler at Joan's coronation.[9] It was not unusual for a Beauchamp to fill this role at a coronation feast as they had a traditional hold on this honour, which was associated with whomever held the manor of Kibworth-Beauchamp. Margaret's husband, Thomas, had been chief pantler at Henry IV's coronation and Walter de Beauchamp served as pantler for Eleanor of Provence's coronation in 1236, the first mention of this role in English records of such a feast.[10] However, the fact that Margaret was a woman made it unusual—she may have been allowed to undertake this role as she held the manor after her husband's death in 1406, or there is the possibility that Joan was served by women at her feast as John, Lord Latymer, was paid 40 marks to release the almoner's dish and his family's traditional occupation of the almoner's role at Joan's coronation. It is thus possible that a woman occupied this position as well, creating an unusual feminine twist on these important ceremonies to install the new queen.[11]

Another tradition associated with the queen's coronation was initiating her role as intercessor, a central facet of medieval queenship. John Carmi Parsons notes that a new queen was "expected to perform" acts of grace and ask for pardons as Eleanor of Provence did on her coronation in 1236 and as French queens did, as they were "specifically granted the power to pardon criminals as part of their coronation honours".[12] Queenly intercession was seen as a key aspect of the female component of monarchy and an expected way for royal women to engage politically, following the models of the biblical queen Esther and the Virgin Mary, the ultimate mediatrix. Joan's predecessors had been active in this regard—the intercession of Philippa of Hainault and Anne of Bohemia was both significant in number and in popular memory, taking on quasi-legendary overtones in contemporary representations.[13] While this has been dismissed by some scholars as either a face-saving mechanism for the king or a purely traditional ritual which did not signify queenly agency, Anthony Musson notes that "it underestimates the numbers of people for whom the queen routinely sought to intercede" and the means through which her role as intercessor and influence on the king gave her enhanced political standing at court as her mediation was greatly valued and sought after.[14] As we have seen in the previous chapter, Joan already had experience in this regard during her marriage to Jean IV and immediately became involved in intercession and petitioning, both for the benefit of others and for herself. She also continued to intercede in Brittany even after leaving the duchy, leveraging her position as dowager duchess and mother of the current duke to ask for the pardon of Guillaume Berthelemer, in conjunction with Yolande of Aragon, in December 1405.[15]

Joan's supplication can be broadly placed into two categories: a means of addressing/righting wrongs or crimes and as a means of securing benefits or acting as a patron. Her first act of intercession came before she even arrived on England's shores in early January 1403 and involved seeking assistance for Navarrese merchants whose ships had been captured by an English captain—it was noted that on Joan's special request, restitution should be made to the merchants and any who refused to do so would be arrested.[16] Shortly after her wedding and coronation, Joan also secured several pardons for John Bayly, Thomas Gilmyn of Tetbury in Gloucester, and for Henry Ade, who was accused of being a counterfeiter.[17] In 1404 she secured some significant pardons, one for Thomas, the abbot of Beeleigh, one for Geoffrey, the abbot of St John, and another for Maud de Vere, countess of Oxford, who had all been involved in a conspiracy against Henry IV based on the premise that Richard II had survived and would return to retake his crown.[18] James Ross has suggested that Joan may have intervened in these cases as the conspirators had been "duped by her kinsman, the duke of Orleans" who they believed would assist them, or that Henry may have encouraged Joan to get involved in these cases to increase her popularity.[19] Alternatively, Joan may have intervened on her own initiative to demonstrate her political engagement and influence in a prominent case, as well as securing a more tangible benefit, the goods and chattels of Abbot Geoffrey which he had forfeited as a part of his prosecution, which she petitioned for in connection with the pardon.[20]

While Joan did not ask for a large number of pardons, she continued to seek them throughout her husband's reign, asking for the pardon of Thomas Barker in October 1406, John Boye of Higham in October 1409, and John Saghier in October 1411—it is possible that the timing of these pardons was linked to the anniversary of Henry IV's coronation, which took place in October 1399.[21] One particularly interesting case in February 1408 involved pardons for several of her own tenants in Thorpe Satchville, Leicestershire.[22] In this particular case, Nicholas Holt, William Bate, Richard Barsby, John Dalby, William Cook, and John Green were all arrested and tried for the death of Richard Bradford and Robert Webster. The two victims had been invited to dine with Nicholas Holt but were then taken prisoner and put in chains, and then the group, "taking upon themselves the royal power and without any legal authority", effectively tried and condemned Bradford and Webster, beheading them and sending their heads to Leicester.[23] Yet Joan interceded to secure their release both as queen and as their liege lord as they were tenants on her dower lands.

This connects with another element of Joan's intercessory activity, acting as a patron or as an aspect of "good ladyship" to secure benefits for others, or again for herself. In chapters 6 and 7 we will explore this further in terms of the gifts, lands, annuities, and positions that Joan used her influence to obtain for those in her service or affinity. She also interceded to help those who were not directly connected to her gain benefits as well, acting as an effective patron. There are two excellent examples of this in 1403 at the start of her tenure: a license granted at her supplication for the king's clerk William Aghton, parson of St Peter's Cornhill in London, and three others to found a perpetual fraternity and guild, and another petition on behalf of the "chancellors, doctors, masters, bachelors and other graduates in the Universities of Oxford and Cambridge" to sue for benefices in England, Wales, and Ireland.[24] She also wisely interceded to assist those who could help her, such as Sir John Tiptoft. At Joan's request, the revenues of the prévôté of Entre-deux-Mers in Gascony were given to Tiptoft in September 1408, and the following year, as we will see in Chapter 5, Tiptoft argued strenuously to rectify the queen's difficulties with her dower to stabilise the finances of her household.[25] Beyond her efforts on behalf of others, Joan frequently petitioned on her own business, of which we will see considerable evidence in the next two chapters, to complain about insufficient returns from her dower, to petition for wardships, to defend her rights to lands and prerogatives that she felt belonged to her, and to ask for lands or goods forfeited by those condemned, such as her request for the Isle of Wight and Carisbrooke Castle, which belonged to the disgraced duke of York, in 1405.[26]

In addition to adapting to her new position as queen of England, Joan also had to take on another new role, that of stepmother to Henry IV's children by his first wife, Mary de Bohun, who had died in 1394, well before his accession. Both Joan and Henry had four sons nearly identical in age: Prince Henry (b.1386), Thomas (b.1387), John (b.1389), and Humphrey (b.1390). Henry had only two daughters—the eldest was Blanche, who was born in 1392, the same year as Joan's daughter Marguerite who came with her to England; however, as Blanche left in 1402 to wed Louis of Bavaria, the two stepsisters never met. Joan's own daughter Blanche also came to England, and it is possible that Marguerite and Blanche of Brittany formed some kind of relationship with Henry's youngest daughter, Philippa, who was born in 1394, putting her between the two Breton sisters in age. Philippa, along with her brothers John and Humphrey, attended their father's wedding to Joan in 1403, and the two boys gave their new stepmother a gift on the day. While Prince Henry did not attend, he did send his father a letter noting "that I moste desirid of the whyche to see that joyfulle day of youre mariage had ben on" and wished the new couple well "Besechyng Godde in all wyse my sovereign lorde to save ande kepe you body ande sowle ande sendde you in thys blissid sacrament of mariage joye, prosperite, longe to endure".[27]

While Joan was now the matriarch of a combined group of 15 children and stepchildren, she and Henry had no children of their own during their ten-year marriage. Indeed, contemporary chronicles noted this, such as Thomas Walsingham who commented,

> In 1403 after the feast of the purification a new queen came to England. She came from smaller Brittany to greater Britain, from a dukedom to a kingdom, from a fierce tribe to a peace-loving people, and I hope her coming was a good omen. She

> had formerly been married to the noble John (IV) de Montfort, duke of Brittany, to whom she had borne children of both sexes. But to Henry, king of England, whom she now married, she bore no children at all.[28]

However, another contemporary account of the royal marriage from the anonymous "Northern Chronicle" claims that Joan "*genuit duos abortivos*", perhaps two miscarriages or stillbirths, although there is no additional evidence to confirm this claim.[29] Yet, the lack of children to the royal couple could be seen as a blessing. If Joan had children with Henry, it might have complicated the succession, creating a cadet line which might have later used the idea of porphytogeniture, or preference given to children born in the reign of their father, and their fully royal blood to contest the rights of Henry's de Bohun sons. While this was unlikely, as porphytogeniture had never been applied to the English succession, on a simpler level, a surfeit of royal children was expensive to maintain, title, and/or dower, thus the lack of issue to the couple was in a way a boon given Henry IV's already challenging finances. In later chapters we will reflect on how Joan's status as a stepmother of kings, rather than a dynastic progenitor, impacted upon her both during her lifetime and her legacy after her death.

The crisis begins: 1403–7

No sooner had Joan been married, crowned, and welcomed into her new family than a series of challenges emerged which would endure in various ways throughout the couple's marriage and define her husband's reign. These issues included the internal challenges of rebellions against Henry's rule and pressure from Parliament to reform royal expenditure, external political issues with Joan's relatives both in Brittany and regarding the increasing division between the Orleans and Burgundian factions in France, and other family strains, including divisions, health difficulties, and deaths. The remainder of the chapter will chart these issues over two periods, that of 1403–7 and the latter years 1408–13. As noted in the introduction, it is impossible to fully capture the complexity of the political landscape of Henry IV's reign and the Hundred Years War here; instead of recounting the detail of these events we will focus on how they affected Joan and her engagement in them.

While February 1403 had been replete with celebration for their wedding and Joan's coronation, "barely had the celebrations finished before Henry was back at work" dealing with the continued issue of rebellions against his rule, concentrated primarily in the North and in Wales headed by Owain Glyndwr.[30] What made the situation more challenging is that Glyndwr had allied himself with two other prominent noblemen who were also alienated from Henry IV, Sir Edmund Mortimer and Harry "Hotspur" Percy, with a goal to dethrone the king and replace him with Mortimer's nephew, the young earl of March who had a claim to the throne via descent from Edward III. Henry fought and won against the rebels at Shrewsbury on 21 July 1403, catching the rebels before the forces of Glyndwr and Northumberland arrived to support them—Hotspur was killed and the earl of Worcester was captured and executed, but Prince Henry suffered a grievous injury to his face and the rebellions against Henry were far from over.

Concurrent with these campaigns came war on a completely different front which was more directly impactful to Joan—the beginning of an extended conflict between Brittany and England. This erupted only months after her marriage to Henry IV which theoretically should have brought the two realms together through the new familial bond. While the conflict was not a direct result of the marriage, it could be said that the simmering tensions and lengthy pirate-style raiding across the Channel was inflamed by the negative reaction of the Breton lords to Joan's marriage and their concern that Henry IV might try to leverage the connection to interfere in Brittany. Matters intensified when the English raided the Breton coast in late June 1403—Joan was immediately drawn into this conflict, as one of the members of her Breton network of service, a William Piedre or "Pedrewe" from Nantes, had his boat *le Seynt Croys* with a cargo of wine taken by an English crew from Wareham. In his petition for the restitution of his ship, William noted his connection to "*la Roigne dengleterre*", which triggered a commission headed by Richard Drax to look into the claim "especially as the said William asserts himself to be a liege man of the king's consort the queen, and if it be true to make restitution", which the master of the English ship was quickly ordered to do.[31]

The conflict developed into a series of raids on the Bretons and counterattacks largely focused on the southwest coast of England. The Bretons quickly responded to the June raid with a reprisal attack on Plymouth, the Isle of Wight, and the Channel Islands of Guernsey and Jersey in August 1403, led by Guillaume de Chastel (or du Châtel).[32] William Wilford of Exeter then was charged with organising a force to respond to the Breton threat and his small fleet seized an impressive number of ships and their cargo and conducted damaging raids near Penmarch, southwest of Quimper. The following year saw another attack headed by de Chastel on Dartmouth, which culminated in the Battle of Blackpool Sands on 14 April 1404, where even the women took part in defending the town—it was a crushing defeat for the Bretons and the "impetuous" and "intrepid" de Chastel, who died shortly after the battle.[33] In an unusual twist, it appears that Joan was given the king's share of the ransom for the prisoners taken at Dartmouth—oddly giving her a potential financial benefit from the defeat of those who were, until very recently, her subjects as regent of Brittany.[34]

As the chronicler Adam Usk noted, the Breton issue was connected to Henry's wider difficulties both with internal rebellions and politics with Joan's Valois relatives as they sent forces to support Glyndwr's rebellion as well:

> The king took as his wife the widow of the Duke of Brittany, who was also the sister of the King of Navarre, hoping through her to gain some assistance. His hopes were promptly dashed, however, because the Bretons, disapproving of the marriage, allied themselves with the French under the command of the count marshal of Aquitaine and the lord of Hugueville in Normandy, and took a large force to Wales to help and support Owen, devastating the entire march with fire and sword and inflicting substantial losses on the English.[35]

While Usk is amalgamating several issues in this brief comment, he does rightly note that Henry's marriage to Joan had resulted in conflict, rather than alliance with her French and Breton relatives, the opposite of the normal scenario with a royal marriage. Another reversal of expectations which would have made Joan less popular with her English subjects is that she did not bring a substantial dowry with her, or indeed any dowry at all. In fact, her original dowry for her marriage to Jean IV had never been fully paid by her father before he died, and in 1404 Joan formally gave Jean V the wherewithal to pursue this with her brother Carlos III—a dispute which rumbled on for several years and ended up in the Parlement de Paris, doing little to improve harmony between the various branches of Joan's family.[36]

The English Parliament of 1404 proved to be another problem for Henry IV to deal with. The members of Parliament effectively took Henry to task for excessive expenditure, both in terms of the household and military matters regarding the vast sums spent quelling uprisings, fighting a cross-Channel war with Brittany, and with threats on nearly every frontier. Thomas Wright summarises the sentiment of the parliamentarians who appear to have felt that "the King had dissipated his revenues and spent too much on his household, while paying insufficient attention to the defence of the realm and so placing it in great peril".[37] Alan Rogers' research on Henry's financial difficulties echoes Wright's sentiment and notes how concern over these issues led to disaffection with the queen: "In the restlessness of the period, Henry's marriage to Joan of Brittany turned out to be a mistake. Not only did it fail to produce political results; the size of her dower and the large foreign personnel of her retinue provided an excuse to the opposition to attack the king's household in detail".[38] In Chapter 6 we will explore this situation further, discussing the petitions from the parliaments of 1404 and 1406, which sought to expel the foreigners from Joan's household, both to reduce excessive royal expenditure and to purge "aliens" from the court. This concern, particularly regarding the sizeable number of Bretons who continued to serve Joan, was clearly tied to the escalation of hostilities with Brittany—these servitors were seen by some as potential enemy agents at the English court.

The first half of 1405 saw Henry fighting rebels and plots on all sides. In February, there was a plot to capture the young earl of

March, Edmund Mortimer, and his brother, to use them as rival claimants by the rebels to unseat Henry IV. The boys were briefly liberated but apprehended again near Cheltenham. While the plot appears to have been masterminded by the king's first cousin, Constance, lady Despencer, who implicated her brother, the duke of York, in her testimony, one contemporary chronicle, the *Eulogium*, claims the boys had been abducted by the queen's ladies, who then blamed the duke of York.[39] Even though this account is clearly erroneous, it may reflect either confusion over which woman was involved or be an attempt to further disgrace the queen's household, which had already been under attack for its excessive cost and number of foreigners.

The quashing of this plot and the favourable outcome of a series of battles in 1405 finally gave the king the upper hand—defeating the Welsh rebels in the battles of Grosmont and Usk (or Pwll Melyn) in the spring and bringing the northern rebels to heel in the battle of Shipton Moor shortly after. While the execution of one particular rebel, Richard Scrope, the archbishop of York, would continue to haunt him, Henry's situation was beginning to stabilise after a very intense and chaotic period following his marriage to Joan; "by the summer of 1405, it must have seemed as if Henry had perfected the art of falling and falling without ever hitting the ground".[40]

A calmer situation may have enabled the royal couple to spend more time together and with their family. The royal couple appear to have remained together a reasonable amount given the political turmoil of the early years of their marriage—Joan had travelled with Henry around the country, and was with him in Cirencester in November 1403 as well as accompanying him to the Midlands, including Leicester and Kenilworth, in the summer/autumn months of 1404.[41] The couple were joined by the king's children at Kenilworth for All Saints Day and kept Christmas at their favourite residence at Eltham with the family in high style. Deborah Codling argued that "the lavish Christmas festivities may have been a way of showing that the king was still very much in control" after his rule had been tested by rebellions, raids, and parliamentary petitions—as well as a bout of ill health shortly after Shipton Moor, which some accounts ominously linked to the execution of the archbishop.[42]

Yet their family was also suffering losses during this period—Joan's sister Maria passed away in 1405 and her two daughters returned to Brittany. While both events would have been difficult for Joan to bear, her daughters' return was likely driven by three elements—pressure in the English court to reduce the expenditure on and number of foreigners, the ongoing hostilities between England and Brittany, and plans afoot to marry the two princesses in a double wedding in June 1407 as discussed in the previous chapter.[43] Nor were they the only princesses or royal women to be married around this time—there were several important weddings which Joan and Henry attended or were connected to. The most significant perhaps was the departure of Henry's daughter Philippa for Scandinavia to marry Erik of Pomerania in August 1406—Henry and Joan travelled with Thomas and Humphrey to King's Lynn to see her off with family feeling as well as the pomp and circumstance needed to underscore the importance of the alliance.[44] While this marriage was diplomatically significant, it highlighted two chronic issues—first, there had been considerable expenditure for the bride's trousseau, proxy wedding, and departure at a time when Henry was struggling with criticism of the royal finances in the "Long Parliament" of 1406, where once again the queen's household was targeted to expel remaining foreigners.[45] Second, Henry had suffered another bout of serious illness with his leg in late April, which had reduced his ability to attend some of the sessions of Parliament—in connection with the trip to King's Lynn for Philippa's departure, Henry visited the shrines of Walsingham and the relics of St Oswald at Bardney Abbey, both sites associated with healing miracles.[46]

Henry and Joan also attended two splendid weddings with international brides in this period, that of Thomas Fitzalan, earl of Arundel, with Beatriz of Portugal, the stepdaughter of Henry's sister Philippa, queen of Portugal, in November 1405, and the wedding of Edmund Holland, earl of Kent, and Lucia Visconti of Milan, a woman who was once a possible bride for Henry himself, in January 1407.[47] Another Beatriz who married in this same period was Joan's niece, who married Jacques de Bourbon, a French lord who was a supporter of the duke of Burgundy—Carlos of Navarre had also been using his daughters Blanca and Juana to contract beneficial "*anglófilo*" alliances in both the French and Iberian orbits with the heir of the king of Aragon and the count of Foix.[48] Joan's familial connections in the region were of potential political benefit to Henry as well—viewing them in the round, his half-sisters Philippa and Catherine (or Catalina) were the queens of Portugal and Castile respectively, while Joan's family gave him connections to Navarre, Aragon, Foix-Béarn, and Armagnac, filling out the Iberian peninsula and giving connections in the Pyrenean region close to the English holdings in Gascony. Another family marriage with regional significance in this period was that of Joan's cousin, Carlos de Beaumont, the alferez of Navarre and chamberlain of her household, whose career will be discussed further in Chapter 6. Beaumont married Anne de Curton (Anna de Guiche) in 1407, a Gascon heiress whose lands reinforced the territory Beaumont had been granted in Mauleon and Soule and Anglo-Navarrese relations, as well as the entrenchment of Navarrese lords in the region.[49]

Returning to the Anglo-Breton relations, the cross-Channel conflict began to improve in 1406. In March there was a flurry of activity related to Joan's network of service in Brittany, making payments and gifts due to them and confirming the powers and prerogatives of some of her officials, a possible indication of greater communication between Jean V and Joan or at least greater co-operation between them.[50] On 11 July a breakthrough in relations came when a one-year truce was signed between Henry and his "well beloved son the duke of Brittany".[51] This pause in hostilities led to negotiations designed to rebuild relations and secure a more durable peace; Henry issued a proclamation on 30 May 1407 in the West Country, which had seen the bulk of the fighting on the English side, that no harm should come to Jean V's subjects while the Breton duke was negotiating with the king.[52] Safe conducts were also issued by Jean V in the same period for Breton and Englishmen to negotiate or send goods for the payment of ransoms for men who had been taken prisoner during the conflict and for Joan's officials to undertake their business.[53] Joan herself appears to have influenced the peace negotiations as Jean V states at the beginning of his acceptance of the Anglo-Breton truce that he was willing to sign the document

> as our very dear and very redoubtable lady and mother, the queen of England, has signified to us several times her desire for all good tranquillity between the very high and excellent prince, and my very redoubtable lord and father, Henry king of England and lord of Ireland, her lord and spouse on one part and ourselves on the other.[54]

While this statement might be a face-saving exercise for the young duke, leveraging the expectation that queens and royal women were peacemakers to belie his own need to negotiate a peace to put an end to a destructive period of conflict, it is extremely likely that Joan did intercede between husband and son to encourage them to renew their truce and rebuild diplomatic relations. She would have had every motive to do so, given not only her personal ties to the two men but her connection to both realms—the destruction caused in both her new kingdom and the duchy she herself had recently governed, which had been partially caused by her second marriage, would have been difficult for her. Moreover, as we have seen, improved relations between both realms improved her access to her Breton dower lands and their revenues—a situation which will be explored further in Chapter 5. Thus, it is quite likely that Jean's statement that he was encouraged to sign the Anglo-Breton truce by his mother's desire for peace was entirely accurate.

While this truce signified a healing between the English and Breton branches of Joan's family, another event in 1407 created a devastating rupture, the assassination of her cousin, Louis, the duke of Orleans, brother of Charles VI, on 23 November by adherents of another cousin, Jean "*sans peur*", the duke of Burgundy.[55] The tension between the dukes of Orleans and Burgundy had been a long-standing issue at the French court, with each seeking to direct the realm given the king's frequent bouts of mental illness. The assassination of Orleans ratcheted the conflict to another level, threatening to convulse France in a civil war and forcing both Henry and Joan's brother Carlos III to consider their alliances carefully. For Carlos, the loss of Orleans was keenly felt as he was a proponent of the Avignonese anti-pope whom Carlos also supported—the death of Orleans pushed him into the Burgundian camp. As a Prince of the

Blood, Carlos was also drawn into resolving the conflict as a member of the family and to protect his own interests and territories in France; accordingly, Carlos entrusted the governance of Navarre to his wife, Leonor de Trastámara, and his heir, Juana, countess of Foix, and travelled to France in July 1408, where he remained until early 1411.[56] For Henry, the next few years would see him courted by Joan's relatives in the Burgundian and the Orleans-Armagnac factions, who both sought his support.

1408–13: Calmer waters or stormy seas?

The latter years of Henry IV's reign could be seen as calmer than the chaos which had marked the first years of his and Joan's marriage. The Gloucester Parliament of 1407 had been far kinder to him than the Long Parliament of 1406 which had put considerable pressures and constraints on the king, particularly in terms of his finances.[57] Henry had also had a stroke of luck when James, the heir to the Scottish throne, fell into his hands in the spring of 1406—the death of his father Robert III shortly after meant that he had the king of Scots in his keeping. In early 1408, Henry had another positive development when the earl of Northumberland and Lord Bardolf were defeated and killed in the Battle of Bramham Moor, which meant that the rebellions and uprisings in the north were finally ended.

Yet only months later Henry suffered a major reversal, a serious bout of ill health which began in June 1408 when he collapsed at Mortlake while visiting his friend and close political ally Thomas Arundel, the archbishop of Canterbury, after mopping up the last of the northern rebels. As his biographer Given-Wilson notes, "Henry IV's great misfortune was to become sick just at the moment when he appeared to have won his dynasty a measure of security".[58] The exact nature of Henry's illness, or indeed illnesses, as he appeared to be suffering from several different ailments, has long baffled historians.[59] Based on the symptoms connected with a disfiguring skin disease described in contemporary accounts as leprosy, it has been suggested that he was suffering from some kind of pox, psoriasis, Hansen's disease, or even syphilis. He also had problems with his leg which had been troubling him in 1406, which may have been connected to circulatory issues or even some kind of coronary or rheumatic heart disease. Whatever the case, Joan would have doubtless been extremely concerned about her husband's poor health—in his youth he had been celebrated as an athletic and attractive prince, but now he was a middle-aged invalid who was becoming increasingly immobile and disfigured. Henry's health, which continued to be poor for the rest of his life, not only debilitated the king personally but led to instability in the government—as Peter McNiven notes, there was an ongoing concern as to what extent Henry would be able to exercise the governance of the realm.[60] Yet Henry himself argued that his mind remained sharp even though his concern about this health, and past sins, weighed upon him—provoking him to make a will and make provisions to ensure the stability of Joan's finances after his death.[61]

Henry's ill health and the possibility that he may indeed die sooner rather than later brought his son and heir, and the prince's followers, into the government of the realm. This led to an effective changing of the guard around the end of 1409 and early 1410, as the treasurer, Sir John Tiptoft, who had supported the queen in stabilising her finances, was dismissed, and Henry's great friend and ally, the archbishop of Canterbury, resigned as chancellor. While there is insufficient space here to discuss the political factions in the government around the two Henrys, from Joan's perspective, managing the familial tension between father and son over the direction of internal and foreign policies would have been difficult. Nor were these the only difficulties in the wider family across the Channel—Henry's daughter Blanche had passed away in 1409 and tensions were high in Joan's Valois and Navarrese family over the Council of Pisa, which sought to heal the Papal Schism and the fallout from the assassination of Louis of Orleans.

Joan's son Jean V "emerged … as a critical player" and an "astute politician" in this family drama in early 1408 when the duke of Burgundy entered Paris and gave a public defence of the assassination of Orleans.[62] Jean V brought Breton forces with him to Paris to support the king and queen and publicly demonstrated his polite hostility to the duke of Burgundy's defence of his actions and desire to interpose himself into the centre of power. While Burgundy's father, Philip "the Bold", had briefly been Jean's guardian after

Joan's remarriage and departure, Jean had broken with his cousin, Jean "*sans peur*", when he allied himself with the Penthièvres in 1406. This resulted in Jean V moving into the Orleanist camp—the marriage of his sister Blanche to the Armagnac heir in 1407 gave him a link to the anti-Burgundian faction after Orleans himself was assassinated. On 9 March 1409, the family attempted to heal the breach through a public reconciliation at the cathedral of Chartres, but it did nothing to stop what had long since escalated from a family crisis into a burgeoning civil war.

Greater cooperation could be seen between England and Brittany at this point, which made a significant change to the earlier cross-Channel conflict. In 1408 English troops under the command of Thomas Holland, the earl of Kent, were brought in to support Jean V against his enemies the Penthiévres—not to demand payment for Joan's Breton dower as Wylie had previously suggested.[63] The assault on the isle of Bréhat by English troops during this campaign appears to have been particularly brutal, and Holland was killed as a result of injuries sustained in the attack, leaving Lucia Visconti, whom he had recently married, a widow. While this created consternation in certain quarters in Brittany and might have provoked renewed hostilities with England, Jean V was keen to keep the peace, renewing the truce in 1409 for two years and sending an embassy to England regarding homage for the long-disputed earldom of Richmond.[64] In 1411, negotiations took place to extend the truce further to ten years, signalling not only a desire to prevent conflict restarting between Brittany and England but perhaps a return to the more Anglophile political leanings of Jean V's father.[65] Indeed the following year, in May 1412, Jean dispatched the lord of Châteaugiron to negotiate a full alliance with England, beginning his justification for the alliance by noting the significance of his familial connection through Joan:

> For the cause of the proximity and connection that we have between the very high and powerful prince my most redoubtable lord and peer Henry, king of England, and for the affinity that is between him and ourselves from the marriage between him and our most redoubtable lady and mother the queen of England.[66]

Ironically then, while Joan's marriage to Henry had initially been a cause for conflict between England and Brittany, it had been invoked, from the truce of 1407 which Joan was credited for inciting, in this proposed alliance of 1412 as a reason for promoting greater harmony and affinity between the two neighbours.

While 1411 and 1412 saw the construction of a longer-term peace with Joan's son in Brittany, more broadly these were fairly turbulent years with significant developments in terms of both internal and international political affairs and continued tensions within her English and Valois family. Over the spring of 1411 envoys arrived from both the Burgundian and Orleans-Armagnac factions who sought English support against the other. While Joan had familial links on all sides, according to one contemporary source she supported the Burgundian embassy—possibly sharing her brother Carlos III's sympathy with that faction, although Carlos as always had a foot in and, like Joan, a tie to both camps and had previously supported Orleans. According to the pro-Burgundian *Livre des Trahisons de France envers la maison de Bourgogne*, Joan asked Henry not to involve himself in the quarrel between the two factions in any way which would be harmful to Burgundy and wrote a letter to the duke of Burgundy, informing him of the embassies of her cousins of Berry and Orleans to the English court.[67] This particular source paints a picture of Joan as a very active agent and intercessor in the affair—"never ceasing" to push the Burgundian case with both her husband and the great lords at court.

While we cannot be certain that this account was completely accurate, this contemporary impression of Joan's influence at court and engagement in politics is worth noting—particularly as this has often been misconstrued or downplayed by modern historians in conjunction with her wider omission from the narrative of the period as noted in the Introduction. While the author of *Le Livre des Trahisons* may have featured Joan as a more central figure to make Henry look weaker or dominated by his wife, there is also the possibility that given Henry's ill health, the queen may have assumed a more substantial role at court to fill the gap, in the same way that Prince Henry did. Yet, there is no sense in these passages that Henry was a henpecked husband, rather that Joan was fully a part of the political discussions around England's position vis-à-vis the Orleans/ Armagnac-Burgundian dispute, which she would have had a natural interest in given her familial connection to all parties. Instead of Joan, Prince Henry is often credited as being the key Burgundian proponent at the English court in this period—Anthony Tuck claims that this was almost in spite of Joan's support, rather than being in concert with her, as "he was likely to prove impervious to the queen's intervention", perhaps looking at their relationship in the light of their later estrangement, although there is nothing to suggest that the prince and his stepmother were on bad terms at this point.[68] In spite of the queen's views, Henry IV was reluctant to offer support to the Burgundians at this point; however, the prince appears to have gone around his father by despatching a force sent out in autumn 1411 under the command of the earl of Arundel, whose archers helped secure a victory over the Orleans-Armagnac forces at St Cloud in November.[69]

This led to two key developments—the first of which was Henry IV reasserting his royal authority and his ability to rule by calling Parliament in early November 1411, dismissing the suggestion of the prince and Bishop Beaufort that he should abdicate on health grounds and replacing the prince's men in government with his own, including Archbishop Arundel, who returned to his previous post as chancellor. The second development was a shift to support the Orleans-Armagnac faction, who offered to not only fully recognise him as king of England but to support his rights in Gascony—both the Burgundian and Orleans-Armagnac proposals included a potential marriage for Prince Henry as well to seal the pact.[70] Again contemporary accounts note Joan's engagement in these events and stress the importance of her familial ties—Monstrelet's chronicle notes that the negotiators had letters of accreditation from Joan's uncle, the duke of Berry. One of these letters was specifically for Joan, calling her "my very redoubtable and honored lady and niece" and Monstrelet comments that while they were all signed by Berry, Joan's letter included two additional handwritten lines to her—perhaps trying to win her help to influence Henry or abandon her Burgundian sympathies.[71]

These negotiations, which on the French side had been pushed forward by Joan's son-in-law the count d'Alençon, led to the signing of the Treaty of Bourges on 18 May 1412, and preparations for a major expedition to support their new Orleans-Armagnac allies led by Henry's son Thomas instead of the pro-Burgundian Prince Henry.[72] Thomas had been gaining increasing prominence, given his controversial marriage to Margaret Holland in late 1411, and the bestowal of the titles of duke of Clarence and earl of Aumale in July 1412, where he was noted as "*praecarissimus filius*".[73] If Thomas was indeed the favourite son—in contrast to Humphrey, who appears to have been Joan's favourite stepson, as will be discussed in the following chapter—the simultaneous rejection of Prince Henry's men and his pro-Burgundian stance with the promotion of Thomas would have certainly been to blame for "a dangerous escalation of the rivalry between the king's two eldest sons" and serious discord in the Lancastrian family, with the heir withdrawing from court to his own estates to brood.[74] While the two Henrys were eventually reconciled after the prince returned to London to ask for the punishment of those who claimed he was trying to undermine Thomas's expedition to France, the notion of tension between the king and his heir has become embedded in popular culture, thanks to William Shakespeare's two *Henry IV* plays—in which Joan is mysteriously absent, although in reality she must have been a key witness to this family drama.[75]

The negotiations of the Orleans-Armagnac faction with England had triggered an angry response from Charles VI and the duke of Burgundy, who attacked the lands of both Alençon and Joan's uncle, the duke of Berry, the leading forces behind the Orleans faction and the English treaty. Alençon was forced to seek the help of his brothers-in-law in Brittany—Joan's son Arthur de Richemont came to his aid with 1,600 men. Yet, Joan's family was bitterly divided—while both Jean V and Carlos III were prevaricating between the Orleanist and Burgundian camps at this point, most of her Breton and Valois family were on opposing sides. Joan's third son, Gilles, was in the Burgundian camp and "exchanged 'high words' when Gilles visited his brother [Arthur] in the hope of detaching him from the Armagnac cause".[76] Bourges, the city for which the Anglo-Armagnac treaty had been named, even though it had been signed in London, was a stronghold of Joan's uncle the duke of

Berry, and became the central focus of the campaign against the Orleans-Armagnac faction as the site of a prolonged siege in the summer of 1412. The Burgundian camp became infected with dysentery and tragically both Joan's son Gilles and her brother Pedro, count of Mortain, were victims of the ravaging illness. Ironically, earlier that year in May, Gilles had been granted a safe-conduct to come to England to see his mother or perhaps argue the Burgundian cause, but it is unclear if he was able to make his visit given the political maelstrom that he was being sucked into at the time.[77] Gilles' body was taken back to Nantes and buried near the tomb in the cathedral that Joan had recently had installed for his father, Jean IV.

The new duke of Clarence left with his forces in mid-August 1412, landing on the Cotentin peninsula in Normandy at a site which "had probably been agreed in advance with the count of Alençon and Arthur de Richemont"—Thomas's stepbrother-in-law and stepbrother through Joan, familial connections which reinforced the political alliance.[78] The three stepbrothers joined their forces at Fougères on the border of Jean V's lands and the English forces helped Alençon to regain some of his territories lost to earlier Burgundian attacks. Yet Thomas's expedition to support the Orleans-Armagnac side arrived too late to relieve the siege of Bourges and his erstwhile French allies were now under pressure from Charles VI to repudiate the Anglo-Armagnac treaty altogether. Thomas and his army moved south, looping through the Loire region, leaving a path of destruction in its wake; a deal was negotiated to pay the English a hefty sum of 210,000 gold écus to leave French territory, after which Thomas headed south to English Gascony and based himself in Bordeaux.[79]

Once in the Midi, Thomas was in close proximity to many of Joan's relatives, including her cousin Carlos de Beaumont's Gascon holdings and the lords of Foix (married to her niece Juana) and Armagnac (whose son was married to Joan's daughter Blanche). The latter two had a long-standing regional rivalry, magnified by Foix's Burgundian allegiance and Armagnac's alliance with Orleans. Bernard d'Armagnac sought Thomas's support against Foix and signed a pact with Thomas which reaffirmed the treaty of Bourges in a more limited fashion in return for armed support for Armagnac.[80] Thomas also made contact with Joan's brother, Carlos III of Navarre, who had continued to "maintain good relations with the English court" throughout the recent Orleans-Burgundian crisis.[81] Like Henry IV, Carlos was also wooed by both sides, but as a French Prince of the Blood, Carlos had to move with extreme caution due to his close ties to all parties and to prevent the loss of his French territories or an attack on Navarre itself if he chose the wrong side. In sum, while Thomas's expedition was driven by the political decisions of his father and impacted by the continually shifting nature of the crisis, he could leverage bonds of blood and marriage which he possessed through his stepmother Joan to smooth his path and reinforce alliances with her sons in the north and her brother and wider familial network in the south as well.

Back in England, Henry IV's precarious health was failing fast—Henry and Joan spent their last Christmas together at Henry's favourite residence of Eltham, where they had passed most of the yuletide seasons over their marriage, "with as much cheerfulness as he could muster" given his continuing illness.[82] While Henry had returned to Westminster, he was too ill to attend the opening of Parliament in February 1413, and collapsed in Westminster Abbey on 20 March while making an offering to the shrine of Edward the Confessor. Famously, he died in the Jerusalem Chamber in the abbot's lodging, fulfilling in an odd way a prophecy that he would die in Jerusalem, although he had never made good on his intention to go on pilgrimage to the Holy Land.[83] It is unclear how much Joan was with him in his final hours and moments but even if Henry's body was as brutally ravaged as some contemporary accounts indicate, it is highly likely that she would have been at his side at his death, as she had been for the majority of the last ten years of their marriage.[84] A lack of detailed accounts of Henry's funeral and interment also means that it is impossible to ascertain Joan's role in events, or whether she accompanied his body from London to Canterbury. However, as will be discussed in the final chapter, much more can be said about her role in commissioning their joint tomb there, although it would be several decades after Henry's own death until Joan joined him in their final resting place.

Conclusion

In this chapter we have seen how Joan transitioned from duchess to queen, crossing the Channel from Brittany to England to take on not only a new royal role but a new husband and stepfamily. She took up the role of queen actively, engaging with ceremonial, petitioning, and politics to make her influence felt at court. All the evidence seems to affirm that Henry and Joan's ten-year marriage was personally strong, given their general tendency to remain together, the lack of even the slightest hint of marital discord or extramarital affairs, and, as we will discuss further in Chapter 5, Henry's desire to dower her generously and support her robustly when she had financial difficulties. While some accounts have assumed that she struggled as a stepmother, given the problems between Joan and her stepson Henry in the latter years of his reign, which will be discussed in the following chapter, there is no indication of any tension or disharmony between her and her stepchildren during this period.[85] Joan also built connections within the court and realm through her network of service, which will be explored in Chapter 6.

In spite of the positive relationships that she forged with her husband, stepfamily, and courtiers, a theme of this chapter has been the constant conflict and continual challenges which Henry and Joan faced together, both within the realm and with their neighbours, and Joan's wider family on the Continent. While Joan's familial connections could be an asset and leveraged to make peace or support alliances and campaigns, a factor which would have made her attractive to Henry as a potential bride, her familial connections could not prevent, or could even be a cause for, conflict, given the negative initial reaction of her Breton and Valois family to her remarriage. The maelstrom of the Orleans-Burgundy crisis offered Joan no familial advantage as she was related to all parties—indeed, as we have seen, her relations were estranged from one another as they chose sides in the conflict, and two of her loved ones, her brother Pedro and her third son, Gilles, died as a result of the fighting. Joan was also affected by Henry's political troubles, with rebellions dominating his attention in the early years of their marriage and later, just as things appeared to stabilise on some fronts, Henry's debilitating illness had a devastating impact on the latter years of his reign and undoubtedly cast a dark cloud over the last years they spent together. In March 1413, Joan was widowed for the second time and transitioned from a consort to a dowager queen—a role which she would retain for the remaining 24 years of her long life. However, as the next chapter will reveal, this final stage of her life and political career was anything but a quiet retirement—Joan would witness the reigns of two further Lancastrian kings and play an important role in the continuing chaos of both English politics and the Hundred Years War.

Notes

1 POPC, I, 188–90.
2 See Michael Jones, "Between France and England: Jeanne de Navarre, Duchess of Brittany and Queen of England (1386–1437)," in *Between France and England: Politics, Power and Society in Late Medieval Brittany* (Aldershot: Variorum, 2003), 12; Ian Mortimer, *The Fears of Henry IV; The Life of England's Self-Made King* (London: Vintage Books, 2008), 259–61. The Brut is one of the few contemporary sources which note her landing at Falmouth: "The iiij yere off Kynge Henry camme Dame Iohn Mountfort, the Duchies off Britayne, into Engelonde, and londed atte Falemouth in Cornwell"; Anon., *An English Chronicle 1377–1461: A New Edition*, ed. William Marx (Woodbridge: Boydell, 2003), 34.
3 Thomas Austin, ed., *Two Fifteenth Century Cookery Books; Harleian MS 279 (ab. 1430) and Harleian MS 4016 (ab. 1450) with extracts from Ashmole MS. 1429, Laud MA 533 and Douce MS 55* (London: Early English Text Society, 1888), 58–9. I would also like to thank Professor Chris Woolgar for his insights into the menu for the wedding feast.
4 A.W. Goodman, *The Marriage of Henry IV and Joan of Navarre in the Cathedral Church of S. Swithun Winchester, Wednesday, 7 Feb. 1403* (Winchester: Warren and Son, 1934), 12; Frederick Devon, ed., *Issues of the Exchequer being a collection of payments made out of His Majesty's Revenue, from King Henry III to King Henry VI inclusive with an appendix* (London: John Murray, 1837), 296, 19 Feb 1403 and E101/404/21.
5 *Signet Letters*, no. 107, 9 February 1403, 41. See also payments to messengers sent with letters requesting the presence of the nobility of the realm at the coronation in Devon, *Issues of the Exchequer*, 296.
6 Robert Fabyan, *The Great Chronicle of London*, ed. A.H. Thomas and I.D. Thornley (London: Corporation and City of London, 1938), 85.
7 The *Liber Regalis* is reprinted in Anon., *English Coronation Records*, ed. Leopold G. Wickam Legg (Westminster: Archibald Constable & Co, 1901), 81–130. For a comparison of Joan's coronation with her sister-in-law Leonor de Trastámara, wife of Carlos III of Navarre, who was also

crowned in 1403, and French and Iberian counterparts, see Elena Woodacre, "The Queen of Navarre and a Queen from Navarre: Comparing the Experience of Queenship of Leonor de Trastámara and Joan of Navarre," *Studia Historica. Historia Medieval* 39, no. 2 (2021): 11–29.

8 Anon., *The Pageants of Richard Beauchamp, Earl of Warwick* (late 15th century), British Library Cotton MS Julius E IV/3, folio 2v.

9 I am grateful to Professor Chris Woolgar for sharing his transcript of Margaret's will with me where she bequeathed her fee as chief pantler at Joan's coronation to Richard; see "Will of Margaret Beauchamp, countess of Warwick, 28 November 1406," in Register of Thomas Arundel, vol. 1, Lambeth Palace Library, f. 234v.

10 J.H. Round, "The King's Pantler," *Archaeological Journal* 60, no. 1 (1903): 268–83.

11 Devon, *Issues of the Exchequer*, 1 March 1403, 297.

12 John Carmi Parsons, "Ritual and Symbol in the English Medieval Queenship to 1500," in *Women and Sovereignty*, ed. Louise Olga Fradenburg (Edinburgh: Edinburgh University Press, 1992), 64.

13 There has been considerable scholarship on queenly intercession and on the activities of later medieval English queens in this regard; see Helen Lacey, *The Royal Pardon: Access to Mercy in Fourteenth-Century England* (York: York Medieval Press, 2009), 46–7 and appendices of intercessory activity; Carolyn P. Collette, *Performing Polity: Women and Agency in the Anglo-French Tradition, 1385–1620* (Turnhout: Brepols, 2006), particularly 99–121 on Anne of Bohemia; Louise Tingle, *Chaucer's Queens: Royal Women, Intercession and Patronage in England, 1328–1394* (New York: Palgrave Macmillan, 2020), chapters 3 and 4, 33–79.

14 Anthony Musson, "Queenship, Lordship and Petitioning in Late Medieval England," in *Medieval Petitions: Grace and Grievance*, eds. W. Mark Ormrod, Gwilym Dodd, and Anthony Musson (Woodbridge: York Medieval Press, 2009), 161.

15 L&M JV, IV, no. 106, December 1405.

16 CPR Henry IV, II, 10 January 1403, 199.

17 CPR Henry IV, II, 15 February 1403, 207; 1 March 1403, 209; 27 May 1403, 229.

18 CPR Henry IV, II, 1 November 1404, 465; 13 November 1404, 472; 5 December 1404, 480.

19 James Ross, "Seditious Activities: The Conspiracy of Maud de Vere, Countess of Oxford, 1403–4," in *The Fifteenth Century III: Authority and Subversion*, ed. Linda Clark (Woodbridge: Boydell, 2003), 35.

20 Petition: SC 8/229/11420 (1404); for the grant of the goods and chattels, see CPR Henry IV, II, 1 November 1404, 468.

21 CPR Henry IV, III, 8 October 1406, 241; IV, 24 October 1409, 114 and 8 October 1411, 351. Helen Lacey notes associations with the anniversaries or jubilees of Henry's predecessors: Helen Lacey, "The

Politics of Mercy: The Use of the Royal Pardon in Fourteenth-Century England" (PhD thesis, University of York, 2005), 81–2, 87.

22 CPR Henry IV, III, 17 February 1408, 435.

23 See the transcript of this case (TNA JUST 3/188 m.49) translated and printed in Anthony Musson and Edward Powell, eds. *Crime, Law and Society in the Later Middle Ages* (Manchester: Manchester University Press, 2013), 36–7.

24 CPR Henry IV, II, 26 April 1403, 260, and 25 November 1403, 325.

25 GSR C61 112, no. 53, m. 12, 8 September 1408.

26 SC 8/231/11512; The grant of the Isle and castle was on 5 April 1405 (CPR Henry IV, II, 501).

27 Letter of Prince Henry to Henry IV (1403) in Colonel Sir Henry James, ed., *Facsimiles of National Manuscripts from William the Conqueror to Queen Anne*, part I (Southampton: Ordinance Survey Office, 1865), 40–41.

28 Walsingham, 325.

29 Anon., "A Northern Chronicle: 1399–1430," in *English Historical Literature in the Fifteenth Century*, ed. Charles Lethbridge Kingsford (Oxford: The Clarendon Press, 1913), 282.

30 Chris Given-Wilson, *Henry IV* (New Haven, CT: Yale University Press, 2016), 216. For contemporary accounts of these uprisings in 1403, see Usk, 168–73, and Walsingham, 326–30.

31 For William's petitions, see SC 8/166/8259 and SC 8/332/15724. On the English response see CCR Henry IV, II, 5 July 1403, 89–90, and CPR Henry IV, II, 14 July 1403, 282 (source of second quotation).

32 Walsingham, 330; Arthur de la Borderie, "La jeunesse de Jean V, duc de Bretagne," *Revue de Bretagne de Vendee et d'Anjou* 23 (Mar 1900): 170–1. Saint-Denys, III, 104–10. Monstrelet, I, 91–2.

33 Walsingham, 331. For a French account of the battle, see Saint-Denys, III, 170–79.

34 Foedera 8, 10 Jan 1405.

35 Usk, 175.

36 Joan's letter to give Jean V all the rights to pursue her dowry, ADLA 9-1, 18 Nov 1404; see also related documents in Catalogo XXVII, no. 112, 17 February 1407; no. 172, 8 March 1407; and no. 920, 1 January 1408. An accord appears to have been reached in 1409, see ADLA E9-16, 28 January 1409.

37 Thomas Edmund Farnsworth Wright, "Royal Finance in the Latter Part of the Reign of Henry IV of England, 1406–13" (unpublished PhD thesis, Merton College, Oxford, 1984), 18.

38 Alan Rogers, "The Royal Household of Henry IV" (PhD thesis, University of Nottingham, 1966), 456.

39 Anon., *Eulogium (historiarum sive temporis): Chronicon ab orbe condito usque ad annum Domini M.CCC.LXCI., a monacho quodam Malmesburiensi ex-aratum* (London: Longman,1858), 402. See also Walsingham, 332, and Given-Wilson, *Henry IV*, 264–65.

40 Given-Wilson, *Henry IV*, 277. For contemporary accounts of the execution of Scrope, see Usk, 202–3, and Walsingham, 336–39.

41 For Henry's full itinerary, see Given-Wilson, *Henry IV*, 542–45. For mentions of Joan's location, see CPR Henry IV, II, 4 November 1403, 327; 28 November 1404, 479; ADLA E9-1, 18 November 1404 at Kenilworth.

42 Deborah Codling, "The Kingly Style of Henry IV: Personality, Politics and Culture" (PhD thesis, Royal Holloway, 2004), 108–9. See also Peter McNiven, "The Problem of Henry IV's Health," *EHR* 100, no. 397 (1985): 747–48.

43 See L&M JV, IV, no. 10, 24 May 1404 for an order for Michel Abraham to go to England to the queen for the coming of the ladies Blanche and Marguerite. Their exact departure is unclear; while Knowlson claims they returned in 1404, there is a record of a payment to Haouys, "femme de Langueffort", who was in England serving the two sisters on 22 January 1406, but it is not clear if this was made on the servants' return from England or while they, and the two princesses, were in England; L&M JV, IV, no. 172, 22 January 1406; George Akenhead Knowlson, *Jean V, duc de Bretagne et l'Angleterre 1399–1442* (Cambridge: W. Heffer & Sons Ltd, 1964), 53.

44 Walsingham, 342; Codling, "Kingly Style," 128; Louise Berglund, "'From Where Few Return Alive': Sending Philippa, Daughter of King Henry IV, to the North, c. 1400–1430," paper given at IMC Leeds, July 2021.

45 Rogers, "Household," 269; Wright, "Royal Finance," 77–78, 323; Mortimer, *Fears*, 306–8.

46 Mortimer, *Fears*, 309; Given-Wilson, *Henry IV*, 293–95.

47 Walsingham, 340; Given-Wilson, *Henry IV*, 75, 302; Mortimer, *Fears*, 312.

48 Eloísa Ramírez Vaquero, *Carlos III, rey de Navarra, Principe de sangre Valois (1387–1425)* (Gijon: Ediciones Trea, 2007), 127, 134–37.

49 Ramírez Vaquero, *Carlos III*, 230–1. Eloísa Ramírez Vaquero, "Estrategias diplomáticas del rey de Navarra en el tránsito al siglo XV," in *Guerra y Diplomacia en la Europa Occidental: 1280–1480 XXXI Semana de Estudios Medievales*, ed. Miguel Angel Ladero Quesada (Pamplona: Gobierno de Navarra, 2005), 398–99. For an example of additional grants and privileges in the area near his wife's lands given to Beaumont around the time of his wedding, see GSR no. 133, 22 August 1409.

50 See L&M JV, IV, nos. 246, 247, 251, 252 and 255, all dated March 1406.

51 ADLA E121-20, 11 July 1406.

52 Foedera 8, 30 May 1407.

53 L&M JV, V, no. 558, 16 April 1407; no. 661, 20 May 1407; nos. 664–67, 21 May 1407; nos. 694–97, 1 June 1407; nos. 733 and 737, 9 June 1407; no. 797, 26 June 1407; no. 873, July 1407. See also a safe conduct for the governor of Nantes, Tristan de la Lande, to come to England for the queen: Foedera 8, 10 May 1407.

54 See Jean V's acceptance, and Henry IV's which follows, in Foedera 8, 11 July 1407. Original text is "*Comme, nostre tres chiere, & tres redoutee Dame & Mere, la Royne d'Angleterre Nous eut, par plusurs foiz, signifie le desir qu'elle a que toute bonne Transquilite feust entre, tres hault & excellent Prince, & mon tres redoute Seigneur & Pere, Henry Roy d'Angleterre & Seigneur d'Irlande, son Seigneur & Espoux, d'une Part, & Nous d'autre part*".

55 For contemporary reactions, see Usk, 217; Walsingham, 361; Monstrelet, I, 154–66.

56 Ramírez Vaquero, *Carlos III*, 180, 185, and "Estrategias diplomáticas," 417–19.

57 For an extended overview of Henry's financial issues and debates with Parliament, see Peter McNiven, "The King's Needs," in *Heresy and Politics in the Reign of Henry IV: The Burning of John Badby* (Woodbridge: Boydell, 1987), 158–84.

58 Given-Wilson, *Henry IV*, 533. Walsingham noted that "a weakness and a trance came upon him so that he was thought to have died", 360.

59 See Given-Wilson, *Henry IV*, 304–5 and particularly McNiven, "Henry IV's Health", *passim* for an extended discussion of Henry's illnesses and the various diagnoses suggested by contemporaries and later historians.

60 McNiven, "Henry IV's Health," 772.

61 See Chapter 5 for further discussion of the provisions made for Joan; Henry's will is printed in Richard Gough and John Nichols, *A Collection of All the Wills, Now Known to be Extant of the Kings and Queens of England, Princes and Princesses of Wales, and Every Branch of the Blood Royal: From the Reign of William the Conqueror to that of Henry the Seventh, Exclusive … With Explanatory Notes and a Glossary* (London: J. Nichols, 1780), 203–5.

62 Jonathan Sumption, *Cursed Kings: The Hundred Years War IV* (London: Faber and Faber, 2016), 240–1; see the chapter "In the Rue Vieille du Temple: The Road to Civil War, 1407–1411" for an excellent summary of this turbulent period, 234–77. See also Monstrelet, I, 175–244 for this episode, including the full recounting of the justification of the murder of Orleans.

63 James Hamilton Wylie, *History of England under Henry the Fourth*, vol. III (London: Longmans, Green and Co, 1896), 102–4. For different contemporary views, see Walsingham, 361, and Saint-Denys, IV, 314–17.

64 Morice, II, 821–22 and 827–30. L&M JV, V, no. 1084, 14 October 1409. Truce in Foedera 8, 11 July 1409.

65 ADLA E121-18, signature on the ten-year truce from Henry IV, signed 21 December 1411 and the articles of the truce, ADLA E121-19. See also L&M JV, V, no. 1125, 27 October 1411, and Given-Wilson, *Henry IV*, 500.

66 L&M JV, V, no. 1132, 10 May 1412. See also ordinances regarding the conservation of the truce, L&M JV, V, no. 1146, 1412 and further documentation of the 1412 negotiations in ADLA E121-16, dated 21 February 1412. On the English side, see an export licence granted to

Châteaugiron and the deployment of Joan's servant William Pomeroy as part of a commission to restore Breton ships and goods captured in the West Country; Foedera 8, 6 July 1412.

67 Anon., *Le livre des trahisons de France envers la maison de Bourgogne*, ed. Joseph Kervyn de Lettenhove (Brussels: F. Hayez, 1873), 73–77, 94–95. Jonathan Sumption has also noted that the Burgundian ambassador was accredited to Joan as well as her husband and stepson, again indicating that the Burgundians sought her influence in the matter: Sumption, *Cursed Kings*, 307.

68 Anthony Tuck, "The Earl of Arundel's Expedition to France, 1411," in *The Reign of Henry IV: Rebellion and Survival, 1403–1413*, eds. Gwilym Dodd and Douglas Biggs (York: York Medieval Press, 2008), 231.

69 Tuck, "Expedition to France," 228–39; Given-Wilson, *Henry IV*, 494–5; Walsingham, 382.

70 Anne Curry, *The Hundred Years War* (Basingstoke: Palgrave Macmillan, 2003), 80–1; Tuck, "Expedition to France," 236–39; Given-Wilson, *Henry IV*, 497–98; Walsingham, 383–85. See also John Milner, "The English Commitment to the 1412 Expedition to France," in *The Fifteenth Century XI*, ed. Linda Clark (Woodbridge: Boydell, 2012), 9–23. Other potential brides who had been offered for the prince during Henry IV's reign included two of Joan's Valois cousins, the French princesses Marie and Catherine—the latter of whom eventually became his wife in 1420; see Given-Wilson, *Henry IV*, 327, 329.

71 Monstrelet, I, 238.

72 Sumption, *Cursed Kings*, 308–11. For the treaty see Foedera 8, 18 May 1412. See also Walsingham, 385.

73 Milner, "1412 Expedition," 16.

74 See also Given-Wilson's note of John Strecche's description of Thomas as "the favoured one" in *Henry IV*, 306, and Peter McNiven, "Prince Henry and the English Political Crisis of 1412," *History* 65, no. 213 (1980): 6–7.

75 Walsingham, 386–7.

76 Sumption, *Cursed Kings*, 312.

77 See Chronicon Brittanicum, in Lobineau, II, 366; Monstrelet, II, 290 (which claims that Gilles and Pedro died when Burgundy moved to Auxerre after the siege). Both Monstrelet and Saint-Denys have extended accounts of the siege of Bourges; see also Sumption, *Cursed Kings*, 312–18. For Gilles' safe conduct, see Foedera 8, 20 May 1412.

78 Sumption, *Cursed Kings*, 324. See also Perceval de Cagny, *Chroniques de Perceval de Cagny*, ed. H. Moranvillé (Paris: Librarie Renouard, 1902), 76–7, on Alençon and Clarence's rendezvous.

79 Given-Wilson, *Henry IV*, 508–12; Walsingham, 387–88. See also John Milner, "The English Enterprise in France, 1412–13," in *Trade, Devotion and Governance: Papers in Later Medieval History*, eds. D.J Clayton, R.G. Davies, and Peter McNiven (Stroud: Sutton, 1994), 80–101.

80 Sumption, *Cursed Kings*, 326–31.

81 Ramírez Vaquero, *Carlos III*, 226–27.
82 Walsingham, 388.
83 Given-Wilson, *Henry IV*, 516–17; Mortimer, *Fears*, 347, 350–51.
84 Michael Evans, *The Death of Kings: Royal Deaths in Medieval England* (London: Hambledon Continum, 2007), 72–4. Usk' s account claims the illness "for five years had cruelly tormented Henry IV with festering of the flesh, dehydration of the eyes, and rupture of the internal organs": Usk, 242–43.
85 See Elena Woodacre, "The Perils of Promotion: Maternal Ambition and Sacrifice in the Life of Joan of Navarre, Duchess of Brittany and Queen of England," in *Virtuous or Villainess? The Image of the Royal Mother from the Early Medieval to the Early Modern Era*, eds. Carey Fleiner and Elena Woodacre (New York: Palgrave Macmillan, 2016), 136–40.

4

DOWAGER: ANYTHING BUT A "QUIET RETIREMENT"

The death of Henry IV in March 1413 was the start of Joan's second widowhood and yet another transition, from consort to dowager queen. While there is often a perception that dowagers exit the stage of court and disappear for a quiet life of "retirement", fuelled perhaps by reduced mentions of royal women after the major ceremonial and lifecycle events such as betrothal, marriage, and the birth of royal heirs are complete, this was hardly the case for Joan and many other elite women in the latter years of their lives. As this chapter and the ones to follow demonstrate, Joan continued to remain active on all fronts over the rest of her long life; she not only outlived two husbands, but many of her relatives by blood and marriage, as her life spanned seven decades. Indeed, her period as dowager queen lasted 34 years and witnessed the reigns of the two remaining Lancaster kings: her stepson Henry V and his son, Henry VI.

This chapter will focus on the turbulent politics of this period between Henry IV's death in 1413 and Joan's own passing in 1437, noting her continued engagement in the events of the period and the conflict generated by the ongoing Hundred Years War. It will be divided into three distinct periods: the early years of Henry V's reign

DOI: 10.4324/9780429261022-6

between 1413 and 1419 when Joan was still the pre-eminent woman at the English court; the "Crisis Years" of 1419–22 when Joan and three of her sons were all placed in various forms of detention; and the final years of 1422–37 during the reign of Henry VI. As this is such a long and significant period of her life, it will also feature heavily in the three thematic chapters to follow. Joan's extensive activity during this period in regard to her lands and the defence of her rights and revenues will be charted in Chapter 5, and in Chapter 6 we will examine her relationships with the members of her household and network of officials in Brittany and England. In the final chapter we will explore the spaces Joan lived in, including the residences of Kings Langley and Havering-atte-Bower, which she favoured in her dowager years, as well as examining her possessions, gift-giving, and her ongoing patronage.

The king's beloved mother: 1413–19

While the death of her husband in 1413 must have been personally devastating, even if it had been long expected due to his ill health, on a practical level it appears to have made little impact on her position in the Lancastrian court. Her stepson, Henry V, was unmarried, so there was no new consort to displace her as the premier woman at court and she appears to have continued to fulfil the female aspect of the monarchy as Henry's "beloved mother". As we will see in the following chapter, Henry initially treated his stepmother with great respect, championing her rights to lands and revenues and generally continuing the work of his father to ensure that she had the financial stability to maintain her household and queenly status.

Tensions were incredibly high regarding relations with Joan's relatives across the Channel—while the latter half of Henry IV's reign had seen improved relations with Brittany, there were still incidents of skirmishes and seizures of English and Breton boats at the outset of Henry V's reign, requiring negotiations, restorations to be made, and the reaffirmation of the truce established between the two realms.[1] Henry was also negotiating with Joan's Valois cousins, sending two unsuccessful embassies to Paris in 1414 to discuss his territorial demands in northern France, including the overlordship of Brittany, and the hand of Katherine de Valois.[2] Joan's brother Carlos III of Navarre may have been concerned about the failure of these talks and how deteriorating Anglo-French relations might impact his realm—in November 1414 he sent a special gift to the English ambassadors and dispatched his cousin Carlos de Beaumont, who had only recently returned from his long posting at the English court as Joan's chamberlain, back to England.[3] Beaumont, an expert diplomat, would have probably conferred closely with Joan and built on his excellent relationship with the new king to ascertain what the English were likely to do next and ensure that Navarre's relationship with England was not jeopardised by Joan's transition from consort to dowager or by the threat of an English invasion of France.

The political drama increased in 1415 with the launch of an English expedition to France which culminated in the famous battle of Agincourt. In June, before Henry's departure, he formally bid Joan farewell and gave her leave to stay in several royal residences during his absence.[4] He did not, however, entrust her with the governance of the realm—while later sixteenth-century chronicles claim this was the case, it is clear that Henry named his brother John, duke of Bedford, as lieutenant in the king's absence.[5]

The momentous battle of Agincourt was a pivotal moment in English and European history and had a significant personal impact on the life of Joan of Navarre. While she would have been pleased for the success of her stepson Henry V, with whom, by all accounts and indications, she had a close relationship, Joan also lost several family members in the battle; it was at the same time a victory over her Valois cousins as well. Joan would have also been torn between supporting her stepsons and her own sons and sons-in-law across the Channel. Her eldest son, Jean V, managed to avoid taking part in the battle as his Breton force had yet to arrive before the battle took place. However, his brother Arthur de Richemont had gone ahead and the prospect that Breton troops might yet arrive had given hope to the French at the very end of the battle.[6]

Yet some of her relations were killed, including her son-in-law Jean I d'Alençon, who had played an important role in the campaign and fought fiercely before he was cut down by one of Henry V's bodyguards in the thick of the fighting around the English king. Alençon's death and valiant efforts in the battle were noted in contemporary accounts—Monstrelet notes that he fought "*moult puissament*", killing Henry's uncle, the duke of York.[7] His role was magnified still further in the seventeenth-century poem of the battle of Agincourt by Michael Drayton, who claims that Humphrey was saved by his brother Henry from Alençon, who "prest [the king] so sore/ That with a stroke (as he was wonderous strong)/He cleft the Crowne that on his Helme he wore".[8] This account of Henry's "providential intervention" to save Humphrey likely originated in the *Vita Henrici Quinti*, which Humphrey himself commissioned and to which he may have contributed his own memories of the event.[9] While this story might be seen as an indicator of the courage of these three men as valiant warriors, from Joan's perspective it could also be seen as a manifestation of her own divided loyalties—her two stepsons (including Humphrey whom she was particularly close to) fighting for their lives against her son-in-law, to whom she may not have been as personally close, but who was the father of several of her grandchildren. If Henry did indeed kill Alençon, as Drayton suggested ("into small peeces cut"), it demonstrates the worst possible outcome of the conflict for Joan, the violent death of her family members.

Back in England, the news of the battle was greeted with jubilation:

> And thenne thorowe London they lette rynge the bellys in every chyrche and song Te Deum; and at Powlys, at ix of the clocke, the tydyngys were oppynly proclaymyd to alle the comeners of [th]e cytte and to alle othyr strangerys. And thenne the Quene [Joan] and alle hyr byschoppys and alle the lordys [th] at were in London that tyme, wentte to Westemyster on hyr fete a prosessyon to Synt Edwarde ys schryne, whythe alle the prestys, and clerkys, and fryers, and alle othyr relygyous men, devoutely syngynge ande saynge the letanye.[10]

While Joan led this service of thanksgiving at Westminster, one wonders if during the Mass she merely contemplated Henry's victory or said prayers for the soul of her son-in-law and for her daughter Marie, now a widow with five young children back in France. As

Agnes Strickland reflected later, "No trifling tax must the widowed queen have paid for greatness, when, instead of putting on her mourning weeds and indulging in the natural grief of a fond mother's heart, for these family calamities, she was called upon to assume the glittering trappings of state".[11] Joan could not openly mourn for her family's losses or call attention to herself as a foreigner with strong ties to the vanquished party—indeed, as will be discussed further later, the remaining aliens in her entourage were targeted yet again in 1416 and openly accused of working as spies for the enemy.[12]

Joan's son Arthur de Richemont was one of a host of elite prisoners along with her cousins the dukes of Orleans and Bourbon, the counts of Vendome and Eu, and Marshal Boucicaut, captured at the battle and brought back to England by Henry V. Jonathan Sumption commented that these high-ranking prisoners "followed in Henry's footsteps to be exhibited like trophies to the crowds in London and Westminster and decorate his court at Windsor. The English King had no intention of admitting them to ransom until it suited him politically".[13] Shortly after the battle, Arthur crossed the Channel in the entourage of the king along with the other prisoners from Calais to Dover on 16 November 1415 and was taken to London on 23 November. Once in London, Joan requested permission to see her son, which was granted by Henry V, even if Georges Toudouze suggests this was done grudgingly.[14]

According to the account of the *Chronique d'Arthur de Richemont*, the encounter between mother and son, long estranged after Joan's departure for England to wed Henry IV in 1403, was somewhat strained. The chronicle claims that Joan was keen to see if Arthur could recognise his mother and so hid among her ladies, placing one of them in her usual spot as if she was the queen. Arthur quite naturally addressed this lady as if she was indeed the queen, at which Joan berated him for being a bad son for failing to recognise his true mother and began to cry.[15] While the veracity of this account cannot be firmly established, the chronicle is a contemporary piece written by a Breton noble, Guillaume Gruel, whose brother Raoul apparently served Arthur and shared his English captivity.[16] However, Paul Strohm and Lisa Hilton have suggested that rather than recounting their actual encounter, this may be a story concocted to leverage tropes of mistaken identity common in medieval romances rather than a comment on her as a mother who had abandoned her son many years previously.[17]

While the chronicler notes that Joan generously provided money and clothing to ensure Arthur's comfort during his confinement, it appears that this was the last time that mother and son met according to his account. Yet there were certainly further opportunities for additional reunions during Arthur's captivity. Arthur was held in a number of places during his English captivity, including the Tower of London, Fotheringhay, Middleham, and Windsor, largely under the care of Sir Thomas Burton who was also responsible for Boucicault, the count of Eu, and later Joan's cousin Charles d'Orleans.[18] The exact conditions of his confinement are unclear—Sumption claims that Arthur and the other prominent prisoners were "accommodated in comfort and allowed some freedom of movement", while Toudouze and Knowlson have claimed that Arthur was held in fairly rigorous and unpleasant conditions, although this would be unusual for such a high-ranking prisoner, particularly given that he was the dowager queen's own son.[19] Whatever the actual circumstances of his imprisonment were, he was not strictly confined to a cell, was allowed to receive visitors such as his servant John Catin who received a safe conduct to visit Arthur in early 1417, and was even brought to court at various points, including for the visit/peace conference of Sigismund of Luxembourg in 1416.[20] The arrival of Sigismund was celebrated with intensive and lavish ceremonial, in which Joan would have no doubt played a prominent role as the premier lady of the land and Sigismund's cousin through her grandmother Bonne of Luxembourg. Arthur and other high-ranking prisoners played a prominent role in the conference as well, with Sigismund "treating them with conspicuous respect as if they were the true representatives of France".[21] It is very likely that Joan and Arthur's paths would have crossed here and potentially at other points when Arthur was brought to court for negotiations or held in any of the major residences such as the Tower or Windsor until at least late 1419.

Arthur's capture put Joan in a very difficult position both as Arthur's mother and as Henry V's stepmother. Queenly intercession was a key part of her role and Joan had successfully requested a number of pardons during the reign of her husband, Henry IV, as discussed in the previous chapter. Yet Arthur's release would be impossible for Joan to effect—he was far too valuable as a political prisoner and Joan had to be careful not to be seen as placing her loyalties to her own children and her relatives in Brittany and France above the good of her adopted realm in England. She did, however, attempt to mediate between the two realms for their mutual benefit and played a significant role in restoring or repairing relations between England and Brittany in the challenging period after Henry's victory at Agincourt.

In April 1417, a safe conduct was issued for Jean V to personally come to England—he does not appear to have crossed the Channel to see his brother and mother, but it did signal the start of another period of intensive contact and negotiation between England and Brittany.[22] Joan's trusted servant John Periaunt was dispatched across the Channel to Brittany instead, and rewarded the following month by Jean V in connection with his mission.[23] Henry crossed the Channel himself in August 1417 to begin another campaign in Normandy. After the brutal sack of Caen in September, Henry turned his focus on the Alençon lands, which were "defended with masculine determination" by Joan's daughter Marie, Alençon's widow and mother of the new young duke.[24] While Marie raised an impressive number of men in an attempt to defend her son's lands from the English, by the end of the month Henry had the territory under his control. Jean V was granted another safe conduct to come to Alençon to meet with Henry in October and promised that Brittany itself would be safe while he came to meet with the king.[25]

Apart from protecting his own duchy, Jean had familial motivations to treat with Henry, given that his sister's and nephew's lands had been seized by the English, as well as impetus from his mother, who was doubtless keen to see Brittany spared, her daughter and grandchildren protected, and her son and stepson reconciled. Indeed, the treaty signed by Henry and Jean in November 1417 was specifically noted as being "at the request and insistence of the most excellent and illustrious lady, queen, our mother as she desires peace and tranquillity" and noted that Jean was "our beloved brother and close relation" through their mutual connection to Joan.[26] In addition, Jean brokered a second treaty between Henry V and Yolande of Aragon, the recently widowed duchess of Anjou and titular queen of Jerusalem, who had recently become a virtual family member as Jean V had affianced his eldest daughter, Isabelle, to Yolande's son, the young duke of Anjou, just a few months earlier. Before his death, Louis II of Anjou had impressed upon his wife the need to ally with Jean V "whom he believed held the key to a lasting peace between the princes [of France]".[27] Yolande appears to have exerted a quasi-maternal influence on Jean and considerable impact on the political events of successive years as the mother-in-law of the dauphin (later Charles VII).

Perhaps Jean's political vacillations during the Hundred Years War could also be seen as the pull of two important women in his life—his mother on the Anglo-Burgundian side and Yolande, who became a significant power in the dauphin's Orleans-Armagnac camp. These near constant shifts might make Jean V appear wily; Richard Vaughan called him "an irresolute intriguer who managed to keep himself out of serious trouble and promote his own interests by shifting in and out of alliances with each of his powerful neighbours, and double-crossing them one after the other".[28] Yet while the Breton historian Saint-Saveur conceded that Jean V's strategies were "*une politique sans grandeur*", it did have the effect of preserving Brittany during a period of intense political turbulence which could have easily resulted in the invasion and destruction of his duchy if he had acted otherwise, and earned him the appellation of "*le Sage*".[29]

Like his nephew Jean V, and indeed like his father, Carlos II, Joan's brother Carlos III has been accused of prevaricating "*politique de bascule*", perhaps a result of having ties on all sides or creating ties on both sides of the conflict in order to ensure his realm's long-term security, which resulted in his reign being hailed as a golden age for Navarre. Sometimes this could result in somewhat contradictory moves—for example, in March 1418, when, as Eloísa Ramírez Vaquero notes, there was a "clear alienation" between Carlos III and the dauphin/Orleans-Armagnac party, he still agreed to contract a betrothal between his daughter Isabel and Jean, the Armagnac heir.[30] Jean d'Armagnac was the widower of Joan's daughter Blanche, so this marriage could be seen as a way of keeping this heir in the extended family. The Armagnac lands were strategically close to both Navarre and England's lands in Gascony and the family itself was obviously at the centre of the internal conflict in France—Jean d'Armagnac himself became even more important when his father, Bernard VII, was assassinated on 12 June 1418, making him the new count. But at the same time as Carlos contracted this betrothal for Isabel, he had dispatched his cousin and trusted diplomat Carlos de Beaumont back to England—indeed, Beaumont himself became involved in the Norman campaign and on 16 March 1418 he received the surrender of the castle of Hommet as the deputy of Joan's stepson Humphrey of Gloucester.[31] Again, this engagement with the campaign could also been seen as contradictory for Navarre, for in 1418 its key Norman port at Cherbourg was taken by the English as was Evreux, the dynasty's ancestral possession, from Joan's grandfather, Philip d'Evreux, husband of Juana II.

However inscrutable Carlos's political moves may have been during this period, Joan may have been the impetus for a further move to bring her homeland and marital home closer together, reinforcing this period of close cooperation, showing that she was an able and agile politician like her brother and son. Another of Joan's nieces, Blanca, the recently widowed queen of Sicily and designated heir to Carlos III's throne in Navarre, was an extremely desirable prize on the European marriage market with suitors across Europe making a play for her hand. In April 1419, Humphrey of Gloucester appointed ambassadors to negotiate a marriage with Blanca—as Humphrey appears to have been quite close to Joan, perhaps even her favourite stepson, it is likely that she encouraged this match, which could have resulted in Humphrey becoming king consort of Navarre. Concurrently, Henry V was continuing his negotiations with France, which included discussions for a marriage of his own with Joan's cousin, Katherine de Valois. Humphrey, however, was clearly too late to secure the Navarrese heiress; Beaumont immediately dispatched a missive to Henry V to inform him that a marriage for Blanca was already being negotiated with Juan, infante of Aragon, softening the rejection perhaps with a personal gift of a book to Henry V.[32]

While this gambit for an Anglo-Navarrese marriage was clearly unsuccessful, Joan was more effective in terms of keeping the peace between her son and stepson. The Anglo-Breton truce was extended in January 1419 and the following month Jean V was issued a safe conduct to come to Rouen, which Henry V had just secured after an extended siege.[33] In March 1419, the two signed another truce—the text of this document largely mirrors the November 1417 version, including the language that the peace had been made at Joan's insistence.[34] In addition to these political negotiations, as highlighted in Chapter 7, Joan was also engaged in a fairly intensive gift exchange between herself, her son, and her stepsons of valuable objects designed to reinforce these diplomatic meetings and ensure continued good relations between Joan's extended brood. With regard to Joan's extended Valois family, 1419 saw an increasingly charged political climate, with Henry negotiating with both sides of the internal division between the king and the duke of Burgundy on one hand and the dauphin and the Orleans-Armagnac faction on the other. The reconciliation of the duke of Burgundy and the dauphin in July threatened the possibility of a united French repulsion of Henry's army, driving him in turn to threaten Paris itself. The murder of the duke of Burgundy in early September changed the landscape once again, triggering a new round of intensive negotiations between Joan's stepson and her Valois relatives.

In this dramatic period we have seen Joan's deep connection to and engagement with political negotiations and the events of the war itself, showing that her familial influence could be felt even while remaining at a physical distance back in England. However, given her close ties to France, Navarre, and Brittany, and the constantly shifting line between being allies, enemies, and neutral regarding England, it was vital that her loyalty to Henry V was unquestioned—any suspicions could have disastrous implications.

Crisis years: 1419–22

After Agincourt, Henry V's biographer Hutchinson noted the heightened state of xenophobia and religious panic and argued that Joan, as a foreign queen who had been an adherent of the anti-pope during the Schism, might be a natural target for persecution.[35] As noted previously, the foreigners in her household had been the object of another round of purges of aliens in 1416 when they were accused of being spies—indeed it has been suggested that the queen may have been the primary suspect as Joan's "subjects believed that she was an enemy agent planted in their midst".[36] In 1419, a specific member of her household was the focus of investigation: her confessor, the Franciscan friar John Randolph. On 16 August, Henry's kinswoman lady Bergevenny was commissioned to seize Randolph's goods from the Franciscan house in Shrewsbury and her man Richard Pepyr duly reported the findings of the raid to the king's council later that month.[37] Randolph himself may have already fled at that point as he was arrested in Guernsey and taken to Henry V in Normandy—after being held at Chateau Gaillard, he was sent to the Tower of London in February 1420.[38]

Randolph's evidence led back to his mistress, Joan, although it is unclear if the friar accused her with evidence which broke the ecclesiastical seal of the confessional. In addition to his testimony, Joan was further implicated by their close relationship and the fact that Randolph clearly had a large quantity of the queen's own goods when an inventory of his possessions in Shrewsbury was taken.[39] At the beginning of October 1419 Joan herself was arrested and it was alleged in Parliament that Joan had "plotted and schemed for the death and destruction of our said lord the king in the most evil and terrible manner imaginable".[40]

The language is vitally important here—what is suggested is that Joan was contriving the king's death, a serious and treasonable act to which Henry would have been particularly sensitive, given the plots against his life and his father's during the previous reign and the assassinations of two Burgundian dukes, the duke of Orleans, and the count of Armagnac across the Channel. What is critically not included here is the word "witchcraft", although that has become intrinsically associated with this charge and, indeed, in many ways has defined Joan's memory as a so-called "royal witch". The accusation of witchcraft was added by chroniclers—the *Brut* and the *Chronicles of London* have virtually identical language here which has been extremely influential on later reporting and perception of Joan's arrest:

> And in this yeer Randolff, Maistre off Dyvynyte, that some time was Quene Johannys confessour, wrouht, as men seyn thurh the excytyng off the sayde Quene, by sorcerye and nygromancye fforto haue dystroyed the king. But as god wolde alle his vnthryffty werking was espyed. Wherfore the same Quene loste her lands, and was putte into the castell off Ledys vndir the kepyng off Sir John Pelham, knyht.[41]

This particular chronicle places much more focus on Randolph; indeed there is far more discussion of Humphrey of Gloucester's failed attempt to spring the Franciscan, whom he also had ties to, from the Tower in 1425 than the queen's arrest or fate. However, it is important to note not all contemporary chronicles described Joan's detainment in the context of supposed "sorcery"—Walsingham's chronicle, one of the most important for this period of English history, notes,

> In this year the widow of the late King Henry, Queen Joanna, was accused of an evil deed, namely of having plotted to harm the king. All her servants were taken from her and she was given into the custody of John Pelham. He allowed her nine serving women and took her into Pevensey castle that he might keep her guarded there under his care.[42]

Walsingham's version of events more closely mirrors the language recorded in Parliament—while both note that Pelham was her jailor, she was in his keeping at Pevensey but was later transferred to Leeds Castle in Kent.[43] And as will be discussed further in the following chapter, she did indeed lose her lands—for some historians, this has been seen as the primary motivation for her arrest.

The motivation—and the context—of Joan's arrest are important to unpick and understand as this move on Henry's part to accuse his stepmother of a serious crime and detain her for several years has long attracted comment for its surprising volte-face after years of good relations and cooperation between the two. E. Carlton Williams has suggested three possible motivations for Joan's arrest. First, as noted above, the repeated calls for the expulsion of foreigners from her household suggests that many may have believed that she was in league with the enemy and conveying information via her servitors.[44] The second reason given was a desire to repurpose Joan's dower for the use of Henry's campaigns, potentially adding another 10,000 marks per annum to the war effort. While many historians have given great credence to this, and indeed this may well have been a key factor in Henry's decision to seize her lands, a counter argument is whether this comparatively small sum in the larger scheme of his military financing would have been worth the approbation of levelling such a serious charge on his aging stepmother.[45] The third rationale given was the possibility that her accusation stemmed from a real concern about witchcraft—Williams notes that only a few weeks before her arrest Archbishop Chichele had ordered prayers to be said in all churches in the realm to protect the king from witchcraft. The Breton historian Toudouze suggests a fourth possibility, that Joan's arrest and the possibility that she could be burned at the stake was blackmail for her sons, to ensure their good behaviour and cooperation with the English.[46]

Yet another possibility was that Henry sought to neutralise her and her influence at court and on the political negotiations of the Hundred Years War by detaining her on a charge as a possible traitor which also tainted her reputation. Henry may have given credence to the repeated accusations of spies in her household, and he may well have worried whether her loyalties lay with him and England or with her Breton, Navarrese, and French relations. Again, Henry had been the focus of several plots and would have been extremely concerned if Randolph had been involved in a genuine conspiracy. As Gwen Seabourne notes, political conflict is often a context for imprisonment, and suspected traitors could be held without trial, which is exactly what happened with Joan.[47] She was never formally charged with the very serious crime of treason—or witchcraft—and thus never had to face the court, so Henry did not need to worry that his stepmother would be found guilty, necessitating the unsavoury prospect of executing her and seriously alienating Brittany and Navarre, nor would she be liberated and restored to her lands, making him look unreasonable for detaining her in the first place.[48] Yet if he was truly concerned that

Joan was a dangerous traitor, Henry would never have allowed her to live in comfortable confinement in a series of royal residences and entertain revered guests including the archbishop of Canterbury, his brother Humphrey of Gloucester, and his friend Thomas, Lord Camoys, who appeared to remain with Joan at Leeds Castle for nearly a year.[49]

However, the lack of trial also meant that Joan could not clear herself of the charge and repair the damage to her reputation as a potential traitor—or this slur that she was a possible witch, which may have been attached to her name thanks to her father's reputation as a poisoner who may have dabbled in necromancy as well. Queens are often brought down or attacked on reputations, often in terms of an allegation of sexual impropriety, although Joan became one of several royal women who were also tainted with an allegation or insinuation of being involved in witchcraft, including her stepdaughter-in-law, Humphrey's second wife Eleanor Cobham, who was tried for the offence in 1441.[50] It has to be said that the arrest of his stepmother on nefarious charges and her prolonged detention has not been beneficial to assessments of Henry V's character and became a stain on his own reputation as a conscientious king. If the king seriously believed that his stepmother was a traitor, a witch, and potential murderer and did nothing more than keep her under house arrest, it would make him look rather weak for failing to punish her for her crimes. Yet it is not weakness that Henry has been accused of by multiple historians, but greed and avarice—the same charge that others have levelled against Joan—as well as a distinct lack of chivalrous behaviour against his stepmother. For example, Hutchison has argued that "Henry's treatment of his step-mother scarcely did him honour", while another biographer, Bryan Bevan, claims that Joan's arrest demonstrates the "hard, very unattractive side" of Henry's character—very much at odds with his reputation as a "conscientious" king.[51]

Returning to the wider picture, by late 1419 both Arthur de Richemont and his mother Joan of Navarre were Henry V's prisoners. However, the situation for Joan and her children was about to escalate significantly. As noted previously, Joan's first husband, Jean IV, had fought a rival branch of the family, the Penthièvres, for the right to the ducal coronet throughout his life and reign. Indeed, Joan's marriage to Jean IV had been motivated by his desire to produce issue which would ensure the continuation of the Montfort line and keep the Penthièvres from retaking the duchy. As Joan produced a large brood of children, including four sons, the success of the Montfort line seemed assured, yet the Penthièvres had never given up hope of regaining the duchy of Brittany. By 1420, Jean V had been on the ducal throne for 20 years and was seemingly secure except for the constantly shifting political landscape of the Hundred Years War. As the count of Penthièvre had "showed great outward marks of affection" to Jean V, the duke may not have suspected that he was, in fact, working with the dauphin to develop a plot to capture him. According to Enguerrand de Monstrelet, the trap was baited with an invitation to dine with the count's mother, Marguerite de Clisson; the date was set for 13 February and the count and his party rode out to meet Jean, his brother Richard, and their entourage at the bridge of la Tuberbe.[52] After the duke and his brother crossed the bridge, the count's fool apparently removed some planks and made a joke that they would not be able to leave, which Jean V found extremely amusing until the count's brother, Charles d'Avagour, sprung out from hiding with his men and ambushed them. Penthièvre claimed that he was arresting Jean in the dauphin's name and to reclaim the duchy which was rightfully his.

Jean and his brother Richard were taken into captivity and like Arthur and Joan across the Channel were moved around a number of secure Penthièvre strongholds and through dauphinist territory during the course of their imprisonment. Sources vary as to how Jean and Richard were treated—Monstrelet claims that they were kept relatively reasonably with a valet to serve them and that "no violence was done to their person", but Sumption argues that Jean was repeatedly coerced by Marguerite and her sons and "threatened with hideous tortures and death" if he refused to cooperate and cede the duchy, particularly as the tide turned against his captors.[53]

FIGURE 4.1 Illustration of Joan and her three sons imprisoned, from Garrett MS. 40, "Missal, Carmelite use (French c. 1440–76)", folio 111r.

Source: Manuscripts Division, Department of Rare Books and Special Collections, Princeton University Library. Image supplied for use courtesy of Princeton University Library.

Jean's wife, the French princess Jeanne de Valois, was at the city of Vannes when she received news of her husband's capture on 15 February. She sprang into action, calling a council and convening the Estates of Brittany to support the duke and work for his immediate release, calling on every possible source of aid from her networks in France and beyond. The decision was taken to confiscate all Penthièvre lands and effectively go to war against the family, attacking their territories, beginning with the castle and town of Lamballe, which surrendered after only 15 days of siege, only to be gutted by the victors, indicating the depth of ferocity with which the Bretons responded to the seizure of their duke. Unsurprisingly, the Penthièvres' allies quickly deserted them as the Breton army continued to attack and take their castles and lands, including Castle Andren and la Motte d'Ebron. Jeanne de Valois also appealed to

Henry V for assistance—using emotional language designed to illicit a chivalric response to assist the duchess as a "damsel in distress", noting multiple times how extremely upset she was and appealing to Henry as a prince who had "a reputation for being honourable and valiant".[54]

The duchess pleaded not just for Henry's general assistance but specifically for the release of Jean's brother, Arthur de Richemont, so that he could come back to Brittany to lead the campaign against the Penthièvres and effect the rescue of Jean V and Richard. Arthur immediately added his request to Henry V to release him so that he could help his brothers and also asked the king to punish the count of Penthièvre for his treasonous actions to his liege lord the duke.[55] A Breton delegation, led by Jean de Malestroit, bishop of Nantes, went to meet with Henry V to negotiate Arthur's release but were unable to bring him home quickly to free his brothers Jean and Richard in turn. While Jonathan Sumption claims that Henry was willing to release Arthur so that he could retake Jean from the count of Penthièvre and his allies, Marie-Hélène Santrot has argued that Henry V hated Arthur and had no intention of liberating him, whether his brothers were in danger or not.[56] Indeed, some historians have questioned whether it was Henry V himself who was behind Jean V's detention, which occurred during the crucial period when the Treaty of Troyes was being negotiated, which resulted in Henry's marriage to Katherine de Valois, effectively securing the French throne. It seems more likely that since the dauphin appears to have been behind the seizure of the duke and his brother, the dauphin was the one who sought to neutralise Jean V and Brittany, but Knowlson argues that even if Henry did not instigate the situation, he "sought to profit from [these] complicated circumstances".[57] Certainly he was holding all the cards at this point, with Arthur and Joan detained under his pleasure, and by withholding Arthur from Brittany, they lacked his strong leadership and the potential that he might be able to quickly secure Jean and Richard's release and crush the Penthièvres.

In the end, Jean and Richard were released fairly swiftly without the assistance of Arthur de Richemont or Henry V. The campaign that the duchess and the Estates waged against the Penthièvres was so successful that the rebel family was effectively brought to its knees, with Marguerite de Clisson under siege in their stronghold at Champtoceaux. Although Jean V agreed fairly outrageous terms for his release with the Penthièvres, which included not only the restoration of all the Penthièvre strongholds but a marriage with the duke's daughter which would include a massive dowry of three major ducal castles, the Estates of Brittany flatly refused to comply with the treaty Jean signed after he was restored to liberty.[58] This situation had a few significant outcomes: it signalled the total domination of the Montfort dynasty in Brittany and the end of the threat of the Penthièvres as their Breton lands were lost, and the count and several of his brothers ended up in exile in Hainault where he had other territory—Marguerite faced trial in Brittany for her part in plotting the seizure of the duke. Another outcome was that Brittany was, temporarily at least, pushed back into the arms of the English. Although Henry V had not released Arthur in time to help his brothers escape from the Penthièvres, he did allow Arthur to meet his brother at Pontorson in the autumn of 1420 to convince him of the need to side with the English—Carlton Williams claimed that Henry believed Arthur's "forceful" personality would be certain to win Jean over.[59] Arthur himself was paroled until Michaelmas 1422 on the condition that he would fight for Henry V "against everyone other than his older brother".[60]

Thus by late 1420, Joan's three sons, Arthur, Jean, and Richard, were back at liberty after their respective detainments. Yet Joan was still held in England, and it appears her release was not high on her sons' or stepsons' agenda—indeed, in 1422 Arthur was attending the festivities for Henry V's wedding in Paris, while in Brittany Jean V worked to seize Joan's lucrative Breton dower, just as Henry V had seized her English lands back in 1419. Joan's Navarrese family do not appear to have protested openly about her imprisonment either—they may have felt unable to do so, given that Henry V was making himself master of France and held some of their own patrimony in northern France. In 1421, a year of intensive diplomatic negotiation in the context of the wider European political situation, Navarrese documents record preparation and expenses for the visits of the ambassadors from France, Burgundy, and England and messengers going back and forth between Brittany and Navarre.[61] It is impossible to say with certainty, however, if Joan's situation was part of these negotiations, messages, and discussions.

Joan's children may not have been any more proactive in trying to secure her release than her Navarrese relatives, which may have been due to political and diplomatic reasons or it could be seen as evidence of alienation from their mother who had left them in Brittany nearly 20 years previously. While Strickland claims that the bishop of Nantes was sent by Jean V to Henry V with an embassy to demand Joan's freedom, it appears that Strickland misunderstood the focus of negotiations on securing the release of Joan's son Arthur, or possibly misinterpreted the duchess of Brittany's appeal to Henry V for the release of Jean V from the Penthièvres.[62] Yet while her children may not have petitioned for her release while in captivity, they do appear to have tagged a rider onto negotiations between the duke of Burgundy and the Estates of Brittany in April 1423, ironically more than seven months after she was actually released, to secure the "pardon of their mother" so that she might be able to return to visit them in Brittany "in innocence and liberty".[63]

Ultimately, Joan's release came in the summer of 1422 in the midst of more political negotiations. Henry drafted a letter to release Joan on 13 July, just as Breton ambassadors were being dispatched to swear fidelity to the terms of the Treaty of Troyes.[64] It is not clear if Joan was released for political expediency, if new evidence came to light, or if the guilt about his treatment of his stepmother as his health was failing from dysentery motivated him to let her go—he died on 31 August 1422, roughly six weeks after this letter was composed. Although Joan is not fully exonerated by the letter, Henry twice notes a lack of certainty over the basis of her arrest—"we doubting lest it shuld be a charge unto our conscience" and "whiche charge we be avisid no longer to ber in our conscience"—indicating perhaps that he did not want to go to his death with Joan's detention weighing on his mind. Henry further notes that her dower and all of her moveable goods should be fully restored to her, along with cloth for five or six gowns and that she should be free to "remoeve thens into what o(th)er place wythin owre roiume that hir lust, and whanne her lust".

Final years: 1422–37

After Joan's release in 1422, she appears to have lived a quieter life in terms of politics and ceremonial, largely away from the court of her step-grandson Henry VI; as we will see in the following chapters, she was still incredibly active, working intensively on the full restoration of her lands and rights and maintaining a sufficiently grand household for a dowager queen. In addition to her multiple petitions regarding her own lands, Joan also continued to engage in intercessory activity for others, including a petition in 1427 to request an inquisition regarding the activities of a member of Parliament, Thomas Makworth, who had been working with a group of local men to prevent the people of Derby from attending the market in the neighbouring town of Ashbourne.[65] Yet she was no longer the only queen in the realm, as her cousin Katherine de Valois was also a dowager after the death of Henry V, and as she was the mother of the new young king, her position at court was clearly going to be superior to the king's step-grandmother. The downgrading of her position can be seen in subtle ways; Joan had once been a member of both the chivalric Breton Order of the Hermine, created by her first husband Jean IV, and became a lady of the Order of Garter in England, receiving robes throughout the reign of her second husband Henry IV and in the early years of Henry V's reign as well. However, she stopped receiving Garter robes when she was detained and did not receive them again in the reign on Henry VI—while Chloë McKenzie's research shows that the overall number of the Ladies of the Garter radically decreased under the reign of Henry VI, other prominent ladies at court such as Katherine de Valois; Humphrey's two wives, Jaqueline of Hainault and Eleanor Cobham; and the countesses of Warwick and Suffolk received robes, thus her omission from the list could still be seen as a sign of her reduced status at court or that her reputation had not fully recovered from the accusation of treason in the previous reign.[66]

In the remaining years of Joan's life, the political landscape continued to be turbulent and relations between England and Brittany fluctuated between periods of war and peace. A year after Henry V's death on 17 April 1423, a treaty of alliance was signed between the dukes of Bedford (on behalf of the young Henry VI), Brittany, and Burgundy.[67] The alliance was reinforced by marriages between the three—Burgundy's two sisters, Anne and Margaret, were married, respectively, to Bedford and Arthur de Richemont. On the other side of the political front, Joan's youngest son, Richard, was confirmed as count d'Etampes by the dauphin (later Charles VII) and made an important marriage around this same time to Marguerite d'Orleans, countess of Vertus and daughter of the murdered Louis d'Orleans and Valentina Visconti.[68]

Joan's stepson Humphrey also made a marriage in 1423 with significant political import, to Jacqueline, the countess of Hainault—in contrast to the previous marriages which had affirmed alliances and allegiances, this marriage threatened to undermine the Anglo-Burgundian relationship as Jacqueline's inheritance in the Low Countries was a matter of active dispute with the duke. Humphrey's campaigns on his new wife's behalf in Hainault the following year did little to relieve the political tension, with Philip the Good challenging Humphrey to a duel in order to resolve the situation—the prospect of a fight between her favourite stepson and her cousin might have seriously worried Joan.[69] Humphrey caused further scandal by abandoning both the campaign and Jacqueline of Hainault to return to England in 1425 with his mistress, Eleanor Cobham, one of Jacqueline's ladies in waiting, whom he eventually wed when his marriage to Jacqueline was declared void in 1428. As we will see in Chapter 7, Joan appears to have been quite close to Eleanor and the couple visited her several times during her later years at her manor of Kings Langley.

In 1425 tensions heightened on various fronts surrounding Joan. Back home in England, Humphrey found himself increasingly pitted against Henry Beaufort, the bishop of Winchester (who had officiated at Henry and Joan's 1403 wedding) for control of the king's council. Across the Channel, Yolande of Aragon had recruited Joan's son Arthur away from the Triple Alliance of Bedford,

Burgundy, and Brittany and back to the side of the dauphin—he was made constable of France on 7 March 1425. As noted previously, Joan's youngest son, Richard d'Etampes, was already an adherent of the dauphin and recruiting Jean V was now vital to create the "triumvirate of Yolande, Brittany and Richemont" that the queen of Jerusalem desired, aided perhaps by the Breton duchess Jeanne de Valois, who was supportive of her brother's cause.[70] On 7 October 1425, Jean V signed the Treaty of Saumur, which effectively broke Brittany's alliance with England and Burgundy and pledged himself to support the dauphin instead—England responded by declaring open war on Brittany in January 1426.[71]

As the mother of the now avowed enemy, Joan's loyalties were again suspect and the following month yet another petition to expel aliens from her household was brought forward to Parliament, arguing that these "foreigners reveal the advice given to the king to his enemies overseas".[72] Brittany itself was invaded as far as Rennes, where Joan had long ago orchestrated Jean V's ducal coronation—and battles were fought at St James de Beuvron and Pontorson on the Breton-Norman border where Arthur sought to help his brother's beleaguered duchy.[73] To bring peace to Brittany, Jean V reopened talks with England in July 1427, and after Henry VI promised to maintain Brittany's privileges if he switched sides again, Jean agreed to a truce on 8 September which reaffirmed both the terms of the Treaty of Troyes and his allegiance to the English king.[74] Again familial language was used as a key element in diplomacy, with Henry referring to Jean as "my very dear and beloved uncle" which he was through both his relationship to Joan and via Jean's marriage to his aunt Jeanne de Valois.

While Joan would have no doubt been relieved both that Brittany was safe from English attack and that her son was allied with her stepsons again, Jean's reunification with England meant a break with his brothers, Arthur and Richard, who remained allied to the dauphin and, along with Joan's grandson, the duke of Alençon, took part in campaigns with Jeanne d'Arc. This was not the only point of animosity between her children, as in September 1431 Alençon took Jean de Malestroit hostage—this was Jean V's trusted councillor who had connections with Joan and had been with him since the start of his reign; Malestroit was so close to the duke of Brittany that de la Martinère suggests he was a father figure for him.[75] Alençon took Malestroit to the castle of Pouancé, which was shortly besieged by his uncles Jean V and Arthur de Richemont and his cousin François, the heir of Brittany, who had recently married Yolande d'Anjou, along with a supporting Anglo-Breton force. Joan's daughter Marie and Alençon's pregnant wife were inside the castle—it is worth considering how Marie must have felt to be besieged by her brothers and nephew or Joan's feelings back in England on hearing of this family debacle. Fortunately, a peace was brokered between Alençon and his uncles, the siege was lifted, and the chancellor returned, but this was a dangerous rift within the family which could have had deadly consequences.

Yet the 1430s were not completely dominated by division in the family. A major olive branch to build connections between England and Brittany came in 1432 with the arrival of Joan's young grandson Gilles, the namesake of her son who died 20 years previously at the siege of Bourges. Gilles was a similar age to the young Henry VI and the two appear to have bonded deeply—creating a lasting Anglophile leaning for Gilles which had profound consequences in later life.[76] This was an effective strategy for creating connections as an alternative to marriage—Jean V also sent his son Richard to be raised at the French court, again always playing both sides and leveraging his own familial connections and his sons' Valois blood through their mother Jeanne.[77] Gilles was brought to England by his father's right-hand man, Jean de Malestroit, who was engaging in ongoing political negotiations in connection with the trip. Joan appears to have been involved with the talks as in the following year letters from Henry VI to Jean V reference Joan "sending charge" to the receivers of her dower lands in Brittany to pay the outstanding balance of the ransom of some English prisoners from the revenues of her lands there in an attempt to heal this bone of contention between the two realms.[78] Gilles was hosted by Richard Beauchamp, earl of Warwick, who had long ago been Joan's champion during the jousting celebrating her coronation. There is no clear record of Gilles' interaction with Joan, but it is highly likely that she met with him during the two years that he was at the English court or that he may have visited her at one of her residences.

Diplomatic links between England and Navarre continued during this period, with flurries of activity; one of these was between 1423 and 1425 when John Gentill was dispatched on a diplomatic trip to visit the courts of all the Iberian monarchs (a repeat of the trip he took around the period of Henry V's Agincourt campaign) and the Navarrese ambassador Johanin Forment also visited England in 1424, shortly after a trip to Brittany.[79] Another Navarrese ambassador, Gracian de Monreal, along with Johan Galindo, the merino of Sangüesa, and Johan de Ezpleta, visited England in early 1430 in conjunction with ambassadors from Aragon—at this point, Joan's brother Carlos III had passed away and the kingdom was ruled by his daughter Blanca I and her husband Juan of Aragon.[80] At this time Navarre and Aragon were in conflict with Castile and appear to have sought an alliance with England to support their position—potentially sealed with a marriage between one of their daughters and Henry VI himself which would have brought another Navarrese queen to England to follow in Joan's footsteps. However, the response of the privy council acknowledged the long-standing good relations between England, the Navarrese, and Aragon, but was somewhat cagey—although Philip Gentill was sent to treat for an alliance with the Navarrese and Aragonese ambassadors at Bayonne later that year, the English concurrently signed a one-year truce with Castile.[81] Further interchange took place between England and Navarre with Navarrese embassies in 1433 and 1436, as well as interesting evidence of an English musician, Master Johan, who spent an extended period at the court of Joan's niece Blanca I as her "royal harper"—while it is impossible to say if Joan's musical patronage extended this far, it does show continued contact between the two realms through various means.[82]

In the 1430s, Joan was clearly reaching her twilight years in her seventh decade—her household records from 1427–8 note a period of serious illness during this time and expenses for doctors and medicine. Yet in spite of this illness, Joan survived many of her peers, children, and stepchildren—her stepson Thomas of Clarence passed away in 1421, his sister Philippa, queen of Sweden, died in 1430, and John of Bedford in 1435, leaving only Humphrey of Gloucester out of her brood of stepchildren. Her cousin, the diplomat Carlos de Beaumont who once served as her chamberlain, died in 1432 in his early seventies. Joan's daughter-in-law and cousin, Jeanne de Valois, duchess of Brittany, passed away a year later in 1433, and her sister Katherine de Valois, the dowager queen of England, followed her only a few years later, in January 1437. Ironically, Katherine's death briefly left Joan once again as the only queen in England and theoretically the most senior woman in the realm, but age and poor health meant she was in no position to take up a strong ceremonial role; instead her daughter-in-law Eleanor Cobham could be seen as filling this space as a "quasi-queen" in this period.

The last ceremonial of Joan's queenly career—and her life—was her funeral at Canterbury Cathedral. We have a letter from Henry VI which gives us an impression of the event. He notes that

> oure counsail have appointed the funerelles of oure graundmodre Quene Johane whom God assoille to be holden and solempnized at Caunterbury the xi (11th) day of August next coming where we have appointed our saide uncle and other lordes and ladyes of this our reaume … to be present at the same day to the worship of God of us and oure saide graundmodre.[83]

A list follows of those who were to attend the funeral, headed by Humphrey, duke of Gloucester, and his wife Eleanor Cobham—a suitable choice as Joan's favourite (and only remaining) stepson who at this time was a key figure in the politics of the realm. The archbishop of Canterbury was also in attendance and likely officiated at the event—possibly along with the three bishops, two abbots, and two priors who were also present. There was also a selection of important nobles, including the duchess of Norfolk and the earls and countesses of Huntington, Northumbria, and Oxford. It could be argued that Joan's funeral was perhaps not as grand or as impactful as that of her predecessors Philippa of Hainault and Anne of Bohemia, as they were consort queens when they died, while Joan was the relic of two reigns past and only the king's step-grandmother. Yet the illustrious guests in attendance and the splendour of the location would have conferred considerable glory to her memory and been a suitably queenly send-off. When word of Joan's death arrived in Navarre in the autumn of 1437, 42 libros were spent on wax and torches and 30 requiem Masses which were said for repose of her soul, a final ceremonial touch which showed that her niece Blanca I and her natal family had not forgotten her either. As noted in the final chapter of the book, Joan was laid to rest alongside her second husband, Henry IV, in the tomb she had created for them both at Canterbury Cathedral, which heralded for all time Joan's many identities—as Navarrese infanta, Breton duchess, and England's queen.

Notes

1 See CCR Henry V, I, 2 June 1413, 21–22 and 12 August 1413, 33. In Foedera 9, see entries on negotiations or reaffirmations of the truce on 14 December 1413, 3 and 4 January 1414, 4 February 1414, 12 February 1414, 18 April 1414, 26 June 1414, 17 October 1414, and 20 August 1415. See also L&M JV, V, nos. 1150–51, 10 August 1413, no. 1196, 25 June 1415, and ADLA E121-17, 17 October 1414.

2 Jonathan Sumption, *Cursed Kings: The Hundred Years War IV* (London: Faber and Faber, 2016), 380 and 394–96.

3 Eloísa Ramírez Vaquero, *Carlos III, rey de Navarra, Principe de sangre Valois (1387–1425)* (Gijon: Ediciones Trea, 2007), 234–6 and Catalogo XXXI, no. 647, 30 November 1414.

4 CPR Henry V, I, 30 June 1415, 342. There is some divergence as to whether Henry took his leave of the queen on the 15th or 16th of June; Harold F. Hutchinson, *Henry V* (London: Eyre and Spottiswoode, 1967), 102; Ian Mortimer, *1415: Henry V's Year of Glory* (London: Bodley Head, 2009), 240.

5 Foedera 9, 11 August 1415. See also John Stow, *The annales, or generall chronicle of England, begun first by maister Iohn Stow, and after him continued and augmented with matters forreyne, and domestique, anncient and moderne, vnto the ende of his present yeere 1614*, ed. Edmond Howes (London: T. Adams, 1615), 346; Edward Hall, *Hall's Chronicle: Containing the history of England during the reign of Henry the Fourth and the succeeding monarchs...* (London: J. Johnson et al., 1809), 59.

6 Anon., *Geste des nobles François* (1420s) and Jean Juvenal des Ursins, "Histoire de Charles VI, roy de France (c.1430s–1440s)," in *The Battle of Agincourt: Sources and Interpretations*, ed. Anne Curry (Woodbridge:

Boydell, 2000), 111 and 131. Note that Philippe Contamine argues that while some French historians have accused Jean V of cowardice, an alternative explanation is that the French refused to wait for the Breton troops which might have saved them: Philippe Contamine, "Bretagne et France a la fin du Moyen Age: le temps de Jean V, de Charles VII et de Jeanne d'Arc," *Bulletin de la Societe Archeologique et Historique de Nantes et de Loire-Atlantique* 127 (1991): 78.

7 Monstrelet, III, 119. However, Rosemary Horrox notes that accounts of the duke of York's death at Agincourt do differ—he may even have suffocated in his armour: Rosemary Horrox, "Edward [Edward of Langley, Edward of York], second duke of York (c. 1373–1415), magnate," ODNB online, 23 Sep. 2004.

8 Michael Drayton, "The Battaile of Agincourt (1627)," in *The Battle of Agincourt: Sources and Interpretations*, ed. Anne Curry (Woodbridge: Boydell, 2000), 326–28.

9 Alessandra Petrina, *Cultural Politics in 15th century England: The Case of Humphrey, Duke of Gloucester* (Leiden: Brill, 2004), 106–7.

10 William Gregory, "Gregory's Chronicle: 1403–1419," in *The Historical Collections of a Citizen of London in the Fifteenth Century*, ed. James Gairdner (London: Camden Society, 1876), 103–28, British History Online, accessed June 7, 2019, http://www.british-history.ac.uk/camden-record-soc/vol17/pp103-128.

11 Agnes Strickland, *Lives of the Queens of England from the Norman Conquest; with Anecdotes of their Courts*. vol. III (Philadelphia: Lea and Blanchard, 1848), 72. Note Strickland wrongly claims that "Her brother, Charles of Navarre, the constable of France, died of his wounds the following day"—her brother Carlos III was not present at the battle, nor was Carlos de Beaumont, the aforementioned alferez who is sometimes referred to in English records as "Charles of Navarre", harmed either, so it is unclear who Strickland is mentioning here.

12 PROME, Henry V: March 1416, IX "Bretons".

13 Sumption, *Cursed Kings*, 466.

14 Georges G. Toudouze, *Du Gueslin, Clisson, Richemont et la fin de la Guerre de Cent Ans* (Paris: Librarie Floury, 1942), 222–23.

15 Guillaume Gruel, *Chronique d'Arthur de Richemont, Connetable de France, Duc de Bretagne (1393–1458)*, ed. Achille le Vavasseur (Paris, Librairie Renouard, 1890), 19–20.

16 Auguste Moliner, *Les Sources de l'Histoire de France* (Paris: Alfonse Picard et Fils, 1904), 255–56.

17 See Woodacre, "Perils of Promotion," 135–36; Lisa Hilton, *Queens Consort; England's Medieval Queens* (London: Phoenix, 2009), 367; Paul Strohm, *England's Empty Throne: Usurpation and the Language of Legitimation 1399–1422* (New Haven, CT: Yale University Press, 1998), 169.

18 See payment to Burton on 20 May 1419 in Frederick Devon, *Issues of the Exchequer being a collection of payments made out of His Majesty's Revenue,*

from King Henry III to King Henry VI inclusive with an appendix (London: John Murray, 1837), 358, and Jean Kerhervé, "Arthur de Richemont, connetable et duc, Entre guerre et politique, dans la France du XVe siècle," in *2000 Ans d'Histoire de Vannes* (Vannes: Archives Municipales, 1993), 106.

19 Toudouze, *Richemont*, 223–24; Sumption, *Cursed Kings*, 491; Knowlson, *Jean V*, 111.
20 Foedera 9, 4 January 1417.
21 Sumption, *Cursed Kings*, 492.
22 Foedera 9, 13 April 1417.
23 L&M JV, V, no. 1241, 29 May 1417.
24 Sumption, *Cursed Kings*, 543. See also Cagny, *Chroniques*, 111–12.
25 Foedera 9, 16 and 27 October. A contemporary chronicle claimed that Jean's motivation was to do homage to Henry, claiming "came the Duke of Brytayne vnto be kynge and became his mon": Anon., *English Chronicle*, 48.
26 Foedera 9, 16 November 1417, original text is "*Precibus & Instantiis, Excellentissimae & Praeclarissimae Dominae, Reginae, Matris nostrae, ac Pacis & Tranquillitatis desiderio*".
27 Foedera 9, 16 November 1417. See also Zita Eva Rohr, *Yolande of Aragon (1381–1442) Family and Power: The Reverse of the Tapestry* (New York: Palgrave Macmillan, 2016), 92 and 97–100.
28 Richard Vaughan, *Philip the Good: The Apogee of Burgundy* (Woodbridge: Boydell, 1970), 9.
29 See E. Durtelle de Saint-Saveur, *Histoire de Bretagne des origines a nos jours* (Paris: Perrin et Armor-editeur, 1975), 287–88, 290–91; Jean Markale, *Les Grandes Heures de la Bretagne* (Paris: Pygmalion, 2008), 374–76.
30 Ramírez Vaquero, *Carlos III*, 242.
31 Foedera 9, 16 March 1418.
32 Foedera 9, 1 April 1419 for the licence to Humphrey to appoint ambassadors for matrimonial negotiations; 28 April 1419 for the missives regarding Blanca's betrothal and the gift of the book.
33 Extension of the truce: Foedera 9, 12 January 1419. Safe conduct for Jean V: Foedera 9, 12 Feb 1419.
34 ADLA E121-24, 19 March 1419.
35 Hutchinson, *Henry V*, 201.
36 E. Carlton Williams, *My Lord of Bedford, 1389–1435* (London: Longmans Green, 1963), 10.
37 CPR Henry V, II, 271, 16 August 1419; Devon, *Issues of the Exchequer*, 20 August 1419, 360.
38 Devon, *Issues of the Exchequer*, 20 February 1420, 365.
39 See A. Keith Thompson, *Religious Confession Privilege, and the Common Law* (Leiden: Martinus Nijhoff, 2011), 3, 49–50, and 99 n56. The contents of the inventory will be discussed further in Chapter 7.
40 PROME, "Henry V: October 1419".

41 Anon., *The Chronicles of London*, introduction and notes by Charles L. Kingsford (Oxford: Clarendon Press, 1905), 73. See also Kingsford's discussion of the relationship between the text of the Brut and this Julius II B version of the *Chronicles of London*: Charles Lethbridge Kingsford, ed., *English Historical Literature in the Fifteenth Century* (Oxford: Clarendon Press, 1913), 118. For a more recent evaluation of the London chronicles and their relationship to the Brut, see Mary-Rose McLaren, *The London Chronicles of the Fifteenth Century* (London: D.S. Brewer, 2002).

42 Walsingham, 434.

43 For payment to John Pelham as her jailor, see Devon, *Issues of the Exchequer*, 27 Nov 1419, 362. Note: her movements during this period will be discussed in connection with her residences in Chapter 7 and the situation of her household in Chapter 6.

44 Carlton Williams, *Bedford*, 48–9.

45 A.R. Myers, "The Captivity of a Royal Witch: The Household Accounts of Queen Joan of Navarre, 1419–21," *Bulletin of the John Rylands Library* 24, no. 2 (1940): 275–76; Labarge, *Henry V*, 151; Hutchinson, *Henry V*, 200–1; Strohm, *Empty Throne,* 163–66; Gemma Hollman, *Royal Witches: From Joan of Navarre to Elizabeth Woodville* (Cheltenham: The History Press, 2019), 63–5. For the context of Henry V's efforts to finance the war effort, see W. Mark Ormrod, "Henry V and the English Taxpayer," in *Henry V: New Interpretations*, ed. Gwilym Dodd (York: York Medieval Press, 2013), 187–216. I would like to thank James Ross for raising this counter argument in our discussions of Joan's arrest.

46 Toudouze, *Richemont*, 227

47 Gwen Seabourne, *Imprisoning Medieval Women: The Non-Judicial Confinement and Abduction of Women in England, c.1170–1509* (Aldershot: Ashgate, 2011), 15–16, 27–30.

48 Hollman, *Royal Witche*, 65. For further discussion of the situation of elite women accused of treason in this period and their treatment, see the chapter "Trying Women: Royal Female Transgression and Treason" in Sarah Stockdale, "Blood on the Crown: Treason in the Royal Kinship Structure of Fifteenth-Century England" (PhD thesis, University of Winchester, 2018), 67–102.

49 For the expenditure related to Joan's guests, see "Account Book of the household of Joan of Navarre," 1420–21, University of Manchester John Rylands Collection Latin MS 238. Camoys appears to have arrived on 12 April 1420 and remained until 31 January 1421—sadly he appears to have died not long after his stay with her. There are multiple rationales for his long stay—Gemma Hollman suggests it might indicate a romantic attachment, but it is equally possible that he was there on Henry V's behalf to keep an eye on Joan as Camoys could be considered one of Henry's "right hand men" or even as Joan's friend as he had

known her since escorting her to England back in 1403; Hollman, *Royal Witches*, 72; Hutchinson, *Henry V*, 75.

50 Ralph A. Griffiths, "The Trial of Eleanor Cobham: An Episode in the fall of Duke Humphrey of Gloucester," *Bulletin of the John Rylands Library* 51 (1969): 381–99; Hollman, *Royal Witches*, 89–177.

51 Hutchinson, *Henry V*, 201; Bryan Bevan, *Henry IV* (London: Rubicon Press, 1994), 152–53. See also Malcolm Vale's biography *Henry V, The Conscience of a King* (New Haven, CT: Yale University Press, 2016).

52 For Monstrelet's account of the affair, see Monstrelet, IV, 28–35.

53 Monstrelet, IV, 31; Sumption, *Cursed Kings*, 690.

54 Foedera 9, 5 April 1420. Joel Cornette notes that she also appealed to her brother the dauphin, to other connections in France, and even to Scotland and Iberia for help: Joel Cornette, *Histoire de la Bretagne et des Bretons*, vol. 1, *Des ages obscurs au regne de Louis XIV* (Paris: Editions du Seuil, 2005), 310.

55 Foedera 9, 13 April 1420.

56 Marie-Hélène Santrot, *Entre France et Angleterre, Le duche de Bretagne; Essai d'iconographie des Ducs de Bretagne* (Nantes: Conseil général de Loire-Atlantique, 1988), 143–45; Sumption, *Cursed Kings*, 691.

57 Knowlson, *Jean V*, 117; Contamine, "Bretagne et France," 79.

58 Sumption, *Cursed Kings*, 706.

59 Carlton Williams, *Bedford*, 98. On the meeting at Pontorson, see Gruel, *Richemont*, 23–4.

60 Foedera 10, 17 January 1421; Sumption, *Cursed Kings*, 712.

61 Ramírez Vaquero, *Carlos III*, 266–69. For relevant expenses related to ambassadors and diplomacy in this period, see Catalogo XXXIII, no. 419, 10 January 1421; no. 598, 28 March 1421; no. 935, 26 August 1421; no. 1000, 15 September 1421; no. 1022, 22 September 1421; no. 1088, 10 October 1421.

62 Strickland, *Lives*, 96. Note: this passage is in a later edition of Strickland's work published in London by Longmans in 1861 and does not occur in the previously cited 1848 edition.

63 "Traité d'Alliance entre le Duc de Bourgogne & les Etats de Bretagne", signed at Amiens, 18 April, 1423, in Morice, II, 1125–28.

64 On the Breton negotiations, see Foedera 10, 9 June 1422 and 17 July 1422. See also Contamine, "Bretagne et France," 79, and Sumption, *Cursed Kings*, 760–61. For a copy of the letter of release see PROME, "Henry VI: October 1423".

65 SC 8/158/7900, 1427, endorsed by the king's council to bring Makworth to answer to them on 6 July 1427.

66 Chloë McKenzie, "Ladies and Robes of the Garter: Kingship, Patronage and Female Agency in Late Medieval England, c. 1348–1445" (PhD thesis, University of Southampton, 2019), 98–104, 189–97, and appendix 2 for a full listing of the Ladies of the Garter. See also James L. Gillespie, "Ladies of the Fraternity of Saint George and of the Society of

the Garter", *Albion* 17, no. 3 (1985): 269–71; Cornette, *Histoire de la Bretagne*, 295. See also Michael Jones, "Les origines de l'Ordre de l'Hermine et son histoire sous les ducs Jean IV and Jean V," in *Des chevaliers de la Table ronde a l'Ordre de l'Hermine, Colloque a Rennes 27 Sept 2008* (Vannes: Institut Culturel de Bretagne, 2009), 75–81.

67 The text of the treaty is printed in Monstrelet, IV, 147–49. See also L&M JV, VI, no. 1556, 17 April 1423, as well as two separate treaties on the 17th and 18th respectively, one just with Bedford (no. 1555) and one with Burgundy (no. 1557). See also Richard Vaughan, *Philip the Good: The Apogee of Burgundy* (Woodbridge: Boydell, 1970), 9–10; Carlton Williams, *Bedford*, 99.

68 There is extensive documentation on the titles and finances of Richard and Marguerite in the ADLA, see E26 to 36; the confirmation of his title is ADLA E31-8, 8 May 1421. Dates for their marriage are given in various sources as both 1423 and 1426.

69 Jehan de Waurin (Jean de Wavrin), *Recueil des Croniques et Anchiennes Istories de la Grant Bretaigne, A Present Nomme Engleterre*, vol. III, *From 1422–1431*, ed. William Hardy (London: Longman and Co., 1897), 125–29 and 134–77, including the text of letters sent between Burgundy and Gloucester. See also Monstrelet, IV, 210–42.

70 Rohr, *Yolande*, 117–27, quote on 124; Wavrin, *Recueil*, III, 88; Gruel, *Richemont*, 35–6.

71 Foedera 10, 15 January 1426. POPC, 3, 181, 15 January 1426. See also Gruel, *Richemont*, 40–2.

72 PROME, "Henry VI: February 1426".

73 Monstrelet, IV, 284–88; Wavrin, *Recueil*, III, 225–34.

74 See ADLA E121-9 and 10, both dated 3 July 1427; see also E121-11, letters vowing mutual assistance between Bedford and Jean V. Also Foedera 10, dated 1427.

75 On Malestroit's relationship with Jean, see J. de la Martinière, "Un grand Chancelier de Bretagne-Jean de Malestroit," *Memoires de la Société d'Histoire et d'Archaeologie de Bretagne* 1 (1920): 9–52; Pierre Thomas-Lecroix, "Jean de Malestroit, Chancelier du duc Jean V, et l'independance de la Bretagne," *Bulletin de la Société Archeologique et Historique de Nantes et de Loire-Atlantique* 115 (1978): 135–94. For three contemporary perspectives on this event, see Monstrelet, V, 11–12; Gruel, *Richemont*, 78–80; and Alençon's chronicler Perceval de Cagny, *Chroniques de Perceval de Cagny*, ed. H. Moranvillé (Paris: Librarie Renouard, 1902), 181–85.

76 Bertram Percy Wolffe, *Henry VI* (New Haven, CT: Yale University Press, 2001), 177–78. See also A. Bourdeaut, "Gilles de Bretagne-entre la France et l'Angleterre-les causes et les Auteurs du drame," *Memoires de la Société d'Histoire et de l'Archaelogie de Bretagne* 1 (1920): 53–145. For documental evidence of Gilles' trip and related political negotations with

Brittany see L&M JV, VII, no. 2023, 29 April 1432; no. 2030, 21 June 1432; no. 2042, 24 August 1432; and Foedera 10, 28 August 1432.

77 Contamine, "Bretagne et France," 82.

78 POPC, 4, 146–51, 18 February 1433.

79 For John Gentill's expenses, see E101/620/21 (1415–16) and E101/322/8 (1423–5). For the Navarrese ambassador's trips to Brittany and England, see Catalogo XXXV, no. 42, 11 January 1423; no. 689, 8 October 1423; and Catalogo XXXVI, no. 151, 18 March 1424.

80 Catalogo XXXVI, no. 161, 30 January 1430; no. 165, 31 January 1430; and no. 433, 28 March 1430.

81 Foedera 10, 7, 8 and 16 November 1430; POPC, 4, 56–9.

82 On the embassies, see Catalogo XLI, no. 37, 18 January 1433; Catalogo XLII, no. 990, 1436. For Master Johan, see Catalogo XLII, no. 267, 14 September 1435 and no. 262, 15 September 1435.

83 POPC, 5, 56.

PART II

5

THE AVARICIOUS QUEEN: THE FIGHT FOR FINANCIAL STABILITY

The link between money and power is a truth which is universally acknowledged. It might be taken for granted that a queen, as the foremost and theoretically most powerful woman of the realm, would have a constant and ample supply of funds to draw from—yet the lives of Joan of Navarre and other medieval queens show that this was not necessarily the case. Money and majesty were also closely linked—queens needed adequate funds to maintain their household and clothe themselves and their retinue in a way which befitted their rank as their lives were constantly under scrutiny from their own court and subjects to foreign visitors. As the female element of the monarchy, it was vital that she represent the power and wealth of the realm as well as affirm her own status through the clothing and jewels that she wore. Moreover, money gave the queen greater agency as patronage was a means for the queen to be a driver of cultural production and enabled her to support favoured religious orders, building links with the church, and demonstrating her piety.

While medieval queens could and did receive money from a variety of sources, a key aspect of her finances was the income received from her dower lands. Dower grants were originally designed to provide for a widowed royal woman in their dowager years—this was

DOI: 10.4324/9780429261022-8

the case in Brittany when Joan was a duchess, but when she became queen of England, she was given a dower to provide income for her both as a consort and after her husband's death. The lands that Joan possessed as part of her dower not only gave her revenue but increased her authority and visibility in the realm as a major landowner. It also allowed her to effectively build her own affinity of those who served her by managing her lands and those who held land from her, which we will explore further in the following chapter. Thus, the economic element of queenship was central to the queen's day-to-day function and her ability to fully exercise her office.

Joan makes an excellent case study for the economic element of queenship due to the heady combination of a very long life during a particularly turbulent political period, which made her time as a consort and dowager queen fiscally challenging. As noted earlier, Joan has often been overlooked by scholars due to her very light presence in the chronicles of the period which gives the erroneous impression that she was of little significance and that there is no material to work on to study her life. However, when one turns to documents and records linked to the economic aspect of her life, there is a wealth of evidence to work with. While this present chapter is too brief to encompass all the surviving documentation, it will draw on a range of examples from records of expenditure, grants of lands and annuities, account books and manorial administration, and more to give an overarching picture of Joan's economic activity and financial challenges.

Previous chapters have reflected on Joan's transitions from infanta to duchess, queen, and dowager—here we will examine the economic impact of these changes in lifecycle stage and status. This chapter will follow the framework laid down by Hilda Johnstone regarding the queen's three sources of revenue: dower grants, supplementary grants (including special/one-off endowments for chamber expenses or other annuities), and queen's gold—giving an overview of all three elements in the context of Joan's life.[1] In the first section, we will discuss both Joan's Breton and English dower in terms of what she was granted, her struggle to hold on to the entirety of her portfolio and realise the revenues from it, and her administration of her lands. Then we will move on to other forms of revenue: supplementary grants, wardships, and the queen's gold. While this means we will go back and forth in time slightly, it gives us the opportunity to clearly dissect the three revenue streams that Joan had access to. In the final section, we will move from revenue to expenditure, looking at account books which reveal how Joan spent her money.

Overall, this chapter will highlight the problems that Joan encountered in realising all of the revenue which she had a right to from her English sources and demonstrate the impact that her inconsistent and often inadequate revenue had on Joan's ability to fund her household, meet her expenses, and maintain her queenly status. As we will see, Joan met these challenges actively, fighting to obtain adequate revenues, maintain her income and portfolio of lands, and retain her rights and prerogatives in her lands. This tenacious behaviour, including petitioning kings and parliaments and bringing suits against those who contested her rights to fees or lands, has earned Joan a reputation as an avaricious queen, perhaps due to the judgement of the Strickland sisters who claimed that "avarice was certainly the besetting sin of Joanna of Navarre".[2] This prompts the question which each reader will have to answer for themselves at the end of this chapter—was Joan greedy or just keen to maintain her position by defending her rights to ensure that she had adequate funds to maintain her household, support her affinity, and effectively exercise the queen's office?

Dower: Developing, maintaining, retaining, and regaining an international portfolio

Yet another unusual aspect of Joan's life and experience as a royal woman is that over the course of her life she held two dowers from her marriages to Jean IV of Brittany and Henry IV of England. Moreover, it was not a case of one dower replacing another when Joan remarried, as she managed to retain the lands granted to her as duchess when she crossed the Channel and gained another dower grant as queen of England. In this section we will work chronologically so that we can see how Joan was able to accrue lands, rights, and revenues first in Brittany and then in England and the struggles she faced due to political and personal turbulence to retain such a wide-ranging portfolio in terms of both geography and the

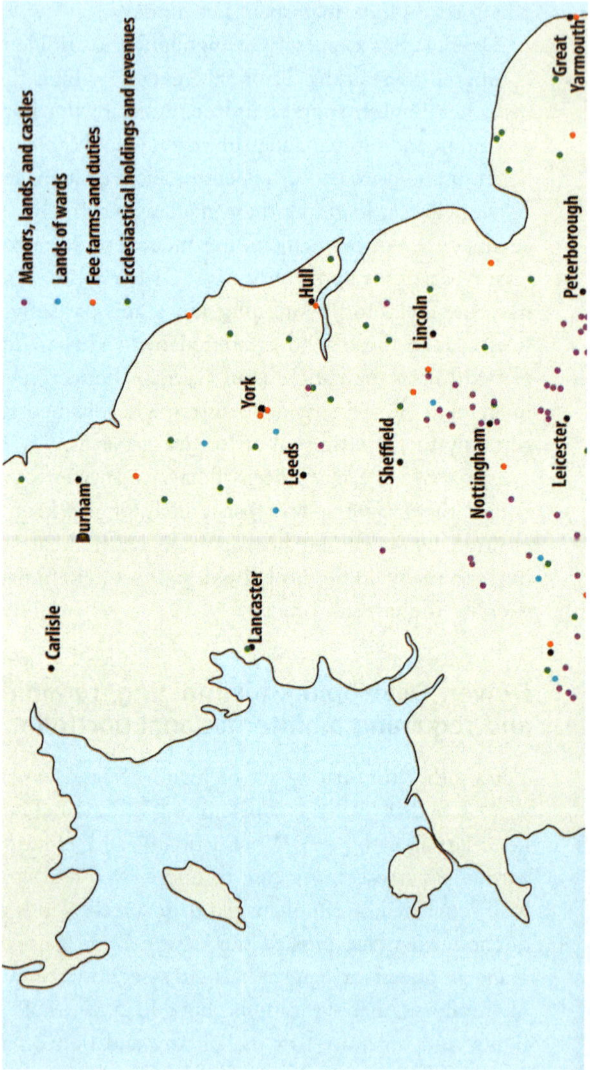
Manors, lands, and castles
Lands of wards
Fee farms and duties
Ecclesiastical holdings and revenues
Great Yarmouth
Peterborough
Hull
Lincoln
York
Leicester
Nottingham
Sheffield
Leeds
Durham
Lancaster
Carlisle

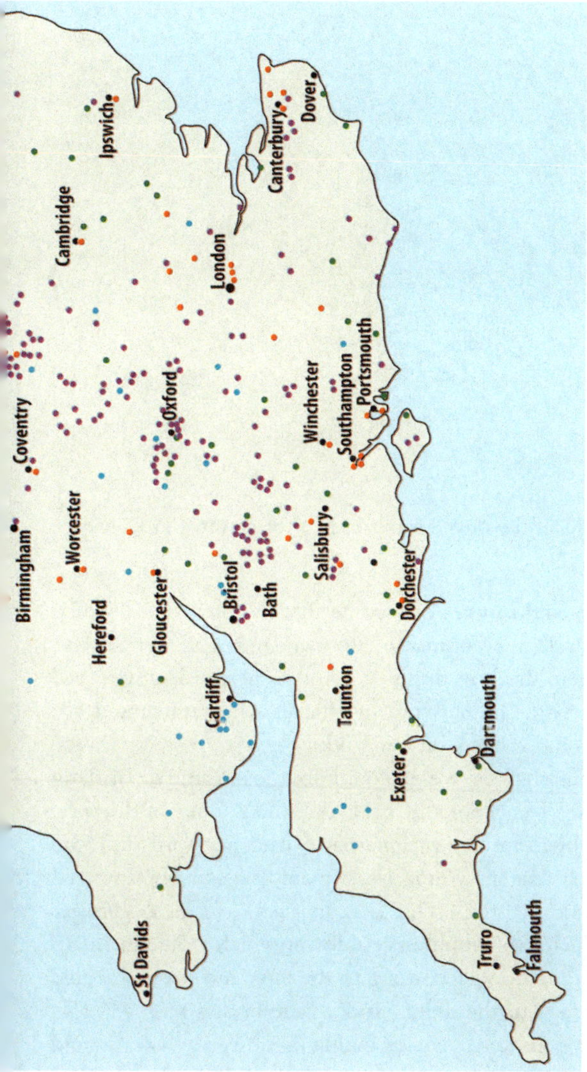

FIGURE 5.1a Map of the dower lands of Joan of Navarre in England.

FIGURE 5.1b Map of the dower lands of Joan of Navarre in Brittany.

types of holdings and sources of income that she possessed. Finally, we will consider Joan's connection to her lands and her role in administering them, both in terms of her own personal activity and her engagement with the network of officials who represented her across the realm and tenants on her lands.

In the previous chapters we explored how Joan came to Brittany in September 1386 to become the bride of Jean IV, duke of Brittany. During the negotiations for the marriage, back in April of 1385, Jean IV promised that his young bride would be suitably dowered according to Breton custom. The *Tres Ancienne Coutume de Bretagne* stipulated that duchesses should have a dower which would maintain them in their widowhood according to the rank and status she held during her marriage to the duke.[3] Indeed the bride's rank was also arguably a factor in terms of assigning a dower which would maintain her station over the long term, and Joan was a royal princess by birth. In return for the dower, the duchess was charged to merit the funds through her loyalty and service to her husband. However, Joan's dower was not granted for six months after the wedding, in February 1387, by which time she was likely pregnant with her first child—perhaps demonstrating to Jean IV, whose need for an heir had motivated the marriage, that she was holding up her end of the bargain. Joan was formally assigned the territories of the entire county of Nantes, the lands of Guérande, the barony of Retz, and the lordships of Touffou and la Guerche, with all dependent revenues, on 24 February 1387.[4] In addition to her lands, Joan had revenues from benefices such as Notre Dame la Blanche de Saillé and fees and customs due to her including a levy on all ships entering the port of Pouliguen.

Jean IV chose the lands for Joan's dower carefully, very deliberately centring her lands in the secure Nantes region where there were several comfortable ducal residences and stable revenues which should assure Joan of a reasonable income in her widowhood.[5] This region had often featured in the dowers of previous duchesses; Guérande, which was an area which had proven its loyalty to Jean in the civil wars in his early reign, was likely to provide consistent revenue. Touffou was a part of the ducal patrimony with a castle in the forest of Bignon, which featured again in the dowers of later duchesses such as Catherine of Luxembourg and Joan's distant relative Marguerite de Foix, mother of Anne of Brittany.

While these territories were secure options for Joan's dower, the barony of Retz was a questionable choice. This was not economically questionable as it had useful forests and drainage schemes and had provided good arable land—even though it had suffered some depopulation during the civil war and due to outbreaks of plague, it still would have been a good source of revenue for Joan's dower. However, the land was disputed as it was claimed by Jeanne Chabot, dame de Rays, who had succeeded her brother Girard V to the territory back in 1371.[6] Jeanne Chabot had struggled to maintain the territories due to two failed marriages which had resulted in conflict with the Church and significant financial difficulties. Jean IV had used her troubles to force her to exchange the lucrative Retz lands for others in western Brittany, promising that she could still have the use of two chateaux, and her heir, Brumor de Laval, was convinced that his rights to the territory would be respected. Giving the territory to Joan for her dower may have convinced Jeanne Chabot and Brumor de Laval that Jean IV had no intention of returning the lands and Jeanne appealed to the Parlement of Paris on 1 February 1393. Given this ongoing dispute over the ownership of the lands, Retz was removed from Joan's dower in her second settlement in 1396.[7] This dower settlement was effectively the same as the original, but the barony of Retz was replaced with lands at Pirmil, Batz, and St Pierre en Retz, which were arguably equitable in terms of revenues. The powerful dukes of Burgundy and Berry favoured Jeanne Chabot's case and forced a settlement in 1399—Jean IV signed an agreement with Chabot on 24 April that year, by July Jeanne retook the Retz castles, and in November of the same year Jean IV died, putting an end to the dispute. However, Joan reaffirmed the accord with Jeanne Chabot after Jean IV's death, ironically confirming Chabot's tenure of lands Joan had once believed would be hers.[8]

As noted previously, in Brittany, in contrast to the situation in England, as will be discussed later, the dower was intended to support the duchess as a widow, not necessarily during the lifetime of her husband. On Jean IV's death in November 1399, Joan not only came fully into her dower possessions but had to cope with governing the duchy itself on behalf of her young son, now Jean V. In the following section on administration, we will see Joan's attention to the management of her dower lands despite the demands of the regency and her clandestine efforts to arrange a match with Henry IV.

When Joan remarried, there were a number of complications as noted in earlier chapters which had to be addressed: Joan's position as regent in Brittany, the custody of her seven surviving children, the fact that they were on different sides of the Schism, the potential reaction of the king of France (Henry's enemy and Joan's first cousin), and, most relevant here, what might happen to her substantial dower and the rights to her dowry from Navarre. We have seen how keen the duke of Burgundy and the French court were to ensure French control of the duchy and stem potential English influence once they were aware of her impending English marriage, thus the custody of her children, particularly the young duke, was a key issue. The Breton historian Fonssagrives claims that the duke of

Burgundy encouraged Joan to exchange the custody of her children for surety on continued rents on the lands of her dower. Indeed, Fonssagrives even claims that immediately prior to her departure in January 1403, Joan attempted to make a lucrative deal with the powerful noble Clisson to give him charge of the city and castle of Nantes in exchange for 12,000 gold ecus, but the deal was foiled by Gilles de Lesbiet, who refused to give charge of the city to anyone but the incoming regent, the duke of Burgundy.[9] These claims have reinforced an impression of Joan as a woman who was both avaricious and ambitious—more concerned with money and titles than retaining the custody of her children.

Ultimately, Joan made the decision to sacrifice the regency and the custody of her sons (though not necessarily her Breton dower) to start a new life in England as Henry IV's queen consort. Henry IV and Joan were married at Winchester Cathedral in February 1403—after the celebration of their wedding and her subsequent coronation at Westminster, the next step in confirming her new status was to formally grant the new queen her English dower in June.[10] Henry IV promised Joan a dower of 10,000 marks per annum (approximately £6,600), a generous sum equivalent to over £4 million a year today, which he could not easily satisfy given the straitened circumstances of the Crown in this period. Anne Crawford notes that before Joan, the precedent for a queen's dower was normally about £4,000–4,500, thus this seems like a considerable increase, yet in the fourteenth century Philippa of Hainaut had an income of £7,000 yearly and her mother-in-law, Isabella of France, had an even more substantial £13,000 at the height of her power as regent for Edward III.[11] Michael Jones argued that compared to the lavish dower of Joan's contemporary Isabeau of Bavaria at 140,000 francs per annum, Joan's dower was not out of line with other queenly dowers of the period.[12] Interestingly, the value of Joan's dower was due in part to Isabeau's daughter, the young Isabella de Valois, second wife of Richard II. Katia Wright has noted that the peace treaty between England and France, which brokered Isabella's marriage, stipulated a dower of 10,000 marks—while Isabella never held a dower of that size due to her very young age during her tenure as queen, it still set a precedent for Joan and her fifteenth-century successors.[13] The generous size of

Joan's dower was also not out of line with Henry's character as he has been described by his biographers Kirby and Bevan to have been both uxorious and generous, perhaps to a fault.[14] While Joan, and possibly Henry, may have felt that this substantial dower was merited by her august royal lineage and in turn enhanced his own fledging kingly status, given the financial difficulties of the Crown in this period, criticism of royal largesse under Richard II and Henry himself, and the fact that she still had another Breton dower as well, this grant was bound to be controversial.

Lands made up a substantial proportion of the dowers of English queens. While Joan did largely come into the lands of Anne of Bohemia as will be discussed later, there was not a fixed set of territory which every queen possessed. All the lands they held came from the larger collection of Crown lands and were held at the king's pleasure—they could be granted or taken away at any time, and at the queen's death any lands she held were reabsorbed into the royal holdings. Joan's dower was not exclusively composed of lands; to satisfy the 10,000 marks per annum of income she had a variety of funding streams including:

- Lands (manors, castles, forests, etc.)
- Wardships (revenues of their lands, rights to their marriage, etc.)
- Fee farms (largely payments from urban centres)
- Duties from ports and customs
- Alien priories and their apports

The focus of the initial 1403 grant was lands, including substantial manors such as the one at Hamstead Marshall, forests, and several castles including Odiham, Devizes, and Rockingham, which had all been commonly held as part of previous queenly dowers.[15] Several important wardships followed later that year, which will be discussed in the following section on supplemental income. It is important to note here, however, that many of the wardships she held included substantial and significant landholdings which both augmented the income of her dower and increased the complexity of administration through the greater number of properties and its wider geographical spread, particularly into Wales where Joan otherwise had little holdings.

As Chapter 3 demonstrated, the royal couple faced a turbulent political landscape at the outset of their marriage, with Henry facing rebellion at home and conflict with Brittany where Joan's young son ruled. This conflict arguably complicated the issue of her dower rights and the fact that she had not only remarried but had been granted an even more generous dower from her new husband. This put into question her right to continue to hold her dower lands in Brittany, as custom varied regarding whether a widow who remarried continued to retain her dower.[16] However, despite these complications, Joan continued to negotiate with her son over her rights in Brittany. In August 1404 her rights as "*usufructaire*" of the county of Nantes were confirmed and she in turn confirmed her son's right to collect outstanding payments from her brother, Carlos III of Navarre, on her original dowry in November of the same year.[17]

In an attempt to satisfy the full 10,000 marks promised to her, Joan received further grants in 1404 for her English dower.[18] The first included several small parcels of land, shares of rent, and some very specific items such as the yearly rent of a leash of greyhounds in the hamlet of Minsterley at Michaelmas valued at 2d per annum. More substantial were two grants received in July 1404 of £1,000 from the customs and subsidies normally reserved for the king from the port of Boston and £3,000 from the tenth granted to the king by the clergy of the provinces of Canterbury and York. However, according to her petition to Parliament in October 1404, Joan was still lacking sufficient income and was not receiving most of what the king had already granted.[19]

Although it had been specifically noted back in June 1403 that Joan would have the same rights and holdings as the late queen, Anne of Bohemia, first wife of Richard II, had, "reversions excepted", it seemed there was a lack of clarity as to exactly what this entailed. Perhaps in response to the queen's petition, entries on the Close Rolls and the findings of contemporary inquisitions show that a commission was sent out to various counties in early 1405 to ascertain what the late queen Anne held and thus what could be ascribed to now fall within Joan's dower as the current consort. Concurrent with this commission Joan continued to accrue more grants between February and August 1405, including the entirety of the Isle of Wight and Carisbrooke Castle on 5 April.[20]

At the same time as the king was attempting to satisfy the generous terms of Joan's dower, Henry was being pressed by Parliament to curb expenditure to address the severe financial problems facing the Crown. Perceptions of excessive household expenditure had been an issue since the reign of Richard II, and Rogers notes in his thesis on the household of Henry IV that expenditure had been extremely high during the early years of Henry's reign as he secured the throne and set up his court.[21] The royal marriage in 1403 had incurred significant expenditure and added to the cost of funding the queen's dower and household. Granting away sources of revenues which could support the household not only to the queen but also to other loyal supporters exacerbated the situation and incurred criticism, though interestingly less of this criticism was directly targeted at the queen herself.

Although there is insufficient space to discuss the challenges of funding the royal household and the Long Parliament of 1406 at length here, it is important to note that Joan's dower was addressed in the wrangling over royal finances. At the beginning of the Parliament in March, the speaker, Sir John Tiptoft, brought another petition to Parliament that the queen was still lacking most of the revenue due to her, apart from some income from her wardships. It was noted that this was an issue of consistency with past queenly dowers.[22] On 19 June Tiptoft called for serious economies in the royal household and the cancellation of all grants made by the king, with the significant exception of those made to the queen and the princes, so that revenues from Crown lands could be diverted to fund the royal household instead. The queen was requested to fund the expenses of her household when she was in residence with the king in order to avoid further drains on the Exchequer, but she clearly needed her own funds coming in consistently in order to do this and make her household self-sufficient. Perhaps in response to all of these elements, the March petition, a desire for the royal household to fund itself through its receipts, and Tiptoft's influence, entries on the Close Rolls as well as from local records between June to October 1406 indicate payments made to the queen as well as requests to pay her what was due, particularly with regard to urban fee farms.[23] From 1406 to 1410 there is also increasing documentation with regard to the administration of her lands and payments of rents such as receivers' accounts from various holdings, including her manor at Havering-atte-Bower and her lands in Staffordshire and around Melton Mowbray and Leicester.[24] Improving relations with Brittany may have helped her gain access to revenues from her Breton dower, with a flurry of orders from Jean V in March 1406 to support her officials and approve her gifts to them, and in May 1407 the governor of the county of Nantes, Tristan de la Lande, was given a safe conduct to transport a flotilla of salt which was due to Joan as part payment for her dower.[25]

However, this uptake in payments does not mean that Joan's struggles to receive what she was owed was over. Indeed, in March 1408 there was a flurry of documentation including two supplications from the queen regarding lands that she believed were rightly hers from the king's grants, including the castle of Barton Seagrove and the patronage of the priory of Ware—the queen won both of these suits.[26] Perhaps in response to the queen's suits and a desire to clarify what rightly belonged to her, two months later, on 20 May 1408, there was a confirmation of the grants made to Joan with specific reference again to her right to the lands previously held by Anne of Bohemia.[27]

As we have already seen, Henry's health, often precarious during their marriage, reached a serious crisis over the winter of 1408–9. Henry made a will on 21 January 1409 which specified that the queen's dower should be paid from the revenues of the duchy of Lancaster on his death. While Henry recovered, both Kirby and Crawford have argued that his ill health may have increased his concerns about the instability and insufficiency of the queen's dower.[28] In April 1409 he dispatched a missive to the chancellor with a handwritten note: "Reverend and well beloved cosin, I send yow a bylle for the Quene towchyng her dower, wych I pray yow micht be sped, and ye shall do us gret ese ther inne, wherefor we woll thank yow with al owre hert".[29] A few months later, on 1 July 1409, a new grant to the queen followed—in contrast to previous grants, it consisted largely of the keeping of alien priories and their apports. Alien priories were religious houses which were tied to mother houses on the Continent—normally in France. The Hundred Years War had provided a pretext for the Crown to begin to suppress or take control of these houses, ensuring that the apports or payments which normally went back across the Channel could be redirected into the king's—or in this case queen's—finances. In the same grant, Joan also received several substantial rights to payments and revenues from urban centres and ports, including London and Southampton of £333 6s 8d each.[30]

Yet it appears that Joan's dower was still failing to produce sufficient income—the queen petitioned Parliament again in January 1410 that she "had yet to receive grants amounting to more than £1,683 of this sum [i.e. her £6,600 dower] and requested that she would receive the remaining £4,983".[31] This appears to be the last of the major grants and petitions regarding the insufficiency of her dower in Henry IV's reign. The following three years did see a steady flow of documentation regarding the administration of her dower. The queen was involved in more suits regarding disputed lands and revenues and the king and queen sent commissions to ferret out profits concealed from them.[32] Records from the later years of Henry IV's reign show that, although she was likely still not receiving her full dues, payments were coming in from various sources such as receivers' accounts from Wiltshire, receipts from the ports of Great Yarmouth and Ipswich, and court rolls from her manor of Willington.[33]

The death of Joan's husband, Henry IV, in early 1413 and her shift in status from queen consort to dowager did not initially make a major change to the documentation generated by her lands and income in England. However, on 27 January 1414, the new king, Joan's stepson Henry V, made a significant grant to the queen, acknowledging that she had still not received the full amount promised by his late father. The majority of the 1414 grant is a confirmation of what she already held, but there were some notable changes. Joan was given more alien priories and their apports, payments of ulnage (a tax on the sale of cloth) from various counties (including £100 each from Somerset and Wiltshire), and also some small fee farms from towns such as Cambridge and sums owed from individuals.[34]

Yet it was also noted in the grant that a few individuals had successfully claimed back lands and revenues from the queen, such as the earl of Suffolk, who reclaimed a disputed portion of the revenues from Rockingham Castle and forest, and that the lands of three of Joan's wards, Fulk Montho, Thomas West, and John de Mowbray, had all been delivered to the heirs. At the end of the grant, it was noted that the total sum of the queen's holdings were 6,089 marks, 3s ½d yearly, nearly 4,000 marks short of what she had been originally promised. However, the grant recognised that there was a considerable shortfall from the income that Henry IV had originally granted her and noted that deficiencies would be rectified. Entries on the Close Rolls from the early years of Henry V's reign also show a series of mandates going out to customs collectors in ports such as Kingston-upon-Hull, Boston, London, Bristol, and Southampton to pay the queen what she was due, and to other tenants who owed Joan money or had usurped her rights to lands, fees, and rents, showing the queen still had strong royal support to collect her revenues.[35]

While Joan's position as dowager was bolstered by this confirmation of her English dower (even if on a reduced scale) by her stepson, her position vis-à-vis her Breton dower was in crisis. Both Kermabon and Knowlson have argued that Joan's son Jean V may have felt that his mother had no need of her Breton dower after being widowed for the second time, as his stepbrother Henry V would assure her comfort as dowager. Moreover, Jean V may have felt that the financial needs of the duchy were greater than his mother's, thus her revenues were fair game to retain for his own needs. However, Joan was unwilling to let her son interfere in the administration of her lands and his assumption of her revenues. When Gontier Col, the secretary of the French king, was despatched on an embassy to the English court in early 1414, Joan met with him and charged him with a message to her son, the duke of Brittany. Gontier duly reported the message to Jean V at an audience on 28 October 1414 in the Chateau de l'Hermine in Vannes.[36] The ambassador reported that Joan sent her loving regards "in true love and maternal affection … as the creature whom she loved best in the world". She in turn hoped that "he would act towards her as an obedient son, a true and loyal friend". Gontier assured the duke that his mother felt that he would never be the one responsible for the actions with regard to her dower which were causing her such dismay and displeasure; indeed he claimed that Joan, crying, told him that she believed that her son "who she had always found to be a true, natural, loyal, humble and obedient son to her" was being led astray by evil counsellors who had turned him against her. However, Gontier also reported that Joan threatened to marry for a third time, to a powerful prince "in England, France or another country" who could press her rights for her or bring war upon Brittany to get back what was owed to her, potentially bringing great damage to her son's beloved duchy. The French ambassador then attempted to broker a deal between mother and son which was very favourable to Joan, not only honouring her rights but offering compensation for back revenues. Jean V refused Gontier's deal, countering that he would respect Joan's dower grant but that he reserved the right to nominate captains and officials in her lands as long as she was living in England. Knowlson suggests that Jean V was insinuating that if she really wanted to fully exercise her dower rights in Brittany, nothing was stopping her from returning to administer her lands in person.[37] However, Jean V did issue a statement in early November in response to Joan's entreaty, which noted her grief at the treatment of her rights and interference with her officials, and that "we want to repair and improve the situation" and that "we desire with all our heart and power, to serve and obey our very formidable lady and mother".[38] The duke stated that "we swear and promise in good faith to our lady and mother, on pain of incurring her perpetual indignation" that her rights to her dower would be respected and her officials would be free to act on her letters and that any of Joan's goods "that we have taken in her absence from Brittany" would be restored to her or she would receive payment in accordance with their value.

Back in England, the initial years of Joan's second widowhood show reasonable activity in terms of receipts and receivers' accounts for her English dower, including a steady stream of income from the ports of Bristol, Yarmouth, and Ipswich.[39] In 1419, as discussed in the previous chapter, Henry V placed the queen under arrest and sequestered her dower, most likely to secure funds for his campaigns in France. Over 1420 and 1421 there followed a series of accounts which took stock of what the queen held in various counties as well as documentation which shows that some of the queen's lands were reassigned to others.[40]

Joan's Breton dowry had continued to be under dispute while she was imprisoned in England, leaving the queen with the serious prospect of being completely landless and without income. Perhaps emboldened by Joan's imprisonment and the obvious lack of support from her powerful stepsons, Jean V dismissed her receiver-general and effectively dispossessed her of her lands in Brittany, with his ducal treasurer only sending Joan part of the revenues that she should have had the rights to.[41] Fortunately for Joan, the crisis abated when Henry V decided in July 1422 to release her and charged three of the greatest prelates of the realm, the archbishop of Canterbury (Henry Chichele) and the bishops of Winchester (Henry Beaufort) and Durham (Thomas Langley—then chancellor), to ensure the restitution of her dower. Henry V died the following month on 31 August 1422, leaving his young son, Joan's step-grandson, to come to the throne as Henry VI. The queen lost no time campaigning for the restitution of her lands, petitioning the king's uncle and Joan's (favourite) stepson Humphrey, duke of Gloucester, and the council in November 1422 to ensure her lands were fully restored to her.[42] Henry V's widow, Katherine de Valois, also petitioned the council regarding her own situation, as her dower settlement was also unclear. Given the need to satisfy the terms of Henry V's decree to restore the lands previously granted to Joan, it was decided that Katherine would be provided for out of the de Bohun lands and the duchy of Lancaster to ensure that both dowagers were suitably dowered. Interestingly, Katherine became the only queen who did not hold lands normally given to queen dowagers, as Joan already held these and, ironically, Joan outlived Katherine by about six months, though both queens died in 1437.[43]

Concurrently with the petition to the council in November 1422, Joan sent her agents out to negotiate over the payment of rents and fees, including fee farms from cities. Some of these fee farms could be theoretically lucrative, for example Joan should have had £200 pounds (or 300 marks) annually from the city of Southampton. However, they had protested at the payment of these fees and in 1415 the city had successfully petitioned Henry V to receive a reduction in their payment to £93 (140 marks) a year for the next ten years.[44] When Joan sought to re-establish her rights to the fee farm in 1422, she cannily chose Thomas Marlborough, a Southampton lawyer who had been part of the 1415 delegation, to negotiate with the city on her behalf. She appointed him on 6 November and by 12 November 1422 an agreement was reached with the mayor, William Nichole—on the same date, a similar agreement was signed with nearby Winchester whose mayor, John Veel, also agreed to resume payment of their £31 annual fee.[45] Despite these successes, Joan faced a sizable challenge to retake the entirety of her dower—her struggle to regain her revenues can be seen in another petition to Parliament in October 1423 which asked for the full restitution of her property and income so "that the said queen shall have and enjoy peaceably her aforesaid dower for the term of her life".[46] While documentary evidence does show that payments to Joan began to resume, once again at the Leicester Parliament of 1426 a petition was made regarding the queen's lands—this is mirrored by entries on the Close Rolls in December 1426 and in 1427 which affirmed that the queen was due restitution of her lands after Henry V's decrees of July 1422.[47]

While Joan's dower had been reconfirmed by Parliament and the Crown and she did enjoy some of the revenues due to her, the remaining years of her life were marked by a series of disputes over property. In 1431 Joan won two disputes over the custody of the alien priories of Modbury in Devon and St Clear in Wales, when letters patent granting the properties to others were annulled after the queen protested that these properties were part of her dower.[48] The queen also brought several suits before the Court of Chancery, but was also challenged by Henry Percy, the earl of Northumberland, over some London properties which had been seized by Henry IV from his father and granted to the queen.[49] Joan succeeded, however, in a long-running dispute with Winchester College: in 1414 the college had been granted the priory of Andover, which had a 20 mark (£13 6s 8d) pension attached to it for Joan. The college fought for decades to be released from paying Joan the pension—petitioning in 1435 that a recent fire at Andover had diminished the profits from the priory making the payment of the pension untenable.[50] However, their protests were unsuccessful, and they had to continue paying Joan until her death in 1437.

During this same period, Joan also continued to dispute with her son Jean V over her rights and revenues for her Breton dower. The situation regarding the county of Nantes, arguably the heart of her dower, had been complicated by the assignment of 500 livres a year from the county to Joan's daughter-in-law, Marguerite d'Orleans, the countess of Étampes (wife of her younger son Richard). The revenues from the county were not substantial enough to support both women and clearly Joan expected that the full revenues from the county would be paid to her. It appears that Jean V found a compromise in this situation, reducing his sister-in-law's pension to 250 livres and agreeing to honour his mother's payments from the county in November 1428.[51] Yet negotiations continued between mother and son with evidence of at least six embassies between Joan and Jean V between December 1429 and August 1432, including payments to her long-standing courtier, Bérart de Montferrand.[52] It appears that a breakthrough was reached in December 1430, when Jean and Joan signed an agreement that the duke could have the revenues of the county of Nantes for five years in return for a payment of 5,500 gold ecus.[53] However, this agreement expired at the end of 1435, and even months before her death in 1437, Joan continued to wrangle with her son over unpaid revenues, claiming she was still owed 2,250 ecus and demanding that 1,000 ecus be immediately paid to her.[54] When Joan died in July 1437, Knowlson suggests that Jean V must have been relieved that the problem of his mother's dower was over at last.[55] In England, her death triggered another wave of documentation to first ascertain what she held in various Inquisitions Post Mortem and then reassign her lands—ultimately some of these lands would again form part of a queen's dower when her step-grandson Henry VI wed Margaret of Anjou in 1445.

The queen's business: Examining the administration of her dowers

Having now established the extent of her Breton and English dowers and Joan's efforts to receive the revenues from them and retain them over her long life, this next section will explore various facets of her connection with her lands and examine her management of her vast collection of land holdings. As it is impossible to thoroughly examine Joan's administration of such a large portfolio of property over four decades in this limited space, we will be focusing on a few key areas and presenting some examples or case studies to demonstrate a sense of connection in various ways. First, we will think about Joan's role in managing her two dowers. Then, we will look at examples of particular types of properties, in this case castles, manors, parks, and forests, noting her physical connection with these places and her efforts to maintain or improve her holdings. The remaining issue which will be explored will be Joan's efforts to preserve and press distinctive and ancient rights she held as a landowner in her parks and forests.

In 1399 Joan came into the possession of her Breton dower on the death of Jean IV, beginning her career as the administrator of what eventually became a large, international portfolio of lands, rights, and revenues. The terms of her dower agreements clearly stipulated that Joan had complete seisin or jurisdiction in her own lands and the power to designate all captains and receivers in her territories.[56] The revenues of her lands in the county of Nantes were ostensibly administered via receivers, but Joan decided to create a new office, that of a *receveur de Baillie*, who sat over these receivers and brought together the receipts from the county, which was an innovation in ducal domains at the time. This innovation arguably gave Joan greater control than previous duchesses over her revenues and even allowed her to bring together receipts from her lands in Nantes and Guérande, potentially thwarting unwanted interference from agents of the duchy—this would prove to be particularly important during her second marriage, as will be discussed later.[57]

The surviving documents in connection with Joan's Breton dower demonstrate her network of officials at work managing and maintaining her sizable dower, as well as her own role in administering her dower lands. For example, two different documents in 1402 show the duchess dealing with issues of inheritance within her lands, one of which concerned the rights of a girl named Jeanne who was the natural daughter of an Englishman known as Jacques Roux.[58]

The receivers' accounts from her holdings in Guérande give a full tally of revenues and the names of her receivers in the area, helping to illuminate the identity and activity of her officials and ascertain the level of revenue that Joan received from the region.[59]

Joan's decision to leave Brittany in early 1403 to marry Henry IV of England made it much more difficult to retain her connection to and administration of her Breton properties. Joan clearly remained engaged with matters in her lands across the Channel, as a letter sent back to Brittany regarding the tenure of a farm in 1418 demonstrates. Interestingly, the letters sent back to Brittany give us some of the best surviving examples of her "letters patent", which have been largely lost. In the heading of the letters sent to Brittany, Joan not only used all her royal and ducal titles (daughter of the king of Navarre, by the grace of God queen of England, duchess of Brittany, lady of Ireland) but notes that she holds the county of Nantes "*en douaire*" or "in dower".[60] While her seal only survives in fragments, Joan hand-signed many of her documents, showing a personal connection to the documentation going out to her lands on both sides of the Channel.

As queen of England, Joan's territorial holding expanded, requiring more of her attention to manage and administer her lands, and the need for dedicated space for this activity. At Westminster Palace, Joan was granted a new tower situated by the great gate in December 1404 which was a specifically designated space for the administration of her lands for both the queen and her officials to work in.[61] Effectively, Joan obtained an office from which she could manage her extensive portfolio of lands and residences and more generally exercise the administrative and financial element of queenship. Brown, Colvin, and Taylor note that this office started a new tradition as it was "subsequently used by later queens in the same way".[62] It is important to note that this space was in close proximity to other administrative areas such as the Exchequer and that a similar space in the northeast tower was given to her stepsons for their "office" use—first to John, duke of Bedford, and later to Humphrey of Gloucester.

The space appears to have consisted of a council chamber on the first floor with a muniment room for storage below. This chamber would have been a vital meeting room for Joan's council who helped her to manage her extensive estates across the realm. Anne Crawford's study of the working of the queen's council in medieval England notes that while the surviving evidence of the workings of these councils is patchy, they played a "judicial, administrative and advisory" role.[63] Indeed, one of their major aspects, which may have been even more pronounced during Joan's tenure, was resolving disputes and enforcing the queen's rights. The membership of the council was often drawn from the queen's wider household and network of officials, reflecting her affinity as we will discuss further in the following chapter.

As part of her dowers, Joan held many castles which offer interesting case studies of her engagement with her lands and the work of the queen and her council to manage her portfolio of properties. These castles ranged from semi-ruinous establishments which had once been important royal residences but had fallen out of favour, to substantial fortified centres which were still frequently used by the royal family and held significant strategic value. Two examples of castles held by Joan and several other medieval queens in their dower are Odiham and Devizes. Odiham, in northern Hampshire, sometimes referred to locally as "King John's Castle", had been a royal residence since the early twelfth century as it was a convenient stopping point for the household as it travelled between the important centres of Windsor and Winchester. By the early fifteenth century it was no longer a key residence and it was in need of considerable work—at the beginning of Henry IV's reign he noted that "we understand from information we have received that our Castle and the lodge situated in our part are very ruinous … and also our Chapel within our said castle is on the point of falling into the fosse of the Castle if speedy measures are not taken by us".[64] Extensive repairs to the building were thus made, including dispatching 15,000 roof tiles and nearly the same number of nails to the site.[65] In 1426–28, during Joan's tenure of the castle, lead was brought by the king's plumber to cover the roof of the staircase of the great tower.[66] Yet, even with this work being done, it appears that Joan and her officials had not sufficiently prioritised the maintenance of Odiham and its estate, as more repairs to the castle were made in 1438–39 shortly after her death, and the roofing work done on the castle had not been replicated elsewhere on the estate. The findings of an Inquisition Post Mortem after the queen's death noted that various buildings at Odiham were unroofed and "ruinous", including a granary, a water mill, and a mill for grinding malt, commenting, "Thus on the day of the queen's death the buildings of the manor were wasted for lack of repair".[67] Other entries also noted that the queen's lands had been poorly managed, for example Joan and her "farmer and minister", Thomas Dene, were criticised for poor management of the lands of the priory of St James in Exeter. It was noted that several buildings on the site had been left unroofed causing considerable damage and that the woods had been cut and sold off.[68]

Devizes Castle in Wiltshire offers a similar example of a castle held by several queens which had once played a key role in royal history as a stronghold of the Empress Matilda during the "Anarchy" or civil war of the twelfth century, but had slowly transitioned from an important defensive fortress to a rarely used residence by the time it was included in several queens' dowers. Brown, Colvin, and Taylor note that "its maintenance consisted a considerable burden on the queen's revenues, and repairs did not always keep pace with dilapidations", necessitating the earmarking of particular rents from nearby forests being dedicated to a maintenance fund.[69] In contrast to Odiham, we can see Joan taking a more engaged role with the maintenance of Devizes over several decades, including major commissions for repairs in April 1410 and February 1433.[70] In particular, 1410 provides an interesting example: we can see an entry in the Patent Rolls for 19 April for a commission to John Brydde, John Bartloit, and Robert Tyndale to take a team of workmen to undertake repairs at Devizes Castle.[71] Brydde (or Brid) and Tyndale were key members of Joan's affinity or network of officials, which will be discussed further in the following chapter. Another important figure in her affinity was Sir William Sturmy, the chief steward of her estates and a powerful figure in the region and at the courts of Henry IV and V to whom Joan rented the manor and castle of Devizes between 1413 and 1417. Tyndale was Yeoman of the Queen's Beds, and Joan made him parker for life at Devizes from

1408; for this role he received 4d daily from the issues of the lordship of Devizes as well as ½d for each animal agisted in the parks and "browsing" rights to ferns, old or windfallen wood and hedges—we will return to these important rights in park and forest land later in this section.[72] Yet even with a team of trusted officials on the case, Joan was not willing to take it on faith that the repairs were undertaken—in the manorial records there is a note about repairs being made in preparation for the queen's arrival and she did visit Devizes castle in September 1411.[73]

Nottingham Castle is an important stronghold that Joan held along with several other significant properties in the region, including the fee farm of Nottingham town, Sherwood Forest, Beckswood Park, and Clipstone Manor, which contained another twelfth-century castle, known, like Odiham, as "King John's Palace". While several sources claim that Nottingham Castle was one of Joan's primary residences, particularly in the later years of her life, there is not a great deal of documentary evidence to securely link her to the site. However, Henry IV did visit Nottingham several times in the early years of their marriage between 1403 and 1407; it is very likely that Joan may have spent time at the castle during one of his visits in the summer of 1403, 1404, or 1405—particularly as we know she was with him in the region in late summer 1404 at Leicester. Even if a visit cannot be securely established, we know that Joan did send "stone cutters, carpenters and other workmen" along with "timber and carriage" to Nottingham, Beskwood, and Clipstone to make necessary repairs in March 1406—if she had visited shortly before this, she might have been made aware of works which needed to be made to her properties in the area.[74] She was also engaged in the repair of the mills in Brewhouse Yard at the castle, known as Sparrow, Donne, Dosse, and Gloff.

Havering-atte-Bower was not only the site of one of Joan's favoured residences as will be discussed in a later chapter, but the property also included a sizeable park. As David Rollason notes, the combination of a royal residence with a surrounding park and/or forest was fairly typical in the Middle Ages.[75] In Joan's portfolio we can see similar combinations including Havering and its park, Woodstock palace with its park and the adjoining Wychwood

Forest, Rockingham Castle and forest, and the aforementioned Nottingham Castle, which Joan held in combination with the nearby parks at Beskwood and Clipstone and Sherwood Forest. In Brittany, Joan also held the forest of Bignon, attached to the lordship of Touffou, which was a key source of timber for the city of Nantes and productive fisheries on the river, making it a profitable holding.[76] Indeed, Rollason notes the ways in which park and forest land not only provided space for hunting but was a means of enhancing the power, and wealth, of rulers through their control of the resources:

> forests were an important tool in the hands of rulers. They could convey messages of bureaucratic power through the sheer administrative control that the ruler was capable of exhibiting with regard to them, and from the resources, in venison and other materials and produce, that he was able to derive from them. They could convey messages of personal power through the hunting that took place in them ... but it is argued here that they could also convey messages of ideological power.[77]

Central to this was the unusual level of control that rulers had over forest areas as land which was outside the normal common law and had a distinct set of administrative offices and its own system of courts to monitor and enforce the rights of the king—or queen in this case. Indeed, Amanda Richardson has collectively examined the role of medieval English queens' engagement with forest and park land, noting both how this was a key aspect of their "lordly authority" and how they "altered the ecological signature of these landscapes".[78] This included ancient rights that the ruler could exercise and extract revenue from in park and forest lands, which could become a bone of contention. These rights, which Joan was keen to exercise and protect, include chiminage, or a toll for carts passing through forest lands, the right to "hamble" dogs or remove some of their claws so that they could not pose a threat to game in the forest, and various pasturing rights including herbage, agistments, and pannage, which allowed pigs to graze in the forest for acorns. The latter right was also known as "garsanage" (or garsanese) and caused considerable conflict during Joan's tenure of Havering. In her study of the manor, Marjorie McIntosh noted that while it was a very profitable fee for previous holders of the manor, the revenues from garsanage had fallen considerably by the time that it came into Joan's hands. Perhaps because of this decline, it appears that Joan "attempt[ed] to collect 'garsanese' more assertively", leading to resistance from local leaders and two suits by the queen against them at the Court of Chancery.[79]

Another interesting example of a dispute triggered by the queen's desire to exercise her rights in park and forest lands comes from Sherwood Forest, where Joan again brought court cases against those who failed to pay fines for the hambling of dogs and chiminage in the forest.[80] Interestingly, these cases come from the later years of Joan's life, in the early 1430s, as does one of the Havering cases on garsanage. To contextualise this, it is worth remembering that after Joan was restored to her English dower in 1422, she fought near-constant battles to regain her rights to properties and revenues which had been taken from her during the period when her English dower was seized. These court cases are only a few examples of a wide range of disputes, suits, and petitions to Parliament to exercise and defend her rights as discussed earlier. It appears that Joan became increasingly aggressive about her rights both to properties and rights pertaining to them, perhaps because she was very aware of her vulnerability in this regard after her period of house arrest—and as we have seen, she was equally keen to defend her rights in Brittany as well, being involved in extended negotiations over the revenues of Nantes in this same period.

However, it must be said that Joan was keen to protect and preserve her rights, revenues, and properties throughout the whole of her life, not just in her later dowager years. An example of her efforts to protect her forest lands from her period as consort can be seen in relation to Wychwood, an ancient forest which bordered on the park and palace of Woodstock. In July 1412, letters patent were issued by her husband Henry IV to commission William Sturmy, Roger Westwood, John Willicotes, John Barton the Younger, Thomas Beckyngham, and John Brid to investigate reports trees had been cut down and damage done to the queen's forest at Wychwood.[81]

Here again we see Sir William Sturmy (chief steward of her estates) and John Brid, who was a member of the Devizes commission and also served as her bailiff and as parker at Woodstock. Another interesting member of the party was John Willicotes, who was likely the son of William Willicotes, who rented four manors from Joan, including Woodstock itself, for which he paid an annual rent of £127 16s.6d—his other son Thomas became controller of works at Woodstock after William's death in 1411.[82] In the next chapter we will be looking at these men again in the context of Joan's networks of service, examining the ways in which appointing men to key, lucrative positions in her administration was a means of building connections at court and across the realm. Here it is important to note the role that Joan's officials played in maintaining her connection to her lands and administering them under her aegis.

As noted previously, the work of Joan and her officials was not always well perceived—we have seen criticism of buildings which became ruinous due to lack of repair on her lands and resistance from her tenants to her desire to collect the full dues owed to her from ancient rights and customs on her lands. Indeed, Joan perhaps went too far at times in her desire to exercise the rights she had as the "lord" of these forests and her exploitation of their resources. In August 1413, she was chastised for contravening the king's order to suspend the felling of "oaks, lopping of boughs or underwoods" in forests belonging to the Crown until further notice.[83] She admitted that "before the writ was made she sold certain underwoods within the said forest, whereof she is tenant for life by the grant of the late king, and that the buyers caused them to be cut down before the writ was made".[84] Again, while criticism of queens and their officials were hardly unique to Joan's tenure, this kind of censure has added to her reputation as an "avaricious" queen who was more interested in extracting maximum profit and revenue than being a good steward of her lands.

Over the course of this section, we have explored a key aspect of Joan's life experience and queenship by looking at how she amassed an extensive international portfolio of lands and revenues. Despite the sheer size of her holdings and the revenue it was supposed to bring her, this examination has also revealed the intense struggles that Joan had to ensure that she had a consistent income, from difficulties collecting amounts due and constant challenge to her right to the lands from disputes with other lords and tenants, to seizures of her lands by her son and stepson. We have also seen how Joan was actively engaged with her dower over several decades by exploring the variety of means through which Joan maintained a connection with her widespread collection of landholdings on both sides of the English Channel. We have seen her defend her rights to lands and revenues—from engaging in lengthy disputes with her son over the revenues from the county of Nantes to bringing suits against those who failed to pay their due for customary rights in her parks and forests. We have seen her efforts, not always successful, to maintain or even improve castles and manors and her physical connection with these sites, which we will explore further when we look at Joan's residences in a later chapter. While Joan could not visit all of the properties that she held and was cut off from her Breton holdings by the Channel and the hostilities of the Hundred Years War, we can see a sense of connection maintained through her administration of them in tandem with her officials, who assisted her and represented her "on the ground", which we will examine further in the following chapter. Next, we turn from her dowers to other forms of income she received—continuing a theme of struggles with inconsistent income and Joan's strident efforts to ensure she received what she was due as duchess and queen.

Supplemental income: Grants, annuities, wardships, and the queen's gold

Having thoroughly examined her English dower, we turn to the additional revenue streams that Joan had access to, starting with supplementary grants, which for Joan took the shape of Lancastrian annuities. As noted previously, Henry IV clearly encountered difficulty in providing Joan with the full 10,000 marks per annum he promised her in income from her dower. Another option that Henry had to provide funding for his wife was to reach into his own purse, as it were, and give Joan an annuity from his own lands—the duchy of Lancaster. Henry's stepmother, Katherine Swynford, had been paid a £1,000 annuity from the duchy during her lifetime. Katherine conveniently died in May 1403, only a few months after Henry and Joan's wedding—Henry lost little time in transferring this grant to Joan on 27 June 1403, roughly six weeks after Katherine's death.[85] Later that same year, in November, a slight adjustment was made to the specific lands in the duchy that the queen's grant was drawn from to ensure that she received the full amount due.[86] The grant broke down to 700 marks (£446 13s 4d) from duchy lands in Lincolnshire, 500 marks (£333 6s 8d) from lands in Staffordshire and Derbyshire, and another 300 marks (£200) from lands in Huntingdonshire. Surviving records of annuities from the duchy of Lancaster show the annuity being consistently paid out—at least the 500 marks (£333 6s 8d) from the Staffordshire and Derbyshire lands can be clearly traced to Joan between 1405 and 1410.[87]

However, Henry V appears to have been keen to preserve the revenues from the duchy and reclaim some of the annuities and Lancastrian lands that had gone to his stepmother and others of his father's supporters. While Somerville notes that she continued to receive grants from the duchy, Joan no longer appears to feature as a key annuity holder in records from Henry V's tenure of the duchy. It seems possible then that Joan may have been part of the £10,000 cut in royal and duchy annuities that Christine Carpenter notes Henry V made at the outset of his reign.[88] Thus it seems that from at least 1415 onwards she was no longer receiving the same Lancastrian annuity—Henry V also refused to honour the request in his father's will that Joan be provided for from the duchy's revenues. Indeed, as we will see in our discussion of Joan's residences in a later chapter, in 1415 Henry also exchanged the manor and palace of Kings Langley for the castle, manor, and town of Hertford, which Joan had been granted from the duchy lands back in September 1404. Altogether it seems that this secondary stream of revenue decreased and may have entirely disappeared once Joan transferred from consort to dowager queen.

Another way that Henry IV sought to satisfy the hefty income that he had promised her was by granting her wardships. Earlier queens, such as Eleanor of Provence, also held many wardships; indeed, Crawford notes that these were a useful way for the king to "augment his wife's income with land without depleting the royal demesne".[89] Michele Seah has also noted that "wardships proved to be another lucrative and important resource" for the finances of Joan's successors, such as Margaret of Anjou, who also held several wardships.[90] The financial benefits of wardship were multiple—first the queen would benefit from the revenues from their lands during their minority and could also reassign revenues to others to build their networks and reward supporters. There were additional monetary aspects if the wardship included the marriage, which could be lucrative to bestow, and the wardship itself could be sold on or reassigned. While these benefits were ultimately temporary, as they would cease when the ward came of age and married, it was a useful way for Henry to try to obtain more income for Joan in the short term. Moreover, there was a greater significance beyond a means to stabilise Joan's financial situation—as Chris Given-Wilson notes, "Henry IV habitually used trusted members of his family to oversee the rehabilitation of his opponent's heirs", thus his assignment of some of the most important heirs of the realm to his wife, whether they were the sons of his opponents or not, indicated his trust in her to bring them up as Lancastrian loyalists.[91]

Joan began to accrue wardships very early on during her tenure, with four substantial ones granted in 1403: John Daubeney on 29 August, Humphrey Stafford on 29 October, and Richard Scrope (or Lescrope) and Fulk Montho, both dated to 14 December 1403 in the Patent Rolls.[92] Henry was very quick to seize on the Daubeney wardship as a means of income for Joan, assigning to the queen the custody of the young John Daubeney's lands and possessions during his minority, as well as the rights to his marriage, only seven days after his father Giles had died on 22 August 1403. John's marriage was later arranged to Elizabeth Scrope, sister of another of Joan's wards, Richard, whose wardship the queen obtained in 1403 as well, but sadly John died shortly after this was arranged in 1409.

The Stafford wardship was a significant one due to both the size of the estate and the long potential for financial benefit, as the heir, Humphrey, was less than a year old when his father died, but perhaps it was an opportunity that Joan took too much advantage of. Within a week of obtaining the wardship, she granted the custody of the manor and town of Rothwell in Northamptonshire to "her knight", John de Assheton, for £56 5s 10 ½d yearly, and she later granted another member of her network, Walter Brigge, £10 a year from the manor of Whatcote in Warwickshire, which was also part of the Stafford lands in 1412.[93] Indeed, her tenure of the Stafford lands was marked by controversy in multiple ways. In 1409 and 1410 commissions were sent out to deal with issues connected to the management of the Stafford lands—the latter was not only related to Joan's tenure of the wardship but a wider pattern of abuses and concealed profits in the lordship of the castle of Caux going back to the time of Richard II.[94] However, the 1409 case was in regard to a complaint brought by the queen over the treatment of her officials on the manor of Callington in Cornwall. It appears that as Joan did not receive the customary £45 fine that the tenants should have paid every 12 years, her officials confiscated some livestock in lieu of payments. Three tenants then broke in to the manor and not only took back the animals but assaulted her official, John Wachet, and threatened several of her servitors.[95] Perhaps in relation to this, Humphrey later brought multiple suits at the beginning of Henry VI's reign against Joan and her tenant farms, claiming that they had exploited his estates during his long minority.[96] At roughly the same time, when Joan was already in a prolonged battle to regain the rights to her lands seized by Henry V, she successfully fought another dispute connected to the Stafford lands over the custody of a messuage, land, and meadow in Levedale belonging to the young John Stafford, son of a knight, and the right to his marriage which Joan felt was part of the wider Stafford wardship, but Lady Bergevenny contested this.[97]

Joan played an active part in the accrual of wardships as well, petitioning for the custody of wards which the king then granted her—this was the case for the wardship of Fulk Montho, for which she petitioned and was granted in December 1403, and for Richard Despencer, which she was granted in April 1405 after another successful petition.[98] Three other wardships were granted to her in 1405 besides Despencer: Thomas West in April, Robert Ughtreth in August, and Thomas Lovell in October.[99] After this date, grants of wardships appear to taper off—while she was granted the marriages of Fulk FitzWarin and Edmund Mortimer in 1407 and 1408, respectively, that appears to mark the end of major wardships given to the queen. Ultimately, wardships seem to have been another of Henry and Joan's strategies to secure her desired income of 10,000 marks per annum—while a useful stop-gap perhaps, these were a short-term solution. In January 1414, it was noted in letters patent that some of her wardships had ended as the heirs reached their majority. Indeed, wardships did not always last long, as we saw with the premature death of John Daubeney or in the case of Thomas Lovell, who reached his majority less than five years after the queen was granted the custody of his lands. Overall, like the annuities, this appears to have been a useful way to supplement Joan's income during her consort years, but may not have been a means to secure her long-term financial comfort as a dowager.

Collecting the queen's gold

Finally, we come to the third revenue stream of Hilda Johnstone's trifecta of queenly revenues—the queen's gold. Effectively this was a levy of 10 per cent on all voluntary fines made to the king. There is a lack of clarity on exactly how large the original fine had to be in order to incur a payment of queen's gold—while the twelfth-century *Dialogus de Scaccario* debated whether the minimum fine was ten marks or a hundred, Kristen Geaman has pointed out records which clearly indicate that the levy was collected on fines of much lower sums.[100] In effect the queen's gold was a payment to the queen which acknowledged her for her intercessory ability, recognising the queen's role as "their future Mediatrix and advocate to the king".[101] The queen's gold had the potential to be a key source of revenue to the queen—Eleanor of Castile took £1,564 17s 4d in 1290; indeed, Louise Tingle has claimed that Eleanor realised more revenue from queen's gold than from her lands at times.[102] Thus, the queen's gold was clearly a key source of revenue that could provide useful funds to support the queen and her household.

Yet, while the levy was affirmed by law and long-standing custom, queens frequently struggled to collect their revenue from it, even though many queens such as Philippa of Hainault and Eleanor of Castile had specific officials designated for exactly this purpose.[103]

Geaman underlines this difficulty noting that "queens did not always directly control this resource"; it was up to the diligence of their officials and the support of the king and his government to ensure that the levy was collected.[104] Johnstone argues that "the first problem [in collecting queen's gold] was the one in which the wits of her friends and officials were pitted against the ingenuity of those from whom the fines were due".[105] Unsurprisingly, there was considerable loathing to pay an extra 10% on top of a voluntary fine and thus people tried to get out of it by any means possible—by merely failing to pay it unless they were forced to or by attempting to argue that their fine was not one to which the queen's gold was applicable. The officials of the Exchequer were not always vigilant to ensure that the levy due to the queen was paid when these voluntary fines were collected and when pressed to account for missing levies, Johnstone notes that the Exchequer's response could be "surprisingly evasive or slow".[106]

Joan found herself in exactly this situation—like many of her predecessors, she struggled to collect the queen's gold throughout her husband's reign. Indeed, Joan wrote to her husband in January 1412 to complain at the lack of revenue that Joan was receiving from the queen's gold levy.[107] Joan's letter to her husband is both frank and forceful—she began by thanking him for raising her to the estate of queen of England and bestowing the crown upon her. She then noted that all queens of England had had the right to claim the levy of the queen's gold for so long that it exceeded living memory—Tingle notes that the phrasing that this levy belonged to "all queens time out of mind" was enshrined at the time of Richard I's coronation and was continually repeated, even into Prynne's treatise in the Stuart era.[108] Joan was leveraging tradition here, calling on ancient and customary rights and also following the footsteps of her predecessors, like Philippa of Hainault, who similarly complained to her husband Edward III in 1338. Joan expressed frustration with the officials of the Exchequer and begged Henry to intercede on her behalf so that she might regain the funds that she had a right to collect as queen of the realm.

Henry did indeed respond to her letter—Prynne argues that Henry was "very zealous, out of his affection to his Queen" to collect the levy owed to her.[109] Tingle has noted that while many kings were enthusiastic supporters of their wife's right to collect the levy, the level of support of kings could be impacted by their personal relationship, noting that Eleanor of Provence and Eleanor of Aquitaine lost their access to the queen's gold during disputes with their husbands.[110] In a document dated 27 April 1412, only three months after the queen's letter, Henry reasserted the rights of the queen to claim these fines generally, but also noted that outstanding fines would be collected retroactively as a list follows of all fines from the fifth year of his reign onwards upon which the queen's gold should have been levied.[111] There are 36 entries on the list; the fines themselves ranged from 15 to 1000 marks. Adding them altogether, the total fines came to £6,287—Joan's levy would have come to approximately £629, which was nearly 1,000 marks, a very tidy sum indeed, if she was able to collect all of the revenue due.

Henry died less than a year later, in March 1413, leaving Joan as a widowed dowager queen who was now at the mercy of her stepson, Henry V, to protect her prerogatives. The situation regarding the rights of dowager queens to collect the queen's gold was somewhat muddy. Dowager queens retained the right to collect the levy on fines which had been due to their husband and/or collected in his reign. But if there was a new queen consort, the levy should in theory go to them—although as Geaman notes, Eleanor of Aquitaine continued to claim queen's gold, perhaps because she was still seen as the primary intercessor during the reigns of her sons Richard and John, leaving Berengaria of Navarre and Isabella d'Angoulême bereft of these funds.[112] Yet, Henry V was not married at this point, leaving the possibility that Joan could continue to collect the levy.

Interestingly, the largest group of slips relating to Joan and the queen's gold levy date to the first year of Henry V's reign. Clearly Henry V and/or his officials were keen to ensure that his stepmother received what she was due.[113] The impetus for this seems to have come from Joan, who petitioned her stepson at the very start of his reign to help her collect what was owed to her in a similar way to how she had entreated Henry IV in the aforementioned letter. In the

Calendar of Close Rolls, an entry from 7 July 1413 notes that the king orders, in response to Joan's petition and in replication of his father's orders on the matter, that

> all business of hers brought before them [the treasurer and the barons] which concerned lands, farms, fees and liberties to her granted by him in dower or for life, the queen's gold or other property, should be treated and furthered as his own [i.e. the king's] … debtors of the queen's gold and of all other moneys or farms should be treated as his debtors … as it is found in divers records thereof in the time of Queen Isabel in her widowhood after the death of King Edward II.[114]

An initial analysis of these records shows some interesting connections. Ninety-eight of the slips are related to collecting queen's gold or a specific fine or amount owed the queen—sometimes noted as being in connection with her dower. Yet only a few, however, can be connected to the debtors noted on Prynne's list from 1412—examples include Humphrey Stafford and the earl of Westmorland. The latter faced a large levy to Joan, for 1,000 marks, and it appears from these records that he may have been paying that to her piecemeal over time. Two more items of interest can be seen in the text of the slips. There is a note that Thomas Feriby was collecting these fines for the queen—this tallies with other records which note that he was her treasurer and receiver-general during this period. Another interesting item is the way that Joan was referred to in these slips—she is noted as "our beloved mother". This is interesting in connection with the other references to Joan as the king's mother rather than the king's widow, and significant given the volte-face of 1419 when her stepson accused her of treason and detained her. Also, in a few places the word "*matris*" or mother appears to have been written in after a rub out—perhaps the clerks were used to putting her in as a "beloved consort" for the last ten years and had to correct their mistakes to note Joan's changed status as "beloved mother".

In sum, this section has not only demonstrated other sources of revenues to which Joan had access but has demonstrated the difference between her relationship with Henry IV and Henry V and the impact of her change from consort to dowager. Henry IV was keen to support his beloved wife and ensure that she had adequate funds at her disposal to support her household and uphold her rights as queen using his funds from the duchy of Lancaster and supporting her claim to the queen's gold. While Henry V was also keen to do right by Joan and continued his father's efforts to support her reclamation of her rights and revenues, he was less willing to support her from the duchy of Lancaster. In addition, while we can see that Henry V continued his father's project to retroactively claim back all the unpaid queen's gold, it does not appear that he allowed Joan to continue to claim the levy as a dowager.

Expenditure: Spending like a queen

Finally, it remains to consider the impact that Joan's long-term struggle to realise the revenues that she was due had on her spending power and ability to maintain herself in a manner befitting her queenly status. It must be noted that it is much easier to trace Joan's revenues from surviving manorial accounts, receipts from ports and fee farms, and other documentation than it is to trace her outgoings, as this documentation has not survived in significant quantities. Indeed, a consistent issue when studying the financial situation of medieval English queens is the patchy survival of their household records and accounts, as there has been greater emphasis on the cataloguing and preservation of material connected to the Crown and the ruler, rather than queens consort and dowager. As noted previously, we have the best understanding of Joan's financial situation, as well as the composition and functioning of her household, during the period when she was under house arrest, as her accounts were being audited by the Crown and thus these records have largely survived.[115] In addition to this, we are fortunate to have one surviving household account book from 1427–28, which is preserved in the collection of the Society of Antiquaries and gives an excellent overview of both her incoming revenue and outgoing expenditure during this period.[116]

TABLE 5.1 Daily average spend across key categories in Joan's surviving household accounts (*in pence = d*)

Category	*1 Oct–15 Dec 1419*	*17 Mar 1420–7 Mar 1421*	*8 Mar–21 Jul 1422*	*4 Apr 1427–4 Apr 1428*
Necessaria	23d	11d	12d	79d
Dona	19d	4d	11d	244d
Wardrobe	130d	N/A	N/A	325d
Queen's Chamber	76d	N/A	63d	565d
Oblaciones	N/A	2d	5d	17d

A review of her surviving account books demonstrates a clear difference between the level of expenditure for her household during the years of confinement versus the "normal" 1427–28 account books. To illustrate this, we can do a comparison of the daily average spend across the surviving account books for the major areas of expenditure: Necessaria (supplies for various departments), Dona (gifts), Wardrobe, the Queen's Chamber, and Oblaciones (offerings/alms). For example, the Wardrobe accounts show a difference of approximately two and a half times higher spending in 1427–28 versus the October–December 1419 accounts. The difference in the Queen's Chamber is even more marked—in this area Joan was spending seven and a half to nine times more in the 1427–28 accounts as she spent in the period of confinement. The average daily spend is also considerably lower for Necessaria and Dona from 1419 to 1422, but this can easily be accounted for with regard to her reduced circumstances—the smaller size of her household necessitated fewer supplies and Joan had less money at her disposal, meaning she could not be as generous in gifting. The Oblaciones section appears to have a less marked difference between the "normal" and detention period due to the smaller sums involved, but Joan was still spending three to six times more on offerings in the 1427–28 period.

There is also a clear trend towards overspending, which is unsurprising if Joan was spending the full extent of what she felt she was due, rather than what was actually coming in. As discussed earlier, revenues were often slow to arrive, in arrears, or even in dispute, but her own creditors would still expect to be paid. While it has to be noted that the majority of the surviving account books date to the period of her confinement when her revenues were considerably depressed given that her lands had been seized by the Crown, the most serious example of overspend actually dates to her later life, from the accounts for 1427–28, which has a significant "surplus" or overspend of £803 18s 7 ½d—a serious amount to be "in the red".

This begs two questions—was her spending out of line with her contemporaries and what was she spending her money on? In connection with the first query, we can do a comparison of the daily diet accounts for food expenditure to place them in the wider context in terms of both royal and elite households, as the table demonstrates, by using accounts from two fifteenth-century bishops' households in Woolgar's *Household Accounts* collection and the royal household account book for 1405–6.[117] However, there is again a significant difference in total spending—as we can see in Table 5.2, Joan's household was much higher than the comparative elite examples but significantly lower than the royal household's expenditure. Even though this comparison comes from the beginning of Joan's period of detention, we can see that her household expenditure was on an entirely different level to that of the bishops' households, spending far more on a daily basis even during a period of captivity with a reduced household. As to be expected, the scale of expenditure is completely different between the combined royal

TABLE 5.2 Comparison between daily household "diet" expenditure

*Household account and date**	*Comparison expenditure*	*Joan's expenditure*
Richard Mitford, 20 Oct 1406	5s 5½d	101s 1½d
John Hales, 2 Oct 1461	5s 5d	119s 7½d
Royal Household, 20 Oct 1405	995s 6d	101s 1½d

Note: All of Joan's examples come from the same day or week in October 1419.

household and the dowager queen's, both in detention and in a "normal" period as we can see using examples from March. For example, on 20 March 1406 the royal household spent £75 21s ½d (1,521s ½d) to the queen's diet of 103s 3d on 20 March 1428—even less was spent during her detention on 20 March 1420, only 32s 9 ½d. Thus we can see that, even as a dowager queen in detention, Joan was spending like a queen at levels which exceeded her ecclesiastical counterparts, but nowhere near the amount of the entire royal household during her marriage to Henry IV.

Looking at how anyone spends their money gives you a good idea of their day-to-day life and what was important to them—Joan's account books are similarly revealing about her life and the pressures of queenship, as the key categories of expenditure demonstrate. The two Dona sections in the 1427–28 manuscript comprise gifts, noted as being "from the hand" or "by the mandate" of the queen. Taken together, Joan spent £383 13s 10d on gifts during this period, equivalent to nearly £240,000 today. Most of these gifts were to servants, such as the queen's chaplain, John Sadyington, who received 40s, or Blanche Chalons, one of her ladies, who was gifted £20. Annuities form another significant element of expenditure, demonstrating that Joan spent a large proportion of her funds on gifts and annuities to those in her service or in her network of connections, who will be discussed in detail in the following chapter—some recipients can be found in both Dona and Annuities. Some of these annuities were very generous, such as the 500 marks a year that she granted her (arguably favourite) stepson, Humphrey, duke of Gloucester. Given the fact that many of the annuities were directly derived from her incoming revenue, such as the 500 marks reassigned to Humphrey from her wool customs from the town of Southampton, this would clearly have a crippling effect on her incoming funds. Even the accounts of the Queen's Chamber show Joan's generosity, with several items purchased noted as being gifts, which will be discussed further in the last chapter, such as the collar with 24 oriental pearls which cost £16 given as a gift to her stepdaughter-in-law Eleanor Cobham. Indeed, John Pattersley, a London jeweller, did very well in the accounts of the Queen's Chamber, though again most of the commissions she gave him were items gifted to others, although it was noted that she did keep one 19oz gold cup from him that cost £29 12s 6d for herself. The Wardrobe section shows much more varied and day-to-day expenditure, including the wages of carpenters making repairs or making a new window for the Queen's Chamber.

Thus, a large amount of Joan's expenditure was spent not on herself directly but on maintaining her household and house itself, as well as generous gifts to those who served her as well as to friends and family. Why was Joan spending way beyond her means—giving away her cash in gifts and grants to others? The answer is in two parts: keeping up appearances and in maintaining networks of service and court connections. A key element of being a queen was having a household and home which was befitting of her rank; being able to pay a large retinue of servants and keep the house in style was important to preserving one's position. Joan had clearly taken a step down from her days as queen consort, but she was still a queen and was determined to continue to live in a queenly manner as a dowager, even if she could not truly afford to do so. She might be living at her manor of Kings Langley, away from the central court circuit, but Joan clearly wanted anyone who visited her home to get the impression that she was regal and royal, with all the accoutrements of queenly status. The following chapters will pick up these two themes and explore the development and maintenance of Joan's networks of service as well as discuss her expenditure on gift giving, possessions, and her residences.

As we will shortly see, maintaining a cosmopolitan and sizable retinue was more than a key part of projecting her status and authority as queen, no matter how challenging the circumstances. Without the support of these long-standing and loyal servants, Joan would have been completely unable to function as queen and certainly would never have been able to survive the years of confinement nor re-establish herself after her release in 1422. Their loyalty and the financial records which chart her generous gifts to her servants demonstrates that Joan was a good mistress, rewarding those in her service with annuities and positions. Beyond her servants, Joan's largest "pensioner", her stepson Humphrey, also showed Joan great loyalty and service—he attempted to get her confessor out of the

Tower of London when he was implicated in the charge of treason, visited her when she was under house-arrest, and supported her petitions to Henry VI's minority council to restore her dower. Thus, while Joan may appear somewhat financially reckless in giving away a substantial portion of her revenues as gifts and annuities, it could also be seen as a shrewd investment in an affinity of servants and supporters who would give her both security and help her to retain or regain her position.

Conclusion

In summary, we can see the economic challenges that Joan faced, particularly over the course of her 34 years as an English queen consort and dowager. She struggled to receive the income from her Breton dower and the generous revenues promised by her husband, despite his steadfast support. Joan's relationship with her stepson was mixed, both economically and generally—on one hand he worked scrupulously to ensure she collected fines due to her and reaffirmed her dower when she was widowed, yet at the same time her dower grant was appreciably reduced by Henry V; he also appears to have cut off her duchy of Lancaster annuity and in 1419 he seized her dower altogether. Was she then his "beloved mother" or just an expensive and expendable foreign hanger-on who was seen by her stepson as a drain on royal finances? While Joan's revenues were eventually restored in the reign of Henry VI, her household account books of 1427 show that she still struggled to make ends meet and balance her queenly budget. Her own son, Jean V of Brittany, disputed her rights to her Breton revenues, leading to decades of disputes and negotiation after she left the duchy for a new life in England.

Regarding the queen herself, we can see that Joan was no shrinking violet—she had no problem protesting when she felt she was not receiving what she was due, keenly defending her rights where money was at stake, issuing letters of protests, petitions to Parliament, and taking matters to court when needed to try to obtain the full revenue that she felt was owed. We have also seen that part of her financial difficulties may have stemmed from maintaining her networks of service, which will be explored further in the chapter to follow—first from the large, costly foreign retinue that caused so much controversy as a consort and later in her generous gifts and revenues to those around her.

Looking at the bigger picture regarding what Joan's situation demonstrates about the economic aspect of queenship, it has highlighted the vulnerability of a queen's finances. She was dependent both on the king (whether it was her husband, son, or even grandson) for their grants of dower and supplements for her revenues. The queen also needed the support of the king and his government to ensure the collection of those revenues—but Joan's case demonstrates that a kingly husband's love and goodwill may not be enough to ensure a steady stream of revenue. As a dowager, a queen was even more financially vulnerable, as Joan's dower was seized under a shaky pretext, and without the support of the most powerful men on the regency council she may never have had her lands and revenues returned to her. In sum, while a queen may have sat at the epicentre of the realm, it does not mean that she was seated on a mountain of money per se. Her financial health depended on several factors—the support of the king and his government, stability in both royal finances and the political landscape, and finally her own prudent spending decisions.

Notes

1 Hilda Johnstone, "The Queen's Household," in *The English Government at Work, 1327–1336*, vol. 1, *Central and Prerogative Administration*, ed. James F. Willard and William A. Morris (Cambridge, MA: Mediaeval Academy of America, 1940), 253.

2 Agnes Strickland, *Lives of the Queens of England from the Norman Conquest; with Anecdotes of their Courts*, vol. III (Philadelphia: Lea and Blanchard, 1848), 67.

3 Jean Kerhervé, *L'état Breton aux 14e et 15e siècles; Les Ducs, l'Argent et les Hommes*, 2 vols. (Paris: Editeur Maloine, 1987), 61; Nicolas Kermabon, "*Ego Dux Britannie Dotavit Eam: Le douaire des duchesses de Bretagne (XIIIe–XVe siècle)*" (PhD thesis, Université de Rennes 1, 2007), 3 vols., I, 22.

4 ADLA E17-11, 12, and 13, dated 24 and 26 February 1387. This donation was ratified by the barons and prelates of Brittany by 18 April 138; see E17-14 and 15, both dated 18 April 1387.

5 Kermabon, "Douaire," I, 114, 122–23. See also Jean-Pierre Leguay and Herve Martin, eds., *Fastes et malheurs de la Bretagne ducale 1213–1532* (Rennes: Ouest France, 1982), 178.

6 See Michael Jones, "Jean IV et le pays de Retz: l'exercise et les limites du pouvoir ducal a la fin du XIVe siècle," in *Echanges et pouvoirs au pays de Retz (Actes du colloque a Machecoul 14 Avril 2007)* (La Bernerie-en-Retz: Societe des Historiens du Pays de Retz, 2008), 31–41.

7 Actes Jean IV, II, no. 1044, 26 February 1396; ADLA E17-13 and E16, f.31-35; Morice, II, 661–64. Note that a codicil of Jean IV's will of 26 October 1399 confirms her dower as per the 1396 settlement; see Kermabon, "Douaire," II, 187–88, and Actes Jean IV, II, no. 1179, 697; Morice, II, 699.

8 Jones, "Pays de Retz," 40. The agreements can be found in Morice, II, 691–93, signed 24 April 1399, and 706, signed 1 September 1400.

9 E. Fonssagrives, *Les Trois femmes de Jean IV; conference donnée à la Société Polymathique du Morbihan le 10 Avril 1923* (Vannes: Imprimerie du Commerce, 1923), 12.

10 CPR Henry IV, II, 4 June 1403, 234–35, 268–69, 271–72.

11 Anne Crawford, "The Queen's Council in the Middle Ages," *EHR* 116, no. 469 (2001): 1194.

12 Michael Jones, "Between France and England: Jeanne de Navarre, Duchess of Brittany and Queen of England (1386–1437)," in *Between France and England: Politics, Power and Society in Late Medieval Brittany* (Aldershot: Variorum, 2003), 12.

13 See Katia Wright, "A Dower for Life: Understanding the Dowers of England's Medieval Queens," in *Later Plantagenet and the Wars of the Roses Consorts: Power, Influence, Dynasty*, eds. Aidan Norrie, Carolyn Harris, J.L. Laynesmith, Danna Messer, and Elena Woodacre (New York: Palgrave Macmillan, 2022).

14 J.L. Kirby, *Henry IV of England* (London: Constable, 1970), 93.

15 John Rickard, *The Castle Community; The Personnel of English and Welsh Castles, 1272–1422* (Woodbridge: Boydell, 2002), 8–10 and tables on pages 79–83.

16 Phifer demonstrates that while a widow was generally able to retain her dower on remarriage, his study of litigation in relation to dower demonstrates that maintaining the dower of a woman who had remarried and gained additional resources could be seen as "an unreasonable imposition" which could be "the cause of social discontent". In addition, he notes that some provisions made for wives by their husbands specifically included a caveat that this would be lost if she remarried. See Michael J. Phifer, "Property, Power and Patriarchy: The Decline of Women's Property Right in England after the Black Death" (PhD thesis, University of Houston, 2014), 177–85.

17 ADLA E9-1, 18 November 1404, on Jean V's rights to pursue dowry payments; see also E9-16, Accord of J V and C III regarding dowry 28 January 1409; Kermabon, "Douaire," II, 231.

18 CPR Henry IV, II, 24 January 1404, 347–49; 18 July 1404, 402 and 418.
19 PROME, Henry IV: October 1404.
20 CPR Henry IV, II, 5 April 1405, 501.
21 Alan Rogers, "The Royal Household of Henry IV" (PhD thesis, University of Nottingham, 1966), 62, 76–7, 95, 120, 348, 369, 383, 399, 408–9.
22 PROME, Henry IV: March 1406, part 1; Rogers, "Household," 49, 124–25. See also Peter McNiven, "The King's Needs," in *Heresy and Politics in the Reign of Henry IV: The Burning of John Badby* (Woodbridge: Boydell, 1987), 174.
23 See a demand for Scarborough to pay the queen 27l 15s 8d a year and the arrears since Michaelmas last in CCR Henry IV, III, 16 June 1406, 41.
24 See SC 6/844/14 from Havering 1407–8, Staffs D641/1/2/48 (1 July 1406), and for Melton Mowbray see SC 6/1092/18 (1405–07), SC 6/1092/17 (1406–7), and SC 6/1092/21 (1408–10).
25 L&M J V, IV, nos. 246, 247, 251 and 252, all March 1406. Foedera 8, 10 May 1407. George Akenhead Knowlson, *Jean V, duc de Bretagne et l'Angleterre 1399–1442* (Cambridge: W. Heffer & Sons Ltd, 1964), 53.
26 CPR Henry IV, III, 2 March 1408, 413–14.
27 CPR Henry IV, III, 20 May 1408, 438–39.
28 See Kirby, *Henry IV*, 222–23; Crawford, "King's Burden," 43.
29 C 81/1362/46 quoted in Kirby, *Henry IV*, 223.
30 CPR Henry IV, IV, 1 July 1409, 85–87.
31 PROME, Henry IV: January 1410.
32 Examples of suits in 1410–11 include C44/23/6 and 8.
33 See SC 6/1093/2 (Wilts), E122/51/34 (Ipswich 1411–13), E122/150/15 (Yarmouth 1411–13), and Bedford and Luton R 6/62/12/13 (22 April 1411). Taxation records from 1412 also show the range of her holdings across several counties. For selected examples see *Inquisitions and Assessments Relating to Feudal Aids, with Other Analogous Documents Preserved in the Public Record Office; A.D. 1284–1431:* vol. VI (London: His Majesty's Stationery office, 1920), 399, 412, 428, 433.
34 CPR Henry V, I, 27 January 1414, 164–67.
35 CCR Henry V, I, 22 June 1414, 127–28; 12 July, 28 October and 4 November 1414, 130–1; 8 November 1414, 15; 14 October 1415, 239–40; 17 February 1416, 258; 28 April 1416, 301.
36 J. de la Martinière, "Un grand Chancelier de Bretagne – Jean de Malestroit," *Memoires de la Société d'Histoire et d'Archaeologie de Bretagne* 1 (1920): 45–9. The full account is reprinted in *Bulletin du Comité Historique des Monuments Écrits de l'Histoire de France. Histoire-Sciences-Lettres* 4 (1853): 73–90. Note the quotations are all my translations in the text above.
37 Knowlson, *Jean V*, 91.
38 L&M JV, V, no. 1182, November 1414.
39 For examples, see receipts from Yarmouth and Ipswich; E122/51/42 and E122/151/10, 1414–15 and 1415–16.

40 For examples of assessment, see E199/19/41 for Kent, and for re-assignment, see CFR XIV, 24 November 1420, 363.
41 Kermabon, "Douaire," II, 255, 266.
42 PROME, Henry VI: November 1422.
43 Crawford, "King's Burden," 44–5.
44 Harry W. Gidden, ed. *The sign manuals, and the letters patent of Southampton to 1422* (Southampton: Cox and Sharland, 1916–1919), 2–7.
45 Hampshire Record Office W/A2/7/1, 12 November 1422 and Southampton SC 1/4/9.
46 PROME, Henry VI: October 1423.
47 CCR Henry VI, I, 5 December 1426, 296–7 and 1427, 363–66.
48 CPR Henry VI, II, 8 May 1431, 119, and 4 July 1431, 141–42.
49 See CPR Henry VI, II, 17 December 1435, 530–31, and C/44/27/12, 1436–37.
50 See Winchester College Archives 2170 a and b, 2171 for protests against the pension, and 2140, 2141, 2143–2150 in regard to payments to the queen. See also 2142, dated 31 July 1414, for a mandate from Henry V to pay Joan the pension.
51 L&M JV, VI, no. 1821, 16 November 1428.
52 Kermabon "Douaire," II, 271. See also L&M JV, VI, nos. 1873, 1876, and 1922, dated 2 December and 26 December 1429 and 1 October 1430, respectively; Morice, II, 1231–32.
53 ADLA B 12838, f.133 v, 134 r; see also Kermabon, "Douaire," II, 272; Kerhervé, *L'Etat Breton*, 66.
54 J. Trevedy, "Le douaire des Duchesses de Bretagne: Contrats de mariage des Ducs (1)," *Revue de Bretagne* 37 (Feb 1907): 37.
55 Knowlson, *Jean V*, 164.
56 See Kermabon, "Douaire," II, 206, 235; ADLA E156-11, 18 May 1401.
57 Kerhervé, *L'Etat Breton*, 62; Kermabon, "Douaire", II, 241.
58 See ADLA B124–10 and ADLA B675-1, both dated 1402. It is unlikely, but it may be possible that this was the same Jehan de Roux who worked for Carlos III as an official in his treasury.
59 ADLA B4245 fols 40r–42v. See also documents for collection of rents in the village of Carvarden and the parish of Avessac in 1401 from her receivers in the region; ADLA B1816, dated 1401.
60 See ADLA B130 (1418) and 152–20 (1437).
61 CPR Henry IV, II, 10 Dec 1404, 473.
62 *King's Works*, I, 533.
63 Crawford, "Queen's Council," 1203.
64 Cited in Patricia MacGregor and Barry Stapleton, *Odiham Castle 1200–1500: Castle and Community* (Gloucester: Alan Sutton, 1982), 114.
65 MacGregor and Stapleton, *Odiham*, 114.
66 *King's Works*, II, 768.
67 CIM VIII, no. 154, 12 September 1438.
68 CIM VIII, 60, no. 108, 3 July 1438.
69 *King's Works*, II, 628.

70 CPR Henry IV, IV, 19 April 1410, 224; CPR Henry VI, II, 14 February 1433, 277; *King's Works*, II, 628.
71 CPR Henry IV, IV, 224.
72 CPR Henry IV, IV, 30 May 1409, 81.
73 *King's Works*, II, 628; SC 6/1062/25; CPR Henry IV, IV, 14 February 1412, 368.
74 CPR Henry IV, III, 30 March 1406, 228. See also Andrew Hamilton, *Nottingham's Royal Castle and Ducal Palace* (Nottingham: Nottingham Civic Society, 1991), 8, 13.
75 David Rollason, *The Power of Place: Rulers and their Palaces, Landscapes, Cities and Holy Places* (Princeton, NJ: Princeton University Press, 2016), 138.
76 Jones, "Pays de Retz," 39.
77 Rollason, *Power of Place*, 166. A similar argument on the importance of revenues is made in John Steane, *The Archaeology of the Medieval English Monarchy* (London: Routledge, 1999), 149–50.
78 Amanda Richardson, "Beyond the Castle Gate: The Role of Medieval Landscapes in Constructions of English Medieval Kingship and Queenship," *Concilium medii aevi* 14 (2011): 43.
79 Marjorie Keniston McIntosh, *Autonomy and Community: The Royal Manor of Havering, 1200–1500* (Cambridge: Cambridge University Press, 2002), 64. Court cases: C/1/69/2 and C/44/24/5.
80 *Records of the Borough of Nottingham*, vol. II (Nottingham: Thomas Forman & Sons, 1882), 122–24, 138–39.
81 CPR Henry IV, IV, 8 July 1412, 373.
82 L.S. Woodger, "Wilicotes, Willliam (d. 1411) of North Leigh, Oxon," in HoP.
83 CCR Henry V, I, 26 April 1413, 16.
84 CCR Henry V, I, 19 August 1413, 32–33.
85 DL 42/15 fol. 150v. Robert Somerville, *History of the Duchy of Lancaster*, vol. 1, *1265–1603* (London: Chancellor and the Council of the Duchy of Lancaster, 1953), 165.
86 DL 42/15 fol. 158. Somerville, *Duchy of Lancaster*, 165.
87 DL 28/27/1 (1402–4) and DL 28/27/3, 9, 10 (1405–10).
88 Christine Carpenter, *The Wars of the Roses: Politics and the Constitution in England* (Cambridge: Cambridge University Press, 1997), 72; Helen Castor, *The King, the Crown, and the Duchy of Lancaster: Public Authority and Private Power, 1399–1461* (Oxford: Oxford University Press, 2000), 36.
89 Crawford, "Queen's Council," 2001.
90 Michele Seah, "The Material Foundations of Queenship in Late-Medieval England, 1445–1509" (PhD thesis, University of Newcastle, Australia, 2019), 59. See also Sue Sheridan Walker, "Royal Wardship in Medieval England" (PhD thesis, University of Chicago, 1966), 122.
91 Given-Wilson, *Henry IV*, 447.

92 CPR Henry IV, II, 29 August 1403, 263; 29 October 1403, 328; 14 December 1403, 329; 1 December 1403, 332; 14 December 1403, 362.
93 CPR Henry IV, II, 4 November 1403, 327 and IV, 19 April 1412, 395.
94 CPR Henry IV, IV, 24 July 1410, 226.
95 CPR Henry IV, IV, 18 July 1409, 111.
96 Carole Rawcliffe, *The Staffords, Earls of Stafford and Dukes of Buckingham, 1394–1521* (Cambridge: Cambridge University Press, 1978), 179.
97 CPR Henry VI, I, 2 December 1423, 155–56.
98 Petition for Montho SC 8/229/11446, and grant CPR Henry IV, II, 1 December 1403, 332. Petition for the wardship of Despencer SC 8/231/11526, and grant CPR Henry IV, III, 6 April 1405, 4.
99 See CPR Henry IV, III, 24 April 1405,11; CPR Henry IV, II, 23 October 1404, 463; CIM VII, no. 432, 233–34.
100 Richard fitz Nigel, *Dialogus de Scaccario (The Course of the Exchequer)*, ed. and trans. Charles Johnson (Oxford: Clarendon Press, 1983), 123; Kristen Geaman, "Queen's Gold and Intercession: The Case of Eleanor of Aquitaine," *Medieval Feminist Forum* 46, no. 2 (2010): 13. See also William Prynne, *Aurum reginae …* (London: Thomas Ratcliffe, 1668), 2.
101 Prynne, *Aurum reginae*, 5.
102 Crawford, "Queen's Council," 1196; Louise Tingle, "Aurum Reginae: Queen's Gold in Late Fourteenth-Century England," *Royal Studies Journal* 7, no. 1 (2020): 83.
103 Johnstone, "Queen's Household," 285; Crawford, "Queen's Council," 1196; fitz Nigel, *Dialogus*, 122; Prynne, *Aurum Reginae*, 7.
104 Geaman, "Queen's Gold," 15.
105 Johnstone, "Queen's Household," 264.
106 Johnstone, "Queen's Household," 264.
107 BL RP 6767, dated 7 January 1412. There is only one slip which appears to date from before this letter, E5/574 (11 Henry IV; 30 September 1409–29 September 1410).
108 Prynne, *Aurum reginae*, 8. Original quote from BL RP 6767 "*apelle Aurum Regine le quel Or as Royns d'Engleterre pur le temps esteantz ad appentuz de droit de lour Corone et elles ount este en possession dicelles du temps dont memorie ne court.*" Tingle, "Aurum Reginae," 80.
109 Prynne, *Aurum reginae*, 64.
110 Tingle, "Aurum Reginae," 80–1.
111 Prynne, *Aurum reginae*, 63. Original E159/288, Memoranda Roll 13 Henry IV, Michaelmas to Trinity.
112 Geaman, "Queen's Gold," 17, 19–23. See also Crawford, "Queen's Council," 1198, which affirms that dowagers should not collect queen's gold if there was a new consort.
113 This would fit neatly with Jonathan Sumption's comment that "Henry V devoted a personal attention to his finances unmatched since the reign

of Edward I". Sumption, *Cursed Kings: The Hundred Years War IV* (London: Faber and Faber, 2016), 419.

114 CCR Henry V, I, 7 July 1413, 25–26.

115 "Account Book of Thomas Lillebourne," TNA E101/406/30, 1 October–15 December 1419; "Enrolled Accounts of Thomas Lilleburne" 1419–20, TNA E364/63, rot. 5; "Account Book of the household of Joan of Navarre", 1420–21, University of Manchester John Rylands Collection Latin MS 238; "Wardrobe Book of Joan Queen of England, 9 Hen. 5", 1422, Leeds Castle Archives E4/1.

116 John Bugge, "Queen Joan. Primus compotus Johannis Bugge (Household Accounts 1427–28)", Society of Antiquaries SAL/MS/216.

117 See C.M. Woolgar, *Household Accounts from Medieval England: Parts 1 and 2* (Oxford: Oxford University Press, 1992–93); Diet account 14: Richard Mitford, Bishop of Salisbury and Diet account 16: John Hales, Bishop of Coventry and Lichfield and BL Harley MS 319.

6

NETWORKS OF SERVICE

The vital importance of a strong and wide-ranging network of service or affinity has long been acknowledged as a key factor in securing and maintaining one's position for elites and royals. Although this has been discussed frequently in the context of elite men and kingship in the Middle Ages, there has been less scholarship with regard to elite and royal women.[1] However, new studies in this area are aiming to fill the gap. Diana Pelaz Flores's impressive doctoral thesis on the Castilian queens of the fifteenth century includes a deep analysis of the queens' households and their affinities, tracing the makeup of and connections between those in the queens' service using social network analysis techniques.[2] Michelle Beer's work on Catherine of Aragon demonstrates the loyalty and support offered by the queen's affinity as Henry VIII sought to strip away this network of service by removing the lands and financial means that Catherine required to maintain it so that he could ultimately remove her from office.[3]

The lengthy career of Joan of Navarre provides an excellent case study for the vital support offered by a network of service or affinity. Her situation demonstrates the role that a cohort of servants can play in navigating both transitions between roles and

DOI: 10.4324/9780429261022-9

treacherous political situations. The support offered by her servants was critical to her survival in terms of retaining familiar faces as she transitioned from infanta to duchess to queen to dowager. We will examine how she was able to extend her networks of service and patronage by cultivating additional personnel and contacts in new areas. Her success in creating and maintaining this affinity is demonstrated through both the records of long service and the loyalty that those in her service maintained to her even when she lost prominence in the English court after the death of her husband and, more significantly, when she was accused of witchcraft and kept under house arrest for several years.

This chapter will trace Joan's networks of service over the course of her long life and many roles. It will extend beyond her immediate household to include those who were involved in the management of her lands in both Brittany and England, and her wider networks of patronage and gift gifting. In addition to a broad analysis of the composition and categories of this network, several case studies of key servitors and families of servitors will highlight the important role they played in the queen's service, their relationships with her over time, and the international makeup of her household. Then we will examine the reaction to her very international household in England by examining various petitions for the expulsion of aliens at court and specifically those in the queen's service over the reigns of all three Lancastrian kings. Finally, we will finish with a look at the officials who helped the queen administer her sizable portfolio of lands as discussed in the previous chapter, before reflecting on the significance of Joan's networks of service.

Finding traces of Joan's networks of service

The sources for this study are challenging because they are quite varied between Navarre, Brittany, and England and rather patchy. Records for the households of queens, duchesses, and infantas are never as well kept as those for their male counterparts. For Navarre, while there is an excellent study of the household of Joan's elder sister Maria in 1365–66 based on surviving records in the Archivo General de Navarra, no similar cache of records appears to have survived to document Joan's establishment as an infanta, if indeed she ever had a household of her own.[4] As discussed in the first chapter, from the few records that survive of Joan's childhood we know that she spent her early years in the Convent of Santa Clara in Estella with other royal children, where she would have had little need for an extensive household. Joan joined the royal Navarrese household in due course, probably after 1380, where several female relatives were based with their servants, including Joan's sister Maria and her aunt Agnes, who had returned to Navarre after her marriage to Gaston Fébus of Foix broke down. Once Joan became the focus of a matrimonial negotiation and was being prepared for her wedding to Jean IV of Brittany, records from the Camara de Comptos mention those in her service more frequently. Through her ongoing connection with her natal family, the Navarrese documents offer glimpses into her household through mentions of rewards for those who served her and acted as go-betweens for the young duchess.

In Brittany, documents which record the makeup of Joan's household as duchess and, later, regent are few. Michael Jones notes in his article on the Breton court that records are generally scarce and those for the duchess's household are rarer still.[5] Yet we can still get a sense of a quasi-royal court in the duchy of Brittany during this period; Marcel Planiol claims that the ducal court had nearly 250 people attached to it during the Montfort period.[6] Surviving documents do give an indication of the size of the household of Joan's immediate successor, Jeanne de Valois, wife of Joan's son Jean V. Jeanne de Valois had 37 people in her household according to documentation from 1416 to 1417 and 1420, including chamberlains, confessors, *ecuyers d'honneur* (esquires or gentlemen), *asséours* (officers of the household), treasurers, garderobe, and a *maréchal de salle*, giving us some indication perhaps of the possible size and composition of Joan's household as duchess. However, it must be noted that Joan followed two largely absentee duchesses, Mary of England and Joan Holland, the first two wives of Jean IV. Thus, there was not a clear framework or pattern for the duchesses' household for Joan to utilise—it would have perhaps been Joan who set the trend for Jeanne de Valois and her successors to follow.

There is a clearer understanding of Joan's household in England as queen consort and dowager, both because of the documentary sources which survive and because there have been several helpful studies of the household of English queens in the Middle Ages which provide a wider context to Joan's situation. Studies of fourteenth-century households include Hilda Johnstone's classic examination of the queen's household, Lisa Benz's comparative study of queens consort in the early fourteenth century, and Caroline Dunn's research on ladies-in-waiting in the Middle Ages, which illuminate the household and wider administrative network of Joan's predecessors, particularly Isabella of France and Phillipa of Hainault.[7] The work of Anne Crawford and Joanna Laynesmith on the household and administration of Joan's successors both provide helpful context for the later fifteenth century.[8] Taken together, while few works have been focused exclusively on Joan and her household to date, there is a clear framework to build upon in terms of how the queen's household and administration functioned generally in the later Middle Ages in England. Johnstone's model of "two interlocked rings" of service to the queen, the smaller being the court, its office, and wardrobe, and the larger being the major and minor officers who administered her lands, has been a particularly helpful concept to apply to this study as a foundation for an analysis of Joan's networks of service.[9]

There is a reasonable amount of evidence from her English household which has survived, particularly as the expenditure on it and the number of aliens that she employed were a source of tension between the king and parliament. While limited records of her household have survived from her tenure as consort, there are repeated mentions of Joan's servitors in various royal records. Those in service to Joan can be found receiving gifts, commissions, positions, and annuities in sources such as issue warrants, and the calendars of various rolls series which helps illuminate the names of those who served her and periods during which they were in service.

Oddly enough, the clearest picture of her household emerges during the period of house arrest. During this period, when the expenses of her household were being closely monitored and effectively charged back to the Exchequer rather than being self-sufficient, the records were well kept and have largely survived. These records include several extant household account books which cover not only the daily expenditure of this period but also significant information on the size and composition of her household and those in her wider network of service from annuities paid.[10] From the reign of Henry V, there are also two extant lists of cloth gifted to her household members which also provide useful information about those who were in service to Joan at this point.[11]

There are very few records of Joan's household in the later years of her life after she was released from confinement, apart from one excellent intact household book for 1427–28 which is currently in the library of the Society of Antiquaries. Again, mentions of her servitors can still be found in the various calendared rolls and in other documents, such as petitions, chancery court cases, and Inquisitions Post Mortem. Working from this piecemeal evidence does make it difficult to ascertain exactly when a particular person entered or left the queen's service—it is only possible to trace the earliest and latest date that a particular servitor is mentioned in connection to Joan and to attempt to fill in the gaps wherever possible with any additional information that can be found from any other sources which might shed more light on their activities in the queen's service and beyond. Several recurring surnames such as Alderwiche, Thorley, du Boiz/Boyas, and Halsham suggest possible families in service to Joan, but the scarce biographical information can make it difficult to make secure connections between servitors. However, we can observe some familial links such as Anthony and Christopher Rys, two brothers who served Joan, or William and Thomas Wilcotes, a father and son pair who managed Joan's estate at Woodstock.[12]

Defining Joan's household then becomes an exercise in drawing together these brief mentions of activity, appointments, or rewards for service and connecting them to the few more detailed glimpses that we get from household books and lists of robes received by those in her service. Taken together, it is possible to get a reasonable, if not a complete, understanding of the continuity and change in Joan's household as both consort and dowager queen and of the wide-ranging networks of service she developed beyond her immediate household. Bringing together the English documents with evidence from Brittany and Navarre demonstrates not only the large number of people in her employ over her long life but the long-term service that many pledged to Joan, as many chose to remain with her as she moved from her natal home to Brittany and when she crossed the Channel to gain a crown. Case studies of several long-serving servitors will be discussed where relevant throughout this analysis in order to highlight the significance of their long-term loyalty to Joan.

Tracing the fluctuating composition of Joan's networks of service

Using Johnstone's model, this next section will investigate the changing composition of the two interlocking "circles" of Joan's network of service, first the smaller circle of her household, office, and wardrobe and then the larger circle of servitors who administered her lands. Each circle will be evaluated separately, moving roughly chronologically in order to discuss changes in size and noting servitors who remained with her over periods of transition between realms and the various roles that Joan played over the course of her long political career.

Ladies-in-waiting

Beginning with women who served Joan, although there are few examples who can be associated with Joan during her early years in Navarre, one of these is Maria Xemeniz de Mendivil, who was first noted as her "*nodriza*" or nurse in a document from April 1371 when she received 52 *libras de carlines* for her care of "*mi seynnora donna Johanna*".[13] The Navarrese records note that Maria was given an annual allowance of wheat plus a house with a garden near Tiebas in 1394 for her service in raising Joan and her sister the Infanta Maria.[14] Later, Joan appears to have personally appealed to her brother Carlos III of Navarre in 1416 to confirm that Maria's son, Gil Pérez de Olcoz, sergeant at arms, would be able to claim his mother's property after her death. This appears to demonstrate some enduring link or at least communication between Joan and Maria long after Joan left Navarre.[15]

Another interesting example which demonstrates some continuity in service from Navarrese women after Joan left Navarre is the case of Jehanne du Boiz who is specifically mentioned in connection with Carlos III's 1398 visit to his sister Joan in Brittany. Jehanne was noted as both currently "*damisela de la duquesa de Bretaña*" and the former wet-nurse of Carlos III (and possibly Joan's as well) and she was rewarded with 20 francs.[16] Jehanne was clearly part of Carlos's inner circle, not only as a consequence of her important role in his early years but because her husband, Guiffroi du Boiz, served in Carlos's household from 1381—both husband and wife were thus closely tied to the Navarrese king.[17] It is interesting then that Jehanne chose to leave Navarre with Joan to become her lady-in-waiting—while it cannot be proven that Jehanne was in Joan's service while she was still resident in Navarre, clearly she transitioned with Joan from the Navarrese court to the Breton one.

As discussed previously, there are few records of Joan's household in Brittany, thus it is only possible to get a partial picture of her ladies in the duchy, ironically mostly from English documents that mention them, and it is not always possible to securely identify in what capacity, if any, that they served Joan. For example, Joan de Bavalen is noted as a Breton woman who delivered the duchess's letter to Henry IV in 1400; while it is likely that she was in Joan's service in some way, it is not clearly stated.[18] The National Archives contains records of two generous pensions granted to women by Joan on 1 January 1403 from Vannes on her departure from Brittany, one of 300 livres to Beatrix de la Lande and another for 100 livres to Joan Chesnel.[19] Again, it appears that these are pensions rewarding these women for service.

It is clear that Joan brought a reasonably sized retinue with her from Brittany to form her new queenly household, which included both women and men from the Breton and Navarrese courts and beyond. Indeed, the foreign component of her household triggered considerable controversy and resulted in multiple attempts to expel her European servants, which will be discussed in more depth shortly. There are several women who served Joan who can be identified as Breton, but due to the lack of records from Brittany, it is difficult to affirm that they served her both as duchess and queen.

One of the most prominent of these women was Marie Sainte or Mary de Sant, who was specifically excluded from an expulsion of aliens demanded by Parliament in January 1404. In 1406 she was noted as Joan's chief damsel and given a grant of a yearly annuity of £20.[20] However, it is possible that Marie Sainte may have been in Joan's service or connected to her even before she became duchess. In the Navarrese household records of Joan's aunt Agnes of Foix and the infantas, there are multiple mentions in 1386 of a "Marie du Sant" or possibly "du Saut".[21] It is therefore possible that Marie may have been in service to Joan as infanta, duchess, and queen and may have even been from Navarre or the Midi region of France instead of Brittany.

While Marie Sainte was protected in the purges of 1404 and 1406, Jonet Dassyne, who was likely a Breton woman, was not as fortunate in the attempts to rid the queen's household of foreigners, as she appears to have left Joan's household in connection with the 1406 wave of expulsions.[22] There is also a vague mention in the expulsion order that in addition to those specifically named an additional "two ladies-in-waiting" and "one mistress" could stay as well as a nurse and a lady-in-waiting for Joan's daughters, so altogether there may have been nine Breton or foreign women in Joan and her daughters' household circa 1404. One of these may have been Peronelle Brocart, who was named as one of her ladies in an account book dating from 1407 to 1409 and was later named as an accessory to the charge of treason laid against Joan in 1419.[23]

While Peronelle is an example of a Breton lady in service to Joan as queen of England, it must be noted that many of her ladies were Englishwomen. For example, six of Joan's ladies were gifted cloth in a household book of Henry IV from 1408; three of these damsels have already been mentioned and were likely Bretons: Petronelle Brocas (likely Brocart), Joan Periaunt, and Alice or Constance Alderwiche. In contrast, the last three names, Alice Mauley (or Maesley), Agnes Hervy, and Margaret Somervile, are likely to have been Englishwomen. Indeed Mauley and Hervy both appear to have familial connections to servitors of the fourteenth-century queen Philippa of Hainault, and Alice may have also served Joan's predecessor Anne of Bohemia, first wife of Richard II.[24] Another

English damsel serving in this period was Isabel Thorley (née Everard), who was not named in this particular list but was given an annuity of £20 for life from the queen's manor of Brigstoke at roughly the same time in July 1408.[25]

The best glimpse of the women who served Joan is again during her dowager years, thanks to the surviving records from Joan's period of house arrest between 1419 and 1422 and the household book in the Society of Antiquaries dating from 1427 to 1428. During the period between 1419 and 1421 the ladies in her household appear to have been very consistently named across three surviving documents as Dame Margaret Trumpyngton, Katherine Wharton, the aforementioned Isabel Thorley, and Agnes Thorley, who may have been related to Isabel.[26] Having only four ladies in her employ, when compared to Isabella of France's 8 to 13 ladies at any given time and Philippa of Hainault's household of 2 to 6 ladies plus another 5 to 14 damsels, likely resulted from Joan's reduced circumstances under house arrest.[27] It should be noted that Isabel Thorley's inclusion demonstrates some continuity during Joan's period of imprisonment—clearly she was allowed to retain long-serving ladies who were close to her. Joan also pushed to have Isabel's annuity of £10 reconfirmed in 1423 at the beginning of the reign of Henry VI, to ensure that Isabel retained this key perk of service, even if Joan's tenure of the manor from which the annuity derived had been disputed during the queen's imprisonment.[28]

In the Society of Antiquaries household accounts which cover 1427–28 there are only four women who are clearly serving Joan as "damsels": Lady Petronelle Halsham, Anne Halsham (again likely a relation), Johanne Swynton, and Massy Uryce. If these were the only women serving her, again this could be due to her reduced financial circumstances as a dowager. Yet there are also mentions of several women in this household book who were gifted cloth, like the specifically named damsels, and/or annuities.[29] Some of these women, like Isabel Thorley and Margaret Trumpyngton, were known to have been in service to Joan only a few short years earlier. While these women are not clearly designated as servants, their presence in the lists of annuities and liveries may indicate that they were still her ladies. These women include the aforementioned

Margaret Trumpyngton and Isabel Thorley, Blanche Chalons, Constance Husee, Johanne Brokysby, Margorie Wentworth, Margaret Skulham, Lady Margaret Veer, and Isabelle Benham. If the nine women who received cloth or annuities were in service along with the four named damsels, then Joan's household would certainly have been comparable in size to her fourteenth-century predecessors. If not, then it is possible that having made do with four women during the period of her confinement, Joan chose not to expand the number after she regained her freedom in 1422.

Case Study: Couples in Joan's service

As Caroline Dunn has rightly noted, marriages between courtiers were both commonplace and encouraged by the royals themselves as beneficial to the construction of robust networks of service.[30] Nor is this trend confined to England; Manuela Santos Silva has discussed this in connection with the early Avis court in Portugal, and Diana Pelaz Flores has also argued for the importance of both couples and families of service in her analysis of the household networks of the fifteenth century queens of Castile.[31] Four of Joan's ladies are identifiable both as Breton born and as wives of male courtiers in her service: Antonyne Dayvar (wife of Perot de Gruer), Peronelle Alderwiche (wife of Anthony Rys), Joan, the wife of John Periaunt, and Alice (or Constance), the wife of Nicholas Alderwiche. The last three women were specifically excepted, along with their husbands and other key foreign members of Joan's household, in the January 1404 expulsion.

Peronelle Alderwiche is a particularly significant figure whose service to Joan and her family can be traced over a long period—she and her husband Anthony Rys make an excellent case study both of long service and facile transitioning between the Breton and English courts. Indeed, though Rys was apparently a Welshman, he was clearly working at the Breton court at least from the 1390s as he was appointed an envoy to England in 1392 and also given a license in the same year to import wine to England.[32] Anthony can be seen in Joan's service from 1402 as a go-between with Henry IV in their marital negotiations and represented the duchess in her proxy marriage in the same year.[33] Once in England, Rys continued to play a key role in her household; indeed, Alan Rogers called Rys Joan's "special agent".[34] While it is clear that Peronelle was Breton born, there appears to be no surviving records of her serving Joan while she was still duchess of Brittany—Peronelle and Rys may have met and married in Brittany or after they were both serving in England. However, the prominence of Rys and his wife at court drew hostile attention in the 1404 expulsion, where both were named as exceptions, but it was specifically noted that Rys "may go to the king's household and return from there, but he should not be continually resident in the aforesaid household".[35] Yet Rys was rewarded for his service to both queen and king with a hefty annuity of £100 from the manor of Petworth in Sussex the following year, in August 1405.[36] In November of the same year Peronelle was specifically granted the "corn, other goods, chattels and estovers" on the same manor, valued at 100 marks.[37]

Rys and Peronelle were top of the list for expulsion in the 1406 purge, testifying to their importance and also a clear backlash to the rewards given to these foreign courtiers. While it is not clear exactly when they left England, they were back in Brittany at the court of Joan's son, Jean V, by 1414. On 24 September 1414, Jean V generously gifted Rys and Peronelle lands and rents in the Guérande, an area which was part of Joan's Breton dower.[38] In this document it notes that Rys was serving as Jean V's maître d'hôtel and that Peronelle was now a lady-in-waiting to Jean's duchess, Jeanne de Valois. It also noted that this gift was in recognition of their service to Jean's mother, the queen of England. While there is no clear indication that Peronelle Alderwiche ever returned to Joan's service, she clearly did maintain a connection with her over the years. This can be seen in documents from 1420 and 1421 when Joan granted Peronelle the rents and customs of the manor of Havering-atte-Bower, one of the queen's primary residences.[39] This gift is unusual not only because Peronelle may not have even been in Joan's service nor resident in England at the time, but more so because Joan was then under house arrest and all of her lands were ostensibly seized by the Crown. Be that as it may, Henry V appears to have acquiesced to the gift as an entry on the Fine Rolls in 1421 records him granting the keeping of Havering to John Burgh, barring the rents due to Peronelle Alderwiche by Joan's letters patent.[40]

Like Anthony Rys, John Periaunt (or Peryant) and Nicholas Alderwiche were two other men who entered the queen's service early on, were very prominent in their roles, and had a long-standing connection with Joan—and with each other. Also like Rys, both were married to damsels of the queen, as mentioned previously. Although the original nationality of the three are murky—Rys may have been originally from Wales, Periaunt appears to have been Breton born, and Alderwiche, while having the most plausibly English name, appears to have had a Breton wife and was treated as an alien at one point—they all had ties of service in both Brittany and England.[41] Rys, Alderwiche, and Periaunt were officials in the honour of Richmond in England, which had belonged to Jean IV, and thus spent time working for him on both sides of the Channel—moreover, Alderwiche and Periaunt retained an annuity from the earl of Westmorland when he was granted the honour after Jean's death.[42] All three men not only knew Joan's first husband, they knew one another—Rys's wife Peronelle Alderwiche appears to have been Nicholas's daughter, and Alderwiche and Periaunt were regular collaborators throughout their careers.

All three men appear to have transferred into the queen's service at some point around the time of the commencement of the negotiations for Joan's second marriage, in which they played an important part. The couples clearly benefited from their service to Joan from the outset—as Joan's chief envoy, Anthony Rys was gifted a gold cup at Berkhamsted worth £31 10s for his efforts in the negotiations during late autumn 1401.[43] Periaunt and Alderwiche may also have taken part in a tournament held during the period of negotiations in London where prizes of gold cups were awarded to foreign participants.[44] Their success in the negotiations resulted in Joan's elevation to queen consort, and when she left Brittany in 1403, all three men were given places in the English royal household, their wives became ladies-in-waiting to a queen, and the rewards of their service to her continued to accrue. In November 1405, the same month that Peronelle Alderwiche had been granted 100 marks a year from the manor of Petworth, Periaunt was awarded a grant of lands in Nottinghamshire worth 40 marks a year and Alderwiche and his wife likewise gained an estate in Essex in January 1406.[45] The Periaunts and Alderwiches hung on through the 1404 and 1406 purges and remained in service—both Jeanne Periaunt and Constance Alderwiche are on a list of the queen's ladies from 1408. In 1411 and 1412, Periaunt and his wife, Joan, obtained papers of denization, perhaps to protect them from further attempts at expulsion, and the couple and their son, Thomas, were granted lands in the honour of Peverel which were valued at £10 per annum.[46] In 1412, Alderwiche was also named Sheriff of Lincoln, and an earlier grant of land in the town of Moreton in Essex was fully confirmed.[47] The two men appear to have been close, as both are noted as standing surety for one another and were involved together in connection with the "purchase" of a Breton prisoner-of-war in 1406, and Jenny Stratford noted that the two appear to have pawned a piece of Isabella de Valois' jewels in order to contribute funds to the Agincourt expedition.[48] Thereafter their paths diverged; Alderwiche's last connection to the queen comes in late 1413 when he was involved in discharging a sum due to Joan from Henry V.[49] Both men appear to have served Henry V during his French campaigns; however, Periaunt appears to have continued in the queen's service as well—while he does not feature in the records of her household from the reign of Henry V, he can be found in the Society of Antiquaries records of 1427–28, where he was named as her Master of the Horse and given both a gift of cloth and an annuity of £5 from the manor of Langley Marish.[50] Assuming this is still the same John Periaunt, this would indicate nearly 30 years connection with Joan, if not continuous service.

Male members of the household

Even though women held key posts in Joan's household, the majority of Joan's servitors were men. There are several Navarrese men who can be linked to her households in both Brittany and England. For example, Johan de Ochagavía is cited in multiple Navarrese records as being "one of the Duchess of Brittany's men" or specifically as an "*escudero*" or esquire/squire.[51] While he is not specifically stated as Navarrese, his distinctive surname and a notation that he was the cousin of Johanico Ruiz, a Navarrese courtier, seems to confirm his origins. A more interesting example, and perhaps the only courtier who can be definitively shown to be in service to Joan as infanta, duchess, and queen, is Guillem Arnault de Saut, otherwise known as Boloyte. Boloyte may have originally been in the service of Joan's aunt Agnes, and served in the "household of the infantas", as discussed in the first chapter, thus he may have simply transitioned from aunt to niece when Joan married and established her own household.[52] In 1384 Boloyte confirmed the receipt of a gift of grain and wine from Carlos II for his service as *escudero* to the Infanta Juana or Joan.[53] This gift was reconfirmed in 1386, at Joan's express supplication, as an amount that Boloyte would receive yearly for life.[54] This may have been due in part to the active role that he played around the time of Joan's wedding to Jean IV, where he turns up several times in the records in connection with preparation for the wedding and collecting the customary "*ayuda*" to help bear the costs of the event. One of his roles during this period, apparently in the context of his role as "*eschuero trinchante*" or "carving esquire" (possibly equivalent to the role of "carver" in the English court), was in the purchase of three sets of carving knives—one for Joan, one for her sister Maria, and another for her aunt Agnes, countess of Foix.[55] He next turns up in 1398, as the *escudero* of the duchess of Brittany (i.e. Joan) and was given a gift of 12 francs and a shield from Carlos III.[56] Finally, we see him again in England as "Sir Guillem Arnaud", one of the specifically named exceptions in the January 1404 expulsion of aliens. Even if he left Joan's service in the expulsions, his record of 20 years of documented service from 1384 to 1404, across three realms, is impressive.

Like Joan's female attendants, it is difficult to find many records of the men who served her in Brittany. Given a lack of definitive lists of her household, only a few male members of her household who are mentioned specifically in various Navarrese, Breton, or English documents have been identified. However, these sporadic mentions do reveal the wide range of men in her employment, such as the aforementioned esquires, messengers, procurers, an *argentier* (silversmith), receivers, and treasurers, as well as clerical staff, who will be discussed in the following chapter. Some of her treasurers seem to have held multiple roles: Alain de Maigne previously served as *mareschal* for Jean IV but then changed over to the duchess's household.[57] He is described as both treasurer and "*garderobier*", possibly a function similar to the keeper of the wardrobe in the English court. Interestingly, in terms of the household, one of the surviving documents in the Breton archives was a request from Joan in April 1392 to Alain, her treasurer and *garderobier*, "to pay the women in her service as per the custom laid out in the last ordinances of the Duke".[58] The other treasurer, Silvester Cleirvaut, appears to have held the post of treasurer and receiver-general. He can be found in several TNA documents from 1402, her last year in Brittany, and 1403, shortly after she arrived in England.[59] The latter document, an entry on the Issue Rolls in April 1403, seems to indicate that Cleirvaut, whose name seems to have been partially Anglicised as Sylvester Chanterowe, served her on both sides of the Channel.[60] It is important to recognise that even after Joan left Brittany, she continued to have a group of officials who administered her dower lands and transmitted her rents to her in England.

As Joan lived in England for the longest period of her life, from 1403 until her death in 1437, it is helpful to break down the analysis of her household in line with the reigns of the three monarchs she was connected to: her husband Henry IV (from her arrival in 1403 to 1413), her stepson Henry V (1413–22), and her step-grandson Henry VI (1422 until her death in 1437). Joan had a variable relationship with the monarch and the royal court in each of these periods, which directly affected the size of her household and the records that we have of its personnel.

In Henry IV's reign, Joan was the queen consort and had a sizeable household in accordance with her rank. Indeed, the number of attendants, particularly the number of foreign attendants that she had, created controversy with Parliament who were desirous to stem royal expenditure and purge the royal household of foreigners. As noted previously, while records of her household are patchy, individual personnel can be identified by gifts, rewards, or mentions of their names in various financial and administrative records. To illustrate this are the examples of two Thomases who served Joan during her reign as consort. One, a Thomas Shirwode, a yeoman of the queen's kitchen, was rewarded for his good service in letters patent issued in September 1403.[61] He was mentioned again in March 1405, with reference to his role in Joan's service, when he was offered protection within a "*clause volumus*" that he was granted in connection in his role in the king's Welsh campaign.[62] Another Thomas, Thomas Feriby, appears in several documents as her clerk and treasurer/receiver-general in connection with the receipt of rents from Joan's manors of Odiham and Havering.[63] As these records date from 1403, the very first year of Joan's arrival, and from 1413, it is clear that he remained in service to her throughout her years as queen consort. Feriby is also an example of an officer who continued to serve Joan after she became a dowager, as a variety of records from Henry V's reign until at least 1416 which testify to his role are still extant, including receipts for the queen's gold, as discussed in the previous chapter, various payments for her lands and revenues, and surviving examples of his seal.[64]

The preponderance of the financial records, which tend to highlight the role of clerical personnel, have helped to identify many of her officers—these are largely treasurers and clerks but also include religious personnel, who will be discussed in the following chapter, as well as specialist members such as the royal physician, Pedro de Alcobaça, and key officers such as Sir Hugh Luttrell, steward of the queen's household. Another prominent officer in Joan's household who appears to have risen from a clerical role at court to a high-profile role in the queen's service was John de Tibbay. Like many courtiers and household staff, Tibbay also held ecclesiastical offices; he was thus both a clerk and a cleric. While Tibbay rose to become one of Joan's treasurers and receiver-generals, and may also have served as her chancellor, he also held canonries and prebends in Lincoln and York, the wardenship of the hospital of St Mary Greatham (Greteham), and was rector of Wensley (Wenslawe). Joan's patronage not only helped him to rise to more prestigious posts within her household, but also outside it; she even sponsored his petition to the Pope in 1411 to hold additional ecclesiastical posts and he became the archdeacon of Huntingdon in March 1414.[65] Joan also sponsored two other de Tibbays, Thomas and Robert, who may have been John's relatives, to hold the post of rector in 1412 and 1414, respectively, in the parish of St John the Baptist with St Mary the Virgin in Devizes, a town centrally placed within her dower lands in Wiltshire.[66] The exact date that John de Tibbay began his service to Joan is unclear, although he is listed as her treasurer and receiver-general in documents from 1409 to 1410, and appears to have been a clerk in royal service from the time of Richard II.[67] However, the end of Tibbay's service can be more securely dated as he was murdered on 22 July 1414. According to the anonymous Chronicle of London, Tibbay was assaulted in London on Lad Lane, near Cheapside—the crime was likely motivated by a desire to control the estate of Richard and Roger Scrope as Tibbay was an executor.[68] Richard and Roger were father and son, respectively the 1st and 2nd barons Scrope of Bolton, who both died in 1403. Interestingly, Joan had been given the wardship of the Scrope heir, Richard, who became the 3rd Lord Bolton—the document granting the wardship to the queen in 1403 commissioned Tibbay, along with Robert Markeley and Peter Grener, to deliver young Richard to Joan, which may have been the point when Tibbay first came into contact with her.[69] Thus while Tibbay did not necessarily die as a direct result of his service to the queen, there was an odd twist here in that the family through which he may have come into contact with Joan may have also held the seeds of his eventual demise.

Other male members of her general household staff have also been identified during her years as queen consort from various sources including some mentions in the surviving household books of Henry IV which recorded grants of cloth or other gifts made to them.[70] The majority of these household members have been securely identified in a particular role, such as Thomas atte Wode, yeoman of the stable, Robert Bele, groom of the hall, and John Lambard, page of the chamber, while other men can only be confirmed to have been in her service. There was considerable crossover between the king's and queen's households—some servitors, such as Bérart de Montferrand, who will be discussed further shortly, are listed as the queen's esquire in some documents and the king's esquire in others, which can make it difficult to securely define their length of service to Joan. Some important figures who held key posts in the king's household and council, such as John Norbury, have also been linked to the queen's service in some documents, but it can be difficult to determine if they can genuinely be considered as part of her household.[71]

As mentioned previously, it is during the reign of Henry V that we can glimpse Joan's household most clearly due to the surviving records from Joan's period of confinement between 1419 and 1422, which give us a good sense of the size and composition of the household. From these surviving records it appears that the size of her household remained fairly constant over this period—in the first three documents, she had 25 to 28 male servitors, 1 to 4 officials, and the 4 women discussed earlier. Records from the last year of her confinement show a drop in the size of her household, listing 16 male servitors, 2 officials, and 3 ladies-in-waiting. This would be expected given the restricted funds available to fund her household—perhaps some either left her service in this period, unwilling to continue their careers in her uncertain situation as an accused criminal, or she may have had to let some staff go due to her straitened financial circumstances.

In spite of this upheaval to Joan's household, we can identify several individuals who remained in her service during her period of detainment. One of these is William Ecclestone, a groom of the Queen's Chamber who is first mentioned in August 1405 in connection with being granted the wardship of Thomas Hardyng, worth 10s a year.[72] William is consistently mentioned as a member of her household across the key records of her captivity, including the account books for 1419–21, and is most likely the William Eylstone mentioned in the 1422 accounts which would appear to indicate at least 17 years of service to the queen. Another servitor of long standing through the reigns of Henry IV and V is her clerk Thomas Lillebourne. He is first listed at almost the same time as William Ecclestone, c. 1405, when he and four other clerks of the queen were gifted robes and hoods as a part of the preparations for the wedding of Princess Philippa.[73] Lillebourne received additional rewards for his service from the queen in April 1410 when she issued letters patent to grant him the manor and lordship of Langley near

Leeds Castle with Thomas Gloucestre, which was confirmed by Henry IV in the same year and again by Henry V in 1413.[74] During the years of Joan's confinement Lillebourne came to greater prominence in the records as it is his name as clerk of the queen's household which is consistently associated with all of the surviving accounts of this period. Not only was he tasked with keeping the records of the queen's household, it appears that he was closely involved with the provisioning for the household too. Lillebourne was at the head of a list of those commissioned in November 1421 to obtain foodstuffs, firewood, and necessities for the queen's household.[75] Some of these provisions may have come from Lillebourne's own lands, as E.E. Dodd in his commentary of the Leeds Castle wardrobe book of 1422 suggested

> Lilleborne himself is the most substantial creditor with £31.19s. under the office of Buyer and 13s.4d. under Hall. Lilleborne had been granted the Manor of Langley by Leeds in 1413 (CPR) and possessed of this he was able, with the Prior of Leeds, to supply, in large measure, the meat required in the castle kitchen and much of the firewood for the hall.[76]

Clearly both Joan and Henry V recognised and appreciated Lillebourne's key role in the maintenance of her household during this difficult period under confinement; in March 1421, the king not only recognised the annuity of £10 from the fee farm of the hundred of Falwesley in Northamptonshire, he granted it to Lillebourne for life.[77] This confirmation was important since Thomas's annuity was ostensibly derived from lands which Henry V had seized from Joan's dower, and without the king's recognition of the annuity, Lillebourne would not have been able to realise the income. Both Lillebourne and Ecclestone seem to have similar tenures of service to the queen of at least 17 years and both demonstrably received rewards for their service, particularly Lillebourne, who served the queen in a key capacity, keeping her household financed and provisioned during a challenging period.

Thanks to the survival of the 1427–28 account books at the Society of Antiquaries, we can get a fairly clear picture of her household in her later dowager years, or at least over the course of the period covered in these accounts. Overall, there were 35 male servitors, another 18 officers/specialists, and 13 women associated with the queen's service over the reign of Henry VI, and almost all of these personnel are named in these accounts. Her servitors were largely valets, grooms, wardens, ushers, and pages as expected, but there are also musical personnel mentioned, who shared the name John. John Bonland and John Saas sang in her choir and the esteemed composer John Dunstable, who will be discussed further in the following chapter, received cloth in these accounts as a member of her household. Dunstable also received a generous annuity from her until her death in 1437 when he appears to have transferred into the service of Joan's stepson, Humphrey, duke of Gloucester. In addition to the musical personnel, there are a number of specialised employees in her service; four physicians received payments for tending to her during a bout of extremely poor health in 1427. Another key member of her personnel noted in the 1427–28 household book is Richard Crek, keeper of her Great Wardrobe in London, who was salaried at 6d per day in addition to an annuity of £9 2s 6d and received a generous gift of cloth as well.

The officers who are easiest to trace in Joan's service in the reign of Henry VI are her financial personnel. One of these is John Bugge, whose appointment as her treasurer and receiver-general is noted at the outset of the 1427–28 account book. Bugge appears to have been in Joan's service previously as she names him as her "*notre bien ame Esquyer*" ("our well-loved esquire"), possibly replacing John Foxholes, who had been her treasurer and receiver-general around 1423/24. Foxholes appears to have come into Joan's service after a stint as receiver-general for Henry, lord Scrope (Lescrop), c. 1415–16, and had experience working in the collection of customs, which would have prepared him well for Joan's service.[78] This can be seen particularly in his connection with Southampton where he first collected customs and subsidies from approximately 1417 to 1424 and can be seen in later documents where he represented Joan's interests in collecting her fee farm of the city c. 1425.[79] Moreover, while Bugge is clearly named to the post of treasurer and receiver-general in 1427, Foxholes appears to have continued in her service in a clerical capacity, as a document regarding the collection of wool customs at Hull for Joan still lists him as her treasurer.[80] There are several documents connected to Bugge which survive to attest to his role in Joan's service, including receipts from ports such as Bristol, Southampton, and Ipswich, where Joan held the rights to levy customs, rents on her fee farm at Queenhithe, and the purchase of a coppice on her manor at Brigstoke.[81] From these documents it is clear that Bugge was in her service at least until 1435 and played a key role, as did Foxholes, in Joan's complicated and somewhat tenuous finances as dowager queen.

Case studies: International courtiers—Pomeroy, Montferrand, and Beaumont

While Bugge and Foxholes provide examples of the many Englishmen in Joan's service, as noted previously, Joan had many international members of her network of service who stayed with her as she transitioned between roles and countries and left their homelands to continue to serve her. These long-serving household members who served Joan in multiple roles and geographical contexts helped her maintain ties and serve her interests across the Channel after she moved to England. An example is William (de la) Pomeroy, who served the queen as her esquire from her earliest days in England in 1403.[82] While it is unclear if Pomeroy served her in Brittany, he appears to have been engaged in Anglo-Breton relations, as he was involved in the ransom of Breton prisoners in 1405, and in 1407 appears to have been a go-between in the conflict between Jean V and the English—possibly in connection with a stint as the captain of Castle Cornet in Guernsey.[83] Pomeroy maintained his connection to Joan but was not badly affected by her imprisonment; indeed, during her confinement in 1421, Henry V not only confirmed an annuity that she had made to him of 20 marks a year from the issues of the manor of Headington (Hedyngton) and the hundred of Bullington (Boleinden) in Oxfordshire, but also made him the constable of the castle of Odiham, a property which had been part of Joan's seized dower.[84] In the 1427–28 account book, Joan reaffirmed the annuity of 20 marks, attesting to his long connection to her of well over 20 years at that point.

Like Pomeroy, Bérart (Berard or Bertrand) de Montferrand can be found in her service from the inception of her queenly reign. He was likely of Gascon origin, but it was unclear if he was already serving her in the Breton court or if he might have come into her service via a Navarrese connection. In 1404 Montferrand was listed as an exception to the expulsion of aliens—possibly because his service to Joan was not exclusive, as he was also listed as a "king's esquire" during the reign of Henry IV, who used him as a go-between to the Breton court in 1410. Indeed, over the course of Henry IV's reign we can see a series of grants and gifts to Montferrand in the Gascon Rolls, such as an annual sum of £20 in 1405, the award of the prévôté of Ombrière in 1408, and in 1410 he was granted all the lands and revenues of the late Bernat Audouin in Aquitaine.[85] Shortly after this, in August 1411, Joan granted him the manor of Foston in Leicestershire as further reward for his service to the king and queen.[86] Montferrand continued his service to the Lancastrian dynasty after the death of Henry IV, transferring his allegiance to his sons, serving Henry V and then forming a close relationship with John, duke of Bedford. Jenny Stratford has examined Montferrand's career in Bedford's service and his value as an internationally mobile courtier with a wide-ranging skill set and connections, noting, "From the first, Bedford understood Montferrand's worth as a diplomatic envoy, especially through his long-standing connections with Brittany".[87] Indeed, Bedford dispatched Montferrand to Brittany in 1422, 1423, and 1424, and also sent him on a diplomatic mission to the kings of Aragon, Castile, and Navarre in 1423, as well as the Count of Foix, to whom the Montferrand family had ties of allegiance. Again, Montferrand's connection to Joan and his experience of serving her would have given him the contacts, context, and perhaps entrée necessary to make him a useful envoy. While Montferrand remained largely in Bedford's service, becoming his chamberlain and reaping significant rewards in terms of lands and titles in both Normandy and Gascony, he also kept up his ties to Joan; indeed, Stratford notes that "through Montferrand there was a clear connection between the households of Bedford and Joan of Navarre".[88] During Montferrand's periods in England, in 1425–27 and in 1428, he clearly renewed his connection to Joan—she gifted him a diamond ring and entrusted him with an important mission as her own envoy to Brittany to negotiate with Jean V over the county of Nantes, as discussed in the previous chapter. There are multiple records of payments from Jean V of Brittany to Montferrand compensating him for journeys to negotiate with the queen—he appears to have led at least two of the five missions sent across the Channel to resolve the dispute.[89] Joan rewarded him for his long and loyal service on multiple occasions, with grants of lands and annuities as queen consort, including revenues from the comté de Nantes in 1429 in recognition of his efforts concerning her dower and a final gift near the end of her life in May 1437 of 1,000 écus.[90]

In sum, Montferrand is the perfect example of an international, or even transnational, courtier who leveraged his connections across England, France, and Iberia to build a very long and successful career. His facility for moving between realms and households greatly aided his rise—transitioning with Joan as she moved across the Channel and became queen, pledging his loyalty to the Lancastrians and serving father, sons, and grandson. Indeed, Montferrand outlived two Lancastrian kings, was at Bedford's deathbed when he died in 1435, and outlived Joan as well, continuing his career into the early 1440s, making him perhaps the longest-serving member of Joan's networks of service.

The final example in our case study of international courtiers in Joan's networks of service is her cousin Carlos de Beaumont, who moved fluidly between the courts of Navarre and England as a diplomat and courtier. As noted in the discussion of Joan's extended family in the first chapter, Carlos was an illegitimate member of the house of Evreux-Navarre, but he was still considered a part of the family and was given important roles to play, beginning with his appointment as alferez to Joan's father Carlos II in 1379, and he continued to serve Carlos III in this role after his accession in 1387. Although many of these diplomatic missions involved negotiations with Navarre's neighbours France, Aragon, and Castile, Beaumont's role also necessitated working with the English kings and their emissaries. Eloísa Ramírez Vaquero has argued that Beaumont was ideally placed to become Navarre's key English envoy given both his royal blood and his maternal connections in the Ultrapuertos region—the area of Navarre on the other side of the Pyrenees which adjoined the English territory in Gascony where many nobles had ties to both Navarre and England.[91]

As noted in the first chapter, some of Beaumont's earliest diplomatic missions involved negotiating with the English, and he continued to play a key role in the lengthy and complicated negotiations over the return of Cherbourg from England back to the Navarrese. This included a trip to England in 1390 and an extensive period of negotiation in 1392–93 to secure the handover of the town from the English in early 1394. Indeed, Eloísa Ramírez Vaquero hailed Beaumont's diplomatic role vis-à-vis the English, noting that he was a "star" ambassador during this crucial period of negotiations.[92] These negotiations also rebounded to Beaumont's own personal benefit as his position in Mauléon and Soule was confirmed as a life grant. This appointment appears to reflect the increasingly complex political situation in England between Richard II and his Lancastrian relatives, as evidence from the Gascon Rolls appears to suggest that this confirmation was made by Richard's uncle, John of Gaunt, now duke of Aquitaine. This grant notes that it was made by Gaunt to Beaumont "for his homage, and because he has been retained by the duke for life, saving at all time his allegiance, as appears in indentures made between the duke and Beaumont, of the place and castle of Mauléon and of Soule", with the approval and confirmation of the king.[93] This grant could be seen as the beginning of Beaumont's long and productive association with the House of Lancaster—Henry IV's coup of 1399 and his ascension to the English throne could demonstrate Beaumont's wisdom in choosing to bind himself to Henry's father, John of Gaunt.

While Beaumont continued to play a vital role in Navarrese politics and diplomacy, including engaging in missions to France and Aragon in 1396, 1398, and 1399, it was in 1403 that his role regarding England made a seismic shift when his cousin Joan became queen. Carlos III intended to take advantage of his sister's elevation as queen consort of England—his most effective means of doing so was the deployment of Carlos de Beaumont. Beaumont's position as a member of the royal family, an accomplished diplomat, and trusted counsellor of the Navarrese king made him the ideal person to accompany his cousin Joan to England as chamberlain of her household, giving Carlos III a direct conduit to the English court and its ruler through his sister and cousin. It is unclear exactly where the dividing line was between carrying out the duties of queen's chamberlain and continuing to work as the alferez—while it might be unfair to label Beaumont as a spy, certainly he was in an ideal position to relay the inner workings of the English court and its fluid politics back to Navarre as well as support Joan in promoting the interests of her homeland.

Beaumont appears to have arrived in England shortly after his cousin; he first appears in letters close issued in July 1403 as the "chamberlain of the queen" where he was already petitioning the English king to assist a Navarrese merchant.[94] While the beginning of his time as chamberlain is fairly clear, the exact length of time that Beaumont remained in his post is harder to define. Alan Rogers has argued that Beaumont stayed in the realm until 1415, yet this cannot be the case as both Navarrese and English records note that he was in Castile on a diplomatic mission in 1411, where he appears to have been working for both Henry IV's and Carlos III's benefit.[95] It seems illogical that Beaumont would have stayed so long in England to serve his cousin, yet there is a period in the Navarrese documents where he is visibly less active, with an effective hiatus in his frequent diplomatic trips between 1403 and 1411, thus it is possible that he spent the entirety of that period at the English court.

Rogers' assertion that Beaumont stayed in England until 1415 may stem from the generous annuity he received from the Crown of 250 marks, which is well documented in the E404 series. This is only one of the benefits Beaumont gained through his service and connections in England, which will be delineated shortly. The first record of this annuity comes in 1405, when it is noted that the king had granted Charles of Navarre an annuity which appears to have been paid in two instalments of 125 marks each.[96] Thereafter, receipts for this annuity turn up with regular frequency at a rate of roughly two a year between 1405 and 1408.[97] At this point there appears to be a break in the confirmation of Beaumont's annuity in the E404 series, but the Gascon Rolls note a part payment of his 250 marks annuity in December 1409.[98] This appears to be the last confirmation of payment during Henry IV's reign, but as will be discussed later, Beaumont's annuity did continue well into the following decade.

This annuity was not the only gift or grant that Beaumont received for his service to the English king. In July 1404, Beaumont and his son Charlot were confirmed as the holders of the baylie (or bailiwick) of Labourd for their lifetime—Miguel Sanz de Villava, Beaumont's proctor, had bought the rights to the baylie from Lop de Saint-Julien and son, but this confirmation from the English king was vital to assure their possession.[99] As Labourd was strategic territory close to Navarrese borders, Beaumont could have been securing the territory both to his own benefit and that of Carlos III. Later, in 1408, Beaumont was given the right to farm the baylie out to the constable of Bordeaux, "as Beaumont has had several troubles and dissent with certain inhabitants of the land of Labourd".[100] Beaumont received other benefits as well—again in the Gascon Rolls it was noted that on 10 June 1407 the king had granted him for 20 years the land of Noaillan with all the lands, tenements, and revenues pertaining to it in the city of Bordeaux and other towns within the duchy of Aquitaine, including Mérignac, Bègles, Villenave[-d'Ornon], and Cadaujac.[101] He also had the "custom on the wine called issac of Bordeaux" for life, as well as the licence to "to bring and carry annually 120 tuns of wine coming from rebel places of the duchy" for 20 years. In August 1409 Beaumont was also granted by the king "at his special request" a right to levy substantial tolls on goods passing through the river Adour and the fishery of Guiche.[102] It was noted that "The king wants Beaumont to have these franchises and liberties in order better to maintain and defend the honor and castle of Guiche against the invasion of the king's enemies", as well as to consolidate his hold on the area, which had been recently improved through Beaumont's marriage to the heiress Anne de Curton, Lady of Guiche.

This evidence from these grants and annuity is a key clue in potentially establishing Beaumont's whereabouts during this period.

Looking at this evidence, it seems likely that he only served Joan at the English court for a brief period, as a maximum from 1403 until 1411 when we can trace his movements back in Iberia again. It is entirely possible that he may have left England in 1409 when the regular payments for his annuity appear to have stopped—1409 is also the year that the last grant was made to Beaumont. Given his activity in the Gascon region, he may have left England itself sooner, serving Henry IV in Gascony rather than serving his cousin in England as her chamberlain. While Joan continued in her role as queen consort until her husband's death in 1413, it is likely that Carlos III decided that Beaumont was better utilised back in Iberia due to the changing situation at the English court and the uncertainty caused by Henry's failing health. Carlos III and Beaumont may have evaluated the situation and decided that in the chaos at the English court, and the fact that Joan was now queen to a man whose health and power were clearly fading, meant that the time was right for Beaumont to be redeployed elsewhere.

Yet Beaumont's preference and influence at the English court did not end when he abandoned his post as chamberlain or when Henry IV died in 1413. While Joan was no longer queen consort, both Carlos III and Beaumont sought to maintain their connections with the new English king; Beaumont's own chaplain, Martin de Cáseda, was dispatched with letters from Carlos III to the newly crowned Henry V just months after his accession.[103] Perhaps connected to these letters Beaumont's annuity was reconfirmed three times between 17 October 1413 and 29 May 1414.[104] Henry V also confirmed the privileges bestowed on Beaumont by his father's letters patent "so long as Beaumont does not become the retainer of anyone other than the king".[105] Beaumont himself appears to have visited England again in 1414—while he was likely there on political motives, it appears he was also negotiating the long-term situation regarding his English annuity. In an entry on the Issue Rolls it was noted on 27 January 1414 that a part payment of £40 was paid to Beaumont's son, Charles (or Charlot), and it appears that on 14 July 1417 the entire annuity was transferred over to Beaumont's son.[106] Beaumont and his son were also reconfirmed as the holders of the bailiwick of La Bourt (or Labourd) in 1415, and in February 1416 Beaumont's rights and lands in Aquitaine were again confirmed by Henry V.[107] Beaumont returned to England again in 1417, when his rights were confirmed once more and Beaumont may have served Henry V in Normandy, as he accepted the surrender of the castle of Hommet on behalf of the duke of Gloucester in the spring of 1418 as noted in Chapter 4.[108] And as discussed previously, in 1419 Beaumont softened the news of Humphrey of Gloucester's rejection as a potential groom for the Navarrese heiress, Joan's niece Blanca, by sending the king one of his own books as a gift.

This interaction marks one of Beaumont's last entries in the English records, which may be explained by other factors and events which took place around this time—namely Joan's period of detention followed by Henry V's death in August 1422. This brought his young son, Henry VI, to the throne and a regency council—with Joan relegated to effective retirement as the somewhat disgraced step-grandmother of the king, and as Beaumont had no personal relationship with Henry VI as he had with his father and grandfather (and even his great-grandfather, John of Gaunt), he had little leverage to push for a reconfirmation of the rights he had been granted in previous reigns. However, Beaumont did not cease all contact with England, as a payment of £10 was paid to Beaumont's messenger, one Johnicot d'Aguerr for letters brought to Henry VI in 1427.[109] His son, Luis de Beaumont, also appears to have voyaged to England in July 1432 and paid homage for his father's lands in Mauléon and Soule.[110] Unfortunately, Luis's relationship with England was not as smooth as his father's—while it is beyond the scope of this work to discuss the detail here, it is worth noting that perhaps Carlos de Beaumont's personal connections and time spent in England may have made a difference to his greater success with the English than his son.

While the English "gravy train" may have stopped for Beaumont, it must be noted that he continued to stand in high favour in the Navarrese court and played an important role in the realm until the end of his life in 1432. While his diplomatic missions appear to have slowed down after 1417, he continued to serve the Navarrese monarchs. During the last years of his life, Blanca I made several payments to Beaumont for his service and that of 15 of his armed men who were guarding the queen.[111] In addition to payments for service rendered, both Beaumont and his family continued to reap the rewards of being in the high favour of the Navarrese crown. While there is not enough space to go into detail here, it is important to note that his sons and daughters, both legitimate and illegitimate, rose to high positions in the governance, court, and church of the realm and made marriages which reinforced Beaumont's position both in Navarre and in Gascony.[112]

The case study of Beaumont demonstrates both similarities and differences with the other international courtiers in Joan's network of service. Clearly a unique factor in this case is his familial ties to Joan as his royal blood and the support of his uncle and cousins gave him opportunities, as alferez and diplomat in Navarre and as chamberlain of the queen's household in England. Beaumont took advantage of these opportunities and built ties of his own with English kings, which increased his holdings in a strategic and disputed corner of southwest France, making marriages for himself and for his children which consolidated his position in the region. Increasing his authority in Gascony arguably also helped Navarre as the lands Beaumont held were close to the Ultrapuertos region where he played a key role as part of his duties as alferez. Generally, it could be argued that Beaumont's appointments and good relations with the English kings not only rebounded to his own benefit, but arguably to that of his Navarrese kin as well by serving both Joan during her queenship and Carlos III by acting as a key conduit to the English court and theoretically improving or stabilising Anglo-Navarrese relations. While his royal blood put Beaumont in a privileged position from the outset, like the other international members of Joan's entourage, we can see that same willingness to move between realms, households, and masters, as well as the impressive rewards that being part of a network of service could bring.

Attacks on Joan's networks of service: Expulsions of aliens

We can see from these examples from the careers of Pomeroy, Montferrand, and, indeed, Carlos de Beaumont the benefits that foreign courtiers in Joan's household brought not only to Joan in terms of helping her maintain connections to Navarre and Brittany but in terms of diplomatic benefits, as her servitors were often leveraged by the Crown in negotiations both during and after their service to the queen. However, these benefits to Joan and to the Crown were not always appreciated by Parliament, who called for the expulsion of aliens in her household four times over the course of her life in England: in 1404, 1406, 1416, and 1426. Wider conflicts between Parliament and the Crown over the expenditure of the royal household provided some of the motivation for expelling the foreigners from her household. Given the straitened state of Crown finances, there was concern about the number of servitors that the queen brought with her from Brittany and the expense associated with her large retinue. The generous rewards to those in her network of service would have further exacerbated this issue, making these courtiers seem even more costly in the short and long term considering some of the lands and annuities granted to them.

Some of this concern was clearly more xenophobic than economic and the preferment given to the foreigners in the queen's household may have upset those who felt that these "aliens" had a stranglehold on some of the most lucrative and important posts in her service. As we have seen, Joan's network of service included not only Navarrese and Breton courtiers but Gascons, Italians (like Gaweyn Trent, her master of the jewels who came from one of the most prominent families in Lucca), and the Portuguese doctor Pedro Alcobaça who served both Henry and Joan and eventually received letters of denization in 1420.[113] While Joan's international entourage caused a stir, the presence of foreigners was hardly new—as Ormrod, Lambert, and Mackman noted, "Royal and princely courts were obvious magnets for aliens as a result of their cosmopolitan outlook, their international dynastic links and their desire to attract the brightest and best artists and scholars of the day", but perhaps because of this international dimension "the royal court continued throughout the later Middle Ages to be a focus for wider culture and political attitudes to foreigners".[114] As the queen consorts of England during this period were generally not native-born, it was commonplace for a foreign bride to bring with her servitors and relatives from her homeland. Yet reactions to these "aliens" at court could be hostile, particularly when they were believed to have excessive influence or gain too many rewards, such as the reaction to the "Savoyard" contingent during the tenure of Eleanor of Provence.[115] Hostilities to Joan's foreign courtiers, particularly the sizable Breton cohort, were inflamed by conflict with Brittany which flared up after Joan and Henry's marriage in 1403 and of course by the hostilities of the Hundred Years War—it is no accident that the timing of these petitions for the expulsion of aliens in the queen's household closely coincided with Breton raids or Henry V's campaigns in France.

The initial 1404 petition called for the removal of aliens and schismatics (adherents of the anti-pope as Joan herself had been), "especially all French, Bretons, Lombards, Italians and Navarrese" from both the king's and queen's households.[116] Yet the petition also included exceptions "for the greater comfort, benefit and well-being of my lady the queen", which protected those close to her in her service including Marie Sainte and "Nicholas Alderwich and John Puryan (Periaunt), and their wives, [who] can also stay in the said households, although they were born in Brittany, provided that they are of the opinion of our aforesaid most holy father, and do liege homage and fealty to our said lord the king". While the text of the 1406 petition did not specifically single out the queen and her household, it included a list of targeted aliens that reversed the earlier exceptions, key members of Joan's household such as Antony Rys, Perot Gruer, her secretaries Robynet and Johan de Boys, as well as her master of the jewels, Gaweyn Trent of Lucca, and several of her ladies, including Peronelle Alderwiche and Antonyne Dayvar.[117] There are also vague mentions which may be incomplete or incorrect spellings of other key servitors such as Nicholas Alderwiche, Marie Sante, and William de la Pomeroy. Lesser members of her household such as the valet Julian Lavender, a cook Nicholas de Brytayn, and Christopher Rys, Anthony's brother, were also on the list. As discussed previously, some of these servitors did leave following the 1404 and 1406 petitions but others managed to cling on through royal favour and protection or may have left briefly, only to return when the anti-foreign fervour calmed down. Ten years later, in 1416, a petition was brought up again in Parliament noting:

> Yet recently, notwithstanding this ordinance [i.e. the expulsion of 1406], many Bretons, having no regard for the aforesaid ordinance and penalty, have returned to the realm, and some are dwelling about the queen's person in her household, and others very close to the said household and elsewhere within the realm, in order to hear, know and learn the secrets of the realm and reveal them to the Bretons, who are the greatest enemies of your realm, and in order to remove the money and treasure from the said realm, to the great harm of the king and the great damage of all the realm.[118]

As this text demonstrates, Joan and her household were clearly marked here as the source of foreign infection. Their diplomatic efforts as trusted intermediaries between the Breton and Navarrese courts had been turned instead into notions of these servitors as spies who were selling the secrets of the realm or thieves who stripped it bare. Clearly tensions would once again have been high given the campaigns of Henry V in France against Joan's own Valois and Breton family. There may have been concern that Joan, who was still the premier woman of the land as the king had not yet married, and the foreigners left in her household, were untrustworthy or disloyal individuals who were too close to the centre of power in the realm. Once again, in 1426, Joan and her household were the subject of a petition for the removal of foreigners, noting "the great damage to the king and his subjects because of the foreigners dwelling in England with Queen Joan" and repeating the entreaty that they be removed as per the statute of 1416.[119] At this stage, Joan was a relatively elderly dowager queen who was struggling to reassert her title to lands and restore her reputation after the years of detention. Yet, the perception that she was still surrounded by foreigners who posed a threat to "national security" was stuck fast, perhaps due in part to the continued presence of foreign servitors in her service who survived these purges or came from abroad to serve her, like the Navarrese esquire Machín de Uriz, who appears to have been in her service shortly before her arrest for witchcraft in 1419.[120]

These repeated petitions bring into question the value of these foreign servants to Joan—was the comfort and connection they brought to courts of her natal family and children worth the damage they caused to her reputation and the leverage that it gave to her enemies to attack her? Overall, while these foreign servants did provide a means to attack Joan, they also made up a critical element of her networks of service. As we have seen in several case studies, Joan built long-term relationships with these courtiers from Navarre, Brittany, France, and beyond, and they in turn served her loyally, remaining in her service or returning to it after these attempts to expel them from her household or attacks on her reputation. Joan rewarded them well for this loyalty, trusting them to not only serve her in the intimacy of her inner household but sending them on vital missions to negotiate on her behalf, like sending Rys to be her proxy in her matrimonial negotiations with Henry or dispatching Bérart de Montferrand to reach an accommodation with her son over her Breton dower. In the end the deep personal and professional connections between Joan and the international group of courtiers in her network of service clearly outweighed the threat of them being used against her or Joan would have abandoned them as soon as Parliament petitioned for their removal instead of continuing to keep them close to her, and persistently rewarding their long service and loyalty.

Joan's administrative network of service: Managing her dower lands

Finally, we move from the inner circle of Joan's household to the outer ring of her network of service—the officials who helped her administer her vast portfolio of lands in England and Brittany. These two rings were closely linked as personnel moved between the two, with some servitors having posts both in her household and as officials on her lands. Joan's household was also theoretically intended to be supported by her dower lands; however, as discussed in the previous chapter, her incoming revenues did not always meet her total expenditure. The last chapter delineated the impressive number of manors, fee farms, alien priories, wardships, custom duties, and more which formed part of her sizable dower in England, and Joan continued to hold dower lands in Brittany, primarily in and around the Nantes region. Maintaining and administering these diverse and far-flung territorial holdings from southern Brittany to northern Yorkshire necessitated numerous servitors, from the recently discussed clerks, treasurers, and receivers to keepers, parkers, stewards, bailiffs, and rangers on both sides of the Channel.

While little is known of the personnel who administered her lands for her in Brittany, as noted previously, the terms of her dower agreements gave Joan complete jurisdiction in her lands, including the power to appoint all receivers and captains in her own territory.[121] It is in the Guérande region where we get the clearest idea of her administrative networks in Brittany, thanks to a clear run of records from this area which lists each of the receivers of the region and the money collected from 1388, just after Joan was granted Guérande as part of her dower as duchess until long after her death in 1437.[122] Thirteen men can be identified from these records as receivers during the queen's tenure of the region, including Jean Andre, who served between 1402 and 1408, and Guillaume du Thuoy, who served over three periods during her dowager years, in 1417–18, 1428–31, and 1433–36. Other than these men, and some of the financial servitors mentioned earlier, such as Maitre Jamet Le Bel, Joan's *procureur* in Nantes, few of the men who administered her Breton dower have yet been identified.[123]

From the impressive number of surviving documents connected with Joan's dower in England, it is possible to get a far clearer picture of those who served the queen by administering her lands. Many of these men held multiple posts and were often also members of the queen's household or the king's or had served them both. They were also frequently men of influence as members of Parliament or members of the king's inner circle. This network of service was carefully crafted, and offering positions on her estates benefited Joan in two ways: first, in getting the assistance she needed to administer her vast and geographically widespread territorial holdings; and second, to ensure that these men of power and authority in the realm had ties to her through both service and the benefits that they accrued as stewards of her lands. Joan appears to have had an eye for spotting up-and-coming men at court and recruiting them into her network of service, as the example of William Porter demonstrates.

William appears to have arrived at court at a similar time to Joan as an esquire to her stepson Henry V and fought with him in campaigns in 1403 and 1404. In 1408, Joan named him as yeoman ranger in her forests of Melksham and Pewsham in Wiltshire. Porter continued to rise in service to Prince Henry and accrue rewards from him—almost immediately after Henry V succeeded to the throne he dispatched Porter on a secret mission to João of Portugal, confirming "that Henry V held Porter in the highest regard".[124] Joan clearly also sought to bind this rising star more closely to her by granting him a plum appointment in Northamptonshire in May 1416, to be the keeper of Rockingham Castle and steward of the forests including the "survey of vert and venison", but excluding the keeping of the park and bailiwick of Brigstock, which she had previously granted to her esquire Ralph Grene.[125] Once again in the reign of Henry VI, immediately after her release from confinement when she was re-establishing her networks at court, she granted Porter another appointment in the same area, this time making him keeper of Kings Cliff park in November 1422.

While Porter's case demonstrates the confluence between the king's (or prince's) household and Joan's own network of service, another strategy Joan used to reinforce her network was giving positions on her lands to those within her own household. Appointing members of her household to serve as administrators of her lands had a double benefit for Joan; it was a useful reward for good service and it also meant that she had reliable, proven servitors in key roles in the administration of her estates. One example is the aforementioned Sir Hugh Luttrell, steward of her household in the reign of Henry IV, who Joan made constable of Bristol Castle and keeper of her forests at Kingswood and Filwood in 1412.[126] Another example is long-serving household member William Ecclestone, groom of the queen's chamber throughout the reigns of Henry IV and V, who was made parker on the queen's manor of Hamstead Marshall.[127]

The career of Robert Tyndale provides an interesting example of a servant who served the queen both in her household and in administering her lands for a lengthy period and whose career appears to have waxed and waned with her. Tyndale was an early entrant into her service as queen consort, serving as yeoman of the beds from 1404.[128] Shortly thereafter, in 1405, Joan named him as parker of her estate at Devizes, at the heart of her sizable and important lands in Wiltshire—this was extended to a life posting by the queen in 1408 and confirmed by Henry IV in 1409.[129] In 1410 he served as part of a commission to repair Devizes Castle as discussed in the previous chapter.[130] Joan's change from consort to dowager did not appear to have any negative impact on Tyndale's career—on the contrary, he rose yet further, being made yeoman of the queen's robes in 1417 and served as MP for Devizes in 1417 and 1419.[131] Yet when the queen was imprisoned on a charge of witchcraft in October 1419, Tyndale's prospects dimmed. He does not appear in the records of her household during her confinement, suggesting that he lost his post as yeoman of the robes. Shortly afterwards Humphrey of Gloucester removed Tyndale from his position as parker of Devizes on charges of mismanaging the vert and venison in the park—a charge that was investigated by a special commission. However, Joan's release in 1422 and the advent of a new king, Henry VI, improved Tyndale's prospects once again. Tyndale was made yeoman of the king's robes in 1426 and although he did not appear to return to Joan's service, he clearly maintained some links with her as she granted him an annuity of ten marks a year from the manor of Clarendon in the account books of 1427–28.

Sir William Sturmy (or Esturmy) provides an interesting case study of the second type of individual that Joan recruited into her administration—men who were influential and at the heart of government. Sturmy was a wealthy landowner with estates in the south and west of England who had served both Richard II and Joan's husband Henry IV. Joan would have been aware of his diplomatic missions, service on the privy council, and his role as steward of her stepdaughter Blanche's household.[132] Sturmy's administrative experience and influence both at Westminster and in the south of England, where the bulk of her most important land holdings were based, may have motivated her to name him as the chief steward of her estates, shortly after her dower was confirmed, c. 1404. Although Sturmy did not serve in her household, he had ties there—Sir Hugh Luttrell, steward of her household, was Sturmy's (step) son-in-law. Sturmy's ties in Wiltshire, where his family had hereditary estates going back to the time of Domesday Book, gave him great familiarity with her lands there. Joan may have benefited from his knowledge of the region and Sturmy clearly benefited from being in her service, leasing a number of her properties, including her manor at Corsham and her estate at Ludgershall, and later being named forester of the queen's lands at Pewsham, Melksham, and Chippenham. Roskell and Kightly, in their biography of Sturmy, claim that "Sturmy's position as Queen Joan's chief steward, combined with his wardenship of Savernake forest and his ownership of substantial estates, made him perhaps the most important commoner in Wiltshire, certainly in the eastern parts of the county", and that Sturmy was able to leverage this position to ensure the election of his associates as MPs across the county.[133] Unlike Tyndale, Sturmy's career was not threatened by Joan's confinement in the latter years of Henry V's reign—ironically, however, it appears he was the head of the commission which looked into the accusation of Tyndale's mismanagement of the park of Devizes. Sturmy, in contrast to Tyndale, did not lose his hold on the lands that he held from the queen; indeed Corsham, Ludgershall, and the alien priory of Clatford, which had all been seized from the queen, were given over to Sturmy—a situation which must have been rather awkward in 1422 when Joan's dower was restored to her.[134] Yet the queen must have gracefully accepted the return of her lands and Sturmy's return to his former position as her chief steward, which he appears to have retained, with the exception of a brief hiatus, until his death in 1427.

This hiatus in Sturmy's tenure as chief steward occurred between Michaelmas 1414 and Michaelmas 1416 when he was briefly replaced by Thomas Tykhill (or Tickhill). Tykhill's brief, and somewhat bizarre, career in Joan's employment is worth a mention as it links to several themes we have explored in connection with her network of service. First, Tykhill is another example of a Crown servant who had served several royal masters as a king's attorney for Henry IV, serving his son on the prince of Wales's council, as chief steward of large portions of the prince's lands in Wales, Cornwall, and the earldom of Chester, and as a justice of the peace. In Maureen Jurkowski's survey of his career, she suggests that Joan may have replaced Sturmy with Tykhill in the hope that his legal experience and skill would mean he was better placed to secure compensation for some of the income that she lost in her 1414 dower grant. Yet in early 1417 Joan had not only fired Tykhill but brought a petition and suit against him alleging "that while he was chief steward, Tykhill had taken her great seal of office as well as various chests containing account books, letters patent and other evidence from her treasury and that he was still retaining them on his own authority for deceitful purposes" and was keeping large sums of money from her as well.[135] Joan brought a further suit against him in 1419 claiming that he and Thomas Davy had forged deeds which had jeopardised her title to the castle and manor of Moor End. It appears that the two men were indeed involved in forging documents which asserted that Joan had granted Tykhill the £34 annual fee farm of Moor End. However, Jurkowski argues that the entire situation stemmed from confusion over who exactly held the rights to Moor End and its fee farm at this juncture, and notes that these suits (and Tykhill's association with Lollard preachers) did not prevent him continuing his career as a Crown servant in other roles. Tykhill's case reinforces the picture of Joan which has been emerging over the previous chapters, of a woman who vociferously defended her rights and revenues—while she was keen to reward those in her service with benefits for loyalty and good service, she was equally quick to react to those whom she felt were taking advantage of her trust or working against her interests.

Other men in Joan's service may not have started as major players at Westminster or as significant nobles but were able to rise through their service to the queen. Richard Bitterley is one example, described as originally "a Sussex man of small means", who began his career in royal service as an esquire and usher of the queen's chamber.[136] In 1416, Joan had granted him an annuity of 100s a year from her manor at Kings Langley and the keeping of the manor house at a salary of 4d daily plus an additional 2d a day from the issues of the manor, as well as "the fees of the office and a robe of the suit of her esquires yearly at her great wardrobe".[137] Both Henry V and VI confirmed that he should have the post for life and be confirmed as a king's esquire in the event of Joan's death.[138] Shortly before Joan's arrest for witchcraft, Bitterley had been elected as knight of the shire for Sussex—Joan's disgrace did not negatively impact upon his career as he retained his position and was given the added benefit of being named warrener at Kings Langley as well. Bitterley continued to work for Joan after her release: she granted him two annuities in the 1427–28 account book, one for £10 and another of 66s 8d yearly. He also continued to work on the keeping and maintenance of her manor at Kings Langley, which became her principal residence until the fire of 1431.[139] Perhaps in compensation for the damage done to his holdings at Kings Langley, Joan made him surveyor of her other principal residence at Havering-atte-Bower before her death in 1437. After her death, Bitterley not only retained the posts that Joan gave him but was awarded the keeping of other estates once held by his former mistress, in acknowledgement of his good service.

These case studies are but a few examples of the careers of the men who served Joan by administering her lands. They illuminate the lives of officials who held several tenancies or positions in her administration concurrently and/or can also be identified as members of her household. Moreover, an interesting correlation can be seen here—those who were in her household and then appointed into her administration and/or those who held multiple positions in her administration all appear to have served her for considerable periods. This could demonstrate that Joan chose well in selecting loyal men who would serve her (or had already served her) for long periods, or alternatively it could be argued that a servitor was more likely to be loyal and serve Joan for a long time if they had multiple ties to her. Either way, it demonstrates an effective strategy for Joan in building her network of service, by reinforcing connections to her in multiple ways, ensuring that those whom she sought to keep in her network were both tightly bound to her and rewarded for their service.

Conclusion

In conclusion, this chapter has illuminated the wide-ranging and complex networks of service constructed by Joan of Navarre over the course of her life as infanta, duchess, and queen. It has highlighted the careers of several men and women who served Joan over long periods of time, remaining with her as she transitioned from one realm to another and from one role to another, as well as servitors who stayed loyal to her and maintained links to her even when she was imprisoned as a potential traitor and rumoured witch. Their loyalty demonstrates that Joan was a good mistress to serve, rewarding those in her service with annuities and positions. It could also be argued that Joan chose her servants well, selecting many who gave good service to her over long periods and many who could offer her political connections as she established herself in the English court or connections to the Breton and Navarrese courts that she emerged from. Yet there was a price to pay for choosing to serve Joan, as some loyal servants faced expulsion as unwanted aliens or, like Robert Tyndale, lost their position when their royal mistress could not protect them in her confinement. Joan paid a price for choosing to retain servants from the Continent as well—part of her enduring obscurity is due to the negative impression she has made through parliamentary petitions, which made her household look like a den of thieves, spies, and foreign miscreants.

On balance, Joan's sheer endurance—managing first to secure promotion from duchess to queen and then to retain and regain her position, navigating the political crises of her husband's reign, imprisonment under the reign of her stepson, and marginalisation as the step-grandmother of the young Henry VI—was due in large part to the support she retained from the affinity of her servitors. Maintaining a cosmopolitan and sizable retinue was a key part of projecting her status and authority as queen, no matter how challenging the circumstances. Her administrators were key to the effective management of her estates, which in turn provided financial support to maintain her household, demonstrating the interlinkage of Johnstone's two rings of service. Without the support of these long-standing and loyal servants, Joan would have been completely unable to function as queen and certainly would never have been able to survive the years of confinement nor re-establish herself after her release in 1422—women like Isabel Thorley, administrators like William Porter, or even more humble valets like John Dudman and

John Willoughby, who stuck by her, serving her before, during, and after her imprisonment. The crucial support offered by these loyal components of the two rings of Joan's network of service helped her navigate treacherous political waters and challenging transitions between infanta to duchess to queen to dowager—and the brief period when she was accused of being a traitor or even a witch.

Notes

1 Chris Given-Wilson, *The Royal Household and the King's Affinity: Service, Politics and Finance in England 1360–1413* (New Haven, CT: Yale University Press, 1986).
2 Diana Pelaz Flores, "'Reynante(s) en vno'. Poder y representación de la reina en la corona de Castilla durante el siglo XV" (PhD thesis, Universidad de Valladolid, 2015).
3 Michelle Beer, "The RSJ Article Prize Winner 2019: A Queenly Affinity? Catherine of Aragon's Estates and Henry VIII's Great Matter," *Royal Studies Journal* 6, no. 2 (2019): 5–25.
4 Nelly Ongay, "El hostal de la Infanta Maria (1365–66)," *Principe de Viana* 64 (2003): 127–58.
5 Michael Jones, "Dukes, Nobles and the Court in Late Medieval Brittany," in *Noblesse et États Princiers en Italie et en France au XVe siècle*, eds. Marco Gentile and Pierre Savy (Rome: Ecole Francaise de Rome, 2009), 253–85.
6 Marcel Planiol, *Histoire des Institutions de la Bretagne*, III (5 vols) (Mayenne: Association pour la publication du manuscrit de M. Planiol, 1981), 43.
7 Hilda Johnstone, "The Queen's Household," in *The English Government at Work, 1327–1336*, vol. 1, *Central and Prerogative Administration*, ed. James F. Willard and William A. Morris (Cambridge, MA: Mediaeval Academy of America, 1940), 250–99; Caroline Dunn, "Serving Isabella of France: From Queen Consort to Dowager Queen," in *Elite and Royal Households in Medieval and Early Modern Europe*, ed. Theresa Earenfight (Leiden: Brill, 2018), 169–201; Caroline Dunn, "All the Queen's Ladies? Philippa of Hainault's Female Attendants," *Medieval Prosopography* 31 (2016): 171–206; Lisa Benz, *Three Medieval Queens: Queenship and the Crown in Fourteenth-century England* (New York: Palgrave Macmillan, 2012).
8 Anne Crawford, "The King's Burden?—the Consequences of Royal Marriage in Fifteenth-century England," in *Patronage, the Crown and the Provinces in Later Medieval England*, ed. Ralph A. Griffiths (Gloucester: Alan Sutton, 1981), 33–56, and "The Queen's Council in the Middle Ages," *English Historical Review* 116, no. 469 (2001): 1193–211; J.L.

Laynesmith, *The Last Medieval Queens: English Queenship 1445–1503* (Oxford: Oxford University Press, 2004).

9 Johnstone, "Queen's Household," 251.

10 E101/406/30, John Rylands Library MS. 238 and Leeds Castle Archives E4/1.

11 E101/407/4 and E101/407/11.

12 L.S. Woodger, "Wilicotes, William (d. 1411) of North Leigh, Oxon," in HoP; CPR Henry IV, IV, 14 February 1412, 368.

13 Catálogo L, no. 677, 12 April 1371.

14 Catálogo XX, no. 877, 12 June 1394.

15 Catálogo XXXII, no. 154, 24 September 1416.

16 Catálogo XXII, no. 1080, 9 September 1398. See María Narbona Cárceles, "Woman at Court: A Prosopographic Study of the Court of Carlos III of Navarre (1387–1425)," *Medieval Prosopography* 22 (2001): 51, for claims she was also Joan's wet nurse.

17 María Narbona Cárceles, *La Corte de Carlos III el Noble, rey de Navarra: espacio domestico y escenario del poder, 1376–1415* (Pamplona: EUNSA, 2006), 80–1.

18 Bryan Bevan, *Henry IV* (London: Rubicon Press, 1994), 92.

19 SC 1/43/133 and 135; Michael Jones "Between France and England: Jeanne de Navarre, Duchess of Brittany and Queen of England (1386–1437)," in *Between France and England: Politics, Power and Society in Late Medieval Brittany* (Aldershot: Variorum, 2003), 12 n52. It is possible that Beatrix was the wife of or related to Tristan de la Lande, Joan's governor of Nantes.

20 CPR Henry IV, III, 12 March 1406, 159; PROME, "Henry IV: January 1404."

21 AGN Reg 187, fols. 63v and 165v. Note Joan also had a chaplain named Bernard de Sant who was gifted a hospital in Aquitaine: CPR Henry IV, III, 30 July 1407, 348. If the two were related, it is possible that they hailed from a family from the Midi region, possibly Foix-Béarn or Ultrapuertos.

22 Alan Rogers, "The Royal Household of Henry IV" (PhD thesis, University of Nottingham, 1966), 458.

23 A.R. Myers, "The Captivity of a Royal Witch: The Household Accounts of Queen Joan of Navarre, 1419–21," *Bulletin of the John Rylands Library* 24, no. 2 (1940): 265.

24 E101/405/22; Rogers, "Household", 458. I would like to thank Caroline Dunn for her insights on the Mauley and Hervy connections to the households of Philippa of Hainault and Anne of Bohemia from her upcoming work on ladies-in-waiting in medieval England.

25 CPR Henry IV, III, 22 July 1408, 464, and on Isabel's marriage to Thomas Thorley (likely in 1399), see CPR Henry IV, IV, 26 June 1410, 215.

26 See E101/407/4 and E101/406/30. It is also possible that the Thorley women were related to Robert Thorley, who served twice as treasurer

of Calais (March 1403–October 1404 and Easter 1406–March 1407) but was accused of financial irregularities.
27 Caroline Dunn, "Philippa," 177, and "Serving Isabella of France: From Queen Consort to Dowager Queen," in *Elite and Royal Households in Medieval and Early Modern Europe*, ed. Theresa Earenfight (Leiden: Brill, 2018), 169–201.
28 CPR Henry VI, I, 8 May 1423, 110.
29 SoA SAL/MS/216, fols 53–55.
30 Dunn, "Philippa," 187; see also "Serving Isabella."
31 Manuela Santos Silva, "The Portuguese Household of an English Queen: Sources, Purposes, Social Meaning," in *Royal and Elite Households*, ed. Theresa Earenfight (Leiden: Brill, 2018), 271–87; Pelaz Flores, "Reynante(s) en vno".
32 Michael Jones, *Ducal Brittany 1364–1399: Relations with England and France during the reign of Duke John V* (Oxford: Oxford University Press, 1970), 128 n3.
33 Bevan, *Henry IV*, 92; Jones, "Between France and England," 10.
34 Rogers, "Household," 452.
35 PROME, "Henry IV: January 1404."
36 CPR Henry IV, III, 1 August 1405, 36.
37 CPR Henry IV, III, 1 November 1405, 103.
38 L&M JV, V, no. 2658, 63.
39 CPR Henry V, II, 1 August 1420, 301.
40 CFR XIV, 20 October 1421, 407.
41 Jones, "Between France and England," 10; Given-Wilson, *Henry IV*, 421.
42 Jones, *Ducal Brittany*, 195–6; Given-Wilson, *Henry IV*, 421.
43 Jenny Stratford, *Richard II and the English Royal Treasure* (Woodbridge: Boydell, 2013), 120 and 172.
44 Stratford, *Royal Treasure*, 119.
45 For the Petworth grant, see SC 8/255/12744 and CPR Henry IV, III, 1 November 1405, 103. For Alderwiche see CPR Henry IV, III, 4 January 1406, 110.
46 CPR Henry IV, IV, 19 December 1411, 368, and 28 December 1412, 460, for wife Joan.
47 CFR, XIII, 13 November 1412, 49.
48 Stratford, *Royal Treasure*, 266, notes that an item of jewellery which she speculates may have belonged to Isabelle de Valois was pawned to Alderwicke and Periant to aid the Agincourt expedition. See E358/6, rot 7d and CCR Henry IV, III, 31 May 1406, 138.
49 Frederick Devon, *Issues of the Exchequer being a collection of payments made out of His Majesty's Revenue, from King Henry III to King Henry VI inclusive with an appendix* (London: John Murray, 1837), 324–25.
50 E101/69/3/374.
51 Catálogo XXIV, no. 817, 15 May 1400 and no. 815, 13 May 1400.
52 Pierre Tucoo-Chala, "L'histoire tragique d'un couple au XIVe siècle:

Agnès de Navarre at Gaston Fébus," *Principe de Viana Anejo: Homenaje José María Lacarra* 2–3 (1986): 751.

53 Catálogo XV, no. 508, 13 October 1384.

54 Catálogo XVIII, no. 681, 12 March 1386.

55 Catálogo XV, no. 1091, 8 September 1385.

56 Catálogo XXII, no. 1117, 29 October 1398.

57 Jean Kerhervé, *L'état Breton aux 14e et 15e siècles; Les Ducs, l'Argent et les Hommes* (Paris: Editeur Maloine, 1987), I, 289.

58 ADLA E210-7, April 1392.

59 SC 1/43/133, 134 and 135 and E403/576.

60 Rogers, "Household," 452.

61 CPR Henry IV, II, 12 September 1403, 261.

62 CPR Henry IV, II, 23 March 1405, 500.

63 See E213/104 and LR 14/1064.

64 PRO 23-2060, Seal of Thomas Feriby.

65 "Lateran Regesta 158: 1411–1412," in *Calendar of Papal Registers Relating to Great Britain and Ireland*: Volume 6, *1404–1415*, ed. W.H. Bliss and J.A. Twemlow (London: His Majesty's Stationery Office, 1904), 302–319, British History Online, accessed June 21, 2021, http://www.british-history.ac.uk/cal-papal-registers/brit-ie/vol6/pp302-319; "Archdeacons: Huntingdon," in *Fasti Ecclesiae Anglicanae 1300–1541*: Volume 1, *Lincoln Diocese*, ed. H.P.F. King (London: Institute of Historical Research, 1962), 8–10, British History Online, accessed July 29, 2021, http://www.british-history.ac.uk/fasti-ecclesiae/1300-1541/vol1/pp8-10.

66 John Pope, "List of Rectors for the Parish of St. John the Baptist with St. Mary the Virgin, Devizes," *Wiltshire OPC Project* (2013), https://www.wiltshire-opc.org.uk/Items/Devizes/Devizes%20-%20Rectors%20List%201310-1960%20(St.%20Mary).pdf.

67 E326/5962 and SC 6/1248/10.

68 Anon., *A Chronicle of London from 1089–1483, Written in the Fifteenth Century*, eds. Sir Nicholas Harris Nicholas and Edward Tyrell (London: Longman, 1827), 98; Christian Oliver Steer, "Burial and Commemoration in Medieval London, c. 1140–1540" (PhD thesis, University of London, 2013), 216.

69 CPR Henry IV, II, 14 December 1403, 362.

70 E101/405/22 and E101/404/21.

71 Rogers, "Household," 469–70: John Norbury was called Joan's esquire (as was Thomas Chaucer) in CPR Henry IV, IV, 15 March 1411, 283.

72 *Signet Letters,* no. 427, 17 August 1405, 98–99. See also CPR Henry IV, III, 18 August 1405, 46.

73 E101/406/10.

74 CPR Henry V, I, 24 June 1413, 48–49.

75 CPR Henry V, II, 16 November 1421, 402.

76 Dodd, commentary on Leeds Castle E4/1, 3.

77 CPR Henry V, II, 27 March 1421, 362.

78 See E40/6094 and E122/140/33.
79 See SC 5/22/2, SC 5/22/3; PROME, "Henry V: November 1414"; CPR Henry V, I, 27 January 1414, 164–67.
80 E213/404.
81 See SC 5/4/2, E213/363/I, E213/97, E122/18/31, and E326/531.
82 *Signet Letters*, no. 147, 4 June 1403, 47–8.
83 *Signet Letters,* no. 239, 11 March 1405, 65 and no. 705, 29 September 1407, 146. See also SC 1/41/195.
84 CPR Henry V, II, 16 September 1421, 396.
85 GSR C 61/110, 22 April 1405; GSR C 61/112, 22 September 1408; GSR C 61/113, 9 January 1410.
86 CPR Henry IV, IV, 12 August 1411, 304.
87 Jenny Stratford, *The Bedford Inventories: The Worldly Goods of John, Duke of Bedford, Regent of France (1389–1435)* (London: Society of Antiquaries, 1993), 415.
88 Stratford, *Bedford Inventories*, 416.
89 Kermabon, "Douaire," 271. See also L&M JV, VI, no. 1876, 29 December 1429 and no. 1880, 6 January 1430; CPR Henry IV, IV, 12 March 1410, 182.
90 See E152-20; CPR Henry IV, III, 27 January 1408, 395; and CPR Henry IV, IV, 12 March 1410, 182; 9 January 1410, 234; 12 August 1411, 304 (noting Joan's letter patent of 16 May 1411), and 24 January 1412, 367. See also L&M JV, VI, no. 1873, 26 December 1429.
91 Eloísa Ramírez Vaquero, "Estrategias diplomáticas del rey de Navarra en el tránsito al siglo XV," in *Guerra y Diplomacia en la Europa Occidental: 1280–1480 XXXI Semana de Estudios Medievales*, ed. Miguel Angel Ladero Quesada (Pamplona: Gobierno de Navarra, 2005), 398.
92 Eloísa Ramírez Vaquero, *Carlos III, rey de Navarra, Principe de sangre Valois (1387–1425)* (Gijon: Ediciones Trea, 2007), 68.
93 GSR C 61/104/20, 20 Feb 1394.
94 CCR Henry IV, II, 23 July 1403, 92.
95 See Foedera 8, 3 November 1411, and Catálogo XXVIII, no. 1108, 5 July 1411 and no. 1414, 12 December 1411.
96 See E404/20/196.
97 See E404/21/273, 22/189, 415 and 536, 23/192 and 24/16.
98 GSR C 61/112/107, 8 December 1409.
99 GSR C 61/109/115, 18 July 1404.
100 GSR C 61/112/57, 10 August 1408.
101 GSR C 61/112/107, 8 December 1409 and GSR C 61/114/42, 29 June 1413.
102 GSR C 61/112/133, 22 August 1409.
103 Catálogo XXX, no. 758, 2 October 1413.
104 E404/29/21, E404/30/104 and 128.
105 GSR C 61/114/42, 29 June 1413.
106 CPR Henry V, I, 29 June 1413, 100.
107 Foedera 9, 5 February 1416.

108 Foedera 9, 16 March 1418; Catálogo XXXII, no. 698, 22 January 1418; GSR C 61/117/55, 10 August 1417.
109 Devon, *Issues of the Exchequer*, 401.
110 Catálogo XL, no. 937, 29 July 1432.
111 Catálogo XL, no. 18, 17 January 1431; Catálogo XXXIX, no. 488, 6 April 1430; no. 881, 16 July 1430; no. 888, 16 July 1430; no. 1046, 26 August 1430.
112 Jean de Jaurgain, "Les Beaumont-Navarre: Notes historiques et généalogiques," *Revista internacional de los estudios vascos (RIEV)* 3, no. 1 (1909): 54–7.
113 W. Mark Ormrod, Bart Lambert, and Jonathan Mackman, eds., *Immigrant England 1300–1550* (Manchester: Manchester University Press, 2019), 119, on Alcobaça; for Trent, see Léon Mirot, "Études lucquoises, Galvano Trenta et les joyaux de la Couronne," *Bibliothèque de l'École des chartes* 101 (1940): 116–56.
114 Ormrod, Lambert, and Mackman, *Immigrant England*, 211 and 209.
115 See Elena Woodacre, "Epilogue: Foreign Women as Consorts," in *Later Plantagenet and the Wars of the Roses Consorts: Power, Influence, Dynasty*, eds. Aidan Norrie, Carolyn Harris, J.L. Laynesmith, Danna Messer, and Elena Woodacre (New York: Palgrave Macmillan, 2022).
116 PROME, "Henry IV: January 1404."
117 PROME, "Henry IV: January 1404" and "Henry IV: March 1406, part 1."
118 PROME, "Henry V: March 1416."
119 PROME, "Henry VI: February 1426."
120 Catálogo XXXIII, no. 346, 16 October 1420.
121 Kermabon, "Douaire," 206, 235.
122 ADLA B4245 fols 40r–42v.
123 ADLA E156–11, 18 May 1401.
124 L.S. Woodger, "Porter, William II (d.1436), of Wimpole, Cambs," in HoP.
125 CPR Henry V, I, 15 March 1416, 401; CPR Henry VI, II, 19 February 1433, 262.
126 CPR Henry IV, IV, 8 November 1412, 448.
127 CPR Henry VI, III, 8 March 1437, 57.
128 CPR Henry IV, II, 15 September 1404, 419.
129 CPR Henry IV, IV, 30 May 1409, 81.
130 CPR Henry IV, IV, 19 April 1410, 224.
131 Charles Kightly, "Tyndale, Robert of Devizes, Wiltshire," in HoP.
132 David Grummit, "Sturmy, Sir William," ODNB, 28 September 2006.
133 J.S. Roskell and Charles Kightly, "Sturmy (Esturmy), Sir William (c. 1356–1427) of Wolf Hall in Great Bedwyn, Wilts and Elvetham, Hants," in HoP.
134 CFR, XIV, 21 February 1420, 321–322.
135 Maureen Jurkowski, "Lancastrian Royal Service, Lollardy and Forgery: The Career of Thomas Tykill," in *Crown, Government and People in the*

Fifteenth Century, ed. Rowena E. Archer (Stroud: Sutton Press, 1995), 41. For Joan's 1417 petition against Tickhill, see *Signet Letters*, no. 796, 163 and SC 8/248/12366.

136 L.S. Woodger, "Bitterley, Richard (d.c. 1456) of Hartling, Sussex," in HoP.

137 CPR Henry V, II, 1 July 1416, 38.

138 CPR Henry VI, I, 8 February 1424, 180.

139 CPR Henry VI, I, 12 July 1426, 360–61.

7

PLACES, PIETY, POSSESSIONS, AND PATRONAGE

While the early chapters of this book have given us a rich understanding of the key events of Joan's life, both in terms her personal milestones and the complex political landscape of the time in which she lived, this chapter will take a completely different approach in connecting with her. Here, we will explore material culture and cultural patronage, using the documentary evidence to reconstruct the objects that Joan possessed and gifted to others and illuminate her role as a patroness, a key aspect of queenship and an important means of image creation.[1] We will also examine the places that Joan inhabited, with particular focus on her major residences. Taken together, these elements will give us a much deeper understanding of her life and of Joan as an individual, helping us to reconstruct the places in which she lived and the objects around her, from the day-to-day to the cherished or ceremonial pieces. Examining gifts given to and by Joan also illuminates her relationships with her family and her network both within and beyond the realm. Her networks are further developed by discussing her patronage activities—demonstrating both her cultural impact and how this resonates with the wider traditions of her natal and marital families.

The tenancy of residences and the possessions of objects are ultimately temporary—whether Joan created or ameliorated them, she

DOI: 10.4324/9780429261022-10

was ultimately a steward of these items of material culture and architecture. The work of queenship scholars and art historians has demonstrated how elite and royal women both created artworks and architecture and moved objects around Europe through their marriages and gifting through their familial networks.[2] Some of these sites and objects survive today, from Leeds Castle in Kent, which was both part of her portfolio of properties and served as her effective prison for several years, to the Trinity Reliquary gifted to her son, which is now in the Louvre, or even her joint tomb with Henry IV, which she likely commissioned, which still stands in Canterbury Cathedral. Other examples have not stood the test of time or are now lost, like her palace at Kings Langley which suffered a disastrous fire during her later years or the breviary given to her by her aunt Blanche of Navarre, queen of France. Yet documentary evidence survives, such as testamentary evidence, expenditure on residences, and household account books, which help us understand the places she inhabited, the possessions with which she interacted, and the people she patronised.

While this chapter contains many diverse elements of her life brought together, it gives us an opportunity to build on the events, politics, and familial dynamics that we looked at in the first section of the book. It will also connect with the examination of the networks of courtiers that Joan built across borders and across the realm and our study of Joan's lands and finances in the previous chapters. Ultimately, it will give us a chance to get to know Joan the woman a bit better, as well as create a clearer picture of how she exercised the offices of duchess and queen.

This chapter will be divided into four sections which follow the major, intertwined themes of this chapter: places, piety, possessions, and patronage. We will start with an examination of places, focusing on her residences and the wide range of places that she inhabited as both duchess and queen. Some of these places were ecclesiastical spaces, which will lead us to a wider consideration of her piety, as well as her engagement with religious patronage and politics. In the possessions section, we will be thinking about the objects within them and how she acquired those objects through gift-gifting and patronage. We will finish our examination of patronage with a particular focus on her commissions of tombs—for both her husbands and for herself, reflecting on the lasting image that Joan wished to create of herself as infanta, duchess, and queen.

Places: Examining the spaces that Joan inhabited as duchess and queen

Over her long life as duchess of Brittany and then as queen of England, Joan of Navarre spent time in a wide range of palaces, castles, manors, and abbeys, in addition to maintaining a considerable portfolio of lands and residences attached to both her Breton and English dowers. This section will look at several aspects of Joan's engagement with the spaces in which she lived and worked. We will look at spaces which were renovated or built for Joan's use, such as the new apartments built for her at her second husband's favourite residence at Eltham. In addition to her use of major royal and ducal residences, we will consider her management of some of the residences which belonged to her—examining her administration, use, and renovation of these spaces, connecting to the discussion of her lands and castles in earlier chapters. Taken together, by examining both the queen's use and development of spaces and the sites she favoured for day-to-day living, we can gain a deeper understanding of how Joan of Navarre constructed, framed, and utilised space as a key element of the exercise of her office, and of her lived experience.

To begin, it is important to recognise and survey the wide range of properties that Joan both inhabited and had a connection with over the course of her life. Broadly speaking, we can group these spaces over three categories: those belonging to her husbands (Crown spaces or ducal/royal residences), those belonging to her (queenly spaces—her own residences and her Westminster "office"), and other spaces, such as ecclesiastical sites or visits to other royal/noble residences.

The most obvious spaces she inhabited were the royal and ducal residences of her two husbands, Jean IV of Brittany and Henry IV of England. As the court was itinerant, which was broadly typical in the later Middle Ages, as a consort Joan moved with her husbands, and on her own, between a selection of properties—from important palaces and castles to smaller manors and hunting lodges. As a dowager queen, the amount of time she spent at court in the major royal residences reduced, particularly after the period of "house arrest", and the amount of time she spent at her own residences increased. It is important to acknowledge that Joan also spent time at locations which were not part of the Crown or her own portfolio, such as abbeys, and had access to spaces which were used for other purposes, such as her aforementioned office, which was previously discussed in connection with the administration of her lands.

One of the most difficult aspects of researching Joan's life has been trying to establish her itinerary from the surviving documentation. The movements of her husbands have been easier to track, particularly Henry IV, as his biographer Chris Given-Wilson has compiled a thorough itinerary. While there is evidence of Joan travelling with her husband, such as documents which demonstrate her presence in Leicester and Kenilworth with Henry IV in 1404, it should not be assumed that Joan was continually with either of her husbands.[3] Indeed, documentation shows that she moved around the realm independently at times and there were periods when husband and wife were necessarily separate, such as during Henry's campaigns against rebels in the early years of their marriage. Yet, there are periods, such as key feast days and court celebrations, notably Christmas and New Year's, when we can be more certain that Joan was likely to be at her husband's side, even if her presence was not always attested to or directly traceable. From the evidence we do have and some reasonable assumptions, we know that Joan spent considerable time during her married life at the key residences of Westminster and Windsor in England and at Nantes in Brittany, which was both a ducal centre and an area which formed a key portion of her Breton dower.

Both of her husbands were keen builders or renovators of their own residences, and we know that Joan both spent time in the particular locations that her husbands favoured and benefited from the ameliorations they made to their properties to heighten their splendour and comfort. In Brittany we can see excellent examples of this at two locations on the southern side of the Breton peninsula around the gulf of Morbihan—the Château de l'Hermine in the city of Vannes and the castle of Suscinio.[4] The city of Vannes played an important role in the reign of Jean IV—he began construction of the château in 1379; in addition to accommodation for the duke and the court, the city was fortified and had a substantial administrative element, including a mint and chancelry, and it frequently hosted the États de Bretagne, which testified to the use of the city as a key governmental centre.[5] The château itself appears to have been fairly substantial in its medieval form, although Bertrand d'Argentré described it somewhat disparagingly as "*un petit bastiment pour un prince*" ("a little building for a prince") in the sixteenth century; the modern scholar Marie Casset termed it "*une vaste residence*".[6] By one estimate, by the end of Jean IV's reign it could accommodate 250–300 people, including the ducal family, the court, and servants.[7] The birth of some of Joan's children at Vannes and Suscinio also testifies to their importance as key ducal residences and perhaps her own desire to be there for her lying-in: her eldest son Jean V was born at Vannes on Christmas Eve 1389 and Arthur de Richemont was born in August 1393 at Suscinio.

While Vannes was a key governmental centre, Suscinio by contrast was a ducal residence where the duke, his family, and court could go to enjoy the beautiful location near the southern coast and partake in the hunting in the extensive enclosed park to the east of the château.[8] It was also close to another spot with sentimental connections, the church of St Gildas de Rhuys, where the tomb of Joan's first child, Jeanne de Bretagne, was located, along with that of other "*petits princes et princesses*" of Brittany.[9] Jean IV made substantial ameliorations to the château in the final two decades of his reign to create a very comfortable princely residence for himself and his duchess. The ducal apartments were in a large four-storey block—the ground floor was for guards and storage and the first-floor rooms contained a hall and more public spaces, with the private apartments of the duke and duchess on the higher floors. Joan's apartments were on the second floor with a bed chamber and an outer withdrawing chamber that "enjoyed a twin room steam bathing facility".[10] A stair from the duchess's chamber led directly to the duke's rooms on the third floor, ending in what appears to have been the duke's private study. The amenities at the châteaux and its decoration, including beautiful faience tiles which have recently been restored, would have made it a comfortable and impressive ducal residence.[11]

Joan's second husband Henry IV was also keen on improvements and ameliorations to royal residences, which may have been both connected to improving creature comforts and his wider efforts to project majesty as a usurper king. His efforts were particularly focused on Eltham, his "favourite retreat" according to his biographer Chris Given-Wilson.[12] Deborah Codling has argued that Eltham gives us a window into Henry himself, as he was "creating both a public and private space there that reflected his tastes and his style of kingship".[13] Henry spent substantial amounts on renovations at Eltham, approximately £1,100 between 1399 and 1407, equal to roughly £675,000 today.[14] Eltham became an important royal centre under Henry IV, as the king brought the court there two or three times a year, often for substantial periods, and it was often used for key celebrations—10 out of the 13 Christmas periods during Henry's reign were celebrated there and 3 Easter courts were held there as well.[15] It was also a place with important sentimental links to the couple as their proxy marriage was celebrated there in April 1402, and Henry and Joan spent an extended period at Eltham as a sort of honeymoon after their wedding in February 1403.

Henry's development of Eltham included practical works like a new kitchen, larder, and saucer capable of providing for the court, and accommodation for courtiers including allotted rooms for key figures such as his family members the duke of York and the earl and countess of Somerset, as well as his friends Thomas Erpingham and John Norbury.[16] It also had spaces for court events such as hosting tournaments and important guests like the Byzantine Emperor in 1400, as well as comforts such as gardens, "dancing chambers", and bathhouses.[17] More significantly, perhaps, he built impressive new apartments—first for himself and then, around the time of his marriage to Joan, a suite of rooms for his new queen. His own rooms were lavishly appointed with glass decorated with themes which resonated strongly with Henry, such as his devotion to the Trinity and St Thomas Becket and heraldic badges including his motto "*Souvenez vous de moi*"—which were also reflected in the couple's joint tomb at Canterbury Cathedral.[18] His rooms also included a study with two desks, including a large one with shelving space for his books—which were important to Joan and his sons Henry V, John of Bedford, and Humphrey of Gloucester as well.[19] Joan's new apartments comprised a two-storey block which was 35 feet wide with a parlour and drawing chamber on the ground floor and a chamber, drawing chamber, and latrine on the first floor. Joan had her own kitchen, chapel, and hall at Eltham as well.[20]

Thus, Joan had comfortable and even beautifully decorated spaces as both duchess and queen in her husband's residences—with dedicated spaces for her every need from her personal comforts of bathing, eating, and sleeping to receiving visitors, praying, and relaxing with courtiers and family. However, Joan also possessed her own residences, including a selection of manor houses, palaces, and castles. As noted in Chapter 5, she held several castles, including Devizes, Odiham, Bristol, Rockingham, Nottingham, and Hertford. While she did not necessarily use all of these sites as residences, we can see documentary evidence demonstrating that Joan was in residence in 1408 and 1413 at Hertford and she may have also spent time there with Henry who was a frequent visitor between 1403 and 1407, particularly in 1406—indeed Deborah Codling claims that Hertford castle was one of Henry's favoured residences.[21] The castle came from the duchy of Lancaster holdings and his father, John of Gaunt, had spent money improving the accommodation and domestic buildings. However, before it was part of Lancaster lands it had been held by two earlier queens, Margaret and Isabella of France, the wives of Edward I and II, respectively. Yet Joan only held the castle until 1415 when she swapped it for Kings Langley palace with Henry V. It is unclear who sought the exchange—Henry V, who may have wanted to return Hertford to the duchy holdings, or Joan herself. There is a petition from the queen in 1415 which requests Kings Langley in compensation for Hertford Castle and subsequent grant of Langley manor from Henry V "in recompense of the castle of Hertford, which was granted to her for life and which the king with her assent has taken into his hands".[22] However, on the same date that he formally took Hertford in exchange for Kings Langley, Henry granted Joan license to live at Hertford in his absence while he was on campaign in France and also gave her leave to "dwell with her men, servants, and minsters" at Windsor, Wallingford, and Berkhamstead as well.[23]

It is the manor or palace of Kings Langley where we can most clearly discern Joan's physical presence. Evidence demonstrates that she did visit Langley even before it belonged to her, as confirmations of her letters patent place her there multiple times in the first half of 1411—without Henry.[24] After she took possession of it in 1415 we can see her there more frequently, with documents noting her presence there in February and March of 1416, and one of her letters patent found in the archives at Nantes testifies to her being in residence at Langley on 1 July 1418.[25] Indeed, from the surviving documentation, it appears that Joan divided her time between London and/or Westminster, presumably at court, and Kings Langley between 1415 and 1419. Like all of her properties, Joan lost access to Kings Langley during her extended period of house arrest from 1419 to 1422, but after her release the palace appears to become her favourite residence—indeed from the surviving evidence she appears to have been there, nearly permanently it seems, between 1425 and 1432, with some breaks, such as a pilgrimage to Walsingham, Norwich, and St Albans in 1427.[26] In the household account book of 1427–28 we have evidence that she hosted important guests there, including her stepson Humphrey of Gloucester and his wife Eleanor Cobham, as well as Cardinal Beaufort, the bishop of Winchester.[27]

Joan was not the only royal to favour Langley—it came into royal hands through Eleanor of Castile, who had held it from the earl of Cornwall, and considerable comforts had been installed there over the years, including a bathhouse, a sizeable wine cellar, and a counting house and clock installed by Edward III in 1368, which "doubtless served to count the hours for the inhabitants of the royal manor as well as for the friars".[28] The Dominican friary adjacent was also the resting place of Edward II's great favourite Piers Gaveston and, during the reign of Henry IV, the initial burial place of his predecessor Richard II.[29] Joan left her own mark on the palace in both positive and negative ways. As noted in the previous chapter she had named Richard Bitterley, one of the ushers of her chamber, as the keeper of the manor in 1416 and he stayed in post, even during the period of Joan's detention, apparently retaining it until his death in 1456. Between 1426 and 1429, in a period we know Joan to have been largely present at Langley, Bitterley was given a commission by the clerk of the King's Works to undertake extensive work on the manor, which cost £94 5s 5 1/2d (more than £61,000 in modern funds)—expensive works which Joan herself was funding.[30]

The works touched on nearly all corners of the palace; Lionel Munby noted that it included "repairs to the Duchess of Gloucester's [Eleanor Cobham's] chamber and 'all the rooms called the Quene chambres', the chamberlain's and comptroller's rooms, the bakery, spicery, cellar and chandlery. Several new chimneys were built, and the Great Hall, the chambers and passages 'to the south' and other buildings outside the Court were also repaired".[31] Sadly, just after these major repair works were undertaken, a terrible accident caused considerable damage to the queen's favourite residence. The contemporary annals of St Albans record that an "*incendium grande et damnosum*" ("a great and destructive fire") swept through the palace in 1431 due to the "negligence and drowsiness of a minstrel and insufficient care of a lighted candle".[32] While there is evidence that Joan returned to Langley in 1432, the damage to the palace must have made it far less pleasant to stay in for the queen and her household. Indeed, a survey made of the manor after Joan's death noted the poor state it was in, as the "roofing of the great hall, the chapel, the king's chamber and of two other chambers was defective, so that their walls and timber-work were rotten and decayed through exposure".[33] Given the heavy toll that the palace took in the fire, it would not have been comfortable for Joan and her household to live in and thus it appears that for the final years of her life she favoured her manor at Havering-atte-Bower.

Havering was another location with a long association with queens and had a very long history, having been noted as a royal manor in Domesday Book.[34] It was first assigned to a queen as a part of her dower in 1273 and was held by the fourteenth-century queens Margaret and Isabella of France, Philippa of Hainault, and Anne of Bohemia prior to Joan's tenure—it continued to be held by queens into the sixteenth century. Joan appears to have used Havering over the entirety of her life—examples of surviving documentation place her there as consort in late September 1407 and she was at Havering for two significant moments during her dowager years—her arrest on a charge of treason at the beginning of October 1419 and her death in July 1437.

It is during the period of her detention, from October 1419 until late summer 1422, that we have the clearest picture of her movements and the spaces that she occupied. As Myers has noted, Joan was not held in close confinement in any form of prison, rather she was held in a sort of house arrest. Initially, between October and December 1419, she was moved around, fairly frequently, between a series of locations: from Havering to Rotherhithe, then to Dartford, Rochester, to Leeds Castle, back to Rochester, Dartford, and Rotherhithe, and then finally to Pevensey in mid-December, where she remained until early March 1420 under the care of John Pelham. After Pevensey, she was moved to Leeds Castle, which, ironically perhaps, had been one of her own residences. It had initially been assigned to her in dower in 1403—another property which had a long association with queens having also been held by Eleanor of Castile who developed the property extensively and then by Margaret and Isabella of France and Anne of Bohemia. However, she had given Leeds to Thomas Arundel, archbishop of Canterbury, who was a great supporter of her husband in 1412. After Arundel died in 1414, the castle was given by Henry V to his grandmother, Joan countess of Hereford, who died there in 1419.[35] By bringing his stepmother Joan to Leeds Castle for her detention in 1420, the castle effectively went full circle and became her residence once again, but in very different circumstances.

In conclusion, this section has touched on many examples of the wide range of places which Joan inhabited over the course of her long life—demonstrating Joan's independent movements to spend time at her own residences, both enjoying their amenities and accommodation for herself and her household and her efforts to maintain, repair, and improve the properties she held. This consideration of Joan's use of space and place has also demonstrated changing patterns of residence in her later years. During Joan's early years as a dowager, prior to her arrest on a dubious charge of treason, it appears that her time was divided between the court and her own residences, when she was still the only queen and the pre-eminent woman in the realm. However, after her release in 1422, with the advent of another queen dowager, her cousin Katherine de Valois, and being demoted to the king's step-grandmother with a slightly tarnished reputation, she appears to have remained more frequently at her own residences at Langley and Havering. It has also demonstrated the importance of the economic aspect of queenship, connecting to our earlier discussion of Joan's management of her queenly portfolio of lands through her engagement with the repair and maintenance of her residences as well as her other castles, manors, and sites. In sum, surveying Joan's connection to space and place gives us both a clearer understanding of how the woman spent her time and how the duchess and queen exercised her office.

Piety: Joan's engagement with religious patronage and politics

In addition to Joan's time spent in her own properties or in other ducal and royal residences, there is evidence that she stayed at ecclesiastical locations as well. In particular, we can see two abbeys which she visited on multiple occasions, Chertsey and Stratford. Chertsey was a Benedictine abbey in Surrey which had been originally founded in the seventh century and had a long history of royal connections and support.[36] However, Henry IV did not appear to have a close bond with the abbey, only staying there once during his reign, on 6 May 1403. It is possible that if Joan was with him on that occasion that she formed more of a connection with the abbey as we know that she stayed there on multiple occasions during her consort years, particularly in March 1410 and April 1411.[37] Her association with the abbey continued in later years as her priest and chaplain, Henry Weston, was one of Chertsey's monks, who was given leave by the Pope in July 1419 to "to engage in the service of the said queen as long as he pleases, even without the monastery".[38]

In her later years, we can see evidence of Joan in residence at Stratford, or St Mary Stratford Langthorne abbey in Essex, in October of 1433 and 1434.[39] She may have stayed here due to religious connections or possibly for convenience as it formed a nearly halfway point between London and her residence at Havering-atte-Bower, thus making it an ideal way to break the journey between court visits and home. In contrast to Chertsey, Stratford was a Cistercian house and it was one which Henry IV had visited frequently, with several stays there in the summer of 1411 and early 1412; it is possible that Joan was also introduced to the abbey if she was accompanying her husband.[40]

However, her stays in ecclesiastical buildings like these, or even Wolvesey Castle, the palace of the bishop of Winchester where she stayed during the wedding festivities of 1403, do not necessarily demonstrate piety—they may purely be circumstantial or for convenience. Yet piety was one of the key qualities of queenship, a virtue which royal women were expected to model to their subjects.[41] Michelle Beer has discussed the idea of performative piety as part of the "sacralisation of queenship"—engaging in public acts of worship and charity, religious patronage, and pilgrimage was a key element of the office itself and a means of fashioning a positive image in the short and long term.[42] Indeed, this was an area which Joan's niece, Blanca I of Navarre, excelled at throughout her reign, engaging in religious patronage, finishing her father's works at Pamplona's cathedral, and even taking her whole court to Zaragoza to celebrate the Assumption of the Virgin at Santa Maria del Pilar—she died in 1441 while on one of her many pilgrimages to another important site of Marian devotion in Castile.[43] Joan's Continental relatives and her English predecessors provide countless examples of significant religious patronage, establishing convents and monasteries—indeed many medieval queens, such as Berengaria of Navarre, chose to be buried at these sites in order to forever link themselves as the patron or foundress of the institution. Supporting a particular site or a particular religious order could also be a means of promoting a queen's sense of natal or dynastic identity—for example Laura Slater has demonstrated how Margaret of France, Isabella of France, and Philippa of Hainault's patronage of Greyfriars in London was a means of highlighting their shared Capetian heritage.[44]

Joan, however, does not appear to have followed in her predecessors' and relatives' footsteps in this sense—we can find no records that Joan founded any religious institution, nor can we see deep, clear links to any site in particular. She also did not appear to favour any religious order exclusively, although there is a clear connection with the Franciscan order which her female Navarrese and French family had a history of patronising. This connection appears to have been fairly consistent over the course of her life, from her early education at the Clarissan convent at Estellla to the presence of Franciscans in the household of the Navarrese infantas in her childhood, and there is evidence of her patronage of the Franciscans with her first husband, Jean IV of Brittany, as well.[45] We know that Joan had at least three Franciscan confessors, and in her accounts of 1427–28 there are payments to several Franciscan friars. Yet she also had religious personnel from other orders, such as Henry Weston, the Benedictine monk from Chertsey who served as one of her chaplains, and she had a connection with the Benedictine abbey at St Albans as well. Joan also had some connection with the Dominican priory adjacent to her residence at Kings Langley; for example, in her accounts of 1427–28, there is a record of a payment to the prior, Henry Waryn, and her accounts also record other payments to Dominicans for preaching.

Many members of her household were ecclesiastics, not just the confessors, chaplains, and almoners, but many of her clerical staff, such as John de Tibbay, her treasurer and receiver-general whom we have already met in previous chapters, who was also canon of Lincoln and York, master or warden of Greatham hospital, and rector of Wensley, among other posts. In the Papal Registers, we can see examples of how Joan supported the clerics in her service to obtain further positions, such as John Leveryche, a Franciscan friar whom she petitioned on behalf of in 1413, or her confessor, William Man, whose petition she supported in 1437 to obtain an additional post.[46] As Helen Maurer has noted, this was part of "good ladyship", but also a savvy financial move as "once the cleric held the benefice, he was assumed to have an adequate income, making it unnecessary to continue paying him wages as a household servant".[47] Perhaps Joan was hoping to save the £20 annuity which she had been paying William from the revenues of her manor of Stoke Bardolph for more than five years by supporting his petition for an additional benefice.[48] Another member of her religious staff who was given a dispensation by the Pope to hold benefices was John Ayleston. Ayleston held a variety of posts; as well as being rector of Stanwell, he held canonries at Windsor, Ely, and Westminster, several rectories, and was also master of St Mary's hospital in Chichester. Ayleston may have obtained these posts thanks to his long-standing service to the queen—the papal dispensation of 1409 names him as "chaplain of Joan, Queen of England", and in the household records of 1427–28 he was named as her almoner and gifted cloth, marking around two decades of association, if not constant service to the queen.[49] Joan not only petitioned the Pope for posts and positions for her clerics, she also petitioned the king for benefits and benefices within his purview, such as her successful supplication to Henry IV to obtain the hospital of Urdiarp in Soule, Gascony, for her chaplain, Bernand de Sant, in 1407.[50] Joan also had some rights attached to her dower to nominate clerics for positions; for example, in 1426 Henry VI granted John Bernyngham the prebend of Shipton on Joan's nomination.[51] Yet Joan could overstep the mark in these matters—in 1428, Walter, the abbot of St Augustine's, Bristol, sued the queen for the restitution of the expenses for his installation when it turned out that his election would be overturned as it had been authorised by Joan in connection with her dower rights in the city, but the king had protested that the patronage of St Augustine's and the right to call elections for a new abbot belonged to him instead.[52]

Supporting the petitions of her clerics was just one of the matters on which Joan corresponded with the papacy—she also requested indulgences or spiritual privileges for the benefit of her eternal soul, and mortal body in some cases. The most frequent privilege that she requested was the power to choose her own confessor, which she requested as both duchess and as queen and both in tandem with her husbands and singly.[53] Not only did she receive confirmation of this privilege, but her confessors were also granted the ability to confer additional benefits to her, such as grant to herself and Henry IV plenary remission of their sins as often as they pleased in 1404 or the ability to eat meat in Lent, which she requested with Jean IV in 1387 as a young bride and again in 1434.[54] It was specifically noted in the 1434 dispensation that her confessors could release her from the need to fast at Lent and other days of abstinence and could allow her to eat meat and dairy products on the advice of her physicians, given her advanced age, although this factor may have been exaggerated in the request.[55] Joan requested the most privileges in 1413, asking for the right to use a portable altar to celebrate Mass, choose her own confessor, and for her confessor to be able to grant absolution, enjoin a salutary penance, and grant her plenary remission of her sins at the hour of her death and one other time as well. The timing of this may have been related to the decline and death of her husband, Henry IV, which may have sharpened her concern for her soul, or as many royals requested privileges in connections with changes in title or status, this may be related to reaffirming her standing as she transitioned from consort to dowager.[56]

Joan's relationship with the papacy was clearly impacted by the Papal Schism. As discussed previously, Joan's Navarrese family had been adherents of the anti-pope in Avignon, and while her first husband, Jean IV, had also been a supporter of the Avignonese pope, the English were allied with the papacy in Rome. This complicated the situation regarding matrimonial dispensations—rather than ones which allowed her to choose her own confessor or eat meat in Lent as discussed previously, these dispensations were papal letters which allowed royal marriages to go ahead, or alternatively refused to support a particular match, and thus could have a major political impact. The first Avignon anti-pope, Clement VII, issued a dispensation for the marriage of Jean IV and Joan on 15 August 1386.[57] While this would seem to indicate good relations with the papacy and support of Jean IV, it should be noted that at almost the same time Clement issued a dispensation for Jean de Penthièvre, scion of the rival Breton clan who contested the Monfort's rule of the duchy, to wed the daughter of Olivier de Clisson, effectively sanctioning the union of Jean IV's greatest enemies.[58] The dispensation for Joan's second marriage was even more complicated given the fact that England was on the other side of the Schism. This required careful manoeuvring on Joan's part—first she obtained a dispensation from the anti-pope, Benedict XIII, to marry an unspecified cousin within the fourth degree in March 1401 while in the midst of negotiating her coming marriage with Henry IV.[59] Then she requested a dispensation to live with heretics, or those on the other side of the Schism, again without specifying her intention to ally herself with the English king. It appears that her agent in

Avignon to secure these dispensations was Bernard du Peyron, one of her closest clerics who had risen from being her almoner or chaplain to become bishop of Nantes under her sponsorship.[60] Once in England, Joan's foreignness, and that of many of the members of her household, was amplified by their connection to the anti-pope in Avignon. While this tension was eventually resolved by the end of the Papal Schism, during Joan's years as consort this added to the concerns regarding the presence of a large number of foreign courtiers in her retinue as discussed in the previous chapter. Indeed, the original 1404 petition to expel foreigners from the royal household noted "that all those who take the part of the antipope … if there are any such around the royal majesty … should go overseas with all possible and decent haste", and particularly noted that the foreigners, "schismatics or not", from Joan's household should be removed.[61]

There is a range of evidence to demonstrate her devotional practices which reflect both Joan's personal piety and the expectations of a queen to model pious behaviour. We do know that Joan went on at least one pilgrimage, as John Amundesham, the chronicler of St Albans, commented that Joan visited the monastery on her way home to Kings Langley after a pilgrimage around several sites in the east of England including Walsingham, Norwich, Peterborough, and "*aliis diversis locis*" in 1427.[62] The account books from 1420–21 demonstrate that Joan had Masses celebrated "in the presense of the queen herself" on all the major feast days such as Corpus Christi, Trinity, and the feast of St John the Baptist at Leeds Castle during her confinement, giving offerings of 6s 8d on each occasion, with the exception of Easter 1422 when Mass was celebrated by two vicars, and the queen offered 13s 4d.[63] She kept religious personnel in her household in order to celebrate Mass regularly—in addition to the aforementioned confessors, her 1427–28 account books list more than a half a dozen chaplains and her almoner, the long-serving John Ayleston, who was charged with distributing £7 3s 4d to the poor that year, equal to nearly £4,500 today.[64]

As noted previously, she had her own chapel at Eltham Palace as consort, and her other residences all had some facility for the devotions for the queen and her household. We can get a glimpse of Joan's chapel at Kings Langley through a list of its furnishings made in her surviving household accounts of 1427–28.[65] Interestingly, this list turns up twice in her account books, first as an inventory of items used to celebrate Mass in the queen's chapel that "for various reasons" Joan and her council decided to move or send away—though these reasons are not explained. Later in the account book, the same inventory of the queen's chapel appears with a note that it has been released, delivered, or put in the care of Eleanor Cobham, the recent bride of Joan's stepson, Humphrey of Gloucester. While it has been suggested that this was simply a gift from Joan to Eleanor, it is not entirely clear from the wording that this is the case.[66] Even if it were more a means of showing support for Humphrey and Eleanor's controversial marriage than a mere gift, giving the new duchess the entire contents of the chapel and all the apparatus needed to celebrate Mass would have been a very generous way to welcome Eleanor to the family. If it was merely put in Eleanor's keeping or "sent away", the question is why—was this in conjunction with renovations at Kings Langley perhaps or, as Jones has suggested, a desire to "shed some regal trappings"?[67] Whatever the case, this inventory gives us a glimpse of the equipment needed by a queen to celebrate Mass in rather lavish style in her private chapel, including several sets of rich vestments including chasubles and copes for her clerical personnel, some made of cloth of gold and others embroidered with roses or flowers in golden thread.

In sum, this section has demonstrated the range of interaction that Joan had with the church, which reflects the centrality of religion to all aspects of life in the Middle Ages. Many of these interactions were in connection with her queenship—from fulfilling expectations of queenly piety as a model to her subjects to engaging with the political aspects of the Papal Schism to secure her marriage to Henry IV. We can also see practical aspects of her piety, from staying at ecclesiastical sites to employing clerics on her staff as both clerks and chaplains. Yet we can also see Joan's devotional practices to some extent by considering the dedicated spaces, objects, and personnel that she kept in order to be able to celebrate Mass regularly and in the dispensations she requested for spiritual privileges, again giving us a window into both the practice of queenship and the day-to-day life of Joan as an individual.

Possessions: Display, status, gift-giving, and networks

Our previous two themes, places and piety, are reflected in our next section, an examination of Joan's possessions. We will be thinking about the objects and possessions which furnished Joan's residences as well as the exchange of objects between Joan and her networks of relatives and servitors through the mechanism of gift giving. Many of these gifts and possessions were objects which were connected to piety: items for her chapel, precious reliquaries, religious jewellery, and books which served a devotional purpose or focused on religious themes. In order to get an understanding of the objects that Joan gifted and possessed, it is necessary to piece together a wide range of evidence—while some queens, like Clémence of Hungary or Joan's aunt Blanche of Navarre, left behind detailed wills and inventories on their death which give us rich information about what they possessed and the network of individuals that they were connected to through their bequests, there is no equivalent surviving document for Joan. What we do have, however, are financial documents—including evidence of expenditure and account books, particularly for her dowager years during her incarceration, and records from 1427 to 1428 which have survived. While a will or testament provides a means for a queen to express the items and individuals that she valued through her bequests, these records of expenditure can be used to build a picture of her taste through documentation of the things that Joan treasured, wore, ate, used, and gifted.

This section will discuss the importance of gift giving, which will underpin an examination of objects and possessions linked to Joan in terms of how she received and gave objects to enhance her status and maintain her familiar and court networks. The importance of display will be particularly highlighted, noting how Joan used jewellery, clothing, and other possessions to demonstrate her exalted status—this was particularly important in times when she was transitioning status from duchess to queen and when she was struggling to maintain her queenly position as an aging dowager. Objects were also a means of maintaining connections with Joan's extended family over the course of her long life, which will be demonstrated by looking at the gifts exchanged and the meanings behind them.

We begin by re-examining Joan's transition from duchess to queen, looking specifically at the role that objects and gift exchange played in affecting this transformation. As Brigitte Buettner has noted, gift giving was absolutely central to the mechanism of the royal court and medieval society more broadly. She argues that gift giving "was so much woven into the medieval *mentalité* that one cannot turn the pages of a literary work, in Latin or the vernacular, religious or secular, history or fiction, without constantly stumbling over its glorified manifestations".[68] Gift exchange was a foundational element of life at court—it played a key role in building and maintaining relationships between peers and bonds of service, it was central to diplomacy and to projecting the wealth, power, and authority of individuals, as well as that of the realm itself in the context of gifts given to ambassadors and between rulers. Here we will examine how gift exchange aided Joan's transformation in status by looking at gifts made between Joan and her new husband and family to establish her both as queen of England as well as his bride and the stepmother of his children. While the focus here is on her transition into queenship, it is important to note that, as discussed at the end of the first chapter, her Navarrese family had also used gifts of material culture, including valuable items of jewels and crowns, to build a trousseau that helped Joan make her first transition from infanta to duchess.

Gifts also form a customary part of courtship rituals—Joan began to receive gifts from Henry IV as their secret matrimonial negotiations gathered pace. November 1401 was a particularly vital point in the negotiations when a team of envoys from the duchess came to London for intensive discussions with the king about the marriage. When they left the following month, Henry sent with them several valuable gifts for his prospective bride. One was a golden pax or "paxbrede" decorated with four balas rubies, a "grand saphir", and pearls, valued at £122 13s 4d, which could have been used for both decorative and liturgical purposes in the duchess's chapel.[69] The other gift was two rings—one which was valued at £100 with a sapphire and ruby and another diamond ring worth £20.[70]

While these were beautiful and valuable gifts, it must be noted that they had not been specifically commissioned for his bride-to-be. Rather, Henry was "regifting"—which did not have the social approbation that is has now—indeed as Marguerite Keane has demonstrated, the links to previous owners could make an object even more meaningful and valuable.[71] The pax was part of Richard II's treasure and had originally been given by Thomas Mowbray, earl marshal.[72] The rings had originally belonged to Joan's predecessor and cousin—Richard II's second wife, Isabella de Valois—ironically or perhaps fittingly, the sapphire ring had been used to contract another royal marriage as it had been part of Isabella's betrothal ceremonial in the Sainte Chapelle in 1396.[73] Henry received these pieces into his possession on 15 December and appears to have promptly chosen a few choice pieces to send immediately on to Joan. Henry also recycled his predecessor's treasure to create gifts for Joan, commissioning Thomas Langport to use gems from brooches which had belonged to Richard II to construct a circlet set with rubies and diamonds. The circlet was sent to Joan in July 1402, perhaps to celebrate their proxy marriage that April or in anticipation of her arrival in England for their wedding.[74]

When Joan did arrive for their wedding in the new year, Henry marked the occasion with a plethora of gifts. Jessica Lutkin has noted that "Henry was readily prepared to indulge his new wife and he lavished expensive gifts on her, perhaps to show his authority and majesty at court, particularly because the gifts would remain within the court, as well as cement their relationship".[75] Henry spent lavishly on more than gifts—as noted in earlier chapters, he also spent considerable sums on their wedding at Winchester and the new queen's coronation. These events, which both took place in February 1403, were not just an opportunity to firmly establish Joan in her role as queen of England; these ceremonies were designed to reinforce Henry's own rather shaky position as the first Lancastrian king—a man whom many in England and across Europe still viewed as an illegitimate usurper. Heralding Joan's arrival with impressive pomp and circumstance, as well as bejewelled gifts, enhanced his own position and reinforced his authority by projecting majesty and magnificence. As Richard Barber has noted:

> Magnificence was applied to everything to do with the ruler: his person, his family, his entourage, his court, the artists, musicians, and architects he employed. Above all it was on show in his public appearances, his feasts and ceremonies. And it was also what inspired the great collections of jewels, manuscripts and holy relics.[76]

Thus the gifts showered on Joan, particularly when they were magnificent objects that she could wear and display in important ceremonies such as their wedding or her coronation, served a very political, as well as personal, purpose.

Moreover, each gift had significance and meaning far beyond their decorative value. On his way to the wedding itself, Henry stopped at Reading to pick up cloth of gold for his new queen—a costly fabric reserved for those of the highest status—which she could wear to emphasise her queenly position.[77] The day before their wedding, on 6 February, Henry gave her a golden hanap or cup and ewer, encrusted with balas rubies, sapphires, and pearls, which had originally been gifts from her own cousin Charles VI of France. These items were not only costly, valued at £357 6s 8d and £111 6s 8d, respectively, but may have also served to underline her familial link to the Valois dynasty.[78]

The same day, Henry also presented Joan with a crown worth £1,313 6s 8d with several "*grosse emerauds*" as well as sapphires, rubies, diamonds, and pearls.[79] This crown had many layers of significance—it was in itself a symbol of royalty and the queen's office which she was assuming. Jenny Stratford also believes that it was worn by Anne of Bohemia, Richard II's first wife, at her own wedding in 1382.[80] Thus the crown had a link to another royal bride—this not only gave Henry and Joan credence by tapping into a form of royal tradition or continuity, but it again highlighted Joan's royal connections as Anne was related to Joan—Joan's grandmother, Bonne of Luxembourg, was a member of the same imperial dynasty. Interestingly, around the time of Joan's departure from Brittany to take up her queenly position in England, she was gifted another costly golden crown with 12 "fleurons", valued at 5,000 écus, by her uncle the powerful duke of Burgundy.[81] This gift also had multiple layers of significance; it could be seen as merely a customary wedding gift from a relative, a gift to soften the blow of her uncle coming to Brittany to take the regency and the custody of her sons from her, or an acknowledgement of her new queenly status or—most likely—all of the above.

Another costly wedding gift to Joan from her new husband underlined her membership in the new Lancastrian dynasty, rather than her ties abroad. This was a large collar which had been made for the queen by John Whitewell, which cost 500 marks, or £333 6s 8d.[82] The collar appears to have featured the Lancastrian SS design—while the meaning of the SS has been debated, it was deeply entwined with the king and his family, instantly identifying the wearer as a member of his family, affinity, or as his ally or supporter.[83] These Lancastrian SS collars, which were given both to members of Henry's affinity in England and gifted diplomatically abroad to allies in Portugal and the Holy Roman Empire, were used by Henry "to place his mark firmly on the English court and send out a message at home and to other European courts that the Lancastrian dynasty was a permanent fixture".[84] This gift was a way of welcoming Joan into the Lancastrian fold—marking her as the king's newest supporter and ally as well as his queen and bride. The expensive jewels and gold that went into its creation would have also advertised both the king's wealth and her own elevated status, but ultimately it was the design and its meaning which had the greater significance. On the tomb that she shares with Henry in Canterbury Cathedral, her effigy sports a similar collar—the effigy may even have been designed to represent the one that she was given the day before she wed, marking her eternal allegiance to her husband as a Lancastrian queen.

Another gift which symbolised her welcome to the family were two golden tablets worth £79, which were given to Joan on behalf of her new stepsons John of Bedford and Humphrey of Gloucester.[85] Tablets were a type of religious jewellery, which sometimes contained relics or depicted religious scenes and could be worn as a pendant on a chain. It appears that they were extremely fashionable in this period; indeed Ronald Lightbown claims that "by the 1390s the tablet was already a favourite type of devotional pendant in England".[86] Joan also gave Henry VI a tablet in her later years which was bejewelled with sapphires and emeralds and had an intricate and interesting design. The design featured "an ymage of Seynt George hauyng a crosse upon hys armure" and 12 enamelled lions—given that St George was the patron saint of England and the king's heraldry featured lions rampant, it was a very fitting present for its king.[87] Henry VI also gave Joan a tablet as a New Year's gift in 1436 with a "great sapphire" on it, which had originally been given to him by "my Lady of Gloucestre", mostly likely Eleanor Cobham—again indicating the cyclical nature of gift exchange by passing on a gift from one member of the royal family to another.[88]

Moving on from Joan's initial period as queen consort, another window into the jewellery that Joan possessed comes from an inventory of the "gold, silver, things, goods, jewels of any kind under the keeping of friar John Raundolf" which Henry V had ordered Joan Beauchamp, Lady Bergavenny, a relative through his de Bohun maternal kin, to seize in August 1419 prior to Joan's arrest.[89] While this list reflects goods in her confessor's keeping, as A.R. Myers notes, most of these items clearly belonged to Joan given their description and the fact that the "gold and silver objects and jewels, which were considerable in quantity and valuable in quality" would not have been appropriate for a humble friar to own.[90] Multiple items are noted to have connections to Brittany, such as two golden spoons "yn a case of silke wroght with the armes of Bretaigne" and one "night cappe for a woman, rede after the gise of Bretaigne"—again the latter item was clearly not something Randolf would have used but Joan certainly might have adopted this fashion during her Breton years and brought it with her to England. There are also many items of jewellery, several of which appear to have personal links and may well have been gifts from either of her two husbands. One is a gold ring with a square sapphire on it, engraved with the motto "*a ma vie*", which, as will be discussed shortly, was linked to the Breton Order of the Ermine, which Jean IV founded and thus may have been a gift from him, or even from Joan's son, Jean V. Two golden brooches also had engravings on them: one said "*a ma vie de cuer entier*" ("you have my whole heart for my life"), which may again have been linked to her Breton husband or his chivalric order, or might indicate a more affectionate or intimate meaning instead; the other brooch was heart shaped and engraved with "*a vous me lie*", which can mean "I bind myself to you" or "it binds me to you"—a motto which was later used by Richard III. While we have to be careful not to read too much into these engravings as these were phrases which were hardly unique and may not have been attestations of intense feeling, they do offer an indication at least of the personal meaning of jewellery beyond displaying wealth and position.

In the 1419 inventory we can also see valuable jewelled items with religious uses or decoration noted previously which might shed further light on Joan's personal piety and devotion, such as a golden tablet with images of St John the Baptist and St Catherine and two silver and gold pax bredes, one "wyth a crucifix and the images of Marie and John pounced and enamelled" and another with four angels at the corners "beryng the armes of the passoun". These particular saints may have had personal meaning for Joan—it is possible that John the Baptist was her own name saint, and devotion to St Catherine of Alexandria was very strong in this period—she was particularly popular with the Valois, including Joan's uncle the duke of Berry.[91] There are also chalices decorated with religious themes which may have been used in Masses performed in her chapel, including a chalice engraved with "*Benedicamus patrem et filium*" ("Let us bless the father and the son") and another chalice and a chafing-pan decorated with emblems of the Trinity, to which Henry IV was particularly devoted. While some of these items might have belonged to or been used by Friar Randolf, particularly a coffer with "diuerses small bokes of the forsaid Freres", it is very likely that many of these items were used by Joan during worship or devotional practices as well.

There are also items of a more personal or practical nature in the 1419 inventory which can shed some potential light on items she used or had around her which can evoke an image or even smells and tastes, such as multiple items decorated with roses and a "tastour of siluer for rose water" and a silver fork "with a dragons hede holding vp the stalke for grene Gynger". We can see reflections of those same items in the 1422 account book held at Leeds Castle where there is a payment of 9s 2d for a pot of green ginger and another for 3s 8d to a certain John Penne for rose water.[92] Again,

Joan's account books, while seemingly dry financial records, are actually a treasure trove of information about her day-to-day life, giving us a window into not only her possessions but what she and her household ate, used, and consumed. Payments for medicines and for physicians can tell us something about the queen's health—for example, evidence in the Society of Antiquaries account books reveal that Joan suffered a period of serious illness in 1427–28.[93] The account books give very precise records of daily and annual expenditure on supplies—while some of this is more interesting in terms of costs and economics, there are also interesting details which give a richer picture. For example, from her period of incarceration the accounts note that supplies of Gascon, Rochelle, and Rhenish wine were brought from the Continent. The Leeds wardrobe account shows that the wine could flow quite lavishly when visitors came—E.E. Dodds notes in his analysis that expenditure in the "Butlery" was double the normal rate when Humphrey, duke of Gloucester, came to visit on 12 June 1422, commenting that "either the duke came with a large entourage or someone in his party was fond of a drink or two".[94] They might have eaten off the sizable selection of silver plate that was inventoried in the Leeds wardrobe book, much of it stamped with the arms of England—as well as that of England and France. Dodd notes that the description of the decoration suggests that much of this plate, though valuable, was "second and third hand pieces" which likely came from the collections of Edward III, Richard II, and Anne of Bohemia and her husband, Henry IV.[95] Yet the connection with previous monarchs and consorts could also be seen as making the items more valuable and reinforcing Joan's status by using items fit for her royal predecessors.

One of the most interesting areas to look at in terms of supplies bought in relates to clothing for Joan and her household. Cloth and clothing were related to the queen's wardrobe in two senses—one in terms of the modern notion of the word "wardrobe" or the garments Joan would have worn, but also in the sense of the "wardrobe" as a department of her household which also encompassed other vital supplies like spices, wax, and other household goods. Indeed, Joan had her own storage facility for these goods in the City of London on St Martins Lane near Aldersgate, St Botolph's church and that of Greyfriars, which became known as "Queen Jane's Wardrobe", as well as a dedicated official, the Keeper of her Great Wardrobe—one of these was Richard Crek who was paid 6d a day in her 1428 accounts.[96]

Clothing is of course another key aspect of display that in tandem with the jewellery discussed previously were vital means of projecting position and status. This was not only important in terms of the clothing that Joan wore personally, but the apparel of those around her was also a means of affirming her own position, demonstrating her wealth and standing. Her surviving account books contain an abundance of information on cloth and clothing, as well as the suppliers and tailors that Joan worked with such as Emma Norton and Matilda Dentone, silkwomen from London; tailors John Fauconer and John Lowes; draper John Skelton; mercer Thomas Denton; furrier Richard Barton; and John Hexman who specialised in socks. This brief discussion can only scratch the surface of the material in these rich sources, which is worthy of its own study, but even a few selected examples can help us to get a better understanding of the functioning of the household and more of a visual image of what Joan and her household wore.

Interestingly, in records from the period of her detention, the cloth or clothing for the queen appears to have been generally all black, but it was enlivened with trim of marten fur and black lace as well as possibly some red silk which was purchased in her Leeds wardrobe book.[97] It appears that Joan's penchant for black dresses had not changed greatly over the 1420s, as the Society of Antiquaries account also lists a least seven black gowns made for the queen as well as black kirtles. Joan's preference for black may have been tied to her dowager status, reminding all who saw her that she was Henry IV's widow, although it must be noted that black cloth was not used exclusively for mourning in this period. Black cloth was becoming increasingly fashionable among the elite classes and could be expensive as it required skill to produce a deep saturated black colour.[98] Her gowns were also richly trimmed as noted above, and black could still be made of expensive, rich fabrics such as a the "damask of Florence" used for one gown. In addition to her dresses, there are also notes in the Leeds account for the purchase of a silken cap and "temples" or "templars", a headpiece arranged at the temples which Joan also wears on her tomb effigy—the 1427–28 accounts note further expenditure for "templerers", again giving us the idea of a fairly consistent "look" for the queen over the decade.

In terms of her household, gifts of cloth were part of the perquisites of the job—this was not only a means of rewarding staff but ensuring they were well dressed in effectively uniform or livery. Caroline Dunn has noted that the members of Philippa of Hainault's household normally received two issues of cloth and fur a year and we can also see examples of Joan's male and female household receiving similar allotments.[99] Even during the period of detention we can find provision for cloth for Joan's household—as noted previously, these lists can be useful not only to see what they were given but because these gifts can help us to reconstruct the composition of her household. From 1421–22 one surviving example shows us that her ladies all received 5–6 ells of coloured cloth as well as trimmings including miniver and doe skin.[100] Her clerks also received a similar allotment of coloured cloth (without the trimmings that the women were given), while other male servants, such as her valets and those who worked in the scullery, received 5 ells of a mixture of coloured and striped cloth.

To bring this section together, we have to imagine the complete package—to assert her queenly position, Joan would have wanted anyone who visited her to be impressed by her residence, the items within it, the personnel who surrounded her, and her own appearance. If the house was crumbling around her and she and her servitors wore threadbare, dowdy clothes, that would demonstrate that she had fallen down the social ladder. Even though it is a thoroughly modern concept, the idea of "conspicuous consumption"—to make a show of her wealth to affirm her queenly status—can be applied here. Given all the threats and challenges to her position and her increasingly marginal and tenuous position in her later years as the king's elderly step-grandmother, whom some may have still perceived as a possible witch or traitor, Joan had to continue to work to keep up appearances, using the power of space, place, and display to do so.

Gift giving and familial connections

Finally, it is worth looking at the gifts given to her family, particularly those that Joan left behind in Brittany when she made her transformation or transition from duchess to queen, with particular focus on her son Jean V. These gifts were doubly important—not only were they a way for Joan to maintain maternal ties with her son after she left the duchy, but they were also important in terms of the diplomatic relationship between Brittany and England, which was under considerable strain during the reign of Henry IV, with open conflict breaking out at various points after Henry and Joan's marriage. However, the first gifts to examine here were from Henry himself to his new stepson Jean at the time of his proxy wedding to Joan in April 1402. Henry sent two lavish gifts to the young duke of a matching golden cup and ewer which were both covered in balas rubies, sapphires, and pearls, valued at £188 13s 4d.[101] After the initial period of transition, Joan continued to use gifts to maintain her relationship with Jean V for decades following her departure. One of the most stunning gifts that she sent to him c. 1412 was the Reliquary of the Trinity, which is now part of the collection of the Louvre Museum. The Louvre claims that this lavish piece, in the international Gothic style, enamelled and encrusted in precious stones, was "precisely the type of gem that royalty purchased for New Year's Day presents or for great occasions. It depicts themes dear to the Valois—the Trinity and the Pietà".[102] Thus this gift could be seen as not only affirming the bonds between mother and son, but of their royal blood and mutual connection to their wider familial network.

Given the increasing tension in cross-Channel politics after the accession of Henry V in 1414 and the king's campaigns in France, including his victory at the battle of Agincourt, it was increasingly important for Joan to maintain her fragile bond with her son and for England to ensure that Brittany would be an ally in their attempt to dominate France. A list compiled of the duke's jewels and gold and silver work acquired between 1414 and 1424 reveals several gifts made from Joan during this period including an "*équierre d'or*" garnished with 6 balas rubies, 15 sapphires, and 16 large pearls, multiple tablets and golden rings, and a diamond which the queen sent to Jean when he met with Henry V in Rouen.[103] There is also a significant mention of a Lancastrian SS collar enamelled with the words "*A ma vie*"—the giver is not listed but this most likely came from Henry V. This collar shows an interesting amalgamation of English and Breton elements—from the design, which as noted previously signalled allegiance to the Lancastrians, to the inclusion of "*A ma vie*" which was the motto of the Breton chivalric Order of the Ermine, an order instituted by Jean IV who was inspired by the English Order of the Garter.[104] Indeed this list also shows considerable gift exchange between Joan's Breton son and her Lancastrian stepsons, including a golden cup the duke gave to Henry V and a crystal goblet for John, duke of Bedford.[105] Joan's servitor John Periaunt also turns up in this inventory, as he was also given "*un esquierre d'or*" when he came to Brittany from Henry V and Joan, in conjunction with diplomatic discussions as noted in Chapter 4.

Linked to the gift of a collar to the Breton duke with both English and Breton elements is a gift given by Joan which also merged heraldic elements, this time that of England, France, and Navarre. Rather than a ceremonial collar, this was a shield which was buried with Henry V in 1422—an indication perhaps of how precious the item was to him or how valuable it was. It is now on display in Westminster Abbey's Triforium Gallery (WA 0837–39). The shield was in the "heater" style, similar to the one which was buried with Edward the Black Prince and was commonly used in the period. What is interesting is the construction and decoration—while the core was oak, it was covered in horsehair and layers of linen with silk as the top layer. The silk was originally azure blue woven with an ivy pattern and has yellow fleurs-de-lys painted on it, alluding to the arms of France and England.[106] A recent examination of the shield by experts at the Victoria and Albert Museum revealed that the silk may be some of the oldest surviving examples of Chinese silk in late medieval Europe. The silk is believed to be of "imperial quality" and "may have been part of a consignment of astounding quality" that may have come into Europe via the Silk Road.[107] The link to Joan can be clearly seen in the interior of the shield which is emblazoned with Navarrese heraldic designs in red velvet. Given the heraldry, Joan would seem the most likely commissioner and giver of the gift—while it is possible that her brother Carlos III of Navarre could have sent it as a suitably royal gift, this would have been recorded in contemporary records in terms of the expenditure, dispatch, and receipt of what would have been an important diplomatic gift. If Joan is the most probable giver of the gift, the question remains, who was the intended recipient—her husband or her stepson? It seems more likely that it was a gift to Henry IV, as a generous gift from one spouse to another. If that was the case, multiple experts have queried why Henry V chose to use it or indeed be buried with it. Was it a sign of his reconciliation with Joan, as he had ordered during his final illness in the summer of 1422 for her to be released and her lands restored to her? Was it chosen by Henry, or even someone else in the royal family, for him to be buried with due to its link to his father or its own inherent value and splendour? While we can never be certain, this piece remains one of the most interesting and impressive extant gifts given by Joan during her lifetime.

Returning to gift exchanges with Joan's biological family, in July 1418 we see what appears to be a familial exchange of gifts between mother and son with the receipt of "sixty pipes of wine, seven baskets of lampreys, two cloths of Joucelyn and a barrel of shad (a type of fish)" which had been sent from Nantes on the *Nostre Dame of St Nicholas*. Joan then sent John de Morin back to Brittany with "eight small barrels of wine of Tire and Malvesye" to her son Jean V.[108] Joan also sent gifts to her daughter-in-law (and cousin), the new duchess Jeanne de Valois, including a parrot (or popinjay, "papegeay"), cloth from London, and four horses along with the shipment of wine.[109] Joan certainly engaged in gift exchange with the rest of her Valois family as well—for example, the Chronicle of Saint Denis notes that when Joan's uncle the duke of Berry paid a visit to Nantes in the early 1390s she gave him bejewelled gifts, which were "of inestimable value" due to their exquisite workmanship and the richness of the materials, to demonstrate her delight at seeing him.[110]

Gift exchange was also a means of retaining connections with her Navarrese family during Joan's years in Brittany and England. Examples include a generous pension of 1,000 livres to her aunt Juana of Navarre, countess of Rohan, and bequests from her aunt

Blanche of Navarre, queen of France, which demonstrate a sense of connection and family feeling between them.[111] While we will discuss books given to Joan by her aunt Blanche shortly, another key bequest to her niece in her will was "a pair of loose bedclothes, the best that I have to put on women in labour".[112] Marguerite Keane, in her analysis of the testament of Blanche of Navarre, stresses the significance of this seemingly mundane gift: "The importance of the bed to the household is an indication of how personal the gift of bedsheets to Jeanne of Brittany [Joan] was; it was an affectionate gift that expressed a close family relationship and the care of an aunt for the wellbeing of a niece".[113] Moreover, Keane notes that this gift was not necessarily intended to be practical or used for childbirth "as Jeanne, mother of seven children by 1396 [when the will was written], surely had plenty of furnishings for childbirth. It was meant to be a symbolic and affectionate gift".[114] Gifts were also given to and received from her brother Carlos III of Navarre; for example, an entry in the Navarrese accounts in May 1414 notes a payment of 38 sueldos for cauldrons bought "to send to the queen of England, sister of the king".[115]

The commissioning and collection of books was an important part of elite culture for men as well as women and offer us another opportunity to explore Joan's piety, personal taste, and possessions and examine the extent of gift exchange with her familial network. As Susan Groag Bell summarises, in the Middle Ages "women frequently bought and inherited religious as well as secular books, and spent considerable time reading them".[116] This applies directly to Joan's own situation—while we cannot be certain how much time she spent reading books, we do know that she was gifted and commissioned books. Most of these books were devotional works or those which provide religious or moral instruction, which was in keeping with trends in elite female book ownership in the period. These books might have been both personally read by the queen herself and/or read with, by, and to her ladies.[117]

While the full extent of Joan's library is unclear as we lack a definitive will or inventory which would help us to trace it, there are eight books which we can link to her, six of which are still extant today. It is entirely likely that she owned many more given the book commissioning and collecting activities of her contemporaries and recent female ancestors, including her grandmothers, Juana II of Navarre and Bonne of Luxembourg, who "initiated what would be a centuries-long trend of female book-collecting".[118] Studies of fourteenth-century royal women have noted extensive book collections: Isabella of France, queen of England, had 34 books in her 1358 inventory; Clémence of Hungary, queen of France, had 44 manuscripts in her inventory; and another French queen related to Joan, Jeanne d'Evreux, had more than 50.[119]

While there is some debate or lack of clarity about Joan's ownership of some of these works, one aspect which has helped to establish connections to her is her tendency to leave her signature in her books, almost like a modern "bookplate" or "ex libris" that people use to denote their ownership. Four of the books believed to be owned by her include examples of her signature or mark of ownership. A great example of this is on folio 2 verso (flyleaf) of a beautiful illuminated thirteenth-century psalter, now in the John Rylands library at the University of Manchester and described as "one of the library's most sumptuous manucripts".[120] Here is clearly written "Royne Jahanne", which Léopold Delisle notes matches several extant documents in the Breton archives.[121] We are fortunate in that Joan was a keen signatory of a wide range of surviving documents in English, French, and Spanish archives, which give us ample opportunity to compare the signatures which survive in these books.[122] Indeed, Michael Jones, Anne Crawford, and several Victorian writers have made the claim that she was the first queen of England to leave a surviving example of her signature.[123] Two manuscripts linked to Joan in the Bibliotheque Nationale in Paris also bear examples of her name inscribed on them—a *Bible historiale* and a translation of a Roman work by Titus Livius (Livy).[124] Finally, there are partially erased indicators "*Ce livre est a Jehan* … (This book belongs to Jehan ...)" and the word "Royne" on multiple folios of a copy of Jean de Meun's *Testament* in Harvard's Houghton Library which have indicated Joan's likely ownership of this book as well.[125]

Another major thread which links many of these books, apart from the predominant themes of the works, is their connection to her family. As Julia Finch has noted, for many royal women "manuscripts served as markers of political and familial identity".[126] As noted in the discussion of familial gift exchange, giving objects to family members either during one's lifetime or as a bequest in a will affirmed and strengthened family networks as well as ensuring that valuable objects stayed within the dynasty.[127] An excellent example of this for Joan's own book collection is a breviary given to her by her aunt Blanche of Navarre—it had previously belonged to another aunt, Jeanne, who had been a nun at the convent of Longchamp, and was rebound by Blanche before being bequeathed to Joan in her will.[128] There may be another connection to Joan's aunt Blanche in a second manuscript owned by Joan, a *Bible historiale*, now also in the Bibliotheque Nationale de France. While it was not bequeathed to Joan by Blanche, the illuminator has been identified as the same artist commissioned by Blanche for her manuscript of *Roman de la dame à la licorne*, potentially suggesting that perhaps this book may have been commissioned by Blanche and gifted in her lifetime to Joan, but the early history of the manuscript is unclear.[129] However, a clearer familial link is that this manuscript went to Joan's favourite stepson Humphrey—an inscription in the book itself notes that it was given to Humphrey in September 1427 at the Abbey of Our Lady (Notre Dame) in Chester by John Stanley, who must have been charged to do so by Joan, the prior owner of the book.[130]

Two other books have tenuous but very interesting familial connections to Joan on multiple levels. What is fascinating is that both are connected to Joan's ancestors and namesakes: Juana I and Juana II, both regnant queens of Navarre and respectively her great-great grandmother and grandmother. The book related to the elder of the two women is a copy of the *Miroir des Dames*, a French translation of the *Speculum Dominarum*, a "mirror" for ladies or queens which was originally written for and dedicated to Juana I of Navarre by Durand de Champagne, her confessor.[131] The book begins with an illumination of the queen herself enthroned with crown, sceptre, and royal robes covered in fleurs-de-lys, receiving the book from a monk, presumably Durand de Champagne, surrounded by her ladies-in-waiting.[132] While the provenance of the book is unclear, there are multiple possibilities of how it may have come into Joan's hands. Diane Booton suggests that this manuscript may have come to Joan from her cousin Charles d'Orleans, who had received it from his mother, Valentina Visconti—as Charles was held prisoner in England for an extended period after the battle of Agincourt, like Joan's son Arthur de Richemont.[133] It is entirely possible that the two might have visited each other during that time and/or exchanged gifts, such as this manuscript. An alternative, but less likely, possibility is that it may have come to Joan through her aunts Blanche and Agnes; Blanche left Agnes her copy of the *Miroir des Dames*—it is possible that Agnes in turn left it to Joan; however, the timing of this is questionable as Agnes died in 1397, a year before Blanche.[134] However it came into her hands, it would have been entirely appropriate for Joan to receive or acquire this manuscript, both because of the familial connection to her ancestor and namesake and because of its content, which offered moral and religious guidance specifically designed to demonstrate how a "queen and other well-born ladies should conduct themselves, not just in the eyes of God, but within society at large", making it ideal reading material for Joan and her female household.[135]

The second book, linked to Joan's grandmother Juana II, was one of her illuminated books of hours. Marguerite Keane has powerfully argued that the imagery in the books of hours Juana II commissioned was not just intended for personal devotion but can be seen as a political statement "motivated by a desire to link Jeanne of Navarre [Juana II] and her children to her Capetian ancestry".[136] This connection was made by the relatively unusual image cycle connected to St Louis in Juana's most celebrated book of hours, which highlights her links to the Capetian king and saint that gave her and her children a strong link to the French crown—as discussed in Chapter 1, Juana's claim had formed a central aspect of Joan's own father, Carlos II's, politics in the Hundred Years War.[137] Again, there is a possible link to Joan's aunt Blanche who bequeathed to Joan's maternal uncle, the duke of Berry, "my most beautiful book of hours, which our very dear lady and mother, may God pardon her, left us at her passing".[138] However, there is some debate about the provenance of Juana II's most famous book of hours and who may have possessed it after her death. Christopher de Hamel also believes that the duke of Berry, one of the most notable book collectors of the later Middle Ages, possessed the book, but he argues that it came into his possession via Joan's maternal grandmother, Bonne of Luxembourg, who died of the Black Death, like Juana II, within weeks of each other in 1349.[139] De Hamel suggests that Berry gifted the book of hours to Joan as an "utterly appropriate" wedding present when she married Henry IV, given the familial link, noting "For a second time, therefore, the prayer '*intercedas pro me ancilla tua Johanna navarre regina*' ['intercede for me your servant Johanna, queen of Navarre'] was applicable to its owner, but this time she was a different Joan and was a queen of England instead".[140] As proof of this connection, de Hamel offers both a link in Berry's inventory and the frontispiece inserted into the book which was created by an English artist c. 1420.[141] Here he suggests one final familial link, noting that this same artist illuminated the hours of Katherine de Valois, offering the possibility that Joan, in turn, may have gifted the book to her successor and cousin, perhaps even around the time of her own wedding to Joan's stepson Henry V in 1420. While all of these possibilities are intriguing, it is impossible to securely establish the line of transmission here—however, what we can clearly say is that Joan's possession of the book demonstrates the importance of family ties and traditions.

Other books which Joan possessed have even more mystery surrounding how she acquired them—one of them also presents a mystery in terms of its survival, a Sarum rite missal which was "newe covered" in baudkin or baldachin, a very rich silken fabric.[142] Given that it was valued at 100 shillings, worth well over £3,000 in modern money, this was clearly a valuable manuscript which may have been similar to a beautifully illuminated contemporary example from early fifteenth-century England, now in a private collection.[143] Another richly decorated devotional work Joan possessed is the aforementioned thirteenth-century psalter, which survives in the collection of the John Rylands library—however, how Joan came to possess it or who originally owned the work is unclear. Similarly unclear is the provenance of a fourteenth-century French version of the Roman author Livy's work translated by Pierre Bersuire—this has been widely linked to Joan thanks to her signature in the book, but again her acquisition of the book is unclear.[144]

While Joan possessed several books which had been previously owned by others and came into her hands as gifts or through purchase, a book which Joan herself may have commissioned is a copy of Jean de Meun's *Testament* combined with Jean Chapuis' *Les Sept articles de la fois* (*The Seven Articles of Faith*). In the early twentieth century Sydney Cockerell identified Joan as the manuscript's original owner and likely commissioner and also noted that the scribe was probably the famous Nicholas Flamel, whom she may have come into contact with via her uncle the duke of Berry, who had also employed Flamel.[145] The manuscript remained at Leeds Castle, one of Joan's own residences where she remained under house arrest for an extended period, from the fifteenth century until it was sold in an estate sale in the early nineteenth century—later owners include William Morris, the book collector Henry Yates Thompson, and Cockerell himself. This devotional work is described as a "spin off" of the highly popular *Roman de la Rose*, which contemplates moral values and the salvation of the soul in verse.[146] Given the contemporary popularity of this work, Joan may have commissioned it in order to have her own copy to add to her personal collection, which would fit nicely with other devotional works and moral treatises that she also possessed.

In sum, Joan's book collection highlights several key elements which tie in with wider observations of her cultural patronage and gifting practices. The importance of Joan's familial ties are clearly stressed here—indeed, the provenance of several of the books discussed demonstrates how Joan, and these objects, acted as a point of connection between the Navarrese and Valois, or paternal and maternal, strands of her family and her marital family in England, who also shared a love of literary works and had important book collections of their own.[147] It also demonstrates how Joan acted as a "cultural ambassador" and circulated objects and artwork across borders through her moves from Navarre, to Brittany, and to England, like so many royal women as "young brides (and widows on remarriage) brought their books across regional and national boundaries, often transmitting artistic style, specific content, and ideas".[148] Finally, we can see both Joan's interests and her own hand in the books she acquired and commissioned, with a clear emphasis on texts with family connections and works which stressed moral behaviour and religious devotion, and very literally we can see her own hand in her "ex libris" signatures that she placed in her manuscripts to denote her ownership of the works.

Patronage: Creating an image and leaving a legacy

Patronage was a key means of agency for elite and royal women—it was enabled by both position and wealth, which gave women the means to fund commissions and support artisans and projects which in turn could enhance their image in life and leave a positive legacy after their death. There are many different forms of patronage—in the previous chapter we explored Joan's extensive political patronage and how she used this to create an extensive network at the Breton and English courts and beyond. In the section on piety, we have explored aspects of her religious patronage—while we noted that Joan did not appear to undertake a major project, such as the foundation or significant amelioration of an institution such as a church, chapel, or convent, we have noted her support of clerics in her service and various religious orders. In our examination of her possessions we have engaged with cultural patronage—her collection and commission of books, for example, particularly those with devotional aspects, can be seen as both religious and cultural patronage. Further examples of her cultural patronage can be seen in her gifting and commissioning of works of great aesthetic value such as the Reliquary of the Trinity, now in the Louvre, and the silk covered shield on display at Westminster Abbey.

Another area where we can see a connection to cultural patronage and familial ties is with music. John Dunstable "was the most eminent of an influential group of English composers active in the first half of the fifteenth century", with around 70 pieces attributed to him, largely works connected with the Mass or liturgical music.[149] Royal patronage likely played a key role in his rise—while there is some debate about his ties to Joan's stepson John, duke of Bedford, there are clearer links to Humphrey, duke of Gloucester, and Joan herself. Andrew Wathey and Judith Stell have studied Dunstable's activity and patronage, revealing that the composer had a relationship with Joan which can be traced over about ten years, as he features both in the household records of 1427–28 and is also recorded as an annuitant of the queen, receiving a generous £80 in 1436.[150] However, the exact nature of the relationship is not completely clear—Wathey notes that while he was often grouped with the ecclesiastical members of her household, he was given a silver cup worth 78s and a furred scarlet gown of a similar style to her clerks and physicians.[151] Nor are there any pieces which Dunstable composed that can be securely linked to Joan or his time under her patronage, although Gillian Gower has made the intriguing suggestion that his works "*Gaude sancta Katerina*" ("Rejoice Saint Katherine") and "*Gaude felix mater Anna*" ("Rejoice fortunate mother Anna") could have possibly been commissioned by the queen.[152] There is more clarity, however, on Dunstable's patronage after Joan's death in 1437, when he transferred into Humphrey of Gloucester's service—Wathey notes that this appears to have been a natural move given Joan and Humphrey's close relationship, his absorption of other members of Joan's household into his own after her death, their shared cultural interests, and association with the abbey at St Albans with which Dunstable also seems to have had a connection.[153]

Joan's interest in music and musical patronage was likely inspired much earlier, however, during her childhood in the Navarrese court. María Narbona Cárceles has noted that Joan's father, Carlos II, "was characterised by his love of music" and patronised Guillaume de Machaut and other musicians and composers—Joan's brother Carlos III shared this interest in music and was also an active patron.[154] Thus, while the evidence of Joan's musical patronage is not completely secure, we can see a clear link to John Dunstable, one of the most important composers in England during this period, and a pattern of musical and cultural patronage in Joan's natal and marital families which would have encouraged and enabled her to do likewise.

Tombs: Joan's role as patron and a "shaper of memory"

A final aspect of Joan's patronage to consider, which incorporates both cultural and religious aspects, was her role in the commissioning of tombs. Joan survived two husbands, giving her the opportunity as a widow to become, as Diane Booton put it, "a shaper of memory" by crafting both men's tombs—including the tomb that she ultimately shared with Henry IV at Canterbury Cathedral.[155] This section will examine Joan's role as a "shaper of memory" in the crafting of both tombs, which she used as an opportunity to not only ensure the legacy of her two husbands but of her marital and natal dynasty and enshrine her own place as a Navarrese infanta, a Breton duchess, and an English queen. It will begin, however, with a consideration of the first tomb commission which she was connected to, for her first child, Jeanne de Bretagne.

As noted previously, Joan's first marriage to Jean IV of Brittany was certainly successful in terms of producing the much needed heirs to ensure the continuation of the Montfort line with four boys and three girls surviving infancy. Jean IV had been married twice previously with no issue and had spent most of his life fighting the claims of a rival branch of the dynasty, the Penthièvres, to the ducal throne. Yet his first child with Joan, Jeanne de Bretagne, had been a girl who had only survived just over a year before she died in December 1388. Her tomb became a means not only of memorialising a lost child, but a political statement in its design and message, as Jean-Yves Copy has demonstrated in his work on this tomb and its significance.[156] Copy notes that Jeanne's tomb was deeply connected to the ongoing threat of the Penthièvres as alternative successors and rivals to the Montfort line—for this to endure according to the agreement in the Treaty of Guérande, it was imperative that Jean IV have a male heir. The birth of a girl and her rapid demise, coupled with the concurrent release of Jean de Penthièvre and his marriage to Marguerite de Clisson, intensified the concern over the Montfort succession. Even though Jeanne was theoretically ineligible to be her father's heir to the duchy, on her tomb she wears a crown supported by angels. Copy notes that this quasi-royal iconography can be compared to the tombs of other heirs who were her contemporaries, such as Wladislas of Poland (d.1389) and Charles, the eldest son of Charles VI (d.1386 at 3 months).[157] Moreover, the use of a crown in the design not only enhanced Jeanne's status as a potential heir, it also emphasised Jean's own ducal power, putting it on an effective par with royal authority. Finally, a last element which must be considered is that the location of the tomb would also have been carefully chosen and is equally important in terms of the messages that the tomb was meant to send in the short and long term. As mentioned earlier in the chapter, Jeanne's tomb was sited at the church of St Gildas de Rhuys, which was both close to her parents' favoured residence at Suscinio and had been the burial site of other ducal children. It was also a monastery built by the celebrated quasi-legendary fifth-century king Gradlon, with relics of the saint-king Judicael and other Celtic saints—these ties to great, royal figures of Brittany's past made Jeanne's tomb even more prominent.[158] Clearly, given the emphasis on the Montfort political agenda, Jean IV must have been involved in the commission—however, Joan was also likely involved or at least consulted. This experience in creating a tomb and, most importantly, reflecting carefully on the message and image-crafting opportunity that a tomb provides, would become incredibly useful to Joan for two tombs she created for her husbands and herself in later years.

When Jean IV died in 1399, even though he and Joan had a large brood of surviving children including four sons, there was still a very strong threat from the Penthièvres, who had never given up their claim against their Montfort cousins for the right to the ducal coronet. Indeed, as there was a concern that they might try to capitalise on the somewhat tenuous position of the young duke, it was vital for Joan to use image crafting in order to strengthen the position of her son and that of the Montfort line. As noted previously, an excellent example of this was her organisation of an impressive ducal coronation for her son which took place at Rennes in March 1401. As we have seen, Joan used quasi-regal staging of this ceremonial and the opportunity it presented to gather the greatest nobles of the realm together to ensure their support of her son and cement his position as the new duke.

A few days prior to the new duke's coronation, Joan had also held a memorial service for her late husband at Nantes Cathedral.[159] This elaborate ceremonial not only demonstrated the queen's piety and respect for Jean IV, but was another element of image crafting to reinforce her son's position by underlining his place as Jean IV's heir and the position of the Montfort dynasty as the rightful ruling house. Nantes Cathedral was both the primary religious seat of the effective ducal capital and the location of Jean IV's burial and eventual tomb. Yet while this might seem to be an obvious location for a ducal burial, there was no central necropolis there or indeed anywhere in the duchy. Instead, as Elizabeth Tingle has noted, the choice of burial site "was an important means of promoting ducal authority against magnate challenges to Montfort lordship and dominion. Thus, in the later fourteenth and early fifteenth centuries, burial occurred in different places of the duchy, to promote ducal legitimacy widely across the province".[160]

Perhaps because of this lack of a necropolis or shifting thoughts on where best to place his tomb for the benefit of the Montfort line, Jean IV had been somewhat vague on the desired location—an earlier will had called for a tomb at the Cistercian abbey of Notre-Dame de Prières at Billiers in Moribihan, but a codicil to his will made shortly before his death named Nantes Cathedral as his preferred burial place.[161] Nantes would have been a location which Joan would have preferred—not only was it the effective capital of the duchy, but the county of Nantes was a key part of her dower lands and effectively a power base for her, as well as a locus of power for the dynasty. Diane Booton has argued that this shift to Nantes may have been the result of persuasion by Joan and her chaplain, Bernard II du Peyron, bishop of Nantes—she argues that

> Joan of Navarre was in a position to persuade the duke. Her engagement in politics on behalf of her husband while he was duke demonstrates that she was strong willed and deeply absorbed in matters of the duchy. Such determined authority no doubt remained during her second marriage in England. The duke's tomb monument therefore could well be seen as a commission by a resolute individual aware of its private association and its broader geo-political overtones.[162]

However, it was some time before a tomb was erected to serve as a focal point for Jean IV's memory. Following Breton custom to inter the deceased members of their family quickly—normally within 24 hours of their death—Jean had been buried at Nantes Cathedral before the great altar. After the late duke was interred, Joan's initial concern appears to have been on establishing her son's ducal authority and ruling on his behalf before commissioning a memorial for her late husband. Indeed, it appears that this was unfinished business when she decamped to England for her second marriage, as the tomb was commissioned and created there before being sent back to Nantes for installation in 1408.

While it might seem unusual that Joan decided to commission the tomb in England and have it sent back across the Channel to Brittany, there were both practical reasons and potential meanings to having the tomb fashioned in England rather than Brittany. As discussed at length earlier, Joan began secret negotiations with Henry IV for their marriage not long after her first husband's death—even though she did not leave Brittany until the beginning of 1403, Joan may have decided that commissioning the tomb from a French or Breton workshop would mean that she would lose sight and control of the project once she left the duchy.[163] Choosing an English workshop for the design and production of the tomb, and alabaster, rather than the limestone or granite often used by Jean IV's predecessors, gave his tomb a different, distinctive feel.[164] It also gave it a clearly English feel due to the design which appears to have been modelled on other alabaster tombs of English knights and may even have drawn inspiration from the design for the tomb of Jean's contemporary and relative through his previous marriages, Edward "the Black Prince".[165] Indeed, as we will see, the Black Prince offers an interesting point of connection between both of the tombs in this study.

Moreover, given Jean IV's extensive personal and political links with England, a kingdom where he himself had lived while in exile and visited frequently, this was not stylistically inappropriate.[166] Indeed, this choice may have had a more political basis as Kim

Woods has argued: "his English tomb would have surely served to visualise the Anglophile leanings of John himself and the continuing alliance between Brittany and England".[167] Yet, ironically perhaps, Joan's second marriage had triggered a period of political discord between England and Brittany, rather than peace—due to a series of skirmishes and ongoing hostilities between the two realms, a safe conduct was issued on 24 February 1408 for three sculptors, Thomas Colyn, Thomas Holewell, and Thomas Poppenhowe, the merchant Jean Guychard, and their party to deliver the tomb on the ship *Saint Nicholas of Nantes.*[168] Ultimately, while no documentation survives to definitively attest to Joan's commission of the tomb, her hand can be clearly seen—as Jean-Yves Copy has noted, the placement, design, and political significance of the tomb were all reflective of Joan and her personality.[169]

When her second husband Henry IV died in 1413, Joan had experience in commissioning tombs and was again ready to make the most of the opportunity that crafting a royal tomb offered to create a lasting legacy for her kingly husband—and, as we will discuss, for herself. Henry IV finally succumbed to the wasting disease which plagued him for several years and left a will which stipulated that he wished to be buried at Canterbury Cathedral. Canterbury was not an obvious choice for the king's burial—he was the first, and indeed remains, the only king to be buried there. Unlike the situation in Brittany, where there was no consistent necropolis, Westminster Abbey was the location where most of England's medieval kings were buried. Historians have debated why Henry rejected this more obvious location and chose Canterbury instead. Christopher Wilson has suggested that Henry rejected Westminster as the Chapel of St Edward the Confessor was too crowded with tombs to fit his in—yet his son Henry V managed to find space for his own tomb.[170] Wilson has alternatively suggested that Henry avoided Westminster over guilt regarding his predecessor, Richard II, whose throne he was accused of usurping. Richard was supposed to be buried at Westminster but his first wife, Anne of Bohemia, had been resting there alone in the joint tomb Richard had commissioned for them. However, Henry IV had buried his cousin at the Dominican friary at Kings Langley instead after Richard died in shady circumstances in early 1400. Ironically, one of the earliest actions of Henry V when he took the throne in 1413 was to move Richard to Westminster Abbey to be with Anne in their joint tomb.

Deborah Codling has suggested Henry sought to create a new royal necropolis at Canterbury for the Lancastrian dynasty—yet none of his successors followed his lead.[171] However, two historians, Christopher Wilson and Jon-Mark Grussenmeyer, have made a convincing argument that Henry chose Canterbury very deliberately to associate himself with two important Thomases—his ancestor Thomas of Lancaster and St Thomas Becket. Both of these Thomases had stood up to—and died—opposing tyrannical rule.[172] In associating himself with these two figures eternally by choosing to be buried at Canterbury, Henry was making a strong statement that he was a legitimate king who had bravely saved England from the tyranny of Richard II, not a political opportunist who had usurped the place of his cousin. Henry was a king who was both very aware of the perception many had of him as an illegitimate monarch and cognizant too of the power of place to confer authority and legitimacy on his reign—in both life and death.

This second tomb commission was then different in two key respects from the tomb of Jean IV: her second husband had a very clear idea of where he wanted to be buried and this time Joan was not only creating her husband's tomb, but also her own. Double tombs—for both king and queen—were a relatively new tradition in England. Indeed, at the time the only precedent for a joint tomb for a royal couple was the aforementioned example of Henry's predecessor—Richard II and his first wife, Anne of Bohemia, at Westminster Abbey. In a way this tomb was doubly radical—both in its choice of location and in the decision to build a double tomb, rather than follow the long-standing tradition of English medieval kings and queens to be buried separately—sometimes not even in the same location. Moreover, Henry could have decided to be buried with Mary de Bohun, his first wife and the mother of his children, as his father John of Gaunt had chosen to be buried with his first wife, Blanche of Lancaster, rather than his royal wife Constanza of Castile or his beloved mistress, then third wife, Katherine Swynford. Yet Henry had not asked to be buried with Mary, nor indeed specifically with Joan, in his will—he had only asked "to be beryed in the chirch at Caunterbury, aftyr the descrecion of my cousin the Archbythcopp of Canterbury".[173] Indeed, Henry left the Archbishop, Thomas Arundel, a great deal of scope, saying only that he wanted to establish a chantry chapel for Masses for his soul, but in terms of his burial he only instructed that it should be "in soch a plase and aftyr soch ordinaunce as it seemeth best to my aforseyd cousin of Canterbury".

However, Thomas Arundel, the archbishop, died in 1414, only a year after Henry, and the tomb had not yet been built, not even, it appears, commissioned or designed, as the evidence indicates that the tomb was installed in the 1420s or possibly the early 1430s. This gave Joan the opportunity to take the reins of the project and shape it in a way that not only spoke to her husband's desire to project majesty and legitimacy, but reinforced her own dynastic background and her role as his queen. While we cannot say with complete certainty that Joan designed the tomb, due to a lack of records, her own prominence in the design certainly suggests that she had control of the commission or at least a great deal of input.[174] Jessica Barker in her book *Stone Fidelity* notes that there are three major identities which are the focus of the tomb's design—Henry's identity as king, their joint identity as a ruling couple, and Joan's identity as not only queen, but as infanta of Navarre and duchess of Brittany.[175] This chimes with the observations of John Carmi Parsons on how the tombs of medieval queens provided an ideal means to "celebrate their capacity to exploit the connections acquired in their lives" by denoting their maternal and paternal ancestry and the titles and positions that they held in their lifetimes.[176]

FIGURE 7.1 The tomb of Henry IV and Joan of Navarre at Canterbury Cathedral

Source: © Angelo Hornak/Alamy Stock Photo.

The tomb chest itself is fashioned from English alabaster, a material which Kim Woods notes was a popular choice for royal and elite tombs in the later Middle Ages due to its "lustre and translucency".[177] Moreover alabaster was closely associated with the Lancastrian dynasty—it had been used for John of Gaunt and for the tombs of other Lancastrian supporters and, conveniently, the two greatest quarries for the stone in England were on Lancastrian lands at Tutbury and Chellaston.[178] Both Henry and Joan have splendid effigies which again project majesty—both are richly dressed and depicted wearing crowns and both were originally holding sceptres, although this—and their hands, have now been lost. Several angels can be seen on the tomb, holding the pillows upon which the king and queen's effigies rest and holding shields on the tomb canopy, although not all of these survive. While tomb depictions were often idealised, it is possible that these effigies have attempted to depict the royal couple in a reasonably accurate and life-like fashion. A few clues suggest this—first is that, as will be discussed shortly, there appeared to be a reasonable resemblance between Henry's well-preserved corpse and his effigy when his tomb was opened in the nineteenth century. Another possible clue may be in the respective size of the royal pair—Joan is depicted as considerably smaller than Henry. While this may be in part a reflection of his masculinity and royal status, effigies on joint tombs often feature figures of roughly equal size, such as those of Joan's relatives Jeanne d'Evreux and Charles IV of France or her predecessors Richard II and Anne of Bohemia, yet Joan looks very petite in comparison to her husband, which may reflect a diminutive stature in life.[179]

Alabaster was also the chosen material for the joint tomb of Joan's brother Carlos III of Navarre and his wife Leonor de Trastámara in Pamplona Cathedral. Interestingly, Carlos and Joan may have been designing their respective joint tombs at the same time—the Flemish sculptor Jehan Lome of Tournai was working for Carlos in Navarre between 1413 and 1419. While we cannot be as precise about the commission and manufacture of Joan and Henry's tomb due to a lack of surviving evidence, the likely installation period of the 1420s or early 1430s means that Joan may have started work on her own shared tomb at a similar time, given that Henry passed in 1413. Alternatively, if she started her commission after her brother's, it is possible that there was some influence or connection—this may have been tenuous as Joan never returned to Pamplona to visit her brother or view his tomb, but as we know that Joan maintained contact with her Navarrese family, it is likely that she was at least aware of the project. Certainly, there are some similarities in terms of material and the basic design of both tombs, which feature the couple recumbent on cushions under gothic canopies with crowns on their heads and animals at their feet. However, this similarity likely owes more to contemporary trends in tomb design than any direct influence from one sibling to another. While alabaster was, as Barker and others have noted, "a Lancastrian stone", it was also popular for tombs, altarpieces, and other sculptural works across Northern Europe and in Iberia at the time, thus again their shared choice of alabaster may not have signalled a conscious choice to create similar tombs.[180]

Even if we cannot demonstrate any concrete evidence of shared inspiration between the siblings' commissions, the design of the wider tomb installation at Canterbury visually attests to Joan's connections with her Navarrese family. This can be clearly seen on the wooden canopy or tester above the tomb, which is arguably even more interesting than the tomb itself because of the significant symbols and the messages that they send to the viewer. It is easily missed in focusing on the tomb chest itself, but the underside of the tester is colourfully painted with significant heraldic designs on a rich blue background. There are three shields on the canopy—one with England's arms, one with Navarre's, and one with the two merged or "impaled" together, representing their individual royal status and celebrating the union of their two houses. Each shield is ringed with a Lancastrian SS collar—and as noted previously, Joan's effigy on the tomb wears an SS collar, perhaps a representation of the one that Henry gave her when they wed.

On the canopy are also Henry's motto "Soverayne" and Joan's "A temperance". In his book *The Fears of Henry IV*, Ian Mortimer discusses the meaning of Henry's motto, which he links to the Lancastrian SS collar. There are multiple potential meanings of "soverayne"—however, Mortimer argues that it shouldn't be seen as linked to the word "sovereign", rather that it is a shortened form of "*souveignez vous de moi*" or "remember me".[181] Joan's motto of "A temperance" is less clear, but a dictionary from the seventeenth century defined the French word "temperance" (which would have been Joan's point of reference as a French speaker) as "temperance, moderation, sobriety—the mean between the extremities of appetite, and affection".[182] Temperance, this idea of self-control and resistance to excess or temptation, was one of the seven virtues (the opposite of the more familiar seven deadly sins) and was stressed both in the Bible and by the classical philosopher Aristotle as the basis for virtuous behaviour.[183]

Also on the canopy are two key symbols—the crowned eagle and the ermine. The crowned eagle has been linked back to the Holy Oil of St Thomas, which Henry was anointed with—again linking him back to St Thomas Becket and a prophecy that a great king would be anointed with this oil who would be a champion of the

Church—perhaps even reclaiming the Holy Land.[184] Deborah Codling has suggested that the hands on Henry's effigy on the tomb, which are now lost, originally clasped an eagle: "According to Walsingham, the note accompanying the oil stated that as long as the king carried the eagle at his chest he would have victory over his enemies and his kingdom would grow and flourish. Henry in death, as in life, appears still to be optimistically clutching his eagle".[185] The symbol of the crowned eagle was clearly important to Henry—there was a subtlety in the menu for Henry and Joan's wedding feast at Winchester which was fashioned in the same design. A painted panel at the head of the tomb depicted the martyrdom of St Thomas Becket to further emphasise the link to the saint.

At the foot of the tomb there was another painted panel with the Coronation of the Virgin—which can be connected with the importance of Marian devotion in the late Middle Ages and has a strong link to medieval queenship—particularly celebrating Mary's role as the Queen of Heaven. The ermine, which one might immediately think of as a symbol of royalty, in this case more likely refers to Joan's Breton connections—the Order of the Ermine was a chivalric order begun by her first husband, Jean IV of Brittany, modelled on the English Order of the Garter. Indeed, on Jean IV's tomb he wears the collar of the order around his neck, and the motto of the order "*A ma vie*" appears in a banderole held by a lion at the duke's feet.[186] Ermines continue—even today—to be a key element of Breton heraldry, thus Joan's position as infanta, duchess, and queen are all clearly referenced on the canopy—another strong case for her hand in the design.

Nor was she the only female patron of a joint alabaster tomb from the workshop of Prentys and Sutton, the most likely candidate for the artisans who produced the tomb. Jessica Barker has compared Joan and Henry's tomb with that of two other tombs commissioned by women which the workshop produced at a similar time (c. 1415–20), that of Beatrice of Portugal and Thomas Fitzalan, earl of Arundel, at the Fitzalan chapel at Arundel Castle, and the tomb of Katherine Clifton and Ralph Green, sheriff of Northamptonshire and Wiltshire.[187] Barker has noted that another key similarity between these tombs is the fact that Beatrice, Katherine, and Joan were all involved in some difficulty over their dowers during their widowhood and that commissioning a tomb with their late husband was a way to make a powerful statement of permanent connection to their spouse and marital family. Certainly, as we have seen, this was the case for Joan—arguably for both of the tombs that she commissioned. With Jean IV, commissioning his tomb and sending it back from England after she remarried was a physical means of displaying her continued connection to the Montforts and Brittany at a time when there was some question of whether she should still be able to claim her Breton dower after her second marriage. After Henry IV's death, commissioning a joint tomb with her royal husband was a means of eternally cementing her position as his queen consort and her connection to him. We know that Joan faced a continual issue with her English dower as dowager, which was particularly acute during the period of seizure and during the reign of Henry VI.

This raises the question again of when the tomb may have been commissioned. Barker has rightly noted that this must have been done at a period when Joan had full access to her funds—so clearly it would not have been commissioned between late 1419 and 1422 when she was under detention. It is possible that it was set in motion earlier, after the death of the archbishop in 1414 but before mid-1419, and was possibly put on hold during the period when her dower was seized, unless Henry V was willing for the tomb to be paid for by the Crown during this period. Yet there is no clear evidence of payments for the tomb in her accounts from her period of detention which have survived, nor in the accounts of 1427–28. Thus it seems there are three possible periods when it could have been commissioned and paid for by Joan: 1414–19, 1422–27, or 1429–37. All three periods may have had similar motivations—in her early widowhood, this would have been a means of trying to emphasise her link to the late king and preserve her queenly status. Immediately after the period of detention, Joan might have used the commission to reassert herself as a queen and enhance her position, which may have been tarnished. In both the 1420s and 1430s, she was fighting vociferously to regain and retain her dower in both England and Brittany. Without clear evidence, we cannot make a certain presumption of when the tomb was commissioned, but her impetus for the creation of the tomb would certainly fit with

Barker's suggestion that it was a key tool for a widow to use when her position and dower were under threat, and perhaps Joan's ultimate opportunity for image creation and the "shaping of memory".

Yet while Joan made impressive efforts to enshrine the majesty and memory of both husbands—and her own—for later generations, there is a brief postscript to this tale regarding the impact that later generations had on these two tombs. In the eighteenth century, the tomb of Jean IV was damaged first by vandals supporting a movement for Breton independence and then by renovations at Nantes Cathedral in 1733 which moved the altar and damaged the monument further. Any remaining elements of the tomb appear to have been lost in the sacking of the cathedral during the French Revolution, although some remnants were found in restoration work on the cathedral in 1888.[188] Across the Channel in England in 1832 there was a decision to open Henry and Joan's tomb to challenge the suggestion in a near contemporary source that Henry's body had fallen into the Thames en route to Canterbury in a freak storm and thus had never been buried there. However, when they did open the tomb they found a smaller lead coffin, presumably Joan's, which they set aside as they were only interested in solving the mystery around Henry's body. They did find a body in his coffin, however, and when they opened up the wrapped shrouding of the king's corpse, "to the astonishment of all present, the face of the deceased King was seen in complete preservation".[189] The observers noted that the king had a thick, russet-coloured beard and nearly all his teeth, but his nose sunk and then disappeared when exposed to the air. Satisfied that the king was indeed buried in the tomb and not wanting presumably to do further damage to his body, they rewrapped him and replaced the lid of his coffin, and presumably Joan's lead coffin as well (although this is not specifically noted) and resealed the tomb.

In summary, this study of three tombs linked to Joan has demonstrated two key aspects: her role as a "shaper of memory" in the creation of tombs for her first child and both of her husbands, as well as the ways in which these tombs serve as a point of comparison and connection between her Navarrese, Breton, and English families. Politics and position were key drivers in all three scenarios—reinforcing the right of the Montfort line in Brittany in terms of the tomb of the young Jeanne and Jean IV and in the timing of the commission and imagery of her joint tomb with Henry IV. All of the tombs were located in sites imbued with meaning—while Jean likely chose St Gildas de Rhuys for its ancient Breton links for the tomb of their first child, Joan may have had some influence on the choice of Nantes for Jean's own tomb, a city that was part of her own power base in the duchy. In contrast, we can see Henry IV's desires and ideology in the choice of their shared tomb at Canterbury Cathedral—the seat of the church in England but not the primary royal necropolis. However, the famous Black Prince is buried there, offering another connection between the two tombs as a possible inspiration for the design of Jean IV's tomb and a man to whom both Jean and Henry shared personal links. Connections can also be seen between Brittany and England in Joan's decision to create an English tomb for Jean IV which reflected both his own political and personal connection to England during his lifetime and the enduring tie that Joan provided between the two realms after her marriage and move across the Channel. Finally, we can see connections between Joan's shared tomb in Canterbury Cathedral and that of her brother and sister-in-law in Pamplona in their material and design as well as the heraldic devises that Joan used to emphasise her Navarrese lineage. Taken together, these tombs demonstrate the power of patronage for Joan to reinforce the status of the Montfort dynasty as the rightful rulers of Brittany and shape not only the memory of her two husbands but her own distinctive position as a Navarrese infanta, a Breton duchess, and an English queen.

Conclusion

Looking back at this chapter as a whole, we can see the importance of places, spaces, and material culture in terms of both how Joan exercised her position as duchess, queen, and dowager, the maintenance of her familial networks and her day-to-day life. We began by examining the wide range of places she inhabited, considering the residences she lived in with her two husbands, as well as those which she personally favoured from her portfolio of dower properties. This gives us a sense of where she lived, the spaces that Joan, her family, and her household inhabited, and the features that were built or improved in order to make them comfortable and suitably impressive for her exalted status. We have also looked at her use of ecclesiastical spaces, from her own private chapels to stays at monasteries during her travels around the realm, which led us to a wider consideration of Joan's relationship with the church and her personal piety. Aspects of piety could also be seen in Joan's possessions, from jewellery with religious motifs to bejewelled liturgical items for celebrating Mass in her chapel, as well as in gifts she commissioned and exchanged with relatives, such as books and the Reliquary of the Trinity given to her son Jean V. We have also seen the importance of gift exchange and material culture in terms of maintaining Joan's familial networks and in establishing and enhancing her position. Patronage, as well, has proven to be another means of ameliorating her position by crafting her image and acting as a "shaper of memory" for both herself and her natal and marital dynasties. In our conclusion to follow, we will consider Joan's memory and how effective her efforts proved to be in terms of creating a lasting legacy.

Notes

1 See Elena Woodacre, *Queens and Queenship* (Bradford: ARC Humanities Press, 2021), especially chapter 3, "Image," 87–120.
2 For example, see Tracy Chapman Hamilton and Mariah Proctor-Tiffany, eds., *Moving Women, Moving Objects (400–1500)* (Leiden: Brill, 2019).
3 CPR Henry IV, II, 28 November 1404, 479.
4 Marie Casset commented that this demonstrated "sans doute le goût des ducs pour cette région si douce à vivre": Marie Casset, "Manoirs de plaisance des ducs de Bretagne XIIIe–XVe siècle," in *Châteaux & Modes de vie au temps des ducs de Bretagne (XIIIe–XVIe siècle)*, eds. Alain Salamagne, Jean Kerhervé, and Gérard Danet (Rennes: Presses universitaires de Rennes, 2012), 169.
5 Jean-Pierre Leguay, *Histoire de Vannes et de sa Region* (Toulouse: Privat, 1988), 62–4.
6 Argentré's quote from Marc Deceneux, "Le chateau de l'Hermine a Vannes: Residence des Ducs de Bretagne," *Association Bretonne* 87 (1978): 58; Casset, "Manoirs de plaisance," 165.
7 Leguay, *Histoire de Vannes*, 70.
8 See Jean-Christophe Cassard, "Suscinio et les chasses des ducs de Bretagne," in *Châteaux & Modes de vie au temps des ducs de Bretagne*

(XIIIe–XVIe siècle), eds. Alain Salamagne, Jean Kerhervé, and Gérard Danet (Rennes: Presses universitaires de Rennes, 2012), 121–49, particularly the map of the park on 123.

9 Cassard, "Suscinio," 138. See also Jean-Yves Copy, *Art, Société et Politique au temps des Ducs de Bretagne; Les gisants haut-Bretons* (Paris: Aux Amateurs de Livres, 1986), 106–10.

10 Anthony Emery, *Seats of Power in Europe During the Hundred Years War: An Architectural Study from 1330–1480* (Oxford: Oxbow, 2016), 105.

11 For more on the tiles, see several chapters in Alain Salamagne, Jean Kerhervé, and Gérard Danet, eds. *Châteaux et modes de vie au temps des ducs de Bretagne (XIIIe–XVIe siècle)* (Rennes: Presses universitaires de Rennes, 2012), including Patrick André, "Le pavement médieval de Suscinio: bilan, conjectures et perspectives," 283–88.

12 Chris Given-Wilson, *Henry IV* (New Haven, CT: Yale University Press, 2016), 389.

13 Deborah Codling, "The Kingly Style of Henry IV: Personality, Politics and Culture" (PhD thesis, Royal Holloway, 2004), 144.

14 Codling, "Kingly Style," 113.

15 John Priestley, *Eltham Palace* (Stroud: History Press, 2013), 41–5.

16 Priestley, *Eltham Palace*, 48–9.

17 Given-Wilson, *Henry IV*, 389–90.

18 Priestley, *Eltham Palace*, 47; *King's Works*, I, 248; *King's Works*, II, 935.

19 See Jeanne E. Krochalis, "The Books and Reading of Henry V and His Circle," *The Chaucer Review* 23, no. 1 (1988): 50–77, particularly 55.

20 Priestley, *Eltham Palace*, 48.

21 Codling, "Kingly Style," 118.

22 CPR Henry V, I, 30 June 1415, 351; SC 8/308/15366.

23 CPR Henry V, I, 30 June 1415, 342.

24 CPR Henry IV, IV, 23 February and 16 May 1411, 283, 298, and 304.

25 CPR Henry V, II, 1 August 1420, 301; CPR Henry V, I, 18 March 1416, 401; ADLA E130 dated 1 July 1418 at Kings Langley.

26 John Amundesham, *Annales Monasterii S.Albani*, vol. 1, ed. Henry Thomas Riley (London: Longmans Green and Co, 1870), 16.

27 SAL/MS/216; Amundesham, *Annales*, 13–14, 28.

28 *King's Works*, II, 975. John Steane, *The Archaeology of the Medieval English Monarchy* (London: Routledge, 1999), 104–6.

29 Lionel M. Munby, ed., *The History of Kings Langley* (Kings Langley branch of the Worker's Educational Association, 1963), 15 and 18.

30 CPR Henry VI, I, 12 July 1426, 360–61.

31 Munby, *Kings Langley*, 19.

32 Amundesham, *Annales*, 61–2.

33 *King's Works*, II, 977.

34 *King's Works*, II, 956.

35 CPR Henry V, I, 10 March 1414, 168; *King's Works*, II, 702.

36 H.E. Malden, ed., "House of Benedictine Monks: Abbey of Chertsey," in *A History of the County of Surrey*, vol. 2 (London: Victoria County History, 1967), 55–64.
37 CPR Henry IV, IV, 29 April 1410, 190, and 8 November 1412, 448.
38 "Lateran Regesta 203: 1418–1419," in *Papal Registers*, 7, 125–31.
39 CPR Henry VI, II, 21 November 1433, 328, and III, 16 February 1437, 38.
40 William Page and J. Horace Round, eds., "Houses of Cistercian Monks: Abbey of Stratford Langthorne," in *A History of the County of Essex*, vol. 2 (London: Victoria County History, 1907), 129–133; Given-Wilson, *Henry IV*, 545.
41 Woodacre, *Queens and Queenship*, 18–20.
42 See chapter 5 "Queenship and Pre-Reformation Piety," in Michelle Beer, *Queenship at the Renaissance Courts of Britain: Catherine of Aragon and Margaret Tudor, 1503–1533* (Woodbridge: Royal Historical Society, 2018), 122–48.
43 Elena Woodacre, *The Queens Regnant of Navarre: Succession, Politics and Partnership, 1274–1512* (New York: Palgrave Macmillan, 2013), 100–1.
44 Laura Slater, "Defining Queenship at Greyfriars London, c. 1300–58," *Gender & History* 27, no. 1 (2015): 53–76.
45 Michael Jones, ed., *Le premier inventaire du tresor des chartes des ducs de Bretagne (1395); Herve Le Grant et les origines du Chronicon Briocense* (Bannalec: Imprimerie Regionale, 2007), 43; Nelly Ongay, "Notas Sobre la Vida Cotidiana de las Infantas Reales en los 'Hospitales' del Reino de Navarra (1365–1400): Alimentos, Vestidos, Religiosidad y Viajes," *Estudios de Historia de España* 17, no. 1 (2015): 67.
46 "Lateran Regesta 165: 1412–1413," in *Papal Registers* 6, 372–387; "Lateran Regesta 350: 1437–1438," in *Papal Registers* 6, 626–33.
47 Helen Maurer and B.M. Cron, eds., *The Letters of Margaret of Anjou* (Woodbridge: Boydell and Brewer, 2019), 17.
48 E210/4175.
49 "Lateran Regesta 136: 1409," in *Papal Registers* 6, 149–60.
50 CPR Henry IV, III, 30 July 1407, 348.
51 CPR Henry VI, I, 15 December 1426, 388.
52 CPR Henry VI, I, 11 July 1428, 486.
53 "Lateran Regesta 167: 1413–1415," in *Papal Registers* 6, 397–410; "Lateran Regesta 306: 1431–1432," in *Papal Registers* 8, 353–366.
54 "Lateran Regesta 118: 1403–1404," in *Papal Registers* 5, 616–627; ADLA E38-1, 5 October 1387.
55 "Lateran Regesta 326: 1431–1434," in *Papal Registers* 8, 510–516.
56 "Lateran Regesta 167: 1413–1415," in *Papal Registers* 6, 397–410. I would like to thank Dr Angela Clark for her input on the link between requests for dispensations and affirmations of royal status.
57 ADLA 37-2, 15 August 1386.
58 Copy, *Art, Société et Politique*, 107.

59 Morice, I, col. 86–87; Michael Jones, "Between France and England: Jeanne de Navarre, Duchess of Brittany and Queen of England (1386–1437)," in *Between France and England: Politics, Power and Society in Late Medieval Brittany* (Aldershot: Variorum, 2003), 10.
60 J. de Kersauson de Pennendreff, *L'episcopat Nantais a travers les siècles* (Vannes: Lafoyle Éditeur, 1892), 704.
61 PROME, "Henry IV: January 1404."
62 Amundesham, *Annales*, 16.
63 Leeds Castle E4/1, John Rylands Library Latin MS238, f. 25v.
64 SoA SAL/MS/216, fol. 34.
65 SoA SAL/MS/216, fols. 45 and 56.
66 I am very grateful to Professor Chris Woolgar for his insightful thoughts on the account book and raising alternative scenarios other than a simple gift from Joan to Eleanor.
67 Jones, "Between France and England," 21.
68 Brigitte Buettner, "Past Presents: New Year's Gifts at the Valois Court, ca. 1400," *Art Bulletin* 83 (2001): 598.
69 Jenny Stratford, *Richard II and the English Royal Treasure* (Woodbridge: Boydell, 2013), 229.
70 Stratford, *Royal Treasure*, 176.
71 Marguerite Keane, *Material Culture and Queenship in 14th-Century France: The Testament of Blanche of Navarre* (Leiden: Brill, 2016), 102–3.
72 Stratford, *Royal Treasure*, 343.
73 Stratford, *Royal Treasure*, 119.
74 Stratford, *Royal Treasure*, 279. See also E101/404/18 m.7.
75 Jessica Lutkin, "Luxury and Display in Silver and Gold at the Court of Henry IV," in *English and Continental Perspectives: The Fifteenth Century 9*, ed. Linda Clark (Woodbridge: Boydell, 2010), 168.
76 Richard Barber, *Magnificence: Princely Splendour in the Middle Ages* (Woodbridge: Boydell, 2020), 3.
77 Codling, "Kingly Style," 126.
78 Stratford, *Royal Treasure*, 164.
79 Stratford, *Royal Treasure*, 146.
80 Stratford, *Royal Treasure*, 121.
81 Jean Kerhervé, *L'état Breton aux 14e et 15e siècles; Les Ducs, l'Argent et les Hommes*. 2 vols (Paris: Editeur Maloine, 1987), 304 n187.
82 E403/576, m. 21. See also Frederick Devon, ed., *Issues of Exchequer being a collection of payments made out of His Majesty's Revenue, from King Henry III to King Henry VI inclusive with an appendix* (London: John Murray, 1837), 294–95.
83 Ronald W. Lightbown, *Mediaeval European Jewellery with a catalogue of the collection in the Victoria & Albert Museum* (London: Victoria and Albert Museum, 1992), 248–49.
84 Lutkin, "Luxury and Display," 164.
85 Codling, "Kingly Style," 126; E403/576, m. 19.

86 Lightbown, *Medieval Jewellery*, 216.
87 Francis Palgrave, ed., *The Ancient Kalendars and Inventories of the Treasury of His Majesty's Exchequer*, II, (London: Commissioners of the Public Records, 1836), 253–54.
88 POPC 5, 1436, 61.
89 CPR Henry V, II, 16 August 1419, 271.
90 A.R. Myers, *Crown, Household, and Parliament in Fifteenth Century England* (London: Bloomsbury Academic, 1985), 128. Note that Myers has given a full transcription of both existing versions of this inventory on pages 128–33.
91 See Stratford, *Royal Treasure*, for a discussion of an image of St Catherine given to the king of England by the duke of Berry, 339. I would like to thank Marguerite Keane for her suggestion of the potential personal links between these saints and Joan.
92 Leeds Castle E4/1, 11.
93 Jones, "Between France and England," 21, referring to SoA SAL/MS/216 fols. 19r, 28v, 32r.
94 Leeds Castle E4/1, 7.
95 Leeds Castle E4/1, 13–14.
96 The building in which Joan's wardrobe was housed had previously belonged to the earl of Northumberland and had been given to Joan when the Percys' possessions were forfeited by treason (CPR Henry IV, III, 22 July 1405, 34), but there was a later dispute over the rights to the property (CPR Henry VI, III, 17 December 1435, 530–1). For later reference to the property's location and denomination as "Queen Jane's Wardrobe," see Christopher Hibbert, Ben Weinreb, Julia Keay, and John Keay, eds., *The London Encyclopaedia* (3rd ed.) (London: Pan Macmillan, 2011), 15; John Strype, *A Survey of the Cities of London and Westminster* (1720), The Stuart London Project, https://www.dhi.ac.uk/strype/TransformServlet?page=book3_112.
97 Leeds Castle E/4, 10-12 and E 101/407/4.
98 Elizabeth Currie, *Fashion and Masculinity in Renaissance Florence* (London: Bloomsbury, 2016), 101.
99 Caroline Dunn, "All the Queen's Ladies? Philippa of Hainault's Female Attendants," *Medieval Prosopography* 31 (2016): 203–4.
100 E101/407/4, also reprinted in A.R. Myers, "The Captivity of a Royal Witch: The Household Accounts of Queen Joan of Navarre, 1419–21," *Bulletin of the John Rylands Library* 24, no. 2 (1940): 284.
101 Stratford, *Royal Treasure*, 170.
102 Isabelle Balandre, "Reliquaire de l'Ordre du Saint-Esprit 'Tableau de la Trinité,'" *The Louvre* website, accessed 27 November 2021, https://collections.louvre.fr/en/ark:/53355/cl010111574.
103 Morice, II, col. 1161–64. Note: also mentioned here are two large silver platters which his sisters brought back from England.

104 Diane E. Booton, "Commemorating Duke John IV of Brittany in Ritual and Image," *Nottingham Medieval Studies* 59 (2015): 171.
105 Morice, II, col. 1163.
106 Council of the London and Middlesex Archaeological Society, *A Catalogue of the Antiquities and Works of Art Exhibited at Ironmongers' Hall, London* (London: Harrison and Sons, 1869), 146–47.
107 Maev Kennedy, "Henry V's Funeral Shield on Show," *The Guardian*, UK News (Museums/Higher Education/Arts), 22 September 2003, https://www.theguardian.com/uk/2003/sep/22/artsandhumanities.arts.
108 CCR Henry V, I, 20 July 1418, 468–69.
109 E. Fonssagrives, *Les Trois femmes de Jean IV; conference donnée à la Société Polymathique du Morbihan le 10 Avril 1923* (Vannes: Imprimerie du Commerce, 1923), 15; CCR Henry V, I, 20 July 1418, 472.
110 Saint-Denys, I, 725.
111 Foedera 8, 1 March 1403.
112 Keane, *Blanche of Navarre*, 180.
113 Keane, *Blanche of Navarre*, 182.
114 Keane, *Blanche of Navarre*, 183.
115 Catálogo XXXI, no. 259, 8 May 1414.
116 Susan Groag Bell, "Medieval Women Book Owners: Arbiters of Lay Piety and Ambassadors of Culture," *Signs* 7, no. 4 (1982): 743.
117 Mariah Proctor-Tiffany, *Medieval Art in Motion: The Inventory and Gift-Giving of Queen Clémence de Hongrie* (University Park, PA: Penn State Press, 2019), 101. For more on the practice of reading to others, see D.H. Green, *Women Readers in the Middle Ages* (Cambridge: Cambridge University Press, 2007), 15–22.
118 Joni M. Hand, *Women, Manuscripts and Identity in Northern Europe, 1350–1550* (Aldershot: Ashgate, 2013), 12. On Juana II, see Julia Finch, "Of Movement, Monarchs, and Manuscripts: The Case for Jeanne II of Navarre's Picture Bible as a Geopolitical Bridge between Paris and Pamplona," in *Moving Women, Moving Objects (400–1500)*, eds. Tracy Chapman Hamilton and Mariah Proctor-Tiffany (Leiden: Brill, 2019), 181–204; Marguerite Keane, "Louis IX, Louis X, Louis of Navarre: Family Ties and Political Ideology in the Hours of Jeanne of Navarre," *Visual Resources* 20, no. 2–3 (2004): 237–52.
119 Proctor-Tiffany, *Medieval Art in Motion*, 80 and 98–9.
120 Anon., "Notes and News," *Bulletin of The John Rylands Library Manchester* 46, no. 1 (1963): 1.
121 Léopold Delisle, "Notice sur un psautier du XIIIe siècle appartenant au comte de Crawford," *Bibliothèque de l'école des chartes* 58 (1897): 389–90.
122 An excellent surviving example is Joan's letter to the king of Aragon, dated 13 February 1413, Archivo de la Corona de Aragón (ACA), COLECCIONES, Autógrafos, I, 7, I, accessed via PARES.
123 Jones, "Between France and England," 1. Anne Crawford repeats the same claim as Mary Anne Everett Wood that Joan's signature is the first

recorded example for an English queen on a letter: Anne Crawford, ed., *Letters of the Queens of England* (Stroud: Sutton, 1997), 115; Mary Anne Everett Wood, ed., *Letters of Royal and Illustrious Ladies of Great Britain* (London: Henry Colburn, 1846), 89.

124 Anon., *Bible historiale Moyenne complete* (late 14th century), BnF ms. Français 2; there is an unusual example of her signature which is almost calligraphic on folio 465 verso "La R. Jahanne. Tout dyz bien" and a partially erased note on folio 511 "Jeanne, royne d'Engleterre, ducesse de Bretagne, fille de roy de Navarre". Titus Livius, *A Urbe condita*, translated into French by Pierre Bersuire (c. 1380), BnF ms Français 269–72; her signature "Jahanne royne" is on the bottom of folio 134 in volume 4 (ms 272).

125 Jean de Meun, *Le testament maistre Jehan de Mehun*, (c. 1400), Houghton Library MS Typ 749. The examples are on folios 1r, 46r, and 80v.

126 Finch, "Of Movement," 181.

127 Proctor-Tiffany, *Medieval Art in Motion*, 131.

128 Keane, *Blanche of Navarre*, 102–3.

129 BnF, "Français 2", *Archives et Manuscripts*, https://archivesetmanuscrits.bnf.fr/ark:/12148/cc485382.

130 BnF ms fr 2, *Bible historiale*, f. 511, "Le dixiesme jour de septembre, l'an mil quatre cens vingt et sept, fut cest livre donné a tres hault et tres puissant prince Humfrey, duc de Gloucestre, conte de Haynnau, Hollande et protecteur etc, deffenseur d'Engleterre, par sir Jehan Stanley, chevalier, ledit prince estant en l'abbaye Nostre Dame a Chestre".

131 Anon. (Durand de Champagne), *Le Livre qui est appellé le Miroer des dames, que fist ung Frere de l'ordre Saint François* (15th century), BnF ms Français 610. Note: this is only one of a dozen surviving copies of the French translation which have survived; see Constant J. Mews, "The *Speculum dominarum (Miroir des dames)* and Transformations of the Literature of Instruction for Women in the Early Fourteenth Century," in *Virtue Ethics for Women, 1250–1500*, eds. Karen Green and Constant J. Mews (New York: Springer, 2011), 22.

132 BnF ms Français 610, folio 1r.

133 Mews, "Transformations," 23.

134 Keane, *Blanche of Navarre*, 95 and 209.

135 Mews, "Transformations," 30.

136 Keane, "Family Ties," 238.

137 Woodacre, *Queens Regnant*, 51–61.

138 Keane, *Blanche of Navarre*, 94–5 and 207.

139 Christopher de Hamel, *Meetings with Remarkable Manuscripts* (London: Penguin, 2016), 412–13.

140 De Hamel, *Meetings*, 414–15.

141 De Hamel, *Meetings*, 417 (see also an illustration of the frontispiece on p. 416).

142 Myers, *Crown, Household and Parliament*, 131.

143 See Anon., *Missal for Selected Feasts (use of Sarum)*, In Latin, illuminated manuscript on parchment, England (London), 1400–1425 (before 1423?), https://www.textmanuscripts.com/medieval/sarum-missal-141427.
144 Note: Joan's possession of the book, while widely noted due to her signature, is disputed by some; see Scot McKendrick, "A European Heritage: Books of Continental Origin collected by the English Royal Family from Edward III to Henry VIII," in *Royal Manuscripts: The Genius of Illumination*, eds. Scot McKendrick, John Lowden, and Kathleen Doyle (London: British Library, 2011), 64 n27.
145 Anon., *A Catalogue of an Exhibition of the Philip Hofer Bequest in the Department of Printing and Graphic Arts* (Cambridge, MA: Harvard College Library, 1988), 22.
146 Laure Miolo, "Medieval Spin-Offs of the Roman de la Rose," *Medieval Manuscripts Blog*, British Library, 9 January 2017, https://blogs.bl.uk/digitisedmanuscripts/2017/01/medieval-spin-offs-of-the-roman-de-la-rose.html. Miolo notes the disputed authorship of these works which were attributed to Meun, but Christine de Pizan suggested that this was a false link.
147 Krochalis, "Henry V and His Circle," 50–77.
148 Groag Bell, "Medieval Women Book Owners," 767. See also Tracy Chapman Hamilton and Mariah Proctor-Tiffany, "Introduction: Women and the Circulation of Material Culture: Crossing Boundaries and Connecting Spaces," in *Moving Women, Moving Objects*, eds. Tracy Chapman Hamilton and Mariah Proctor-Tiffany (Leiden: Brill, 2019), 1–12.
149 Margaret Bent, "Dunstable (Dunstable), John," ODNB online.
150 See Andrew Wathey, "Dunstable in France," *Music & Letters* 67, no. 1 (1986): 1–36; Judith Stell and Andrew Wathey, "New Light on the Biography of John Dunstable?," *Music & Letters* 62, no. 1 (1981): 60–3.
151 Wathey, "Dunstable in France," 6.
152 Gillian Gower, "The Iconography of Queenship: Sacred Music and Female Exemplarity in Late Medieval Britain" (PhD thesis, UCLA, 2016), 241.
153 Wathey, "Dunstable in France," 23 and 28.
154 María Narbona Cárceles, "La actividad musical en la corte de Carlos III de Navarra, 1387–1425: mecenazgo o estrategia politica?", *Principe de Viana* 67, no. 238 (2006): 315.
155 Booton, "Commemorating," 157.
156 See Jean-Yves Copy, "Du nouveau sure la couronne ducale bretonne: le temoignage des tombeaux," *Memoires de la Societe d'Histoire et d'Archeologie de Bretagne* 59 (1982): 171–91, and *Art, Société et Politique*, 106–10.
157 Copy, "Couronne ducale bretonne," 173.
158 Copy, "Couronne ducale bretonne," 186.

159 Chronicon Briconese in Morice, I, col. 80.

160 Elizabeth Tingle, "The Afterlives of Rulers: Power, Patronage and Purgatory in Ducal Brittany 1480–1600," in *The Image and Perception of Monarchy in Medieval and Early Modern Europe*, eds. Sean McGlynn and Elena Woodacre (Newcastle upon Lyme: Cambridge Scholars, 2014), 285–86.

161 Morice, II, col. 699.

162 Booton, "Commemorating," 180.

163 Booton notes, "She could have commissioned the monument from Breton or French sculptors working in local materials perhaps in a more familiar style; instead, she chose an English-made sculpture in alabaster, a decision that may have allowed better oversight of its production." Booton, "Commemorating," 179.

164 Booton, "Commemorating," 177.

165 Kim Woods, *Cut in Alabaster: A Material of Sculpture and its European Traditions 1330–1530* (Turnhout: Harvey Miller, 2018), 175; Copy, *Art, Société et Politique*, 174.

166 Rachel Dressler, "Identity, Status and Material: Medieval Alabaster Effigies in England," *Peregrinations: Journal of Medieval Art and Architecture* 5, no. 2 (2015): 95–6.

167 Woods, *Alabaster*, 175.

168 Foedera 8, 24 February 1408.

169 Copy, *Art, Société et Politique*, 174. Original quote "Le choir de cet emplacement, la factor de l'oeuvre et sa signification politique ont été conditionnés par la personnalité de Jeanne de Navarre".

170 Christopher Wilson, "The Tomb of Henry IV and the Holy Oil of St. Thomas of Canterbury," in *Medieval Architecture and its Intellectual Context: Studies in Honour of Peter Kidson*, eds. Eric Fernie and Paul Crossley (London: Hambledon, 1990), 181.

171 Codling, "Kingly Style," 215.

172 Jon-Mark Grussenmeyer, "The Tomb of a King and the Ideology of a Dynasty: Henry IV and the Lancastrian Connexion to Canterbury Cathedral" (MA diss., University of Kent, 2012), 21.

173 "Will of Henry IV," in Richard Gough and John Nichols, *A collection of all the wills, now known to be extant of the Kings and Queens of England* (London: J. Nichols, 1780), 203.

174 Wilson notes, "the absolute equality of Joan and Henry's heraldic commemoration suggests strongly that she was the patron": Wilson, "The Tomb of Henry IV," 182.

175 Jessica Barker, *Stone Fidelity: Marriage and Emotion in Medieval Tomb Sculpture* (Woodbridge: Boydell, 2020), 163.

176 John Carmi Parsons, "'Never was a body buried in England with such solemnity and honour': The Burials and Posthumous Commemoration of English Queens to 1500," in *Queens and Queenship in Medieval Europe*, ed. Anne Duggan (Woodbridge: Boydell, 2002), 329.

177 Woods, *Alabaster*, 147.

178 Woods, *Alabaster*, 234; Dressler, "Identity, Status and Material," 68–9.
179 I would like to thank Eloísa Ramírez Vaquero for drawing this possibility to my attention.
180 Barker, *Stone Fidelity*, 185. On the wider popularity of alabaster, see Woods, *Alabaster*, 145.
181 See Mortimer's extended discussion of the motto and the SS collar in Ian Mortimer, *The Fears of Henry IV; The Life of England's Self-Made King* (London: Vintage, 2008), Appendix Seven, 384–87.
182 Randle Cotgrave, *A French-English Dictionary* (London: Printed by W.H for Luke Fawne, 1650), unpaginated.
183 Kasey Evans, *Colonial Virtue: The Mobility of Temperance in Renaissance England* (Toronto: University of Toronto Press, 2012), 16.
184 For an extended discussion, see Wilson, "The Tomb of Henry IV," 181–90.
185 Codling, "Kingly Style," 215.
186 Booton, "Commemorating," 171.
187 Jessica Barker, "The Funerary Programme of Beatrice of Portugal (d. 1439) at the Fitzalan Chapel in Arundel," paper given at *Espacios de memoria y representation: Reinas, infantas y damas de la corte ante la muerte en las monarquías ibéricas medievales*, 29 April 2021.
188 P. de Lisle du Drenuc, *Les Tombeaux des Ducs de Bretagne* (Vannes: Editeur Lafolye, 1894), 42–44.
189 Anon. (J.H.S), "Tomb of King Henry IV in Canterbury Cathedral," *Archaeologia Cantiana* 8 (1872): 298.

CONCLUSION: REMEMBERING JOAN

Royal marriages were designed to create alliances—bonds of blood which were meant to create connections to promote unity and peace. Joan herself was a product of generations of dynastic marriages, which meant she was closely related to many of the greatest families of Western Europe, and her marriages, along with those of her children, stepchildren, and grandchildren, only increased these connections over the years. Not only was Joan herself an active participant in creating peace between her family members through intercession and diplomacy, the connections created by her marriages and maternity were repeatedly cited in peace treaties as a pretext for familial relationships which should preclude unity. While the use of the terms used in diplomatic documents like "brother", "father", "mother", "cousin", "uncle", and "*carissimus consanguineous noster*" or "our most beloved close relative" could be seen as formulaic; they were employed to reinforce family bonds—bonds which had been created through Joan.

Yet these connections did not prevent war and conflict, which were near constant during the entirety of Joan's life through both the Hundred Years War and the internal rifts in Brittany between the Penthièvres and Montforts, the Valois internecine strife between

DOI: 10.4324/9780429261022-11

the Orleans/Armagnacs and Burgundy, and in England, with rebellions, plots, and tensions between the Lancastrians themselves. Ultimately it seems that there was never a point in Joan's long life when she could claim that all of the various branches of her family in Navarre, Brittany, France, and England were in harmony—her life witnessed conflict after conflict both between and within the branches. The decisions that Joan herself made—to marry Henry IV, to involve herself in brokering peace, to intercede with her relatives to incline them to a side or encourage them to back down from warfare—always alienated at least one group within her family and made her loyalties suspect both to them and her subjects.

This suspicion has led to a negative perception of Joan, particularly in English history, where she barely features in the contemporary chronicles. This scant mention by chronicles has in turn informed both later historiography and popular culture, where Joan is largely missing from the memory of the Lancastrian era. Henry IV has generally been given less focus than his heroic son Henry V, the victor of Agincourt—many generations have only been acquainted with his reign via the history or so-called "Hollow Crown" plays of William Shakespeare. Joan is completely absent from *Henry IV, parts I and II*, as well as those on the later Lancastrian kings—yet we cannot fault Shakespeare entirely for this as she was largely missing in the chronicles that he himself was using to construct his own work.[1] And so it goes on—this pattern of omission continues through to Jane Austen, who claimed in her potted history of England that "it is supposed that Henry [IV] was married, since he had certainly four sons, but it is not in my power to inform the Reader who was his wife".[2] Today, as noted in the introduction, she remains one of England's least known queens—another royal woman with a fascinating life whose existence is a mystery to many.

Although Joan has not resonated strongly in the written record or in popular culture, there are still some tangible reminders in terms of material culture and architectural remains which give the modern world evidence of her existence in the present day. Sadly, many of the residences where Joan spent most of her time are lost to us now, such as Kings Langley, Havering-atte-Bower, and the monasteries of Stratford and Chertsey. A few locations which were becoming ruinous in Joan's time, such as Odiham Castle, are even more of a ruin now. However, others such as Suscinio in Brittany have been the focus of major restoration efforts to try to recapture the way they might have been in Joan's lifetime. In a more extreme sense, Eltham Palace has been subject to so much work by later kings and owners that the building as Joan would have known it has been nearly erased. Still, three surviving castles deliberately highlight their connection to her, even if briefly, in the story they tell of the sites' history: Nottingham, Pevensey, and Leeds. Pevensey and Leeds include Joan in relation to the charge of treason and her detention there—an interesting tale which makes an exciting anecdote for visitors by highlighting that she was suspected, in some sources at least, of witchcraft. While Joan gets only a brief mention on the website for Leeds Castle and the guidebook, her household account from the castle's archives has featured in their displays, providing some physical link to her presence there.[3] English Heritage has written up a reasonable overview of Joan's life in their website for Pevensey, which explains her detention there and gives some context of her life before and after the accusation of treason or witchcraft.[4] Nottingham Castle also includes a mention of Joan in their online literature, particularly in the context of the mills in Brewhouse Yard and has used the idea of Joan as a potential witch for Halloween-inspired tie-ins for their blog.[5] Joan also physically featured in an event for the reopening of the castle during a set of performances from Theatre Design students at Nottingham Trent University in 2021, titled "Ghosts" which "brought to life six forgotten, denied, and unexpressed stories from Nottingham Castle's history".[6]

Objects connected to Joan, such as the Trinity Reliquary she gifted to Jean V or books that she once possessed, are kept safe in collections around the world, from the Louvre in Paris to the special collections of libraries such as the University of Manchester and Harvard University. Perhaps the best place to encounter Joan or where her presence is most physically evident is at her shared tomb with Henry IV in Canterbury Cathedral—here we can see the power of Diane Booton's notion of Joan being a "shaper of memory". While Joan was not able to shape popular memory in the way she might have wished to ensure that she would have a lasting legacy as one of the most renowned queens of the Middle Ages, her tomb forever represents the image that she wanted to endure—not as a "royal witch" but as an infanta of Navarre, duchess of Brittany, and queen of England.

While it is impossible to do complete justice to a life as long and complex as Joan of Navarre's in this short space, it is hoped that this biography—the first full-length scholarly treatment of her life—will start to raise awareness of this important yet overlooked royal woman. By reconsidering the intense political landscape of the Hundred Years War with Joan at the centre, instead of on the sidelines or in the footnotes, a new perspective has been offered which demonstrates Joan's deep connection to and involvement in the events of the period. By moving beyond what happened during her lifetime to consider her agency as an able and engaged administrator of a vast portfolio of lands on both sides of the Channel, which made her one of the most significant landholders in both England and Brittany, we can see not only Joan's economic acumen but her fierce defence of her rights and position—perhaps one of her most defining character traits. Through an examination of her networks of service, we can understand her relationships with those around her—who she trusted and the loyalty of those who served her, even when that meant following her to foreign lands or sharing her exile from court life. Finally, by thinking about the spaces she inhabited, the people and institutions she patronised, and the possessions she possessed and gifted to others, we have gained a greater understanding of her day-to-day life and what was important to her. Taken together, it is hoped that this work has begun to draw Joan of Navarre out from the shadows of history and back into the light where she belongs, and in so doing, encourage others not only to learn more about her but to seek out and bring to light the many other royal women like Joan whose stories also desperately need to be told.

Notes

1 For further discussion of this omission and the "invisible queenship" in the whole history cycle, see Kavita Mudan Finn and Lea Luecking Frost, "'Nothing Hath Begot my Something Grief': Invisible Queenship in Shakespeare's Second Tetraology," in *The Palgrave Handbook of Shakespeare's*

Queens, eds. Kavita Mudan Finn and Valerie Schutte (New York: Palgrave Macmillan, 2018), 227–49.

2 Jane Austen, *The History of England*, The British Library Add. MS 59874, 3.

3 Chrissie Charlton and Jessica Hodge, *Leeds Castle* (London: Scala, 2009).

4 Anon, "Joan of Navarre", *English Heritage: Pevensey Castle*, accessed 13 November 2021, https://www.english-heritage.org.uk/visit/places/pevensey-castle/history/joan-of-navarre/

5 Anon, "A Witch at Nottingham Castle?," *Nottingham Castle*, 25 October 2021, accessed 13 November 2021, https://www.nottinghamcastle.org.uk/a-witch-at-nottingham-castle/

6 Joan's story, called "The Invisible Queen," was performed by Justine Emma Moore with a costume designed by Mea Catherine Fenwick who researched the queen's life with support from Dr Natasha Hodgson in the History department, see Anon, "Theatre Design Students Work with Nottingham Castle as Part of its Landmark Re-opening," *Nottingham Trent University*, accessed 13 November 2021, https://www.ntu.ac.uk/about-us/news/news-articles/2021/05/theatre-design-students-work-with-nottingham-castle-as-part-of-its-landmark-re-opening

SELECTED BIBLIOGRAPHY

Primary sources: Manuscript and archival sources

Archival documents from The National Archives (Kew, London), Archives départmentales de Loire-Atlantique (Nantes), Archivo General de Navarra (Pamplona).

Austen, Jane. *The History of England.* BL Add. MS 59874.

"Account Book of the household of Joan of Navarre," 1420–21, University of Manchester John Rylands Collection Latin MS 238.

Anon. *The Pageants of Richard Beauchamp, Earl of Warwick* (late 15th century). BL Cotton MS Julius E IV/3.

Anon. *Bible historiale Moyenne complete* (late 14th century). BnF ms. Français 2.

Anon. (Durand de Champagne). *Le Livre qui est appellé le Miroer des dames, que fist ung Frere de l'ordre Saint François* (15th century). BnF ms Français 610.

Anon. *Missal for Selected Feasts (use of Sarum).* In Latin, illuminated manuscript on parchment, England (London), 1400–1425 (before 1423?). https://www.textmanuscripts.com/medieval/sarum-missal-141427.

Bugge, John. "Queen Joan. Primus compotus Johannis Bugge (Household Accounts 1427–28)." Society of Antiquaries SAL/MS/216.

Livius, Titus. *A Urbe condita,* translated into French by Pierre Bersuire (c. 1380). BnF ms Français, 269–272.

de Meun, Jean. *Le testament maistre Jehan de Mehun* (c. 1400). Houghton Library MS Typ 749, Harvard University.

"Response of Charles VI to agreement signed between Joan of Navarre, Olivier de Clisson and the Vicount of Rohan." Nantes Mediatheque ms 1695, no. 18, dated 22 Jan 1400.

"Wardrobe Book of Joan Queen of England, 9 Hen. 5," 1422, Leeds Castle Archives E4/1.

"Will of Margaret Beauchamp, countess of Warwick, 28 November 1406," in Register of Thomas Arundel, vol. 1, Lambeth Palace Library, f. 234v.

Printed primary sources

Amundesham, John. *Annales Monasterii S. Albani*. Vol. 1, edited by Henry Thomas Riley. London: Longmans Green and Co, 1870.

Anon. *A Chronicle of London from 1089–1483, Written in the Fifteenth Century*, edited by Sir Nicholas Harris Nicholas and Edward Tyrell. London: Longman, 1827.

Anon. *The Chronicles of London*. Introduction and notes by Charles L. Kingsford. Oxford: Clarendon Press, 1905.

Anon. *Chronique des quatre premiers Valois (1327–1393)*, edited by Siméon Luce. Paris: Jules Renouard, 1862.

Anon. *An English Chronicle 1377–1461: A New Edition*, edited by William Marx. Woodbridge: Boydell, 2003.

Anon. *English Coronation Records*, edited by Leopold G. Wickam Legg. Westminster: Archibald Constable & Co, 1901.

Anon. *Eulogium (historiarum sive temporis): Chronicon ab orbe condito usque ad annum Domini M.CCC.LXCI., a monacho quodam Malmesburiensi exaratum*. London: Longman, 1858.

Anon. *Le livre des trahisons de France envers la maison de Bourgogne*, edited by Joseph Kervyn de Lettenhove. Brussels: F. Hayez, 1873.

Anon. "A Northern Chronicle: 1399–1430." In *English Historical Literature in the Fifteenth Century*, edited by Charles Lethbridge Kingsford. Oxford: The Clarendon Press, 1913.

Anon. *A Catalogue of an Exhibition of the Philip Hofer Bequest in the Department of Printing and Graphic Arts*. Cambridge, MA: Harvard College Library, 1988.

Archives de Bretagne. *Lettres et Mandements de Jean V, Duc de Bretagne de 1402 à 1406*. Vol. IV. Introduction and notes by René Blanchard. Nantes: Société des Bibliophiles Bretons, 1895.

Archives de Bretagne. *Lettres et Mandements de Jean V, Duc de Bretagne de 1407 à 1419*. Vol. V. Introduction and notes by René Blanchard. Nantes: Société des Bibliophiles Bretons, 1890.

Archives de Bretagne. *Lettres et Mandements de Jean V, Duc de Bretagne de 1420 à 1431.* Vol. VI. Introduction and notes by René Blanchard. Nantes: Société des Bibliophiles Bretons, 1892.

Archives de Bretagne. *Lettres et Mandements de Jean V, Duc de Bretagne de 1431 à 1440.* Vol. VII. Introduction and notes by René Blanchard. Nantes: Société des Bibliophiles Bretons, 1895.

Archivo General de Navarra. *Catálogo de la Seccion de Comptos, Documentos.* Vol. VII: *Años 1368–1369*, edited by José Ramón Castro. Pamplona: Editorial Aramburu, 1954.

Archivo General de Navarra. *Catálogo de la Seccion de Comptos, Documentos.* Vol. XV: *Años 1384–1385*, edited by José Ramón Castro. Pamplona: Editorial Aramburu, 1956.

Archivo General de Navarra. *Catálogo de la Seccion de Comptos, Documentos.* Vol. XVI: *Años 1386–1387*, edited by José Ramón Castro. Pamplona: Editorial Aramburu, 1956.

Archivo General de Navarra. *Catálogo de la Seccion de Comptos, Documentos.* Vol. XVII: *Años 1388–1380*, edited by José Ramón Castro. Pamplona: Editorial Aramburu, 1956.

Archivo General de Navarra. *Catálogo de la Seccion de Comptos, Documentos.* Vol. XVIII: *Año 1391, Adiciones: 1341–1390*, edited by José Ramón Castro. Pamplona: Editorial Aramburu, 1956.

Archivo General de Navarra. *Catálogo de la Seccion de Comptos, Documentos.* Vol. XIX: *Año 1392*, edited by José Ramón Castro. Pamplona: Editorial Aramburu, 1957.

Archivo General de Navarra. *Catálogo de la Seccion de Comptos, Documentos.* Vol. XX: *Años 1393–1394*, edited by José Ramón Castro. Pamplona: Editorial Aramburu, 1957.

Archivo General de Navarra. *Catálogo de la Seccion de Comptos, Documentos.* Vol. XXI: *Años 1395–1396*, edited by José Ramón Castro. Pamplona: Editorial Aramburu, 1958.

Archivo General de Navarra. *Catálogo de la Seccion de Comptos, Documentos.* Vol. XXII: *Años 1397–1398*, edited by José Ramón Castro. Pamplona: Editorial Aramburu, 1958.

Archivo General de Navarra. *Catálogo de la Seccion de Comptos, Documentos.* Vol. XXIV: *Año 1401; Adiciones 1385–1400*, edited by José Ramón Castro. Pamplona: Editorial Aramburu, 1959.

Archivo General de Navarra. *Catálogo de la Seccion de Comptos, Documentos.* Vol. XXVII: *Años 1407–1408*, edited by José Ramón Castro. Pamplona: Editorial Aramburu, 1961.

Archivo General de Navarra. *Catálogo de la Seccion de Comptos, Documentos.* Vol. XXVIII: *Años 1409–1411*, edited by José Ramón Castro. Pamplona: Editorial Aramburu, 1961.

Archivo General de Navarra. *Catálogo de la Seccion de Comptos, Documentos.* Vol. XXX: *Año 1413*, edited by José Ramón Castro. Pamplona: Editorial Aramburu, 1962.

Archivo General de Navarra. *Catálogo de la Seccion de Comptos, Documentos.* Vol. XXXI: *Años 1414–1415*, edited by José Ramón Castro. Pamplona: Editorial Aramburu, 1963.

Archivo General de Navarra. *Catálogo de la Seccion de Comptos, Documentos.* Vol. XXXII: *Años 1416–1418*, edited by José Ramón Castro. Pamplona: Editorial Aramburu, 1963.

Archivo General de Navarra. *Catálogo de la Seccion de Comptos, Documentos.* Vol. XXXIII: *Años 1419–1421*, edited by José Ramón Castro. Pamplona: Editorial Aramburu, 1963.

Archivo General de Navarra. *Catálogo de la Seccion de Comptos, Documentos.* Vol. XXXV: *Año 1423*, edited by José Ramón Castro. Pamplona: Editorial Aramburu, 1964.

Archivo General de Navarra. *Catálogo de la Seccion de Comptos, Documentos.* Vol. XXXVI: *Años 1424–1425, Adiciones: 1330–1423*, edited by José Ramón Castro. Pamplona: Editorial Aramburu, 1964.

Archivo General de Navarra, *Catálogo de la Seccion de Comptos, Documentos.* Vol. XXXIX: *Año 1430*, edited by Florencio Idoate. Pamplona: Editorial Aramburu, 1965.

Archivo General de Navarra. *Catálogo de la Seccion de Comptos, Documentos.* Vol. XL: *Años 1431–1432, Adiciones 1406–1430*, edited by José Ramón Castro. Pamplona: Editorial Aramburu, 1965.

Archivo General de Navarra. *Catálogo de la Seccion de Comptos, Documentos.* Vol. XLI: *Años 1433–1434*, edited by José Ramón Castro. Pamplona: Editorial Aramburu, 1966.

Archivo General de Navarra. *Catálogo de la Seccion de Comptos, Documentos.* Vol. XLII: *Años 1435–1436, Adiciones 1331–1434*, edited by José Ramón Castro. Pamplona: Editorial Aramburu, 1966.

Archivo General de Navarra. *Catálogo de la Seccion de Comptos, Documentos.* Vol. L: *Años 1092–1618, Adiciones 1361–1412*, edited by Florencio Idoate. Pamplona: Editorial Aramburu, 1970.

Archivo General de Navarra, *Catálogo de la Seccion de Comptos, Registros*, Vol. LII: *Años 1365–1535*, edited by Florencio Idoate. Pamplona: Editorial Aramburu, 1974.

Austin, Thomas, ed. *Two Fifteenth Century Cookery Books; Harleian MS 279 (ab. 1430) and Harleian MS 4016 (ab. 1450) with extracts from Ashmole MS. 1429, Laud MA 533 and Douce MS 55.* London: Early English Text Society, 1888.

Bellaguet, Louis, ed. *Chronique du Religieux de Saint-Denys contenant le régne de Charles VI de 1380 a 1422.* Vol. I. Paris: Imprimerie de Crapelet, 1839.

Bellaguet, Louis, ed. *Chronique du religieux de Saint-Denys: contenant le règne de Charles VI, de 1380 à 1422.* Vol. III. Paris: Crapelet, 1841.

Bellaguet, Louis, ed. *Chronique du religieux de Saint-Denys: contenant le règne de Charles VI, de 1380 à 1422.* Vol. IV. Paris: Crapelet, 1842.

Bouchart, Alain. *Grandes Croniques de Bretaigne.* Vol. III, edited by Marie-Louise Auger, Gustave Jenneau, and Bernard Guenee. Paris: Editions du Centre National de la recherche scientifique, 1986.

de Cagny, Perceval. *Chroniques de Perceval de Cagny*, edited by H. Moranvillé. Paris: Librarie Renouard, 1902.

Calendar of Close Rolls, Henry IV: Volume 1, 1399–1402, edited by A.E. Stamp. London: His Majesty's Stationery Office, 1927. British History Online. Accessed November 17, 2021. http://www.british-history.ac.uk/cal-close-rolls/hen4/vol1.

Calendar of Close Rolls, Henry IV: Volume 2, 1402–1405, edited by A.E. Stamp. London: His Majesty's Stationery Office, 1929. British History Online. Accessed November 17, 2021. http://www.british-history.ac.uk/cal-close-rolls/hen4/vol2.

Calendar of Close Rolls, Henry IV: Volume 3, 1405–1409, edited by A.E. Stamp. London: His Majesty's Stationery Office, 1931. British History Online. Accessed November 17, 2021. http://www.british-history.ac.uk/cal-close-rolls/hen4/vol3.

Calendar of Close Rolls, Henry IV: Volume 4, 1409–1413, edited by A.E. Stamp. London: His Majesty's Stationery Office, 1932. British History Online. Accessed November 17, 2021. http://www.british-history.ac.uk/cal-close-rolls/hen4/vol4.

Calendar of Close Rolls, Henry V: Volume 1, 1413–1419, edited by A.E. Stamp. London: His Majesty's Stationery Office, 1929. British History Online. Aaccessed November 17, 2021. http://www.british-history.ac.uk/cal-close-rolls/hen5/vol1.

Calendar of Close Rolls, Henry V: Volume 2, 1419–1422, edited by A.E. Stamp. London: His Majesty's Stationery Office, 1932. British History Online. Accessed November 17, 2021. http://www.british-history.ac.uk/cal-close-rolls/hen5/vol2.

Calendar of Close Rolls, Henry VI: Volume 1, 1422–1429, edited by A.E. Stamp. London: His Majesty's Stationery Office, 1933. British History Online. Accessed November 17, 2021. http://www.british-history.ac.uk/cal-close-rolls/hen6/vol1.

Calendar of Close Rolls, Henry VI: Volume 2, 1429–1435, edited by A.E. Stamp. London: His Majesty's Stationery Office, 1933. British History

Online. Accessed November 17, 2021. http://www.british-history.ac.uk/cal-close-rolls/hen6/vol2.

Calendar of the Fine Rolls Preserved in the Public Record Office, Henry IV 1405–1413. Volume XIII. London: His Majesty's Stationery Office, 1933.

Calendar of the Fine Rolls Preserved in the Public Record Office, Henry V 1413–1422. Volume XIV. London: His Majesty's Stationery Office, 1934.

Calendar of Inquisitions Miscellaneous (Chancery) Preserved in the Public Record Office. Volume VII: *1399–1422*. London: Her Majesty's Stationery Office, 1957.

Calendar of Inquisitions Miscellaneous (Chancery) Preserved in the Public Record Office. Volume VIII: *1422–1485*. Woodbridge: Boydell, 2003.

Calendar of Papal Registers Relating to Great Britain and Ireland. Volume 5, *1398–1404*, edited by W.H. Bliss and J.A. Twemlow. London: His Majesty's Stationery Office, 1904. British History Online. Accessed November 27, 2021. http://www.british-history.ac.uk/cal-papal-registers/brit-ie/vol5.

Calendar of Papal Registers Relating to Great Britain and Ireland. Volume 6, *1404–1415*, edited by W.H. Bliss and J.A. Twemlow. London: His Majesty's Stationery Office, 1904. British History Online. Accessed November 25, 2021. http://www.british-history.ac.uk/cal-papal-registers/brit-ie/vol6.

Calendar of Papal Registers Relating to Great Britain and Ireland. Volume 7, *1417–1431*, edited by J.A. Twemlow. London: His Majesty's Stationery Office, 1906. British History Online. Accessed November 27, 2021. http://www.british-history.ac.uk/cal-papal-registers/brit-ie/vol7.

Calendar of Papal Registers Relating to Great Britain and Ireland. Volume 8, *1427–1447*, edited by J.A. Twemlow. London: His Majesty's Stationery Office, 1909. British History Online. Accessed November 27, 2021. http://www.british-history.ac.uk/cal-papal-registers/brit-ie/vol8.

Calendar of the Patent Rolls Preserved in the Public Record Office, Henry IV. Volume II, *1401–1405*. London: His Majesty's Stationery Office, 1905.

Calendar of the Patent Rolls Preserved in the Public Record Office, Henry IV. Volume III, *1405–1408*. London: His Majesty's Stationery Office, 1907.

Calendar of the Patent Rolls Preserved in the Public Record Office, Henry IV. Volume IV, *1408–1413*. London: His Majesty's Stationery Office, 1909.

Calendar of the Patent Rolls Preserved in the Public Record Office, Henry V. Volume I, *1413–16*. London: His Majesty's Stationery Office, 1910.

Calendar of the Patent Rolls Preserved in the Public Record Office, Henry V. Volume II, *1416–1422*. London: His Majesty's Stationery Office, 1911.

Calendar of the Patent Rolls Preserved in the Public Record Office, Henry VI. Volume I, *1422–1429*. London: His Majesty's Stationery Office, 1901.

Calendar of the Patent Rolls Preserved in the Public Record Office, Henry VI. Volume II, *1429–36*. London: His Majesty's Stationery Office, 1907.

Calendar of the Patent Rolls Preserved in the Public Record Office, Henry VI. Volume III, *1436–41*. London: His Majesty's Stationery Office, 1907.

Calendar of Signet Letters of Henry IV and Henry V (1399–1422), edited by J. L. Kirby. London: HMSO, 1978.

Cotgrave, Randle. *A French-English Dictionary*. London: Printed by W.H. for Luke Fawne, 1650.

Council of the London and Middlesex Archaeological Society. *A Catalogue of the Antiquities and Works of Art Exhibited at Ironmongers' Hall, London.* London: Harrison and Sons, 1869.

Crawford, Anne, ed. *Letters of the Queens of England.* Stroud: Sutton, 1997.

Curry, Anne, ed. *The Battle of Agincourt: Sources and Interpretations.* Woodbridge: Boydell, 2000.

Devon, Frederick, ed. *Issues of the Exchequer being a collection of payments made out of His Majesty's Revenue, from King Henry III to King Henry VI inclusive with an appendix.* London: John Murray, 1837.

d'Eugui, Garcia. *Crónica d'Espayña de Garcia de Eugui*, edited by Aengus Ward. Pamplona: Gobierno de Navarra, 1999.

Everett Wood, Mary Anne, ed. *Letters of Royal and Illustrious Ladies of Great Britain.* London: Henry Colburn, 1846.

Fabyan, Robert. *The Great Chronicle of London*, edited by A.H. Thomas and I.D. Thornley. London: Corporation and City of London, 1938.

Fasti Ecclesiae Anglicanae 1300–1541: Volume 1, *Lincoln Diocese*, edited by H.P.F. King. London: Institute of Historical Research 1962. British History Online. Accessed November 25, 2021. http://www.british-history.ac.uk/fasti-ecclesiae/1300-1541/vol1

fitz Nigel, Richard. *Dialogus de Scaccario (The Course of the Exchequer)*, edited and translated by Charles Johnson. Oxford: Clarendon Press, 1983.

Froissart, Jean. *Chronicles*, translated and edited by Geoffrey Brereton. London: Penguin Books, 1978.

Froissart, Jean. *Chronicles of England, France, Spain, and the adjoining countries, from the latter part of the reign of Edward II to the coronation of Henry IV, by Sir John Froissart.* Vol. 2, edited by Thomas Johnes. London: H.G. Bohn, 1852.

Gidden, Harry W., ed. *The sign manuals, and the letters patent of Southampton to 1422*, edited with introduction, notes, and index. Southampton: Cox and Sharland, 1916–1919.

Gough, Richard, and John Nichols, eds. *A Collection of All the Wills, Now Known to be Extant of the Kings and Queens of England, Princes and Princesses of Wales, and Every Branch of the Blood Royal: From the Reign of William the*

Conqueror to that of Henry the Seventh, Exclusive... With Explanatory Notes and a Glossary. London: J. Nichols, 1780.

Gregory, William. "Gregory's Chronicle: 1403–1419." In *The Historical Collections of a Citizen of London in the Fifteenth Century*, edited by James Gairdner, 103–128. London: Camden Society, 1876. British History Online. Accessed June 7, 2019. http://www.british-history.ac.uk/camden-record-soc/vol17/pp103-128.

Gruel, Guillaume. *Chronique d'Arthur de Richemont, Connetable de France, Duc de Bretagne (1393–1458)*, edited by Achille le Vavasseur. Paris: Librairie Renouard, 1890.

Hall, Edward. *Hall's Chronicle: Containing the history of England during the reign of Henry the Fourth and the succeeding monarchs*. London: J. Johnson et al., 1809.

Inquisitions and Assessments Relating to Feudal Aids, with Other Analogous Documents Preserved in the Public Record Office; A.D. 1284–1431. Volume VI. London: His Majesty's Stationery Office, 1920.

Inventaire Sommaire des Archives Communales antérieures à 1790 Vol. 1: *Ville de Nantes*. Nantes: Imprimerie du Commerce, 1888.

James, Colonel Sir Henry, ed. *Facsimiles of National Manuscripts from William the Conqueror to Queen Anne* part I. Southampton: Ordinance Survey Office, 1865.

Jones, Michael, ed. *Recueil des actes de Jean IV, duc de Bretagne*, Vol. II, nos. 431–1196 (1383–1399). Torquay: Devonshire Press, 1983.

Lobineau, Guy Alexis. *Histoire de Bretagne*. Vol. I. Paris: François Muguet, 1707.

Lobineau, Guy Alexis. *Histoire de Bretagne*. Vol. II. Paris: François Muguet, 1707.

Maurer, Helen, and B.M. Cron, eds. *The Letters of Margaret of Anjou*. Woodbridge: Boydell and Brewer, 2019.

Moliner, Auguste. *Les Sources de l'Histoire de France*. Paris: Alfonse Picard et Fils, 1904.

de Monstrelet, Enguerran. *La Chronique d'Enguerran de Monstrelet en deux livres avec pièces justificatives 1400–1444*. Vol. I, edited by L. Douët d'Arcq. Paris: Jules Renouard, 1857.

de Monstrelet, Enguerran. *La Chronique d'Enguerran de Monstrelet en deux livres avec pièces justificatives 1400–1444*. Vol. II, edited by L. Douët d'Arcq. Paris: Jules Renouard, 1858.

de Monstrelet, Enguerran. *La Chronique d'Enguerran de Monstrelet en deux livres avec pièces justificatives 1400–1444*. Vol. III, edited by L. Douët d'Arcq. Paris: Jules Renouard, 1859.

de Monstrelet, Enguerran. *La Chronique d'Enguerran de Monstrelet en deux livres avec pièces justificatives 1400–1444.* Vol. IV, edited by L. Douët d'Arcq. Paris: Jules Renouard, 1860.

de Monstrelet, Enguerran. *La Chronique d'Enguerran de Monstrelet en deux livres avec pièces justificatives 1400–1444.* Vol. V, edited by L. Douët d'Arcq. Paris: Jules Renouard, 1861.

Morice, Dom Hyacinthe. *Memoires pour servir de preuves a l'histoire ecclesiastique et civile de Bretagne.* Vol. I. Paris: Charles Osmont, 1742.

Morice, Dom Hyacinthe. *Memoires pour servir de preuves a l'histoire ecclesiastique et civile de Bretagne.* Vol. II. Paris: Charles Osmont, 1746.

Morice, Dom Hyacinthe. *Histoire ecclesiastique et civile de Bretagne.* Paris: De l'imprimerie de Delaguette, 1750.

Nicolas, Nicholas Harris, ed. *Proceedings and Ordinances of the Privy Council of England: 10 Richard II. MCCCLXXXVI to 11 Henry IV. MCCCCX.* Vol. 1. London: Eyre & Spottiswoode, 1834.

Nicolas, Nicholas Harris, ed. *Proceedings and Ordinances of the Privy Council of England: 12 Henry IV. MCCCCX to 10 Henry V MCCCCXXII.* Vol. 2. London: Eyre & Spottiswoode, 1834.

Nicolas, Nicholas Harris, ed. *Proceedings and Ordinances of the Privy Council of England: 1 Henry VI. MCCCCXXXII to 7 Henry VI MCCCCXXIX.* Vol. 3. London: Eyre & Spottiswoode, 1834.

Nicolas, Nicholas Harris, ed. *Proceedings and Ordinances of the Privy Council of England: 8 Henry VI MCCCCXXIX to 14 Henry VI MCCCCXXXVI.* Vol. 4. London: Eyre & Spottiswoode, 1835.

Nicolas, Nicholas Harris, ed. *Proceedings and Ordinances of the Privy Council of England: 15 Henry VI MCCCCXXXVI to 21 Henry VI MCCCCXLIII.* Vol. 5. London: Eyre & Spottiswoode, 1835.

Palgrave, Sir Francis, ed. *The Ancient Kalendars and Inventories of the Treasury of His Majesty's Exchequer.* Vol. II. London: Commissioners of the Public Records, 1836.

Parliament Rolls of Medieval England, edited by Chris Given-Wilson, Paul Brand, Seymour Phillips, Mark Ormrod, Geoffrey Martin, Anne Curry, and Rosemary Horrox. Woodbridge: Boydell, 2005. British History Online. Accessed November 17, 2021. http://www.british-history.ac.uk/no-series/parliament-rolls-medieval.

Perroy, Edouard, ed. *The Diplomatic Correspondence of Richard II.* London: Royal Historical Society, 1931.

Pope, John. "List of Rectors for the Parish of St. John the Baptist with St. Mary the Virgin, Devizes." Wiltshire OPC Project (2013). https://www.wiltshire-opc.org.uk/Items/Devizes/Devizes%20-%20Rectors%20List%201310-1960%20(St.%20Mary).pdf.

Prynne, William. *Aurum reginæ, or, A compendious tractate and chronological collection of records in the Tower and Court of Exchequer concerning queen-gold evidencing the quiddity, quantity, quality, antiquity, legality of this golden prerogative, duty, and revenue of the queen-consorts of England.* London: Thomas Ratcliffe, 1668.

Records of the Borough of Nottingham. Vol. II. Nottingham: Thomas Forman & Sons, 1882.

"Relation de l'ambassade de Gontier Col, secrétaire du roi de France, auprès de Jean VI, duc de Bretagne, en 1414." In *Bulletin du Comité Historique des Monuments Écrits de l'Histoire de France. Histoire-Sciences-Lettres* 4 (1853): 73–90.

Ruiz San Pedro, Maria Teresa, ed. *Fuentes documentales medievales del País Vasco. Archivo General de Navarra (1349–1387).* V. *Documentación Real de Carlos II (1368–1369).* Donostia: Eusko Ikaskuntza, 2003.

Rymer, Thomas, ed. *Foedera, conventiones, literae, et cujuscunque generis acta publica*... Vol. 3, part 2. London: Johannem Neulme, 1740.

Rymer's Foedera. Volume 8, edited by Thomas Rymer. London: Apud Joannem Neulme, 1739–1745. British History Online. Accessed November 17, 2021. http://www.british-history.ac.uk/rymer-foedera/vol8.

Rymer's Foedera. Volume 9, edited by Thomas Rymer. London: Apud Joannem Neulme, 1739–1745. British History Online. Accessed November 17, 2021. http://www.british-history.ac.uk/rymer-foedera/vol9.

Rymer's Foedera. Volume 10, edited by Thomas Rymer. London: Apud Joannem Neulme, 1739–1745. British History Online. Accessed November 17, 2021. http://www.british-history.ac.uk/rymer-foedera/vol10.

de Saint-André, Guillaume. *Chronique de l'État Breton,* edited by Jean-Michel Cauneau and Dominique Philippe. Rennes: Presses universitaires de Rennes, 2005.

de Sainte Marie, Pere Anselme. *Histoire généalogique et chronologique de la maison royal de France,* Vol. 1. Paris: Compagnie des Libraries, 1712, 220.

Secousse, Denis-François. *Recueil de pièces servant de preuves aux Mémoires sur les troubles excités en France par Charles II, dit le Mauvais.* Paris: Durand, 1755.

Stow, John. *The annales, or generall chronicle of England, begun first by maister Iohn Stow, and after him continued and augmented with matters forreyne, and domestique, anncient and moderne, vnto the ende of his present yeere 1614,* edited by Edmond Howes. London: T. Adams, 1615.

Strype, John. *A Survey of the Cities of London and Westminster* (1720). The Stuart London Project. https://www.dhi.ac.uk/strype/TransformServlet?page=book3_112.

The Gascon Rolls Project (1317–1468). http://www.gasconrolls.org/en/

Usk, Adam. *The Chronicle of Adam Usk 1377–1421*, translated and edited by Chris Given-Wilson. Oxford: Clarendon Press, 1997.

Walsingham, Thomas. *The Chronica Maiora of Thomas Walsingham 1376–1422*. Translated by David Prest and notes and introduction by James G. Clark. Woodbridge: Boydell, 2005.

de Waurin, Jehan (Jean de Wavrin). *Recueil des Croniques et Anchiennes Istories de la Grant Bretaigne, A Present Nomme Engleterre*. Vol. III, *From 1422–1431*, edited by William Hardy. London: Longman and Co., 1897.

Secondary sources

André, Patrick. "Le pavement médieval de Suscinio: bilan, conjectures et perspectives." In *Châteaux & Modes de vie au temps des ducs de Bretagne (XIIIe–XVIe siècle)*, edited by Alain Salamagne, Jean Kerhervé, and Gérard Danet, 283–288. Rennes: Presses universitaires de Rennes, 2012.

Anon. "Joan of Navarre." *English Heritage: Pevensey Castle*. Accessed November 13. 2021. https://www.english-heritage.org.uk/visit/places/pevensey-castle/history/joan-of-navarre/.

Anon. "Notes and News." *Bulletin of The John Rylands Library Manchester* 46, no. 1 (1963): 1.

Anon. (J.H.S.). "Tomb of King Henry IV in Canterbury Cathedral." *Archaeologia Cantiana* 8 (1872): 294–299.

Anon. "Theatre Design Students Work with Nottingham Castle as Part of its Landmark Re-opening." *Nottingham Trent University*. Accessed November 13, 2021. https://www.ntu.ac.uk/about-us/news/news-articles/2021/05/theatre-design-students-work-with-nottingham-castle-as-part-of-its-landmark re opening.

Anon. "A Witch at Nottingham Castle?" *Nottingham Castle*, 25 October 2021. Accessed November 13, 2021. https://www.nottinghamcastle.org.uk/a-witch-at-nottingham-castle/.

Arzoz Mendizábal, Íñigo. "Juana de Valois." In *Reinas de Navarre*, edited by Julia Pavon, 615–644. Madrid: Silex, 2014.

Balandre, Isabelle. "Reliquaire de l'Ordre du Saint-Esprit 'Tableau de la Trinité.'" The Louvre website. Accessed November 27, 2021. https://collections.louvre.fr/en/ark:/53355/cl010111574.

Barber, Richard. *Magnificence: Princely Splendour in the Middle Ages*. Woodbridge: Boydell, 2020.

Barker, Jessica. *Stone Fidelity: Marriage and Emotion in Medieval Tomb Sculpture*. Woodbridge: Boydell, 2020.

Beer, Michelle. *Queenship at the Renaissance Courts of Britain: Catherine of Aragon and Margaret Tudor, 1503–1533*. Woodbridge: Royal Historical Society, 2018.

Beer, Michelle. "The RSJ Article Prize Winner 2019: A Queenly Affinity? Catherine of Aragon's Estates and Henry VIII's Great Matter." *Royal Studies Journal* 6, no. 2 (2019): 5–25. DOI: 10.21039/rsj.223.

Bent, Margaret. "Dunstable (Dunstable), John." *Oxford Dictionary of National Biography Online*, 25 May 2006. 10.1093/ref:odnb/8286.

Benz, Lisa. *Three Medieval Queens: Queenship and the Crown in Fourteenth-century England*. New York: Palgrave Macmillan, 2012.

Bevan, Bryan. *Henry IV*. London: Rubicon, 1994.

Booton, Diane E. "Commemorating Duke John IV of Brittany in Ritual and Image." *Nottingham Medieval Studies* 59 (2015): 157–186.

de la Borderie, Arthur. "La jeunesse de Jean V, duc de Bretagne." *Revue de Bretagne de Vendee et d'Anjou* 23 (Mar 1900): 161–186.

Bothwell, James. "An Emotional Pragmatism: Edward III and Death." In *Monarchy, State and Political Culture in Late Medieval England: Essays in Honour of W. Mark Ormrod*, edited by Craig Taylor and Gwilym Dodd, 39–70. York: York Medieval Press, 2020.

Bourdeaut, A. "Gilles de Bretagne-entre la France et l'Angleterre—les causes et les Auteurs du drame." *Memoires de la Société d'Histoire et de l'Archaelogie de Bretagne* 1 (1920): 53–145.

Boulaire, Alain. *Les Rohan "Roi ne puts, duc ne daigne, Rohan suis"*. Paris: Editions France-Empire, 2001.

Brondarbit, Alexander. "Review of Christopher Given-Wilson, Henry IV (New Haven, CT: Yale University Press, 2016)." *Royal Studies Journal* 4, no. 2 (2017): 247–49.

Brown, R. Allen, H.M. Colvin, and A.J. Taylor, eds. *History of the King's Works*. Vol. I *The Middle Ages*. London: HMSO, 1963.

Brown, R. Allen, H.M. Colvin, and A.J. Taylor, eds. *History of the King's Works*. Vol. II *The Middle Ages*. London: HMSO, 1963.

Brundage, James A. "Widows and Remarriage: Moral Conflicts and their Resolution in Classical Canon Law." In *Wife and Widow in Medieval England*, edited by Sue Sheridan Walker, 17–32. Ann Arbor: University of Michigan Press, 1993.

Buettner, Brigitte. "Past Presents: New Year's Gifts at the Valois Court, ca. 1400." *Art Bulletin* 83 (2001): 598–625.

Carlton Williams, E. *My Lord of Bedford, 1389–1435*. London: Longmans Green, 1963.

Carmi Parsons, John. "'Never was a body buried in England with such solemnity and honour': The Burials and Posthumous Commemoration of English Queens to 1500." In *Queens and Queenship in Medieval Europe*, edited by Anne Duggan, 317–338. Woodbridge: Boydell, 2002.

Carmi Parsons, John. "The Pregnant Queen as Counsellor and the Medieval Construction of Motherhood." In *Medieval Mothering*, edited by John Carmi Parsons and Bonnie Wheeler, 39–63. New York: Garland, 1996.

Carmi Parsons, John. "Ritual and Symbol in the English Medieval Queenship to 1500." In *Women and Sovereignty*, edited by Louise Olga Fradenburg, 60–77. Edinburgh: Edinburgh University Press, 1992.

Carpenter, Christine. *The Wars of the Roses: Politics and the Constitution in England*. Cambridge: Cambridge University Press, 1997.

Castor, Helen. *The King, the Crown, and the Duchy of Lancaster: Public Authority and Private Power, 1399–1461*. Oxford: Oxford University Press, 2000.

Carrasco Perez, Juan. "Fiscalidad y circulación moneta en el Reino de Navarra: La dote de la infanta Juana, duquesa de Bretaña." *Anuario de Estudios Medievales* 22 (1992): 641–664.

Carrasco Perez, Juan. "Le Royaume de Navarre et Le duché de Bretagne au cours du dernier tiers du XIVe siècle: politique matrimoniale et circulation monétaire." In *1491: La Bretagne, terre d'Europe*, edited by Jean Kerhervé and Tanguy Daniel, 205–221. Brest: Centre de recherche bretonne et celtique, 1992.

Cassard, Jean-Christophe. "Suscinio et les chasses des ducs de Bretagne." In *Châteaux & Modes de vie au temps des ducs de Bretagne (XIIIe–XVIe siècle)*, edited by Alain Salamagne, Jean Kerhervé, and Gérard Danet, 121–149. Rennes: Presses universitaires de Rennes, 2012.

Casset, Marie. "Manoirs de plaisance des ducs de Bretagne XIIIe–XVe siècle." In *Châteaux & Modes de vie au temps des ducs de Bretagne (XIIIe–XVIe siècle)*, edited by Alain Salamagne, Jean Kerhervé, and Gérard Danet, 161–176. Rennes: Presses universitaires de Rennes, 2012.

Castañeda y Alcover, Vicente. "El Condado de Beaumont-le-Roger." *Revista de Archivos, Bibliotecas y Museos* 88 (1926): 232–239.

Cazilhac, Jean-Marc. *Jeanne d'Evreux, Blanche de Navarre: Deux reines de France, deux douairieres durante la Guerre de Cent ans*. Paris: L'Harmattan, 2010.

Chapman Hamilton, Tracy, and Mariah Proctor-Tiffany, eds. *Moving Women, Moving Objects (400–1500)*. Leiden: Brill, 2019.

Charlton, Chrissie, and Jessica Hodge. *Leeds Castle*. London: Scala, 2009.

Charon, Philippe. "Jeanne de Valois, reine de Navarre et comtés d'Evreux (1343–1373)." *En la España Medieval* 32 (2009): 7–50.

Collette, Carolyn P. *Performing Polity: Women and Agency in the Anglo-French Tradition, 1385–1620*. Turnhout: Brepols, 2006.

Contamine, Philippe. "Bretagne et France a la fin du Moyen Age: le temps de Jean V, de Charles VII et de Jeanne d'Arc." *Bulletin de la Societe Archeologique et Historique de Nantes et de Loire-Atlantique* 127 (1991): 71–86.

Cook, Petronelle. *Queen Consorts of England: The Power behind the Throne.* New York: Margot Arnold, 1993.

Copy, Jean-Yves. *Art, Société et Politique au temps des Ducs de Bretagne; Les gisants haut-Bretons.* Paris: Aux Amateurs de Livres, 1986.

Copy, Jean-Yves. "Du nouveau sure la couronne ducale bretonne: le temoignage des tombeaux." *Memoires de la Societe d'Histoire et d'Archeologie de Bretagne* 59 (1982): 171–191.

Cornette, Joel. *Histoire de la Bretagne et des Bretons,* Vol. 1 *Des ages obscurs au regne de Louis XIV.* Paris: Editions du Seuil, 2005.

Crawford, Anne. "The King's Burden?—the Consequences of Royal Marriage in Fifteenth-century England." In *Patronage, the Crown and the Provinces in Later Medieval England,* edited by Ralph A. Griffiths, 33–56. Gloucester: Alan Sutton, 1981.

Crawford, Anne. "The Queen's Council in the Middle Ages." *English Historical Review* 116, no. 469 (2001): 1193–1211.

Currie, Elizabeth. *Fashion and Masculinity in Renaissance Florence.* London: Bloomsbury, 2016.

Curry, Anne. *The Hundred Years War.* Basingstoke: Palgrave Macmillan, 2003.

Deceneux, Marc. "Le chateau de l'Hermine a Vannes: Residence des Ducs de Bretagne." *Association Bretonne* 87 (1978): 58–62.

Delisle, Léopold. "Notice sur un psautier du XIIIe siècle appartenant au comte de Crawford." *Bibliothèque de l'école des chartes* 58 (1897): 381–393.

Drayton, Michael. "The Battaile of Agincourt (1627)." In *The Battle of Agincourt: Sources and Interpretations,* edited by Anne Curry, 326–28. Woodbridge: Boydell, 2000.

Dressler, Rachel. "Identity, Status and Material: Medieval Alabaster Effigies in England." *Peregrinations: Journal of Medieval Art and Architecture* 5, no. 2 (2015): 65–96.

Dunn, Caroline. "All the Queen's Ladies? Philippa of Hainault's Female Attendants." *Medieval Prosopography* 31 (2016): 171–206.

Dunn, Caroline. "Serving Isabella of France: From Queen Consort to Dowager Queen." In *Elite and Royal Households in Medieval and Early Modern Europe,* edited by Theresa Earenfight, 169–201. Leiden: Brill, 2018.

Emery, Anthony. *Seats of Power in Europe During the Hundred Years War: An Architectural Study from 1330–1480.* Oxford: Oxbow, 2016.

Evans, Kasey. *Colonial Virtue: The Mobility of Temperance in Renaissance England.* Toronto: University of Toronto Press, 2012.

Evans, Michael. *The Death of Kings: Royal Deaths in Medieval England.* London: Hambledon Continum, 2007.

Finch, Julia. "Of Movement, Monarchs, and Manuscripts: The Case for Jeanne II of Navarre's Picture Bible as a Geopolitical Bridge between

Paris and Pamplona." In *Moving Women, Moving Objects (400–1500)*, edited by Tracy Chapman Hamilton and Mariah Proctor-Tiffany, 181–204. Leiden: Brill, 2019.

Fonssagrives, E. *Les Trois femmes de Jean IV; conference donnée à la Société Polymathique du Morbihan le 10 Avril 1923.* Vannes: Imprimerie du Commerce, 1923.

García Arancon, Maria Raquel. "Carlos II de Navarra: El circulo familiar." *Principe de Viana* 48 (1987): 569–608.

Gasche, Etienne. *Petite Histoire des duchesses de Bretagne.* Fouesnant: Yoran Embanner, 2011.

Geaman, Kristen. *Anne of Bohemia.* London: Routledge, 2022.

Geaman, Kristen. "Queen's Gold and Intercession: The Case of Eleanor of Aquitaine." *Medieval Feminist Forum* 46, no. 2 (2010): 10–33.

Gillespie, James L. "Ladies of the Fraternity of Saint George and of the Society of the Garter." *Albion* 17, no. 3 (1985): 269–271.

Given-Wilson, Chris. *Henry IV.* New Haven, CT: Yale University Press, 2016.

Given-Wilson, Chris. *The Royal Household and the King's Affinity: Service, Politics and Finance in England 1360–1413.* New Haven, CT: Yale University Press, 1986.

Goodman, A.W. *The Marriage of Henry IV and Joan of Navarre in the Cathedral Church of S. Swithun Winchester, Wednesday, 7 Feb. 1403* (Winchester: Warren and Son, 1934).

Graham-Goering, Erika. *Princely Power in Late Medieval France: Jeanne de Penthièvre and the War for Brittany.* Cambridge: Cambridge University Press, 2020.

Green, D.H. *Women Readers in the Middle Ages.* Cambridge: Cambridge University Press, 2007.

Griffiths, Ralph A. "The Trial of Eleanor Cobham: An Episode in the fall of Duke Humphrey of Gloucester." *Bulletin of the John Rylands Library* 51 (1969): 381–399.

Groag Bell, Susan. "Medieval Women Book Owners: Arbiters of Lay Piety and Ambassadors of Culture." *Signs* 7, no. 4 (1982): 742–768.

Grummit, David. "Sturmy, Sir William." *Oxford Dictionary of National Biography Online*, 28 September 2006. 10.1093/ref:odnb/92978.

Hamilton, Andrew. *Nottingham's Royal Castle and Ducal Palace.* Nottingham: Nottingham Civic Society, 1991.

de Hamel, Christopher. *Meetings with Remarkable Manuscripts.* London: Penguin, 2016.

Hanawalt, Barbara A. "Widows." In *The Cambridge Companion to Medieval Women's Writing*, edited by Carolyn Dinshaw and David Wallace, 58–69.

Cambridge Companions to Literature. Cambridge: Cambridge University Press, 2003.

Hand, Joni M. *Women, Manuscripts and Identity in Northern Europe, 1350–1550.* Aldershot: Ashgate, 2013.

Henneman, John Bell. *Olivier de Clisson and Political Society in France under Charles V and Charles VI.* Philadelphia: University of Pennsylvania Press, 1996.

Hibbert, Christopher, Ben Weinreb, Julia Keay, and John Keay, eds. *The London Encyclopaedia.* 3rd ed. London: Pan Macmillan, 2011.

Hilton, Lisa. *Queens Consort; England's Medieval Queens.* London: Phoenix, 2009.

Hollman, Gemma. *Royal Witches: From Joan of Navarre to Elizabeth Woodville.* Cheltenham: The History Press, 2019.

Horrox, Rosemary. "Edward [Edward of Langley, Edward of York], second duke of York (c. 1373–1415), magnate." *Oxford Dictionary of National Biography*, 23 Sep. 2004. Accessed November 20, 2021. 10.1093/ref:odnb/22356.

Howitt, Mary. *Biographical Sketches of the Queens of England.* London: Henry Bohn, 1851.

Hutchinson, Harold F. *Henry V.* London: Eyre and Spottiswoode, 1967.

de Jaurgain, Jean. "Les Beaumont-Navarre: Notes historiques et généalogiques." *Revista internacional de los estudios vascos (RIEV)* 3, no. 1 (1909): 46–62.

Johnstone, Hilda. "The Queen's Household." In *The English Government at Work, 1327–1336*, Vol. 1: *Central and Prerogative Administration*, edited by James F. Willard and William A. Morris, 250–299. Cambridge, MA: Mediaeval Academy of America, 1940.

Jones, Michael. "Between France and England: Jeanne de Navarre, Duchess of Brittany and Queen of England (1386–1437)." In *Between France and England: Politics, Power and Society in Late Medieval Brittany*, 1–23. Aldershot: Variorum, 2003.

Jones, Michael. *Ducal Brittany 1364–1399: Relations with England and France during the Reign of Duke John V.* Oxford: Oxford University Press, 1970.

Jones, Michael. "Dukes, Nobles and the Court in Late Medieval Brittany." In *Noblesse et États Princiers en Italie et en France au XVe siècle*, edited by Marco Gentile and Pierre Savy, 253–285. Rome: Ecole Francaise de Rome, 2009.

Jones, Michael. "'En son habit royal': Le Duc de Bretagne et son image vers la fin du Moyen Âge." In *Representation, Pouvoir et Royaulté*, edited by Joël Blanchard, 253–278. Paris: Picard, 1995.

Jones, Michael. "Jean IV et le pays de Retz: l'exercise et les limites du pouvoir ducal a la fin du XIVe siècle." In *Echanges et pouvoirs au pays de Retz (Actes du colloque a Machecoul 14 Avril 2007)*, 31–41. La Bernerie-en-Retz: Societe des Historiens du Pays de Retz, 2008.

Jones, Michael. "Marguerite de Clisson, comets de Penthievre et l'exercise du pouvoir." *In Femmes de pouvoir, femmes politiques durant les derniers siècles du Moyen Âge et au cours de la premiere Renaissance*, edited by Éric Bousmar, Jonathan Dumont, Alain Marchandisse, and Bertrand Schnerb, 349–368. Brussels: de Boeck, 2012.

Jones, Michael. "Les origines de l'Ordre de l'Hermine et son histoire sous les ducs Jean IV et Jean V." In *Des chevaliers de la Table ronde à l'Ordre de l'Hermine, Colloque à Rennes 27 Sept 2008*, 75–81. Vannes: Institut Culturel de Bretagne, 2009.

Jones, Michael, ed. *Le premier inventaire du tresor des chartes des ducs de Bretagne (1395); Herve Le Grant et les origines du Chronicon Briocense.* Bannalec: Imprimerie Regionale, 2007.

Jones, Michael. "The Rituals and Significance of Ducal Civic Entries in Late Medieval Brittany." *Journal of Medieval History* 29 (2003): 287–314.

Jones, Michael. "Le voyage de Pierre de Lesnerac en Navarre, 1386." In *The Creation of Brittany: A Late Medieval State*, 175–196. London: Hambledon, 1988.

Jurkowski, Maureen. "Lancastrian Royal Service, Lollardy and Forgery: The Career of Thomas Tykill." In *Crown, Government and People in the Fifteenth Century*, edited by Rowena E. Archer, 33–52. Stroud: Sutton, 1995.

Keane, Marguerite. "Louis IX, Louis X, Louis of Navarre: Family Ties and Political Ideology in the Hours of Jeanne of Navarre." *Visual Resources* 20, no. 2–3 (2004): 237–252.

Keane, Marguerite. *Material Culture and Queenship in 14th-Century France: The Testament of Blanche of Navarre (1331–1398).* Leiden: Brill, 2016.

Kennedy, Maev. "Henry V's Funeral Shield on Show." *The Guardian*, UK News (Museums/Higher Education/Arts), 22 September 2003. https://www.theguardian.com/uk/2003/sep/22/artsandhumanities.arts.

Kerhervé, Jean. "Arthur de Richemont, connetable et duc, Entre guerre et politique, dans la France du XVe siècle." In *2000 Ans d'Histoire de Vannes*, 95–120. Vannes: Archives Municipales, 1993.

Kerhervé, Jean. *L'état Breton aux 14e et 15e siècles; Les Ducs, l'Argent et les Hommes.* 2 vols. Paris: Editeur Maloine, 1987.

de Kersauson de Pennendreff, J. *L'episcopat Nantais a travers les siècles.* Vannes: Lafoyle, 1892.

Kightly, Charles. "Tyndale, Robert of Devizes, Wiltshire." In *The History of Parliament: the House of Commons 1386–1421*, edited by J.S. Roskell, L. Clark, and C. Rawcliffe (1993). http://www.historyofparliamentonline.org/volume/1386–1421/member/tyndale-robert.

Kirby, J.L. *Henry IV of England*. London: Constable, 1970.

Knowlson, George Akenhead. *Jean V, duc de Bretagne et l'Angleterre 1399–1442*. Cambridge: W. Heffer & Sons Ltd, 1964.

Krochalis, Jeanne E. "The Books and Reading of Henry V and His Circle." *The Chaucer Review* 23, no. 1 (1988): 50–77.

Lacarra, Jose Maria. *Historia Politica del Reino de Navarra desde sus origenes hasta su incorporacion a Castilla*. Vol. 3. Pamplona: Editorial Aranzadi, 1973.

Lancelott, Francis. *The Queens of England and their Times from Matilda, Queen of William the Conqueror to Adelaide, Queen of William the Fourth*. Vol. 1. New York: D. Appleton, 1859.

Lacey, Helen. *The Royal Pardon: Access to Mercy in Fourteenth-Century England*. York: York Medieval Press, 2009.

Lawrance, Hannah. *Historical Memoirs of the Queens of England, from the Commencement of the Twelfth Century*. Vol. 2. London: Edward Moxon, 1840.

Laynesmith, J.L. *The Last Medieval Queens: English Queenship 1445–1503*. Oxford: Oxford University Press, 2004.

Leguay, Jean-Pierre. *Histoire de Vannes et de sa Region*. Toulouse: Privat, 1988.

Leguay, Jean-Pierre, and Herve Martin, eds. *Fastes et malheurs de la Bretagne ducale 1213–1532*. Rennes: Ouest France, 1982.

Leroy, Béatrice. "Neutralité ou double jeu? Le rôle du royaume de Navarre dans les relations internationales de la fin du XIVe siècle et du début de XVe siècle." In *Terres et Hommes du Sud*, edited by Christian Desplat, 487–500. Biarritz: J&D Editions, 1992.

Lethbridge Kingsford, Charles, ed. *English Historical Literature in the Fifteenth Century*. Oxford: Clarendon Press, 1913.

Lightbown, Ronald W. *Mediaeval European Jewellery with a Catalogue of the Collection in the Victoria & Albert Museum*. London: Victoria and Albert Museum, 1992.

de Lisle du Drenuc, P. *Les Tombeaux des Ducs de Bretagne*. Vannes: Lafolye, 1894.

Lutkin, Jessica. "Luxury and Display in Silver and Gold at the Court of Henry IV." In *English and Continental Perspectives: The Fifteenth Century* 9, edited by Linda Clark, 155–178. Woodbridge: Boydell, 2010.

MacGregor, Patricia, and Barry Stapleton. *Odiham Castle 1200–1500: Castle and Community*. Gloucester: Alan Sutton, 1982.

Malden, H.E., ed. *A History of the County of Surrey*: Vol. 2. London: Victoria County History, 1967.

Markale, Jean. *Les Grandes Heures de la Bretagne*. Paris: Pygmalion, 2008.

Martin Duque, Angel J. "Monarcas y Cortes Itinerantes en el Reino de Navarra." In *Viajeros, Peregrinos, Mercadores en el Occidente Medieval, XVIII Semana de Estudios Medievales*, 245–270. Pamplona: Gobierno de Navarra, 1992.

de la Martinière, J. "Un grand Chancelier de Bretagne-Jean de Malestroit." *Memoires de la Société d'Histoire et d'Archaeologie de Bretagne* 1 (1920): 9–52.

McIntosh, Marjorie Keniston. *Autonomy and Community: The Royal Manor of Havering, 1200–1500*. Cambridge: Cambridge University Press, 2002.

McKendrick, Scot. "A European Heritage: Books of Continental Origin Collected by the English Royal Family from Edward III to Henry VIII." In *Royal Manuscripts: The Genius of Illumination*, edited by Scot McKendrick, John Lowden, and Kathleen Doyle, 42–65. London: British Library, 2011.

McLaren, Mary-Rose. *The London Chronicles of the Fifteenth Century*. London: D.S. Brewer, 2002.

McNiven, Peter. "The King's Needs." In *Heresy and Politics in the Reign of Henry IV: The Burning of John Badby*, 158–184. Woodbridge: Boydell, 1987.

McNiven, Peter. "Prince Henry and the English Political Crisis of 1412." *History* 65, no. 213 (1980): 1–16.

McNiven, Peter. "The Problem of Henry IV's Health." *English Historical Review* 100, no. 397 (1985): 747–772.

Mews, Constant J. "The *Speculum dominarum (Miroir des dames)* and Transformations of the Literature of Instruction for Women in the Early Fourteenth Century." In *Virtue Ethics for Women, 1250–1500*, edited by Karen Green and Constant J. Mews, 13–30. New York: Springer, 2011.

Milner, John. "The English Commitment to the 1412 Expedition to France." In *The Fifteenth Century XI: Concerns and Preoccupations*, edited by Linda Clark, 9–23. Woodbridge: Boydell, 2012.

Milner, John. "The English Enterprise in France, 1412–13." In *Trade, Devotion and Governance: Papers in Later Medieval History*, edited by D.J. Clayton, R.G. Davies, and Peter McNiven, 80–101. Stroud: Sutton, 1994.

Miolo, Laure. "Medieval Spin-Offs of the Roman de la Rose." *Medieval Manuscripts Blog*, British Library, 9 January 2017. https://blogs.bl.uk/digitisedmanuscripts/2017/01/medieval-spin-offs-of-the-roman-de-la-rose.html.

Mirot, Léon. "Études lucquoises, Galvano Trenta et les joyaux de la Couronne." *Bibliothèque de l'École des chartes* 101 (1940): 116–156.

Mortimer, Ian. *The Fears of Henry IV; The Life of England's Self-Made King*. London: Vintage, 2008.

Mortimer, Ian. *1415: Henry V's Year of Glory*. London: Bodley Head, 2009.

Mudan Finn, Kavita, and Lea Luecking Frost. "'Nothing Hath Begot my Something Grief': Invisible Queenship in Shakespeare's Second Tetraology." In *The Palgrave Handbook of Shakespeare's Queens*, edited by Kavita Mudan Finn and Valerie Schutte, 227–249. New York: Palgrave Macmillan, 2018.

Munby, Lionel M., ed. *The History of Kings Langley*. Kings Langley: Worker's Educational Association, 1963.

Musson, Anthony. "Queenship, Lordship and Petitioning in Late Medieval England." In *Medieval Petitions: Grace and Grievance*, edited by W. Mark Ormrod, Gwilym Dodd, and Anthony Musson, 156–172. Woodbridge: York Medieval Press, 2009.

Musson, Anthony, and Edward Powell, eds. *Crime, Law and Society in the Later Middle Ages*. Manchester: Manchester University Press, 2013.

Myers, A.R. "The Captivity of a Royal Witch: The Household Accounts of Queen Joan of Navarre, 1419–21." *Bulletin of the John Rylands Library* 24, no. 2 (1940): 263–284.

Myers, A.R. *Crown, Household, and Parliament in Fifteenth Century England*. London: Bloomsbury Academic, 1985.

Narbona Cárceles, María. "La actividad musical en la corte de Carlos III de Navarra, 1387–1425: mecenazgo o estrategia politica?" *Principe de Viana* 67, no. 238 (2006): 313–331.

Narbona Cárceles, María. "Les bâtards royaux et la nouvelle noblesse de sang de Navarre (fin XIVe siècle – début XVe siècle)." *Revue du Nord* 31 (2015): 421–438.

Narbona Cárceles, María. *La Corte de Carlos III el Noble, rey de Navarra: espacio domestico y escenario del poder, 1376–1415*. Pamplona: EUNSA, 2006.

Narbona Cárceles, María. "La 'Discreción hermosa': Blanca de Navarra, reina de Francia (1331?–1398). Una dama al servicio de su linaje." In *La dama en la corte bajomedieval*, edited by Martí Aurell, 77–118. Pamplona: EUNSA, 2001.

Narbona Cárceles, María. "Leonor de Trastámara." In *Reinas de Navarra*, edited by Julia Pavón, 645–680. Madrid: Silex, 2014.

Narbona Cárceles, María. "Woman at Court: A Prosopographic Study of the Court of Carlos III of Navarre (1387–1425)." *Medieval Prosopography* 22 (2001): 31–64.

Ongay, Nelly. "La boda de la infanta Juana con el duque Bretón Juan IV (1386). Las relaciones diplomáticas con Carlos II Evreux." *Estudios de Historia* 20 (2018): 141–152.

Ongay, Nelly. "De Evreux a Olite: la condesa de Foix y su viaje de regreso de Francia." *Príncipe de Viana* 67, no. 239 (2006): 873–900.

Ongay, Nelly. "El Hostal de la Infanta Maria (1365–66)." *Principe de Viana* 64 (2003): 127–158.

Ongay, Nelly. "Testamento y exequias de Carlos II de Navarra." *Arqueologia, historia y viajes sobre el mundo medieval* 25 (2008): 72–82.

Ongay Gambarte, Nelly. "Notas Sobre la Vida Cotidiana de las Infantas Reales en los 'Hospitales' del Reino de Navarra (1365–1400): Alimentos, Vestidos, Religiosidad y Viajes." *Estudios de Historia de España* 17, no. 1 (2015): 49–74.

Ormrod, W. Mark. "Henry V and the English Taxpayer." In *Henry V: New Interpretations*, edited by Gwilym Dodd, 187–216. York: York Medieval Press, 2013.

Ormrod, W. Mark, Bart Lambert, and Jonathan Mackman, eds. *Immigrant England 1300–1550*. Manchester: Manchester University Press, 2019.

Page, William, and J. Horace Round, eds. *A History of the County of Essex*: Vol. 2. London: Victoria County History, 1907.

Palmer, J.J.N. "The Background to Richard II's Marriage to Isabel of France (1396)." *Bulletin of the Institute of Historical Research* 44 (1971): 1–17.

Petrina, Alessandra. *Cultural Politics in 15th century England: The Case of Humphrey, Duke of Gloucester*. Leiden: Brill, 2004.

Plaisse, André. *Charles, dit Le Mauvais, Comte d'Evreux, Roi de Navarre, Capitaine de Paris*. Evreux: Société Libre de L'Eure, 1972.

Planiol, Marcel. *Histoire des Institutions de la Bretagne*, Vol. III. Mayenne: Association pour la publication du manuscrit de M. Planiol, 1981.

Poupart, Jeanne-Marie. "Un mariage Anglo-Breton au XVe siècle." *Nouvelle Revue de Bretagne* 2 (1951): 81–91.

Priestley, John. *Eltham Palace*. Stroud: History Press, 2013.

Proctor-Tiffany, Mariah. *Medieval Art in Motion: The Inventory and Gift-Giving of Queen Clémence de Hongrie*. University Park, PA: Penn State University Press, 2019.

Ramírez Vaquero, Eloísa. "Carlos II. La Nobleza." *Principe de Viana* 48 (1987): 645–656.

Ramírez Vaquero, Eloísa. *Carlos III, rey de Navarra, Principe de sangre Valois (1387–1425)*. Gijon: Ediciones Trea, 2007.

Ramírez Vaquero, Eloísa. "Estrategias diplomáticas del rey de Navarra en el tránsito al siglo XV." In *Guerra y Diplomacia en la Europa Occidental: 1280–1480 XXXI Semana de Estudios Medievales*, edited by Miguel Angel Ladero Quesada, 373–421. Pamplona: Gobierno de Navarra, 2005.

Rawcliffe, Carole. *The Staffords, Earls of Stafford and Dukes of Buckingham, 1394–1521*. Cambridge: Cambridge University Press, 1978.

Rawcliffe, Carole. "Norbury, John (d.1414), of Hoddesdon and Little Berkhampstead, Herts." In *The History of Parliament: the House of Commons 1386–1421*, edited by J.S. Roskell, L. Clark, and C. Rawcliffe (1993). http://www.historyofparliamentonline.org/volume/1386-1421/member/norbury-john-1414.

Richardson, Amanda. "Beyond the Castle Gate: The Role of Medieval Landscapes in Constructions of English Medieval Kingship and Queenship." *Concilium medii aevi* 14 (2011): 35–53.

Rickard, John. *The Castle Community; The Personnel of English and Welsh Castles, 1272–1422*. Woodbridge: Boydell, 2002.

Rohr, Zita Eva. *Yolande of Aragon (1381–1442) Family and Power: The Reverse of the Tapestry*. New York: Palgrave Macmillan, 2016.

Rollason, David. *The Power of Place: Rulers and their Palaces, Landscapes, Cities and Holy Places*. Princeton, NJ: Princeton University Press, 2016.

Roskell, J.S., and Charles Kightly. "Sturmy (Esturmy), Sir William (c. 1356–1427) of Wolf Hall in Great Bedwyn, Wilts and Elvetham, Hants." In *The History of Parliament: the House of Commons 1386–1421*, edited by J.S. Roskell, L. Clark, and C. Rawcliffe (1993). http://www.historyofparliamentonline.org/volume/1386-1421/member/sturmy-%28esturmy%29-sir-william-1356-1427.

Ross, James. "Seditious Activities: The Conspiracy of Maud de Vere, Countess of Oxford, 1403–4." In *The Fifteenth Century III: Authority and Subversion*, edited by Linda Clark, 25–41. Woodbridge: Boydell, 2003.

Round, J.H. "The King's Pantler." *Archaeological Journal* 60, no. 1 (1903): 268–283.

de Saint-Saveur, E. Durtelle. *Histoire de Bretagne des origines à nos jours*. Paris: Perrin et Armor-editeur, 1975.

Salamagne, Alain, Jean Kerhervé, and Gérard Danet, eds. *Châteaux et modes de vie au temps des ducs de Bretagne (XIIIe–XVIe siècle)*. Rennes: Presses universitaires de Rennes, 2012.

Santos Silva, Manuela. "The Portuguese Household of an English Queen: Sources, Purposes, Social Meaning." In *Royal and Elite Households in Medieval and Early Modern Europe. More than Just a Castle*, edited by Theresa Earenfight, 271–287. Leiden: Brill, 2018.

Santrot, Marie-Hélène. *Entre France et Angleterre, Le duche de Bretagne; Essai d'iconographie des Ducs de Bretagne*. Nantes: Conseil général de Loire-Atlantique, 1988.

Seabourne, Gwen. *Imprisoning Medieval Women: The Non-Judicial Confinement and Abduction of Women in England, c.1170–1509*. Aldershot: Ashgate, 2011.

Slater, Laura. "Defining Queenship at Greyfriars London, c.1300–58." *Gender & History* 27, no. 1 (2015): 53–76.

Somerville, Robert. *History of the Duchy of Lancaster*. Vol. 1: *1265–1603*. London: Chancellor and the Council of the Duchy of Lancaster, 1953.

Steane, John. *The Archaeology of the Medieval English Monarchy*. London: Routledge, 1999.

Stell, Judith, and Andrew Wathey. "New Light on the Biography of John Dunstable?" *Music & Letters* 62, no. 1 (1981): 60–63.

Stratford, Jenny. *The Bedford Inventories: The Worldly Goods of John, Duke of Bedford, Regent of France (1389–1435)*. London: Society of Antiquaries, 1993.

Stratford, Jenny. *Richard II and the English Royal Treasure*. Woodbridge: Boydell, 2013.

Strickland, Agnes. *Lives of the Queens of England from the Norman Conquest; with Anecdotes of their Courts*. Vol. III. Philadelphia: Lea and Blanchard, 1848.

Strohm, Paul. *England's Empty Throne: Usurpation and the Language of Legitimation 1399–1422*. New Haven, CT: Yale University Press, 1998.

Strohm, Paul. *Hochon's Arrow: The Social Imagination of Fourteenth-Century Texts*. Princeton, NJ: Princeton University Press, 1992.

Sumption, Jonathan. *Cursed Kings: The Hundred Years War IV*. London: Faber and Faber, 2016.

Sumption, Jonathan. *Divided Houses: The Hundred Years War III*. London: Faber and Faber, 2009.

Thomas-Lecroix, Pierre. "Jean de Malestroit, Chancelier du duc Jean V, et l'independance de la Bretagne." *Bulletin de la Société Archeologique et Historique de Nantes et de Loire-Atlantique* 115 (1978): 135–194.

Thompson, A. Keith. *Religious Confession Privilege, and the Common Law*. Leiden: Martinus Nijhoff, 2011.

Thornton-Cook, Elsie Prentys. *Her Majesty: The Romance of the Queens of England, 1066–1910*. London: Murray, 1926.

Tingle, Elizabeth. "The Afterlives of Rulers: Power, Patronage and Purgatory in Ducal Brittany 1480–1600." In *The Image and Perception of Monarchy in Medieval and Early Modern Europe*, edited by Sean McGlynn and Elena Woodacre, 281–297. Newcastle upon Lyme: Cambridge Scholars, 2014.

Tingle, Louise. "Aurum Reginae: Queen's Gold in Late Fourteenth-Century England." *Royal Studies Journal* 7, no. 1 (2020): 77–90. DOI: 10.21039/rsj.227.

Tingle, Louise. *Chaucer's Queens: Royal Women, Intercession and Patronage in England, 1328–1394*. New York: Palgrave Macmillan, 2020.

Toudouze, Georges G. *Du Gueslin, Clisson, Richemont et la fin de la Guerre de Cent Ans*. Paris: Librarie Floury, 1942.

Travers, Nicolas. *Histoire civile, politique et religieuse de la ville et du comté de Nantes*. Nantes: Forest, 1836.

Trevedy, J. "Le douaire des Duchesses de Bretagne: Contrats de mariage des Ducs (1)." *Revue de Bretagne* 37 (Feb 1907): 22–42.

Tuck, Anthony. "The Earl of Arundel's Expedition to France, 1411." In *The Reign of Henry IV: Rebellion and Survival, 1403–1413*, edited by Gwilym Dodd and Douglas Biggs, 228–240. York: York Medieval Press, 2008.

Tuck, Anthony. "Henry IV and Europe: A Dynasty's Search for Recognition." In *The McFarlane Legacy: Studies in Late Medieval Politics and Society*, edited by R.H. Britnell and A.J. Pollard, 116–122. Stroud: Alan Sutton, 1995.

Tucoo-Chala, Pierre. "L'histoire tragique d'un couple au XIVe siècle: Agnès de Navarre et Gaston Fébus." *Principe de Viana Anejo: Homenaje José María Lacarra* 2–3 (1986): 741–753.

des Ursins, Jean Juvenal. "Histoire de Charles VI, roy de France (c. 1430s–1440s)," in *The Battle of Agincourt: Sources and Interpretations*, edited by Anne Curry, 128–134. Woodbridge: Boydell, 2000.

Vale, Malcolm. *Henry V, The Conscience of a King*. New Haven, CT: Yale University Press, 2016.

Vaughan, Richard. *Philip the Good: The Apogee of Burgundy*. Woodbridge: Boydell, 1970.

Vernier, Richard. *Lord of the Pyrenees: Gaston Fébus, Count of Foix 1331–1391*. Woodbridge: Boydell, 2008.

Videgain Agos, Fernando. *Los Bastardos de la casa real Navarra*. Pamplona: Ediciones y Libros S.A., 1979.

Wathey, Andrew. "Dunstable in France." *Music & Letters* 67, no. 1 (1986): 1–36.

Whaley, Derek. "From *a* Salic Law to *the* Salic Law: The Creation and Re-creation of the Royal Succession System of Medieval France." In *The Routledge History of Monarchy*, edited by Elena Woodacre, Lucinda H.S. Dean, Chris Jones, Russell E. Martin, and Zita Eva Rohr, 443–464. London: Routledge, 2019.

Wilson, Christopher. "The Tomb of Henry IV and the Holy Oil of St. Thomas of Canterbury." In *Medieval Architecture and its Intellectual Context: Studies in Honour of Peter Kidson*, edited by Eric Fernie and Paul Crossley, 181–190. London: Hambledon, 1990.

Wolffe, Bertram Percy. *Henry VI*. New Haven, CT: Yale University Press, 2001.

Woodacre, Elena. "Epilogue: Foreign Women as Consorts." In *Later Plantagenet and the Wars of the Roses Consorts: Power, Influence, Dynasty,* edited by Aidan Norrie, Carolyn Harris, J.L. Laynesmith, Danna Messer, and Elena Woodacre. New York: Palgrave Macmillan, 2022.

Woodacre, Elena. "The Perils of Promotion: Maternal Ambition and Sacrifice in the Life of Joan of Navarre, Duchess of Brittany and Queen of England." In *Virtuous or Villainess? The Image of the Royal Mother from the Early Medieval to the Early Modern Era*, edited by Carey Fleiner and Elena Woodacre, 125–148. New York: Palgrave Macmillan, 2016.

Woodacre, Elena. "The Queen of Navarre and a Queen from Navarre: Comparing the Eexperience of Queenship of Leonor de Trastámara and Joan of Navarre." *Studia Historica. Historia Medieval* 39, no. 2 (2021): 11–29.

Woodacre, Elena. *Queens and Queenship*. Bradford: ARC Humanities, 2021.

Woodacre, Elena. *The Queens Regnant of Navarre: Succession, Politics and Partnership, 1274–1512*. New York: Palgrave Macmillan, 2013.

Woodger, L.S. "Bitterley, Richard (d.c. 1456) of Hartling, Sussex." In *The History of Parliament: the House of Commons 1386–1421*, edited by J.S. Roskell, L. Clark, and C. Rawcliffe. Woodbridge: Boydell and Brewer, 1993. http://www.historyofparliamentonline.org/volume/1386-1421/member/bitterley-richard-1456.

Woodger, L.S. "Porter, William II (d. 1436), of Wimpole, Cambs." In *The History of Parliament: the House of Commons 1386–1421*, edited by J.S. Roskell, L. Clark, and C. Rawcliffe. Woodbridge: Boydell and Brewer, 1993. http://www.historyofparliamentonline.org/volume/1386-1421/member/porter-william-ii-1436.

Woodger, L.S. "Wilicotes, Willliam (d. 1411) of North Leigh, Oxon." In *The History of Parliament: the House of Commons 1386–1421*, edited by J.S. Roskell, L. Clark, and C. Rawcliffe. Woodbridge: Boydell and Brewer, 1993. http://www.historyofparliamentonline.org/volume/1386-1421/member/wilcotes-william-1411.

Woods, Kim. *Cut in Alabaster: A Material of Sculpture and its European Traditions 1330–1530*. Turnhout: Harvey Miller, 2018.

Woolgar, C.M. *Household Accounts from Medieval England: Parts 1 and 2*. Oxford: Oxford University Press, 1992–93.

Wright, Katia. "A Dower for Life: Understanding the Dowers of England's Medieval Queens." In *Later Plantagenet and the Wars of the Roses Consorts: Power, Influence, Dynasty*, edited by Aidan Norrie, Carolyn Harris, J.L. Laynesmith, Danna Messer, and Elena Woodacre. New York: Palgrave Macmillan, 2022.

Wylie, James Hamilton. *History of England under Henry the Fourth*. Vol. III. London: Longmans, Green, 1896.

Yanguas y Miranda, D. José. *Dicconario de Antigüedades del Reino de Navarra.* Vol 1. Pamplona: Javier Goyeneche, 1840.

de Ybarra, Fernando. *Matrimonios Reales Hispano-Británicos el el Medievo.* Vol. I: *Póker de Reinas.* Salamanca: Universidad Pontificia de Salamanca, 1999.

Zunzunegui, José. "El Matrimonio de la Infanta Juana con el Duque de Bretaña: Navarra a fines de siglo XIV." *Principe de Viana* 4 (1943): 51–68.

Unpublished works

Barker, Jessica. "The Funerary Programme of Beatrice of Portugal (d. 1439) at the Fitzalan Chapel in Arundel." Paper given at Espacios de memoria y representation: Reinas, infantas y damas de la corte ante la muerte en las monarquías ibéricas medievales, 29 April 2021.

Berglund, Louise. "'From Where Few Return Alive': Sending Philippa, Daughter of King Henry IV, to the North, c. 1400–1430." Paper given at IMC Leeds, July 2021.

Codling, Deborah. "The Kingly Style of Henry IV: Personality, Politics and Culture." PhD thesis, Royal Holloway, 2004.

Farnsworth Wright, Thomas Edmund. "Royal Finance in the Latter Part of the Reign of Henry IV of England, 1406–13." PhD thesis, Merton College, Oxford, 1984.

Gower, Gillian. "The Iconography of Queenship: Sacred Music and Female Exemplarity in Late Medieval Britain." PhD thesis, UCLA, 2016.

Gray, Fabia Anne. "Formal and Informal Contacts between the House of Navarre and the English during the 14th century Phase of the Hundred Years War." PhD thesis, University of Nottingham, 2005.

Grussenmeyer, Jon-Mark. "The Tomb of a King and the Ideology of a Dynasty: Henry IV and the Lancastrian Connexion to Canterbury Cathedral." MA diss., University of Kent, 2012.

Kermabon, Nicolas. "Ego Dux Britannie Dotavit Eam: Le douaire des duchesses de Bretagne (XIIIe–XVe siècle)." PhD thesis, Université de Rennes 1, 2007, 3 vols.

Lacey, Helen. "The Politics of Mercy: The Use of the Royal Pardon in Fourteenth-Century England." PhD thesis, University of York, 2005.

McKenzie, Chloë. "Ladies and Robes of the Garter: Kingship, Patronage and Female Agency in Late Medieval England, c. 1348–1445." PhD thesis, University of Southampton, 2019.

Pelaz Flores, Diana. "'Reynante(s) en vno'. Poder y representación de la reina en la corona de Castilla durante el siglo XV." PhD thesis, Universidad de Valladolid, 2015.

Phifer, Michael J. "Property, Power and Patriarchy: The Decline of Women's Property Right in England after the Black Death." PhD thesis, University of Houston, 2014.

Rogers, Alan. "The Royal Household of Henry IV." PhD thesis, University of Nottingham, 1966.

Seah, Michele. "The Material Foundations of Queenship in Late-Medieval England, 1445–1509." PhD thesis, University of Newcastle, Australia, 2019.

Sheridan Walker, Sue. "Royal Wardship in Medieval England." PhD thesis, University of Chicago, 1966.

Steer, Christian Oliver. "Burial and Commemoration in Medieval London, c. 1140–1540." PhD thesis, University of London, 2013.

Stockdale, Sarah. "Blood on the Crown: Treason in the Royal Kinship Structure of Fifteenth-Century England." PhD thesis, University of Winchester, 2018.

INDEX

Printed in Great Britain
by Amazon

45878690R00198